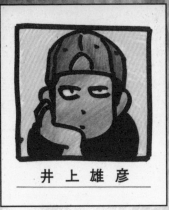

井上雄彦

Takehiko Inoue

1) I THINK IN JAPAN, MANGA IS AN ESTABLISHED CULTURE. I CAN'T DENY THE ACHIEVEMENTS OF THIS THING WE CALL THE "MEDIA MIX STRATEGY," BUT I'M ALSO UNCERTAIN ABOUT THE TENDENCY TO BE OVERLY THANKFUL.

2) I'M SURE THERE ARE MANY PEOPLE BESIDES MYSELF THAT ARE EXCITED ABOUT (HIDEO) NOMO'S PERFORMANCE IN THE MAJORS. HOW GREAT IT WOULD BE IF SOMEBODY LIKE HIM SHOWED UP IN BASKETBALL.

Takehiko Inoue's *Slam Dunk* is one of the most popular manga of all time, having sold over 100 million copies worldwide. He followed that series up with two titles lauded by critics and fans alike—*Vagabond*, a fictional account of the life of Miyamoto Musashi, and *Real*, a manga about wheelchair basketball.

SLAM DUNK
Vol. 25: Greatest Challenge

SHONEN JUMP Manga Edition

STORY AND ART BY TAKEHIKO INOUE

English Adaptation/Stan!
Translation/Joe Yamazaki
Touch-up Art & Lettering/James Gaubatz
Cover & Graphic Design/Matt Hinrichs
Editor/Mike Montesa

© 1990 - 2012 Takehiko Inoue and I.T. Planning, Inc.
Originally published in Japan in 1995 by Shueisha
Inc., Tokyo. English translation rights arranged with
I.T. Planning, Inc. All rights reserved.

The SLAM DUNK U.S. trademark is used with
permission from NBA Properties, Inc.

Some scenes have been modified from the original
Japanese edition.

The stories, characters and incidents mentioned in this
publication are entirely fictional.

Printed in Canada

Published by VIZ Media, LLC
P.O. Box 77010
San Francisco, CA 94107

10 9 8 7 6 5 4 3 2 1
First printing, December 2012

www.viz.com

THE WORLD'S
MOST POPULAR MANGA

www.shonenjump.com

STORY AND ART BY TAKEHIKO INOUE

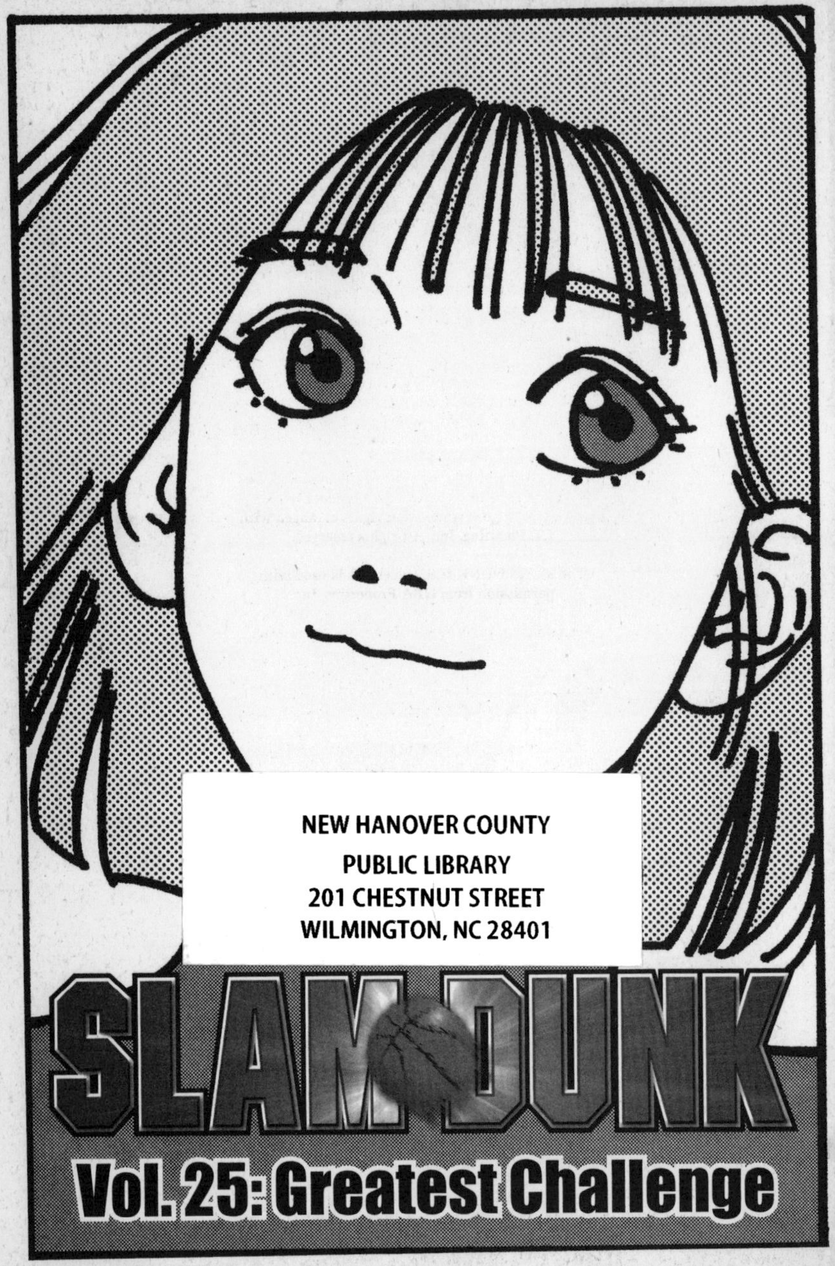

SLAM DUNK

Vol. 25: Greatest Challenge

Character Introduction

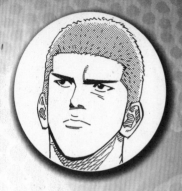

Hanamichi Sakuragi
A first-year at Shohoku High School, Sakuragi is in love with Haruko Akagi.

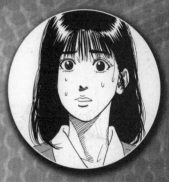

Haruko Akagi
Also a first-year at Shohoku, Takenori Akagi's little sister has a crush on Kaede Rukawa.

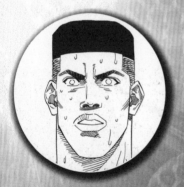

Takenori Akagi
A third-year and the basketball team's captain, Akagi has an intense passion for his sport.

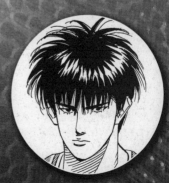

Kaede Rukawa
The object of Haruko's affection (and that of many of Shohoku's female students!), this first-year has been a star player since junior high.

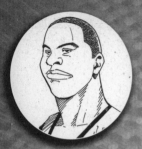

Kawata

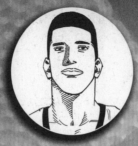

Fukatsu

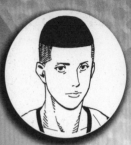

Sawakita

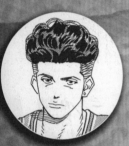

Ryota Miyagi
A problem child with
a thing for Ayako.

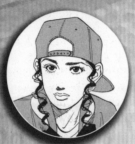

Ayako
Basketball Team
Manager

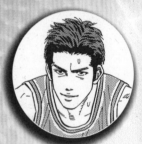

Hisashi Mitsui
An MVP during
junior high.

Our Story Thus Far

Hanamichi Sakuragi is rejected by close to 50 girls during his three years in junior high. He joins the basketball team to be closer to Haruko Akagi, but his frustration mounts when all he does is practice day after day.

Shohoku advances through the Prefectural Tournament and earns a spot in the Nationals.

In a weeklong secret training session, Sakuragi shoots 20,000 shots to prepare for the Nationals.

Shohoku defeats Osaka's Toyotama High in the first round, and now must face Akita's Sannoh Kogyo, last year's national champions and the team that represents the pinnacle of Japanese high school basketball.

Vol. 25:
Greatest Challenge

Table of Contents

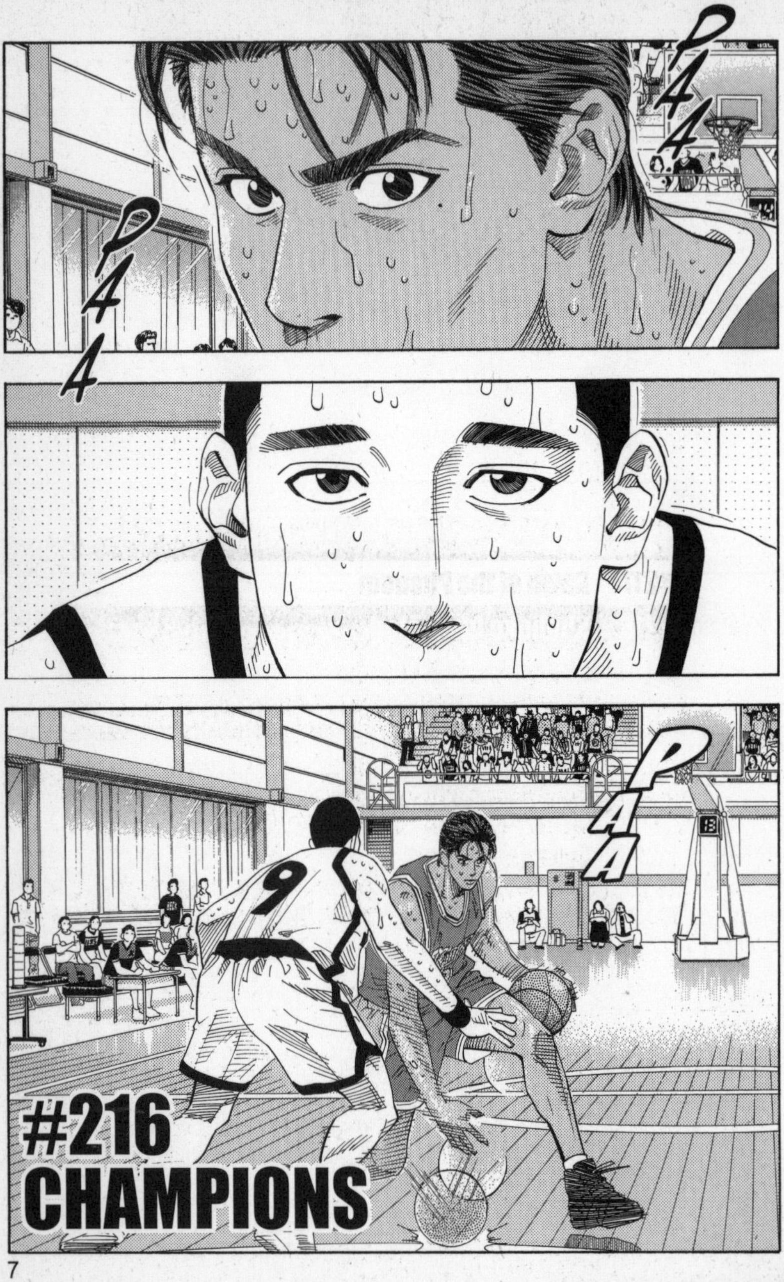
PAA
PAA
PAA
#216
CHAMPIONS

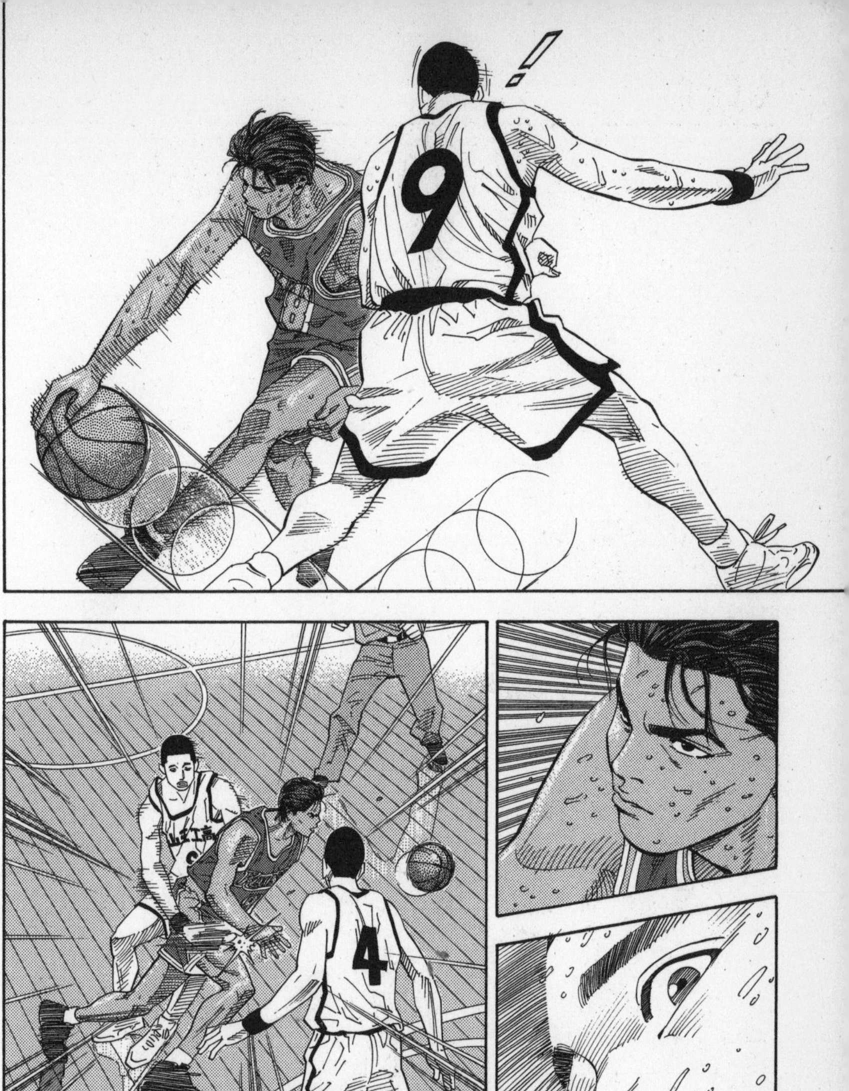
!
!

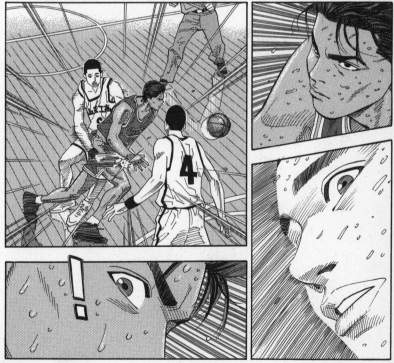

READ THIS WAY

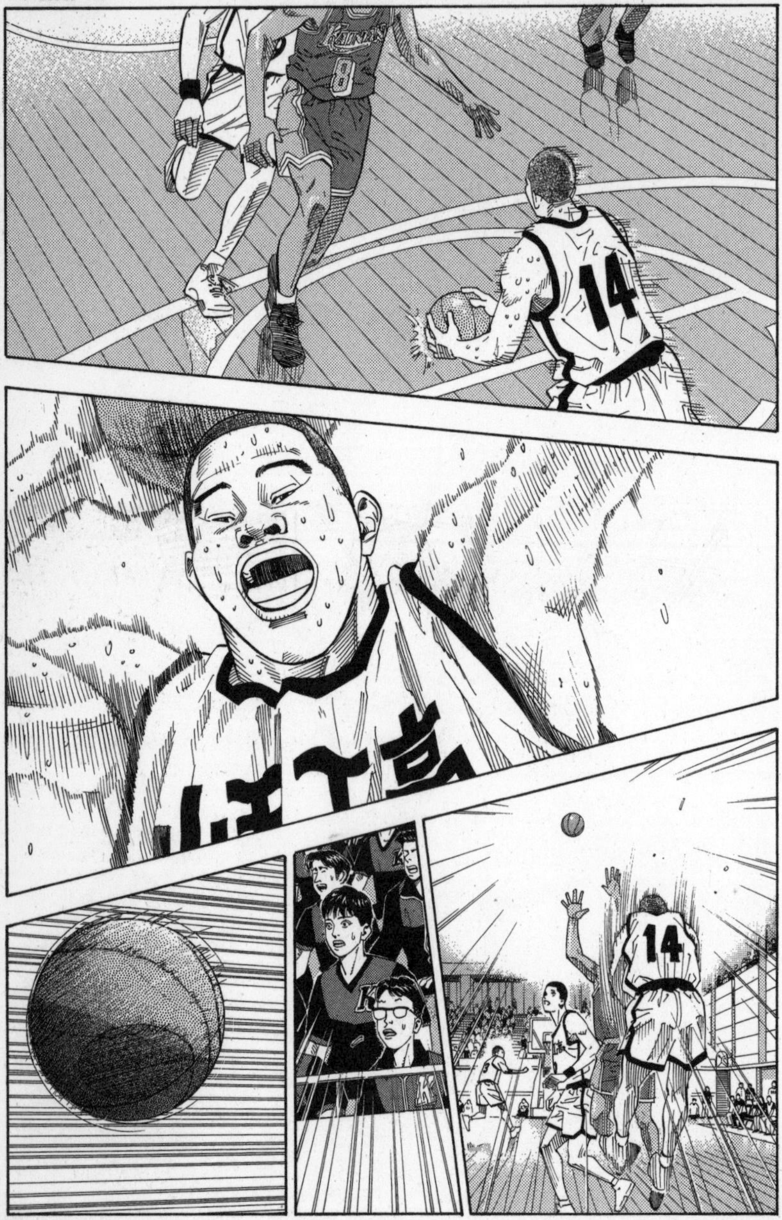

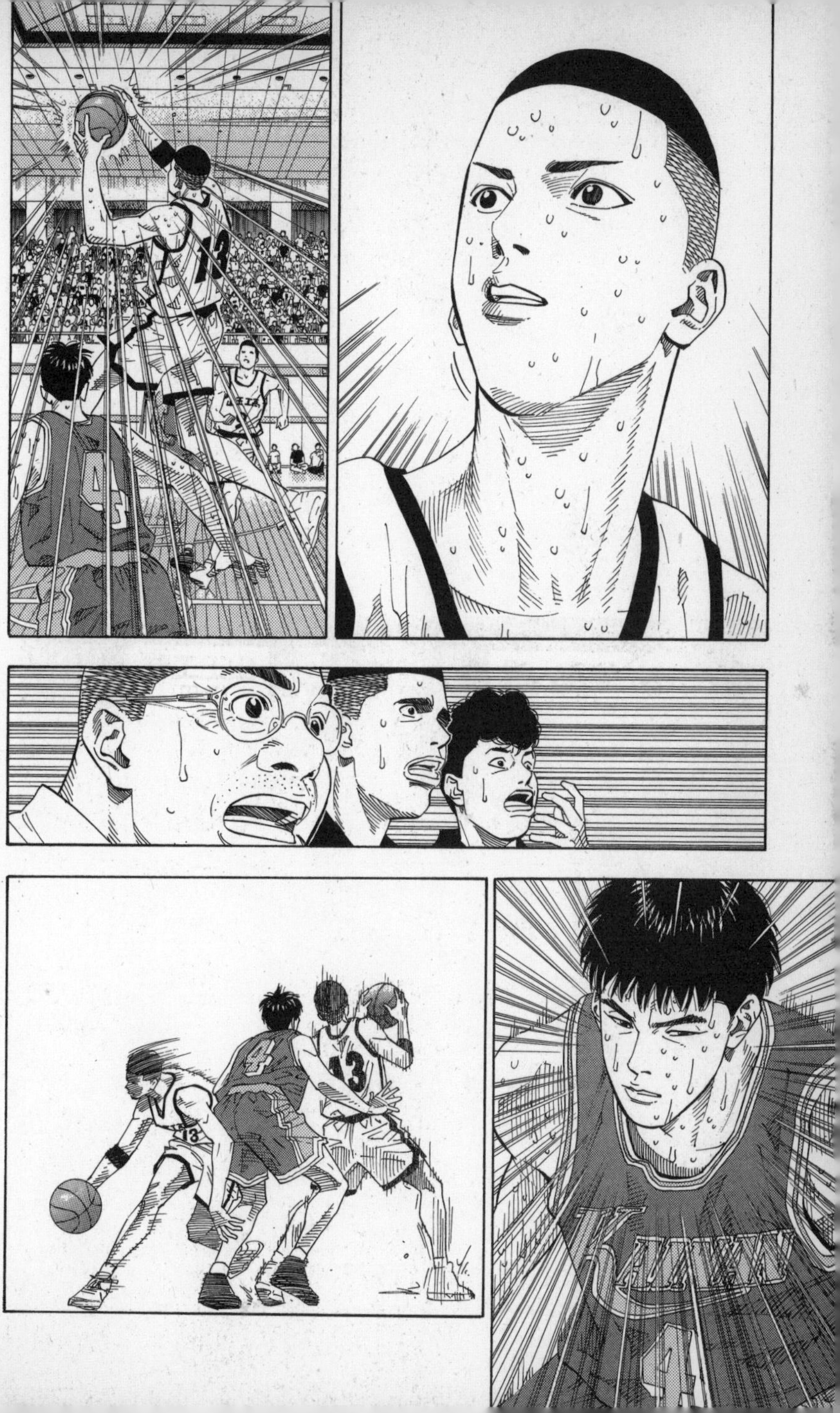

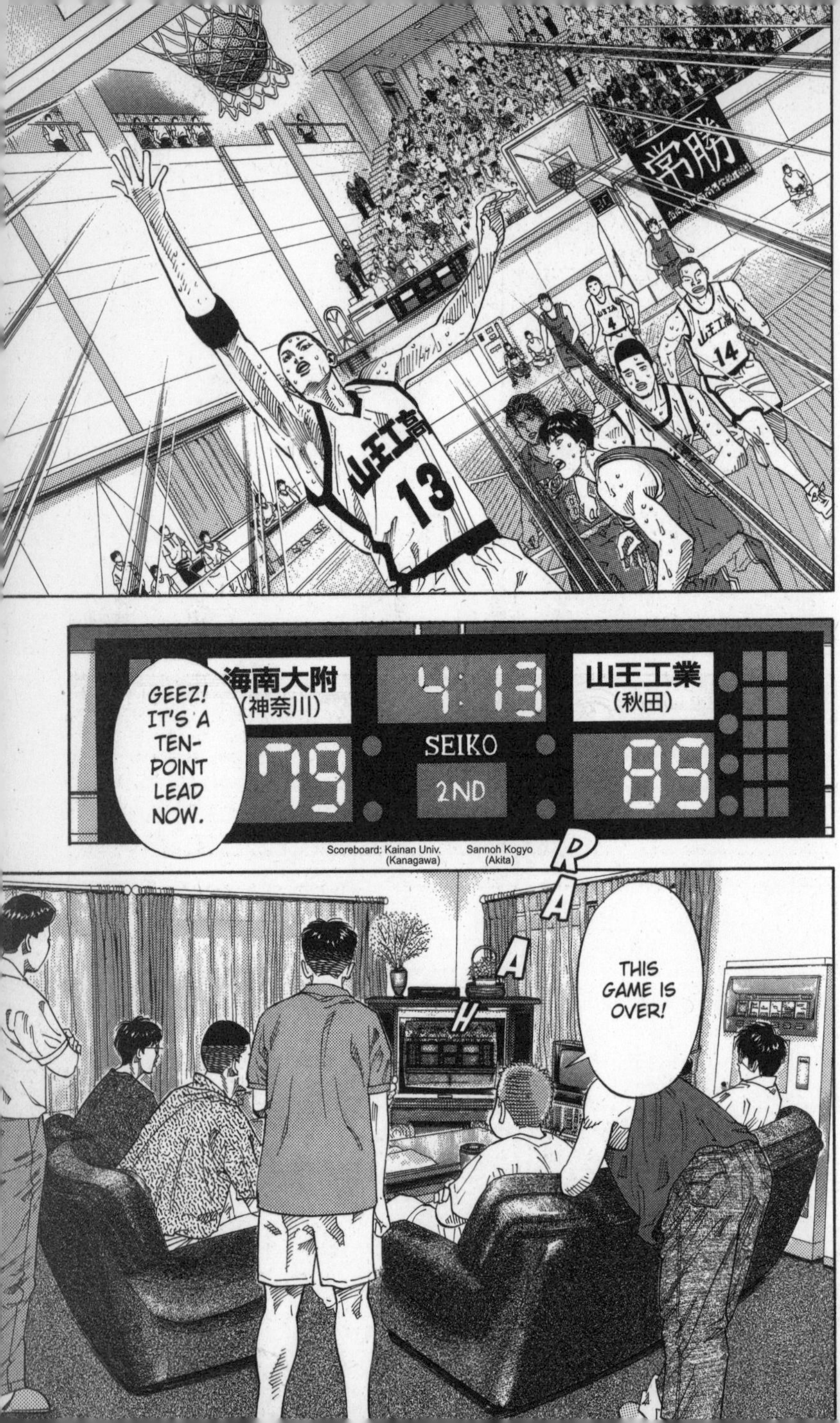
常勝
山王工高
13
4
14
山王工業
(秋田)
89
4:13
SEIKO
2ND
海南大附
(神奈川)
79
GEEZ! IT'S A TEN-POINT LEAD NOW.
Scoreboard: Kainan Univ. (Kanagawa) Sannoh Kogyo (Akita)
RAAH
THIS GAME IS OVER!

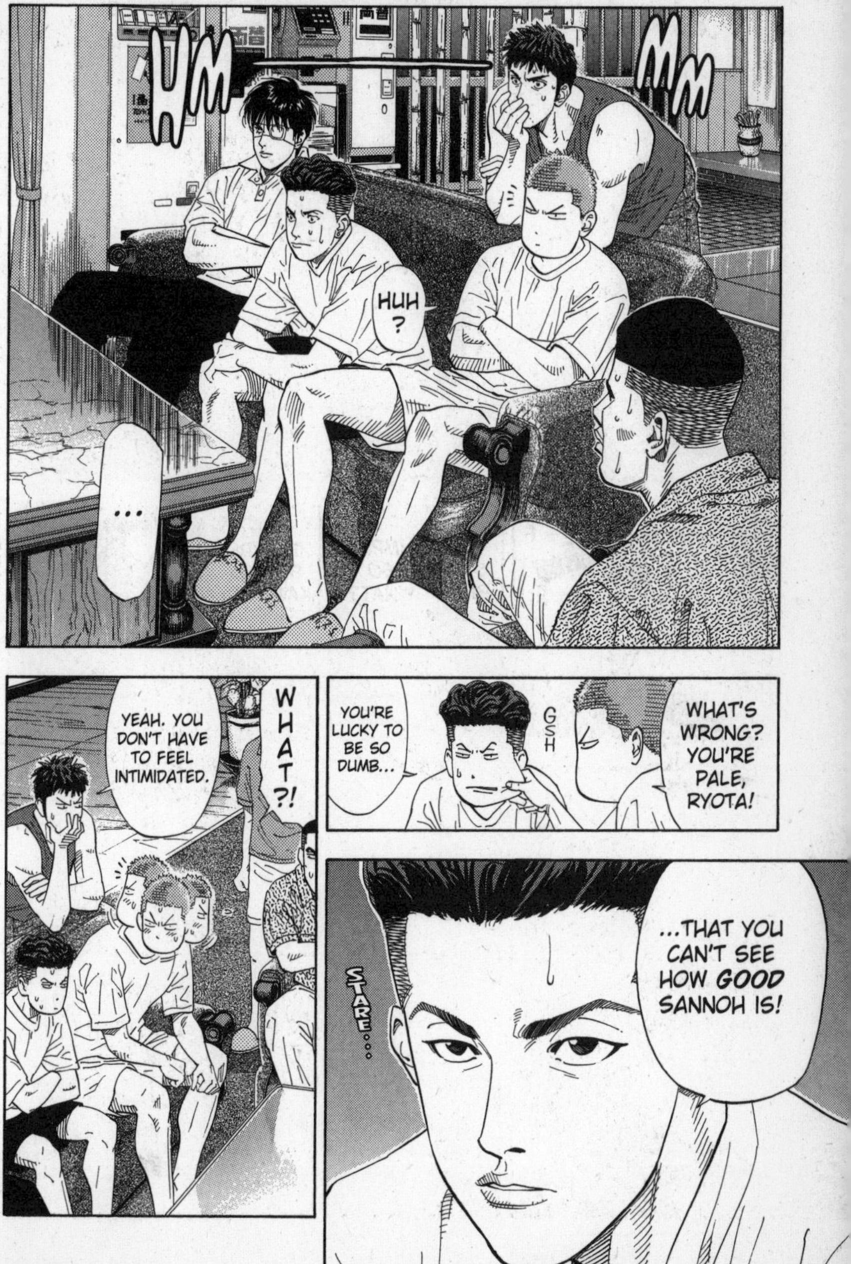
MM
HM
HUH?
...
WHAT'S WRONG? YOU'RE PALE, RYOTA!
GSH
YOU'RE LUCKY TO BE SO DUMB...
...THAT YOU CAN'T SEE HOW GOOD SANNOH IS!
STARE...
WHAT?!
YEAH. YOU DON'T HAVE TO FEEL INTIMIDATED.

READ THIS WAY

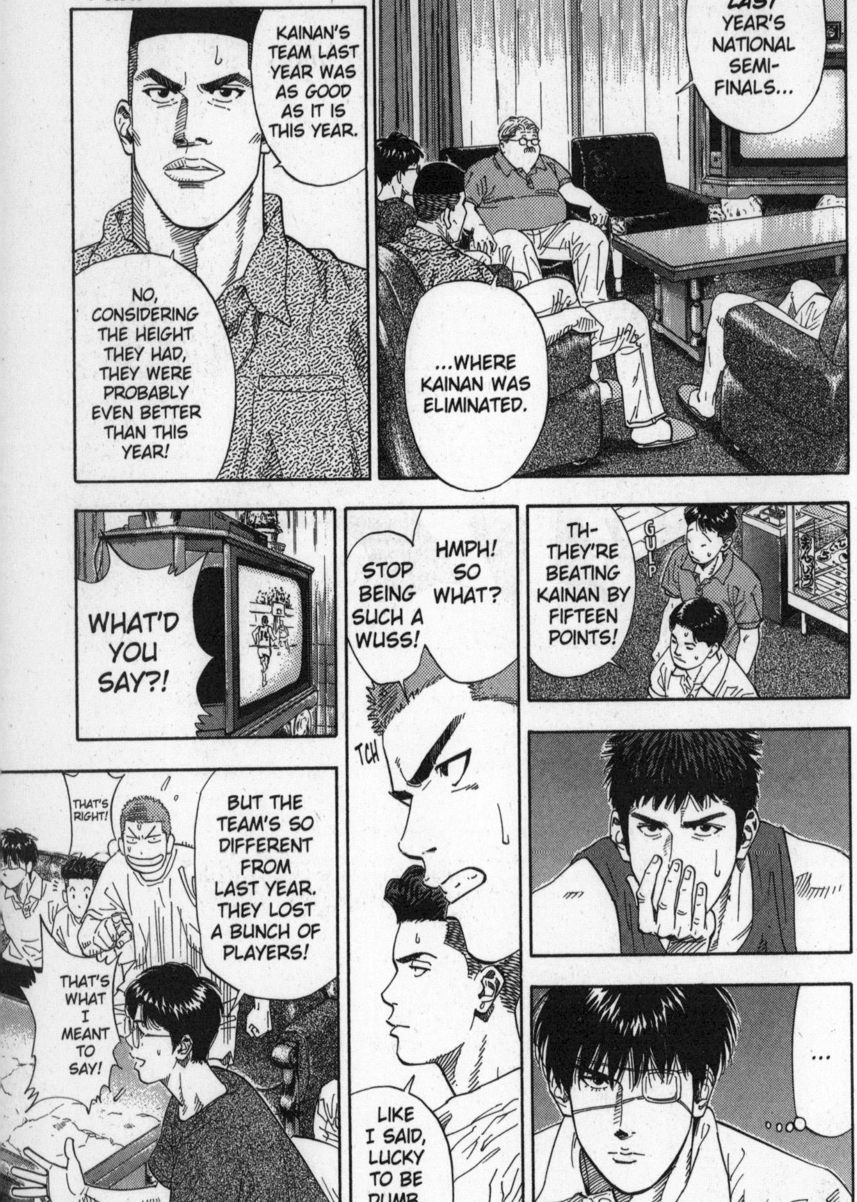
THIS IS LAST YEAR'S NATIONAL SEMI-FINALS...
...WHERE KAINAN WAS ELIMINATED.
KAINAN'S TEAM LAST YEAR WAS AS GOOD AS IT IS THIS YEAR.
NO, CONSIDERING THE HEIGHT THEY HAD, THEY WERE PROBABLY EVEN BETTER THAN THIS YEAR!
GULP
TH-THEY'RE BEATING KAINAN BY FIFTEEN POINTS!
...
HMPH! SO WHAT?
STOP BEING SUCH A WUSS!
TCH
LIKE I SAID, LUCKY TO BE DUMB.
WHAT'D YOU SAY?!
BUT THE TEAM'S SO DIFFERENT FROM LAST YEAR. THEY LOST A BUNCH OF PLAYERS!
THAT'S RIGHT!
THAT'S WHAT I MEANT TO SAY!

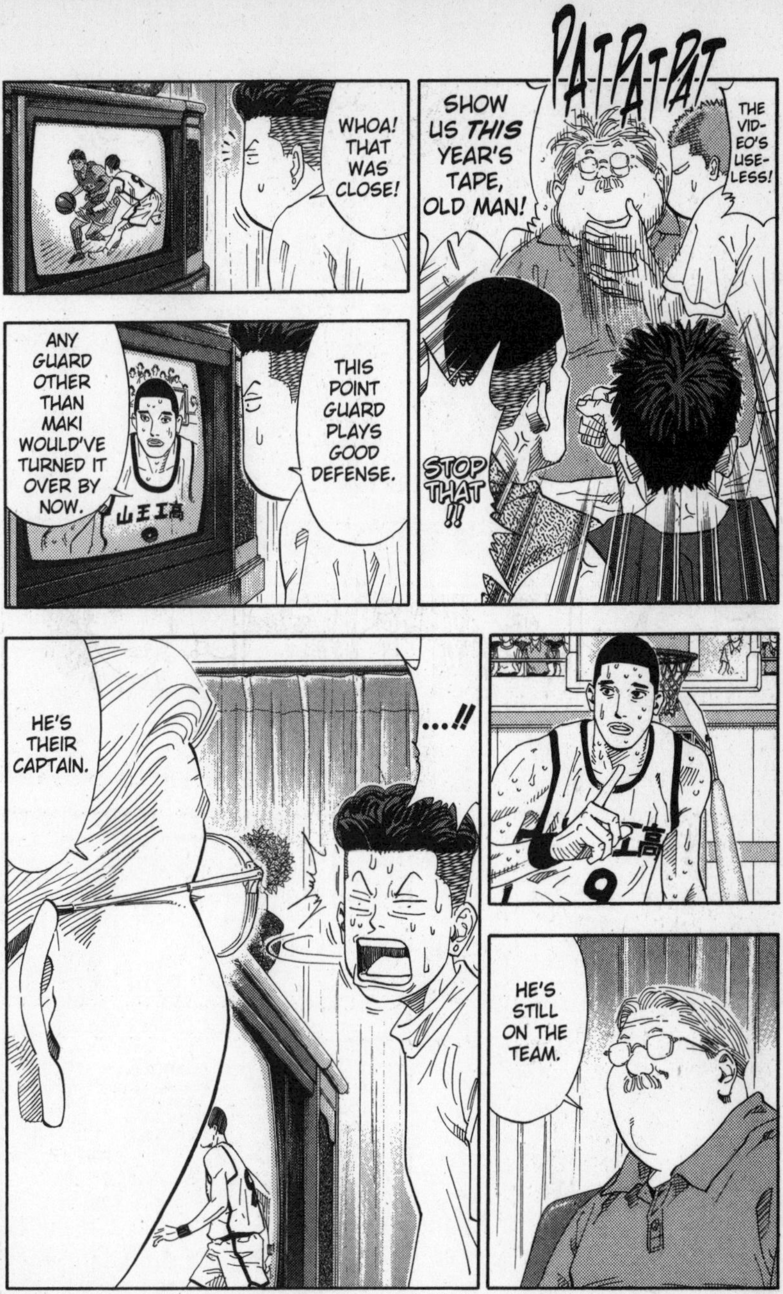
PATPATPAT
THE VIDEO'S USELESS!
SHOW US THIS YEAR'S TAPE, OLD MAN!
STOP THAT!!
WHOA! THAT WAS CLOSE!
THIS POINT GUARD PLAYS GOOD DEFENSE.
ANY GUARD OTHER THAN MAKI WOULD'VE TURNED IT OVER BY NOW.
山王工高
HE'S STILL ON THE TEAM.
...!!
HE'S THEIR CAPTAIN.

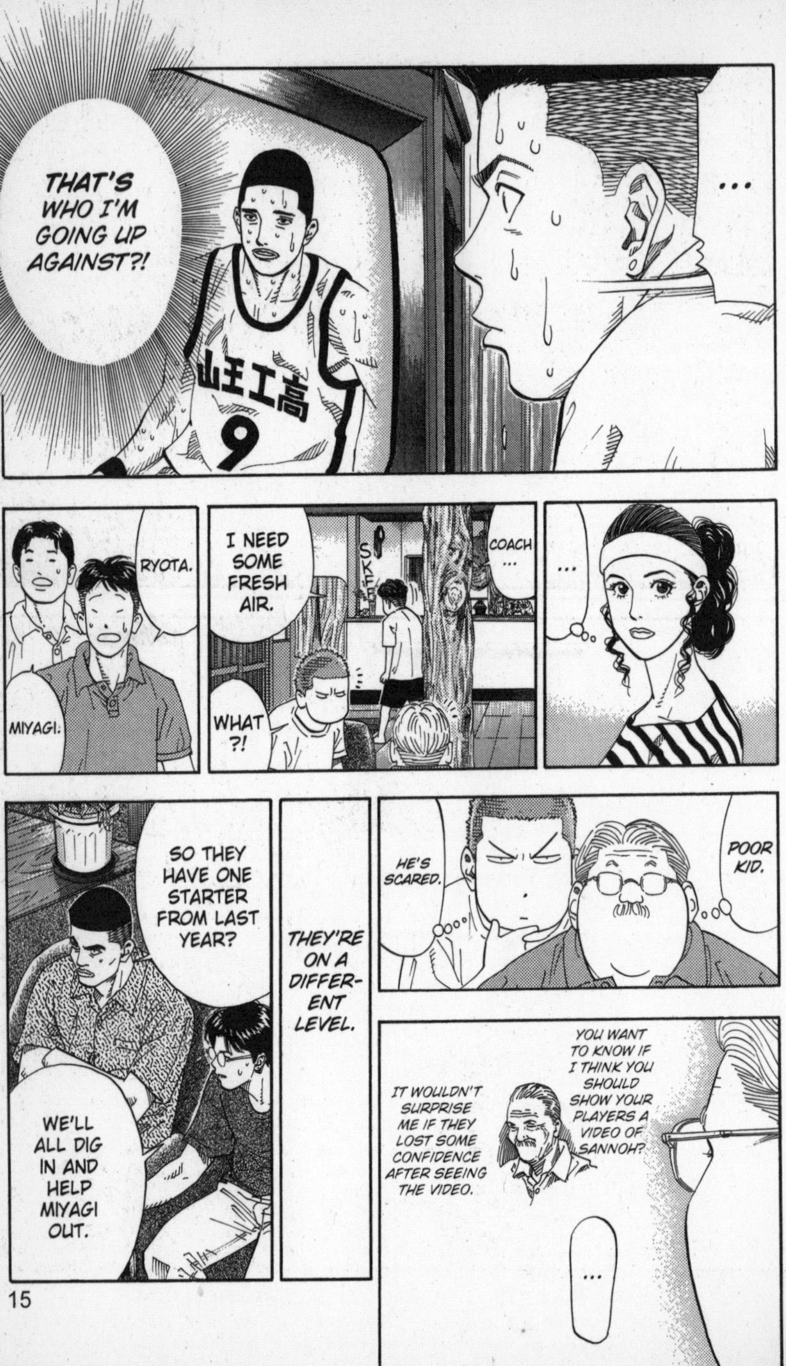
...
THAT'S WHO I'M GOING UP AGAINST?!
...
COACH ...
I NEED SOME FRESH AIR.
SKFF
WHAT ?!
RYOTA.
MIYAGI.
POOR KID.
HE'S SCARED.
YOU WANT TO KNOW IF I THINK YOU SHOULD SHOW YOUR PLAYERS A VIDEO OF SANNOH?
IT WOULDN'T SURPRISE ME IF THEY LOST SOME CONFIDENCE AFTER SEEING THE VIDEO.
...
THEY'RE ON A DIFFER-ENT LEVEL.
SO THEY HAVE ONE STARTER FROM LAST YEAR?
WE'LL ALL DIG IN AND HELP MIYAGI OUT.

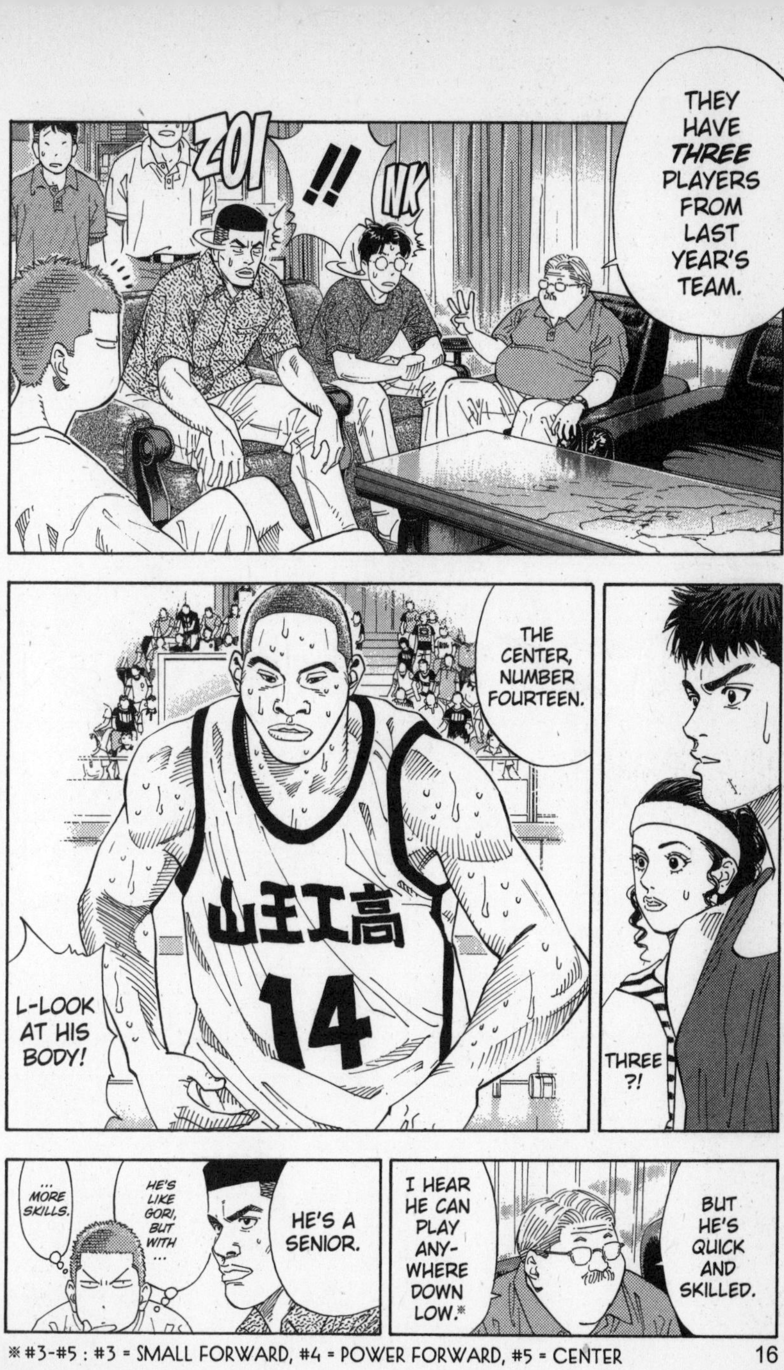
THEY HAVE *THREE* PLAYERS FROM LAST YEAR'S TEAM.
NK
!!
ZOI
THREE ?!
THE CENTER, NUMBER FOURTEEN.
山王工高
14
L-LOOK AT HIS BODY!
BUT HE'S QUICK AND SKILLED.
I HEAR HE CAN PLAY ANY-WHERE DOWN LOW.※
HE'S A SENIOR.
HE'S LIKE GORI, BUT WITH ...
... MORE SKILLS.

※ #3-#5 : #3 = SMALL FORWARD, #4 = POWER FORWARD, #5 = CENTER

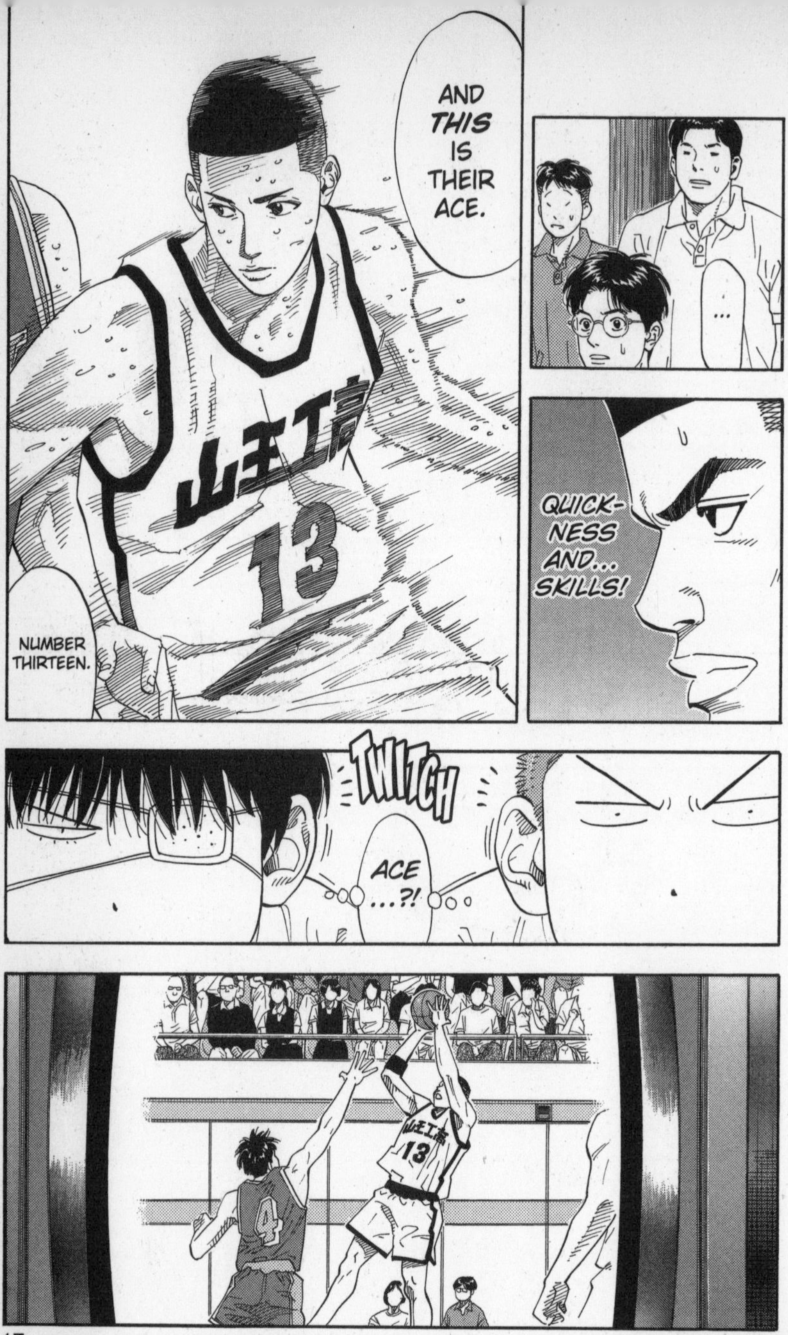
...
QUICK-
NESS
AND...
SKILLS!
AND THIS IS THEIR ACE.
NUMBER THIRTEEN.
TWITCH
ACE ...?!

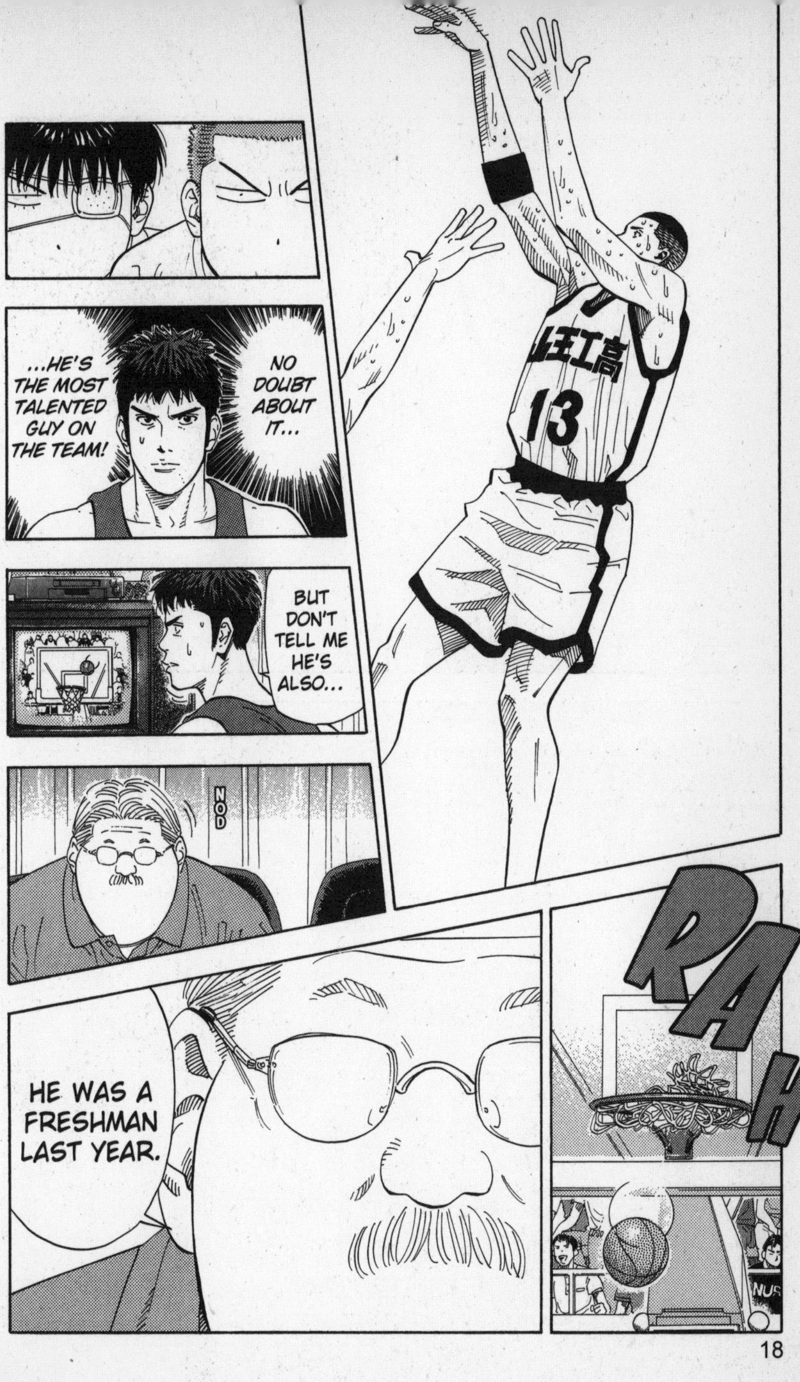
NO DOUBT ABOUT IT...
...HE'S THE MOST TALENTED GUY ON THE TEAM!
BUT DON'T TELL ME HE'S ALSO...
NOD
RAH
HE WAS A FRESHMAN LAST YEAR.

READ THIS WAY

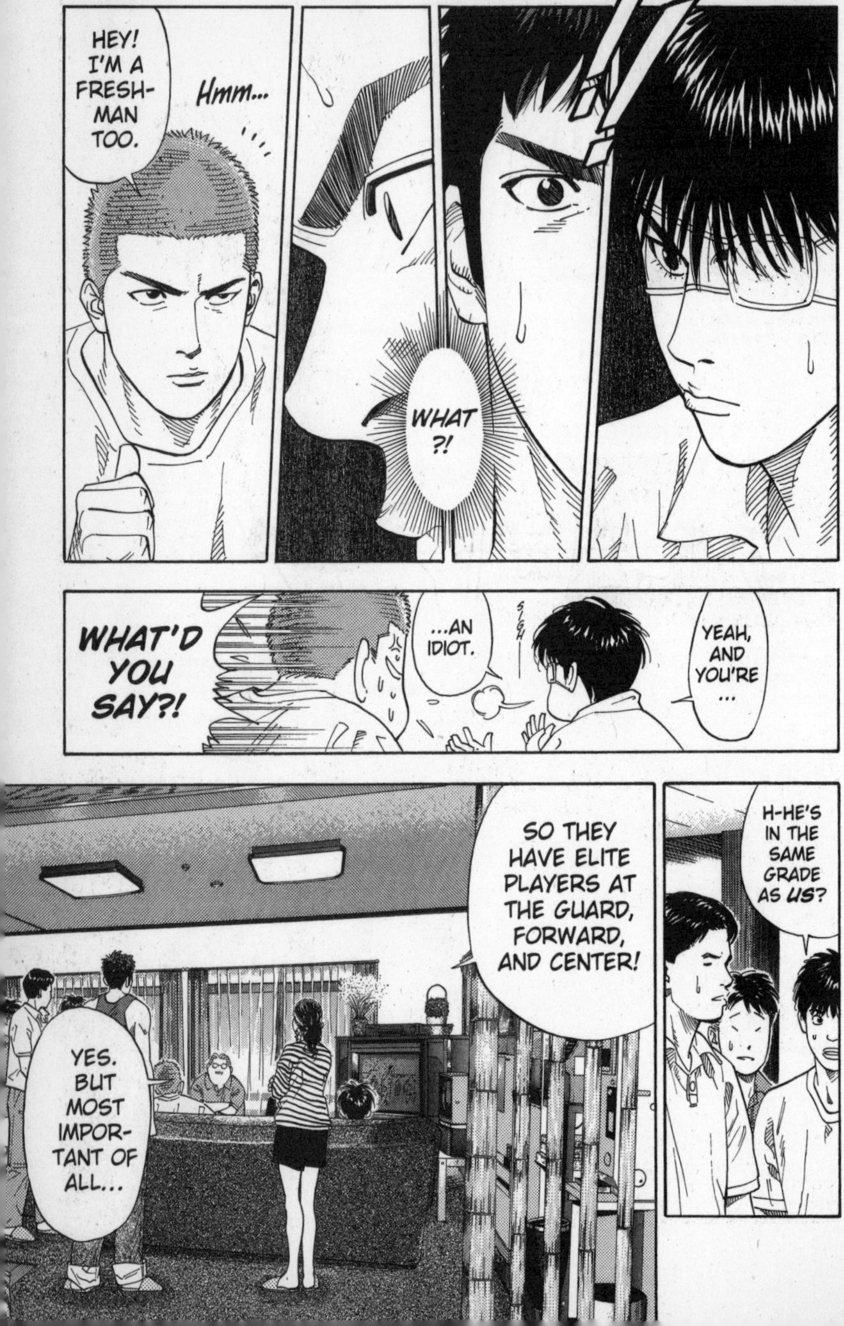
WHAT ?!
HEY! I'M A FRESHMAN TOO.
Hmm...
YEAH, AND YOU'RE ...
SIGH
...AN IDIOT.
WHAT'D YOU SAY?!
H-HE'S IN THE SAME GRADE AS US?
SO THEY HAVE ELITE PLAYERS AT THE GUARD, FORWARD, AND CENTER!
YES. BUT MOST IMPORTANT OF ALL...

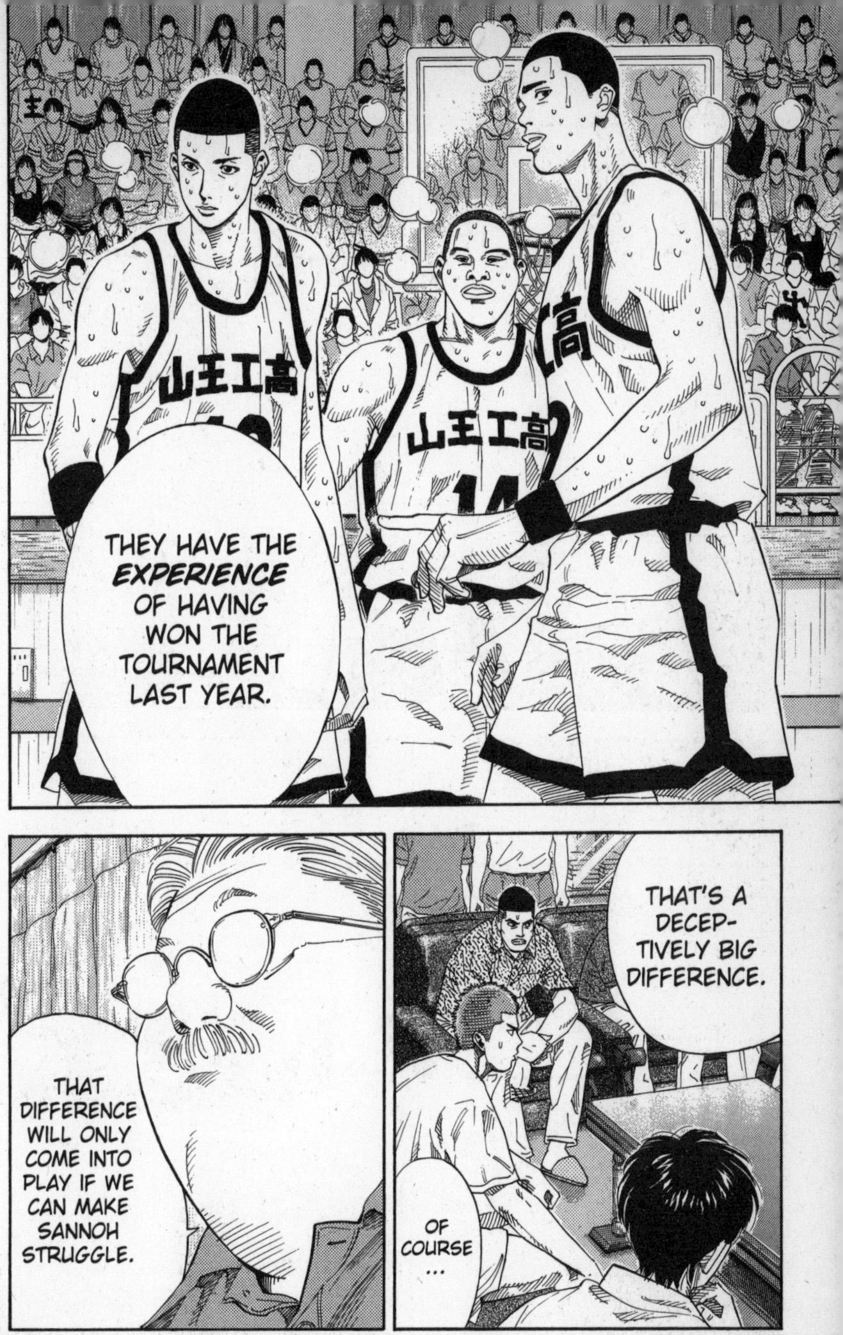

THEY HAVE THE *EXPERIENCE* OF HAVING WON THE TOURNAMENT LAST YEAR.
THAT'S A DECEPTIVELY BIG DIFFERENCE.
OF COURSE...
THAT DIFFERENCE WILL ONLY COME INTO PLAY IF WE CAN MAKE SANNOH STRUGGLE.

READ THIS WAY

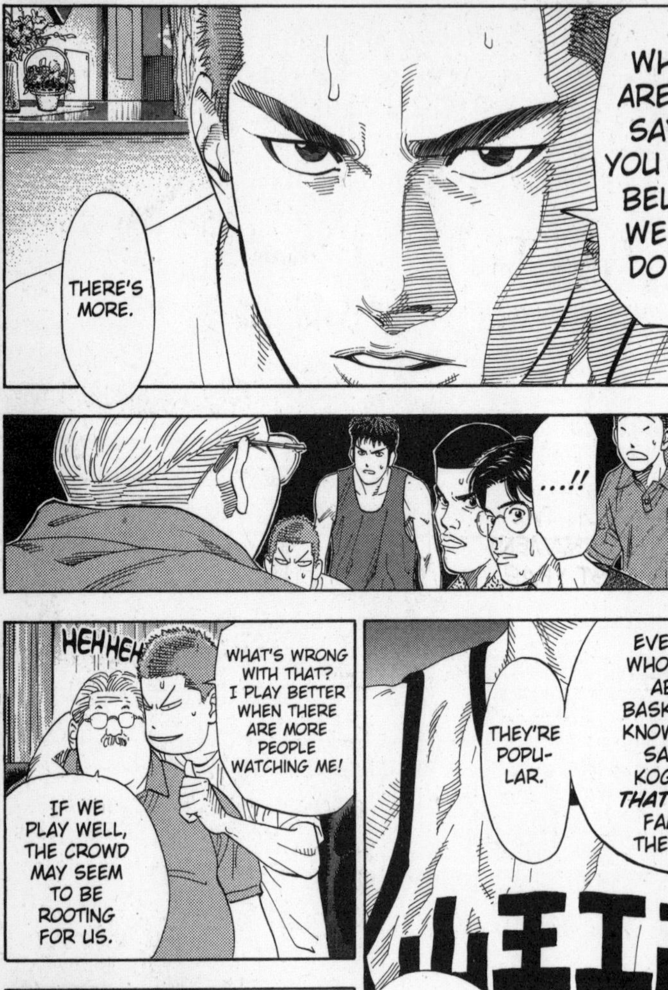
WHAT? ARE YOU SAYING YOU DON'T BELIEVE WE CAN DO IT?!
THERE'S MORE.
...!!
EVERYONE WHO CARES ABOUT BASKETBALL KNOWS WHO SANNOH KOGYO IS. *THAT'S* HOW FAMOUS THEY ARE.
THEY'RE POPU-LAR.
山王工高
THE STANDS WILL BE FILLED TOMORROW.
HEHHEH
WHAT'S WRONG WITH THAT? I PLAY BETTER WHEN THERE ARE MORE PEOPLE WATCHING ME!
IF WE PLAY WELL, THE CROWD MAY SEEM TO BE ROOTING FOR US.
BUT IF WE GET TO A POINT WHERE WE MIGHT ACTUALLY BEAT THEM...

Scoreboard: Shohoku (Kanagawa) Sannoh Kogyo (Akita)

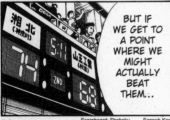

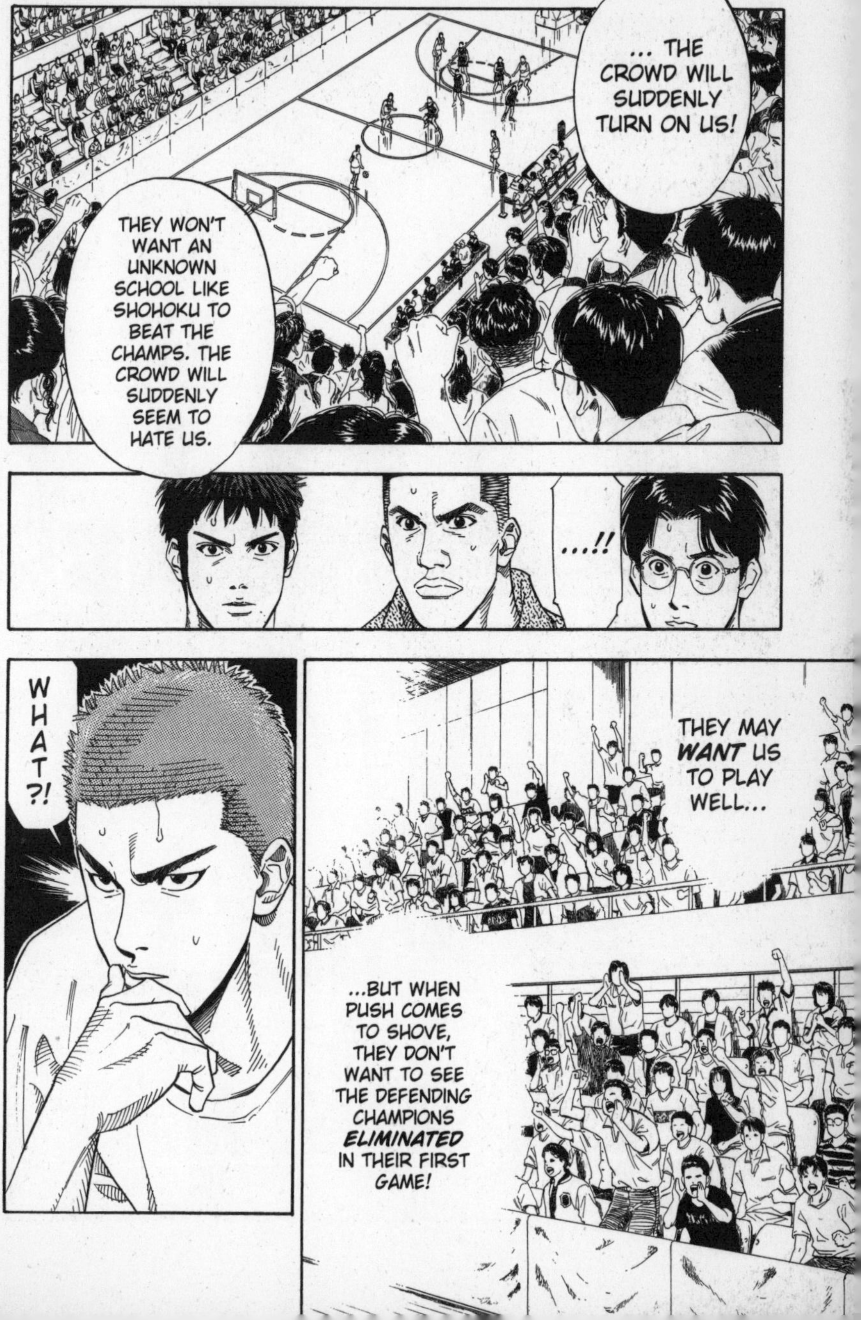
... THE CROWD WILL SUDDENLY TURN ON US!
THEY WON'T WANT AN UNKNOWN SCHOOL LIKE SHOHOKU TO BEAT THE CHAMPS. THE CROWD WILL SUDDENLY SEEM TO HATE US.
...!!
THEY MAY WANT US TO PLAY WELL...
...BUT WHEN PUSH COMES TO SHOVE, THEY DON'T WANT TO SEE THE DEFENDING CHAMPIONS ELIMINATED IN THEIR FIRST GAME!
WHAT?!

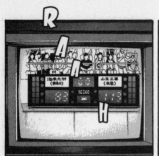

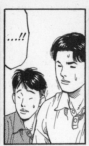

....!!

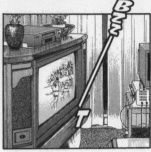

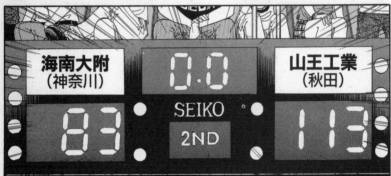

海南大附 （神奈川）	0.0	山王工業 （秋田）
83	SEIKO 2ND	113

Scoreboard: Kainan Univ.   Sannoh Kogyo
(Kanagawa)   (Akita)

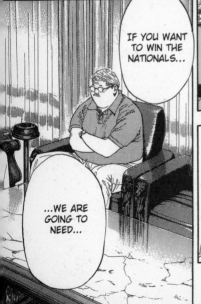

IF YOU WANT TO WIN THE NATIONALS...

...WE ARE GOING TO NEED...

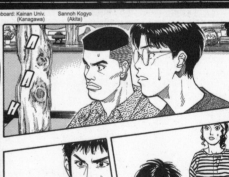

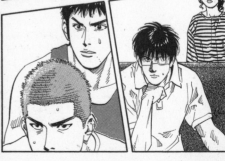

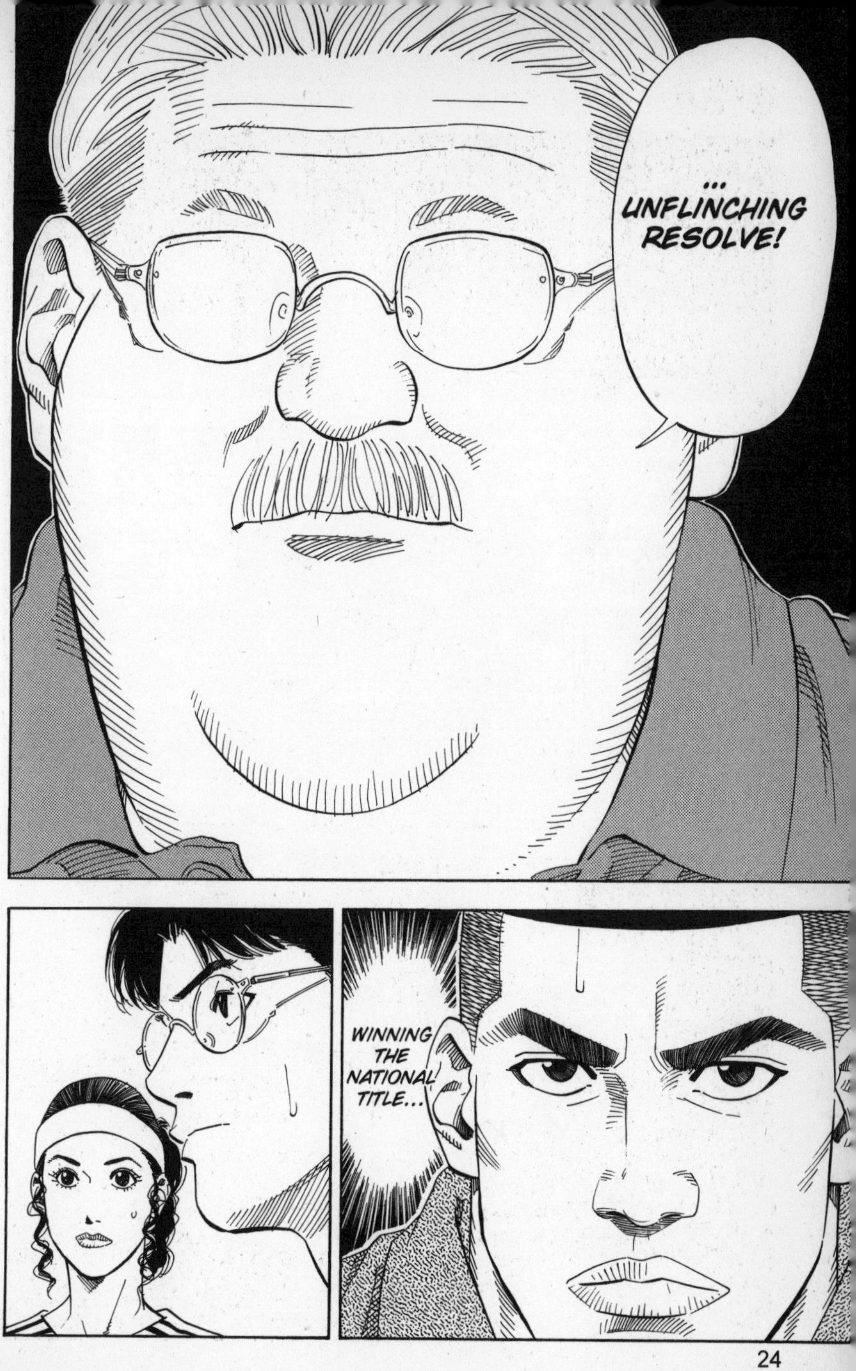
... UNFLINCHING RESOLVE!
WINNING THE NATIONAL TITLE...

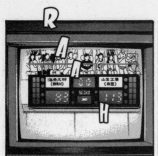

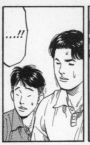

....!!

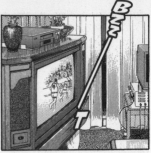

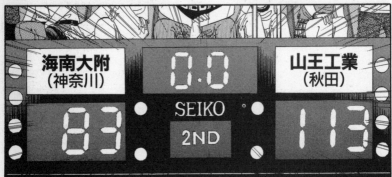

海南大附 （神奈川）	0:0	山王工業 （秋田）
83	SEIKO 2ND	113

Scoreboard: Kainan Univ.　　Sannoh Kogyo
(Kanagawa)　　(Akita)

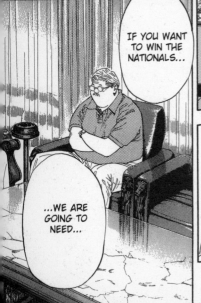

IF YOU WANT TO WIN THE NATIONALS...

...WE ARE GOING TO NEED...

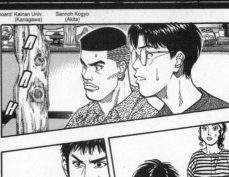

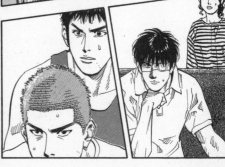

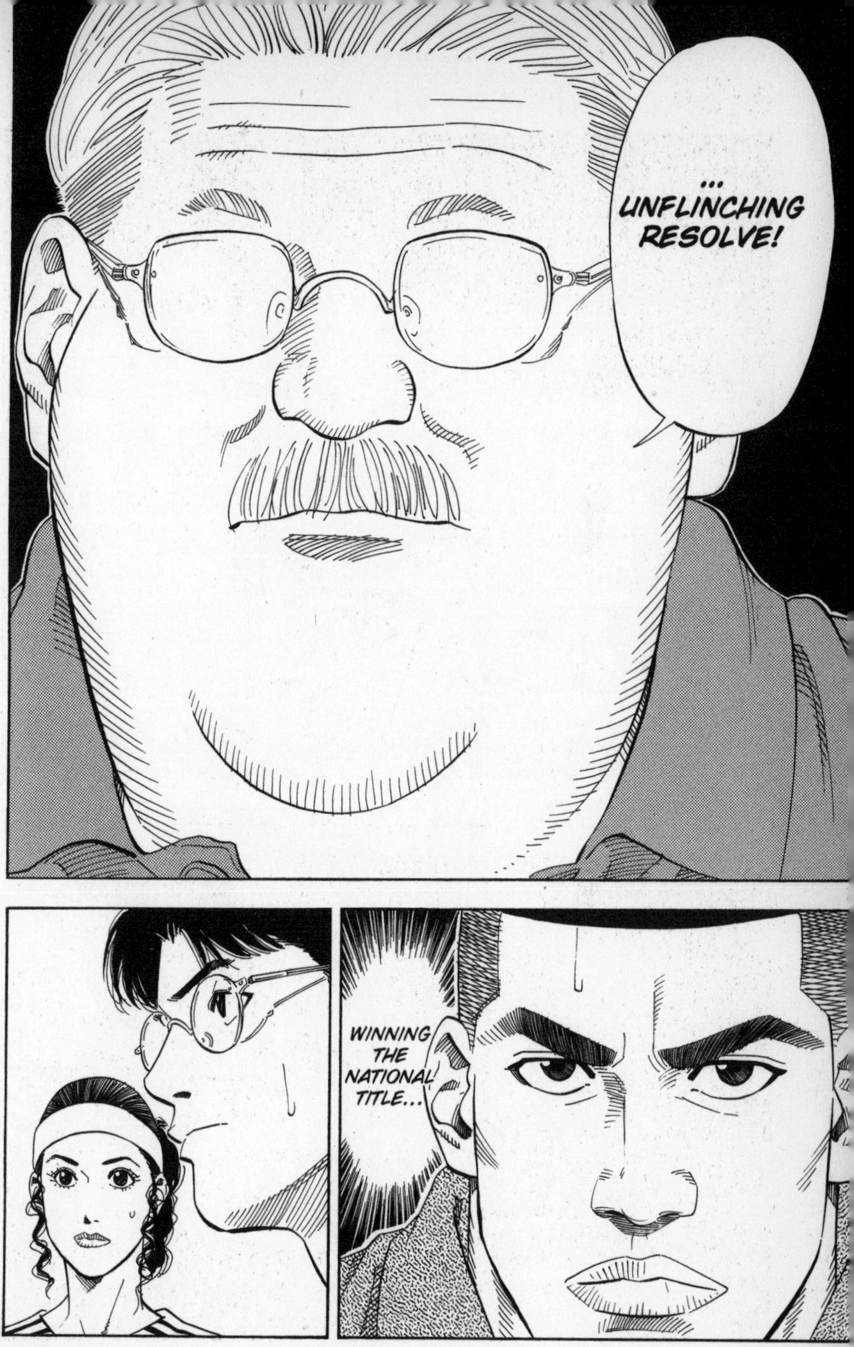
... UNFLINCHING RESOLVE!
WINNING THE NATIONAL TITLE...

READ THIS WAY

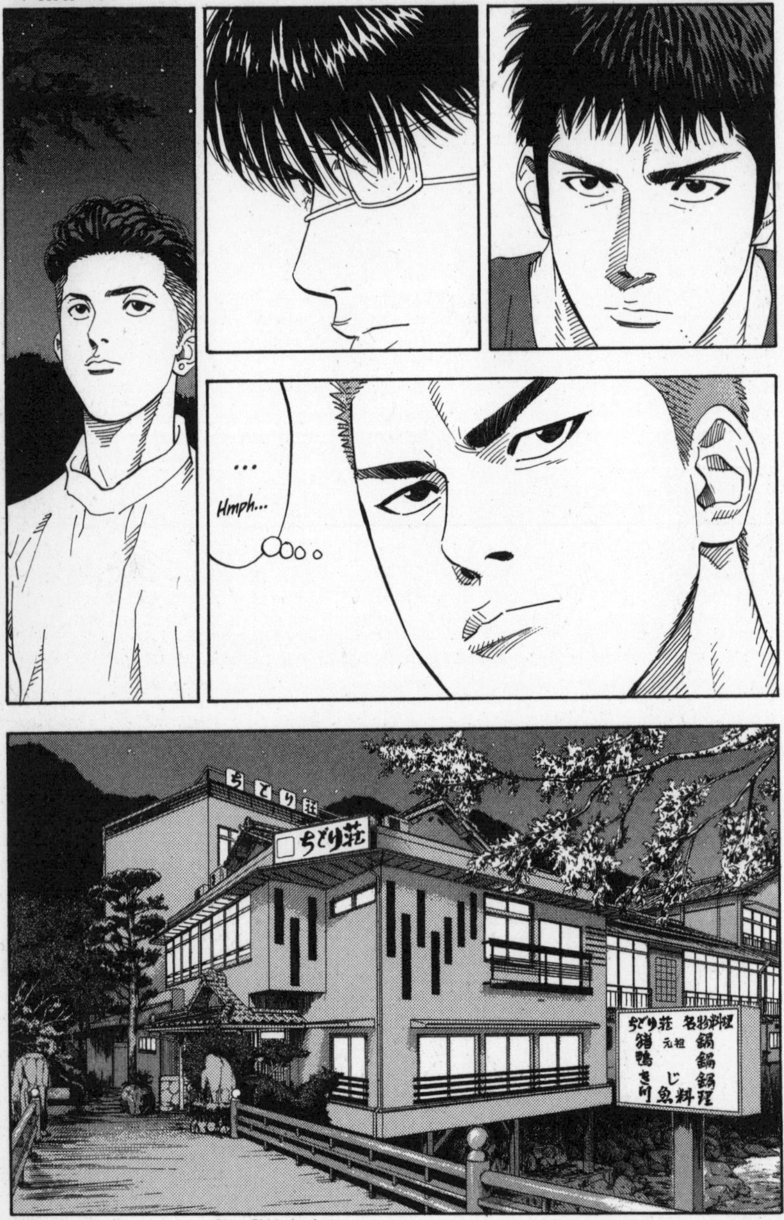
...
Hmph...
ちどり荘
ちどり荘
ちどり荘 名物料理
猪 元祖 鍋
鴨 鍋
きじ 鍋
川魚料理

Sign: Chidoriso Inn

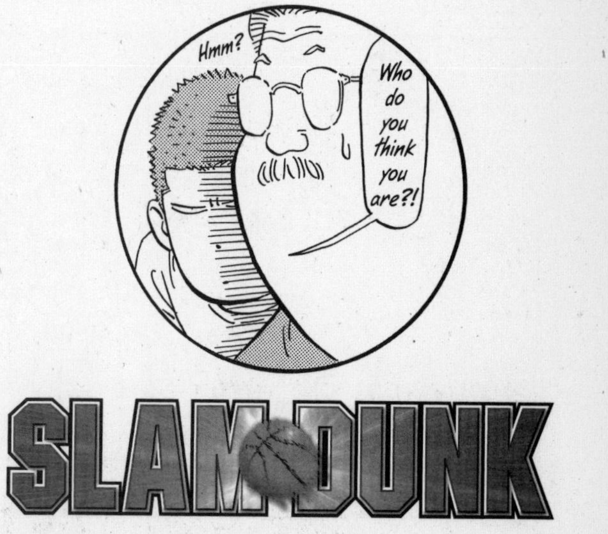
Who do you think you are?!
Hmm?

READ THIS WAY

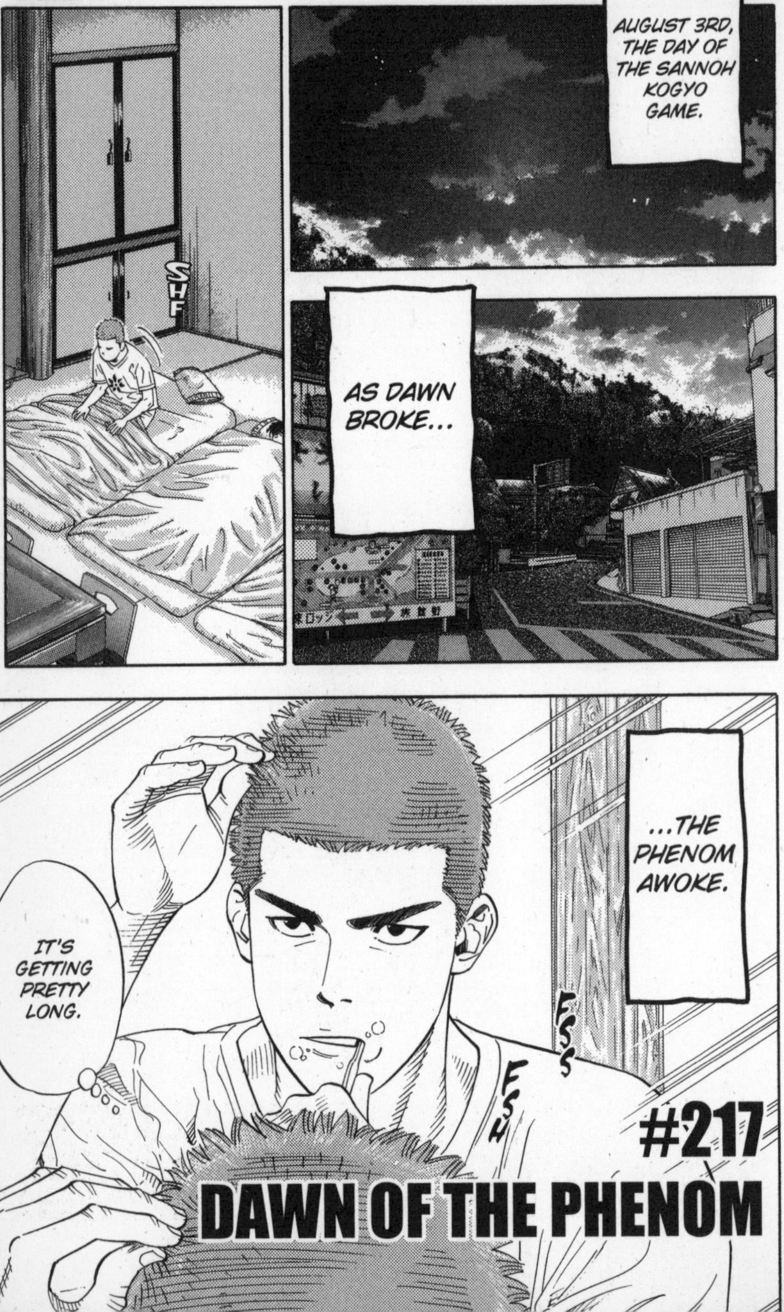
AUGUST 3RD, THE DAY OF THE SANNOH KOGYO GAME.
AS DAWN BROKE...
SHF
...THE PHENOM AWOKE.
FSS
FSH
IT'S GETTING PRETTY LONG.
#217
DAWN OF THE PHENOM

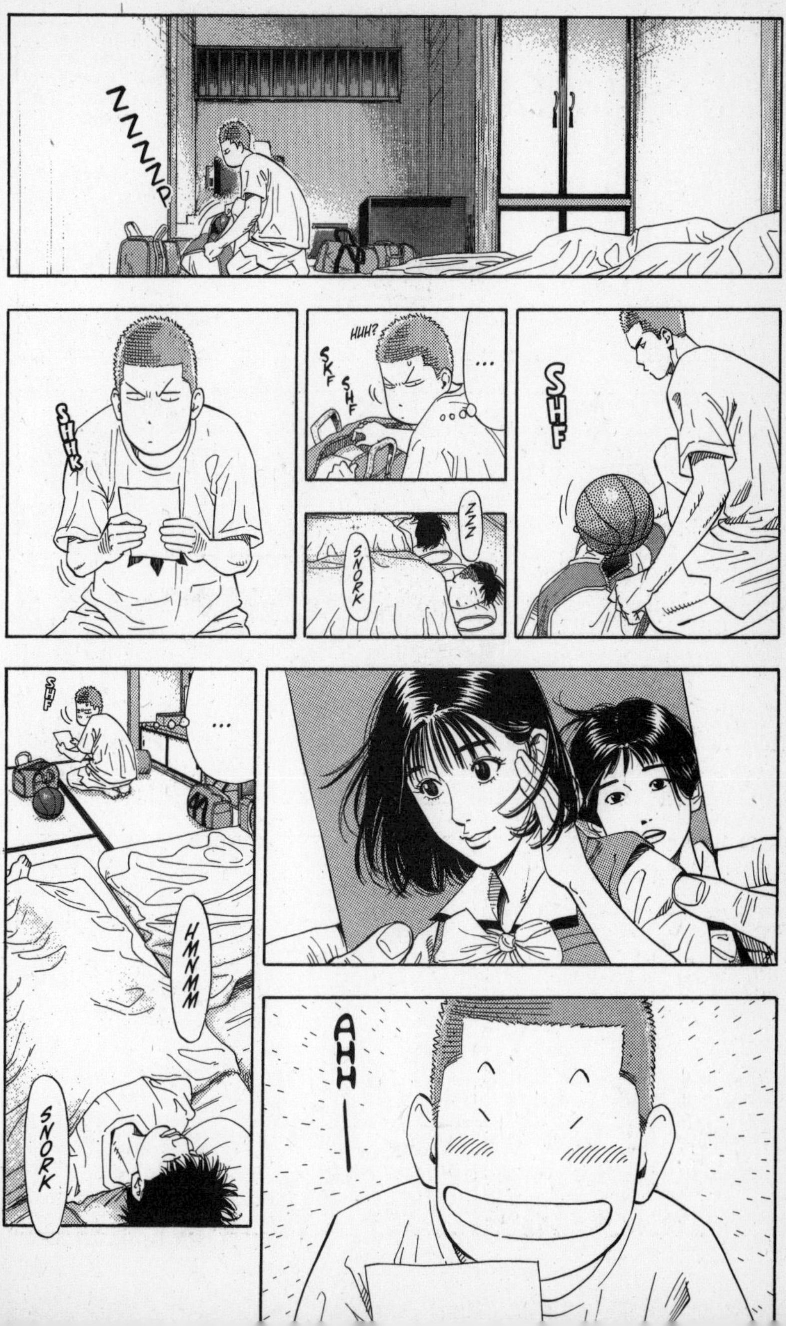
ZZZZZP
SHF
...
HUH?
SKF
SHF
ZZZ
SNORK
SHHK
AHH—
...
SHF
HMNMM
SNORK

READ THIS WAY

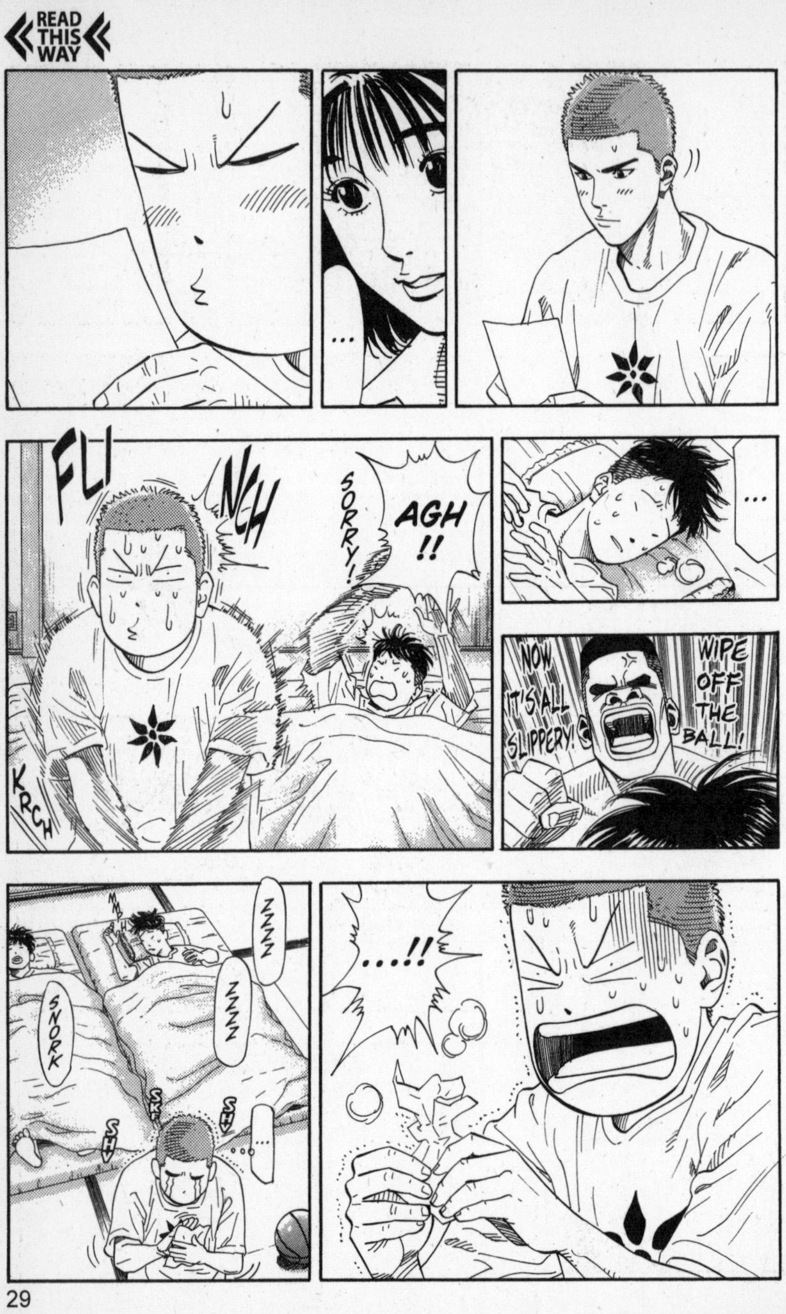
...
...
WIPE OFF THE BALL!
NOW IT'S ALL SLIPPERY!
AGH !!
SORRY!
FLINCH
KRCH
...!!
ZZZZ
MMPH
ZZZZ
SNORK
SHV
SKI
SHV
...
...

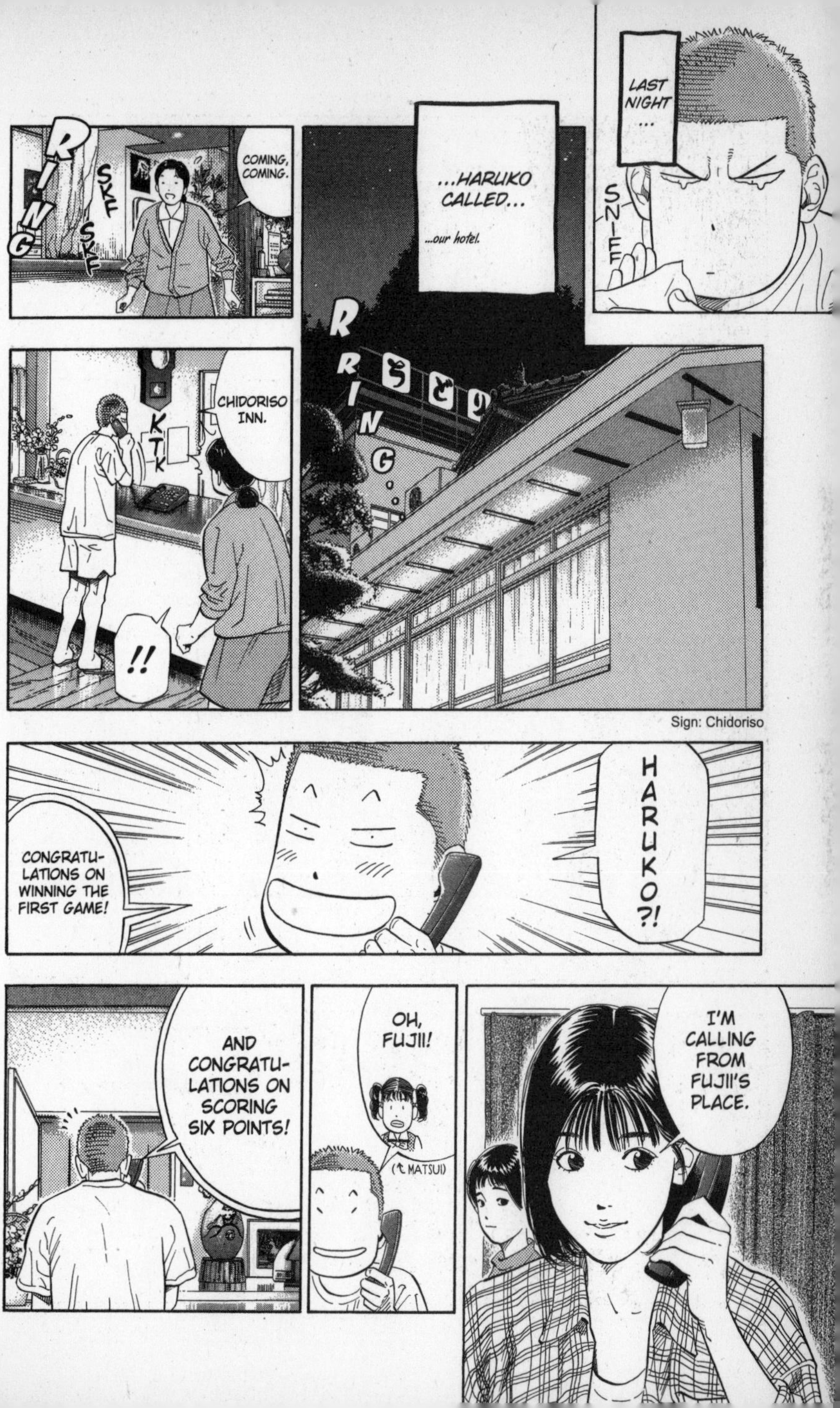
LAST NIGHT ...
SNIFF
...HARUKO CALLED...
...our hotel.
RRING
ちどり
Sign: Chidoriso
COMING, COMING.
RING
SKF SKF
CHIDORISO INN.
KTK
!!
HARUKO?!
CONGRATULATIONS ON WINNING THE FIRST GAME!
I'M CALLING FROM FUJII'S PLACE.
OH, FUJII!
(← MATSUI)
AND CONGRATULATIONS ON SCORING SIX POINTS!

READ THIS WAY

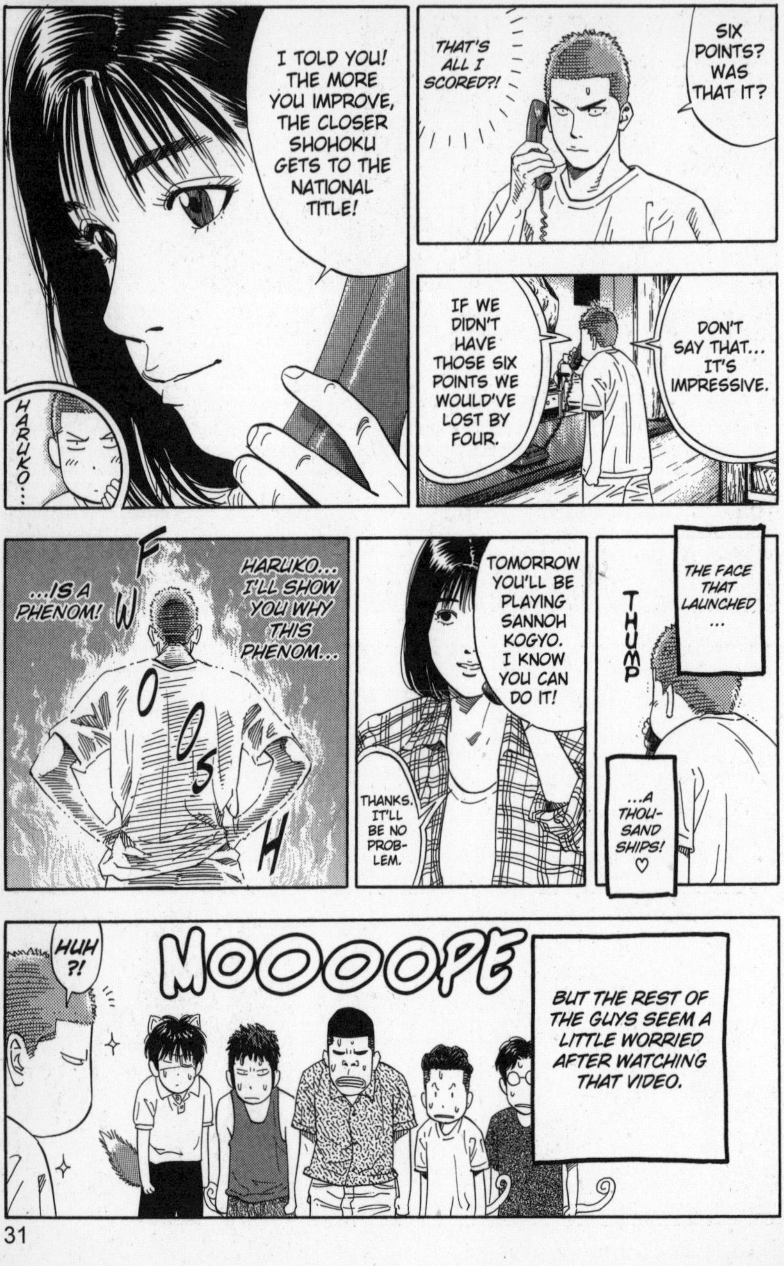

SIX POINTS? WAS THAT IT?
THAT'S ALL I SCORED?!
DON'T SAY THAT... IT'S IMPRESSIVE.
IF WE DIDN'T HAVE THOSE SIX POINTS WE WOULD'VE LOST BY FOUR.
I TOLD YOU! THE MORE YOU IMPROVE, THE CLOSER SHOHOKU GETS TO THE NATIONAL TITLE!
HARUKO...
THE FACE THAT LAUNCHED...
THUMP
...A THOUSAND SHIPS! ♡
TOMORROW YOU'LL BE PLAYING SANNOH KOGYO. I KNOW YOU CAN DO IT!
THANKS. IT'LL BE NO PROBLEM.
HARUKO... I'LL SHOW YOU WHY THIS PHENOM...
FWOOOSH
...IS A PHENOM!
BUT THE REST OF THE GUYS SEEM A LITTLE WORRIED AFTER WATCHING THAT VIDEO.
MOOOOPE
HUH?!

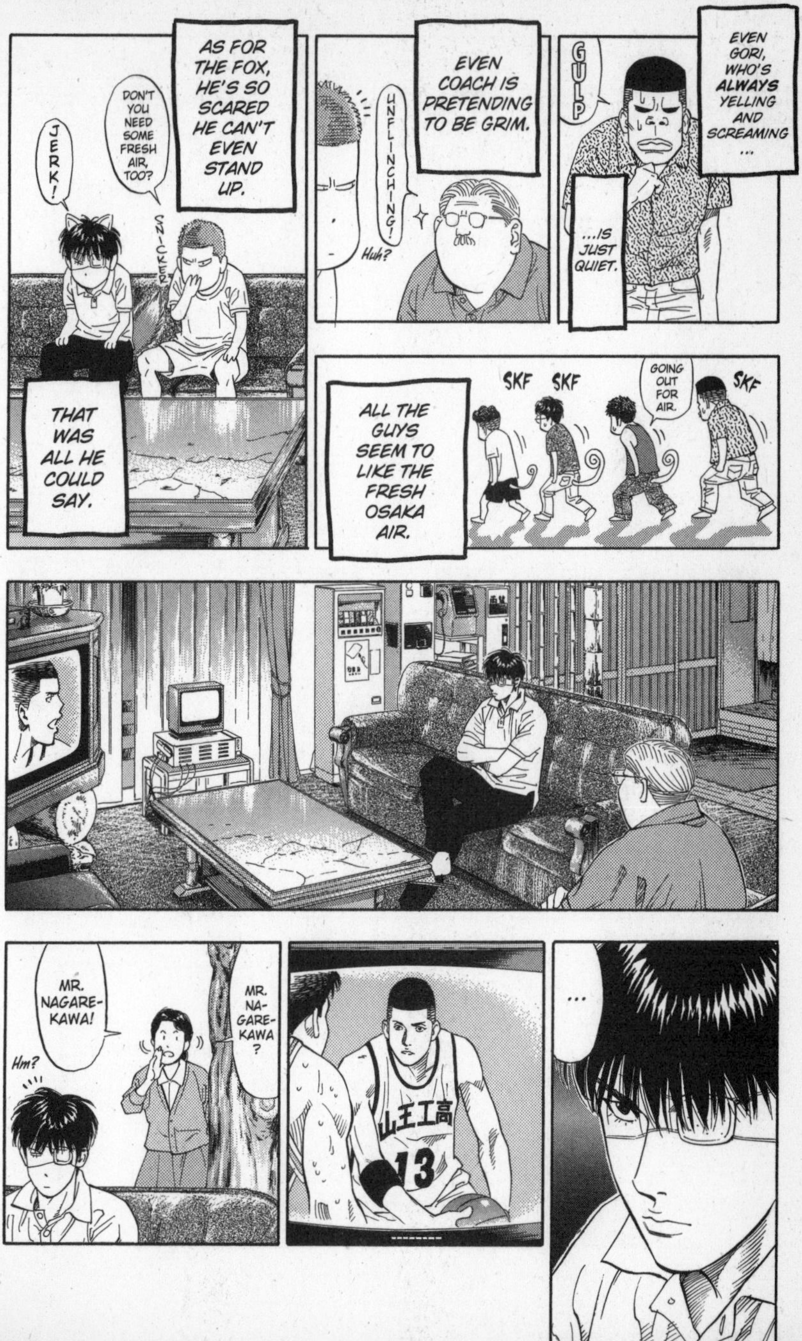
EVEN GORI, WHO'S **ALWAYS** YELLING AND SCREAMING...
GULP
...IS JUST QUIET.
EVEN COACH IS PRETENDING TO BE GRIM.
UNFLINCHING!
Huh?
SKF
GOING OUT FOR AIR.
SKF
SKF
ALL THE GUYS SEEM TO LIKE THE FRESH OSAKA AIR.
AS FOR THE FOX, HE'S SO SCARED HE CAN'T EVEN STAND UP.
DON'T YOU NEED SOME FRESH AIR, TOO?
SNICKER
JERK!
THAT WAS ALL HE COULD SAY.
...
MR. NAGARE-KAWA?
MR. NAGARE-KAWA!
Hm?

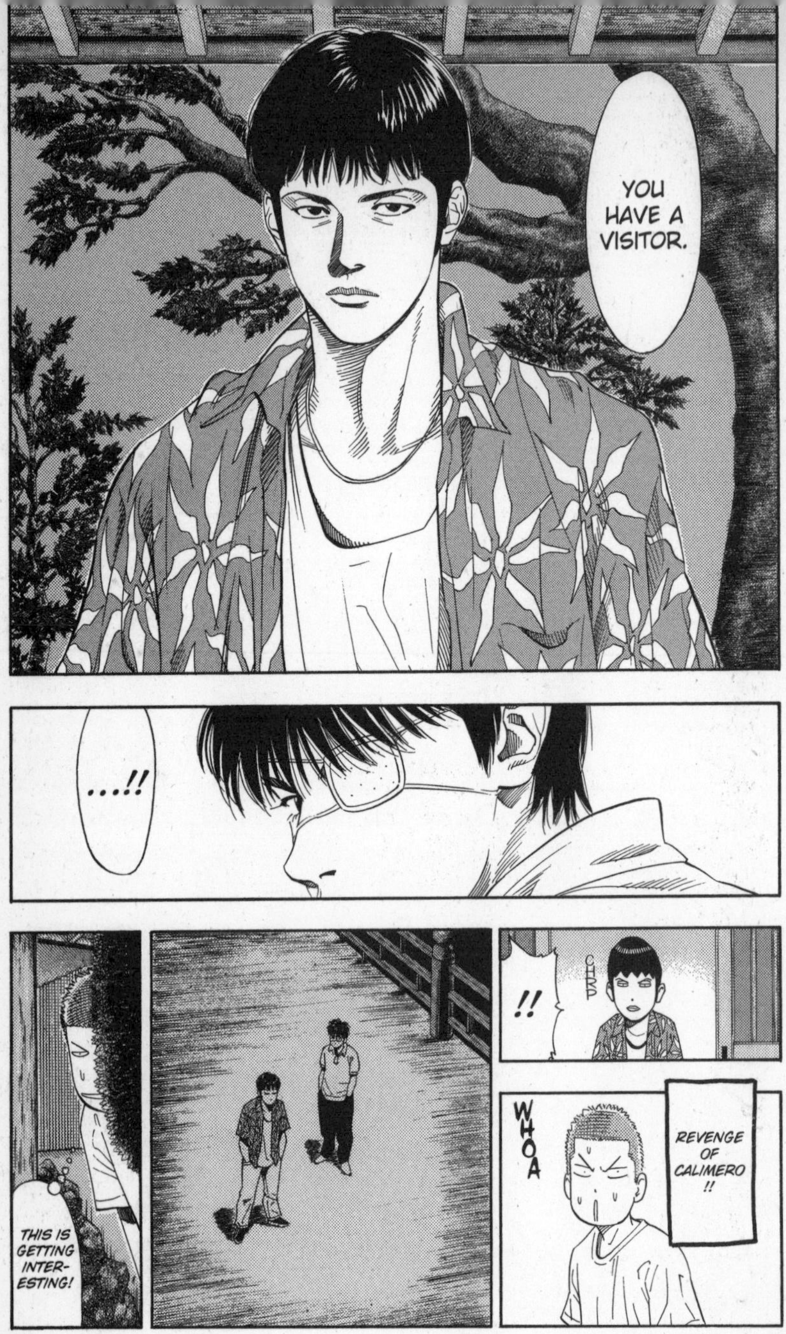
YOU HAVE A VISITOR.
...!!
!!
CHRP
WHOA
REVENGE OF CALIMERO !!
THIS IS GETTING INTER-ESTING!

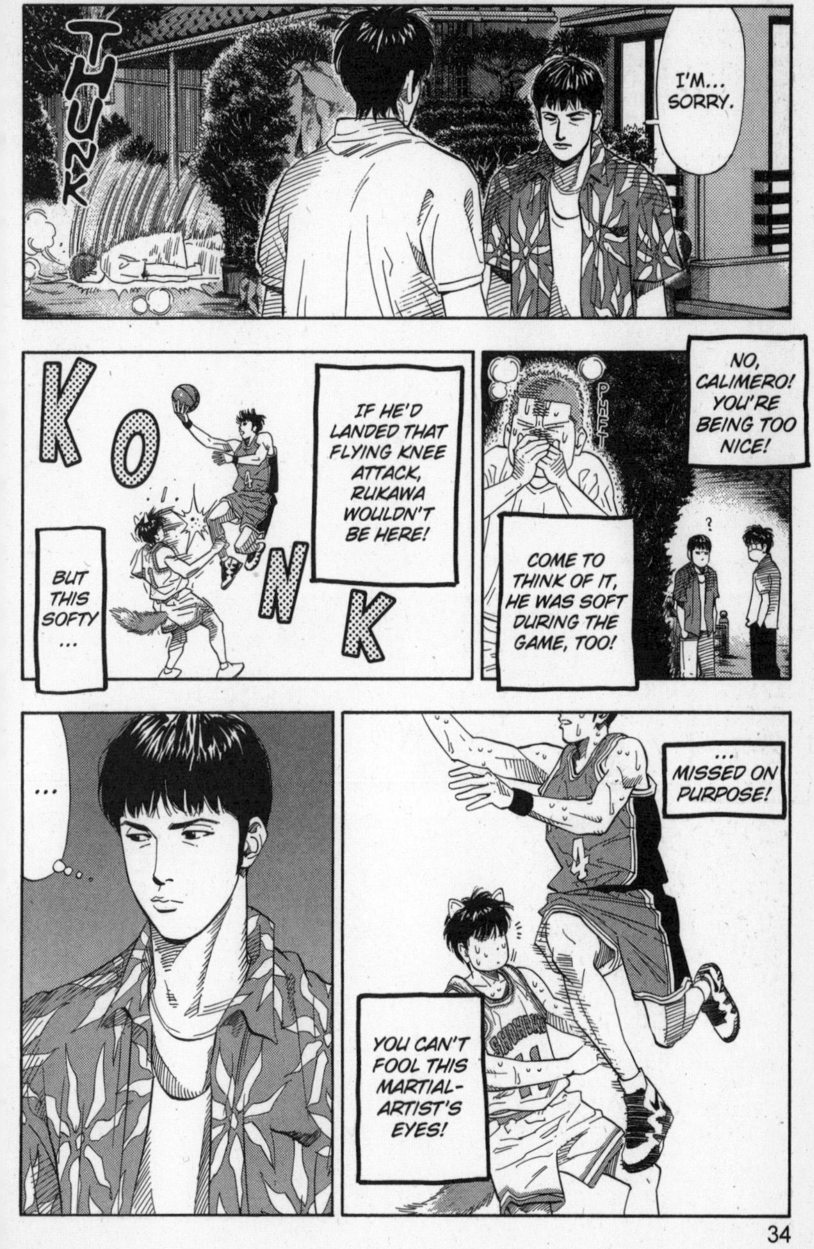
I'M... SORRY.
THUNK
NO, CALIMERO! YOU'RE BEING TOO NICE!
PHFFT
COME TO THINK OF IT, HE WAS SOFT DURING THE GAME, TOO!
?
IF HE'D LANDED THAT FLYING KNEE ATTACK, RUKAWA WOULDN'T BE HERE!
KONK
BUT THIS SOFTY ...
... MISSED ON PURPOSE!
YOU CAN'T FOOL THIS MARTIAL-ARTIST'S EYES!
...

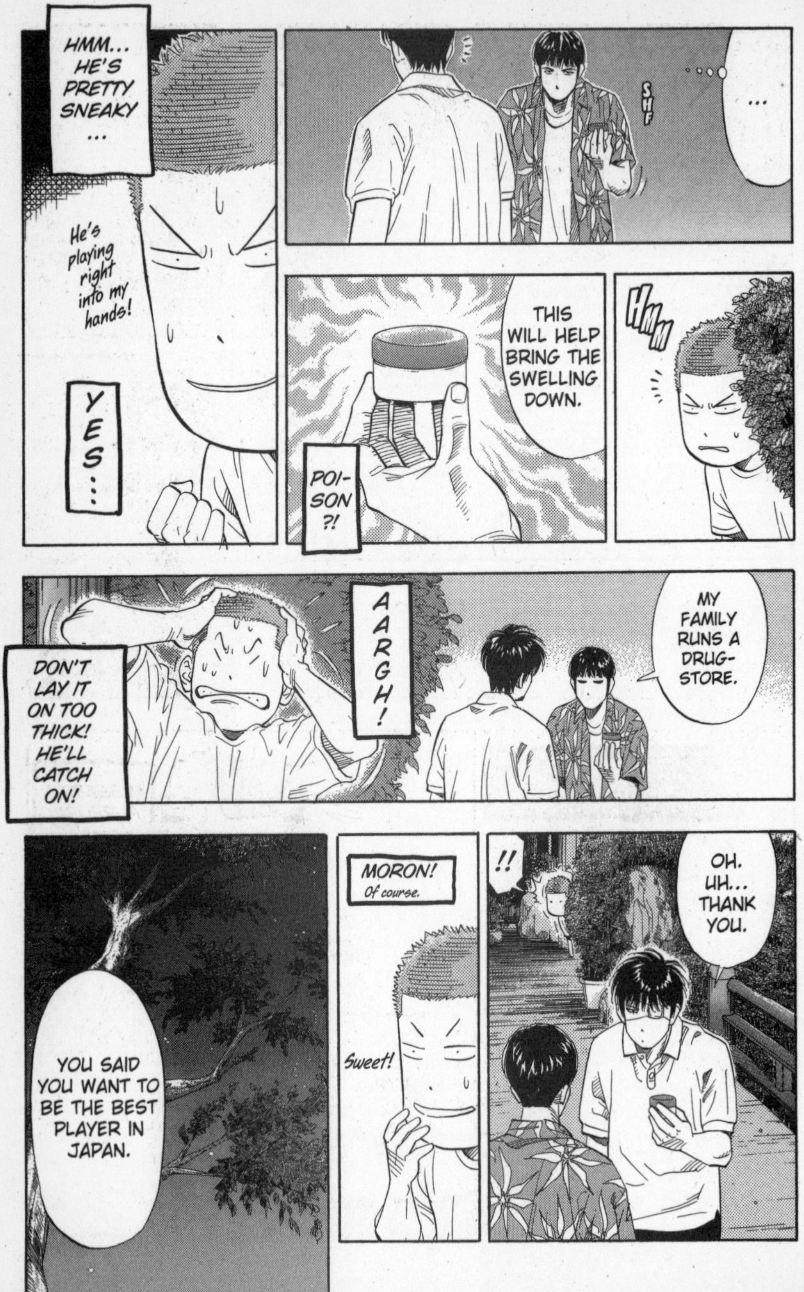
...
SHF
HMM
THIS WILL HELP BRING THE SWELLING DOWN.
POI-SON?!
HMM... HE'S PRETTY SNEAKY...
He's playing right into my hands!
YES...
MY FAMILY RUNS A DRUG-STORE.
AARGH!
DON'T LAY IT ON TOO THICK! HE'LL CATCH ON!
OH. UH... THANK YOU.
!!
MORON!
Of course.
Sweet!
YOU SAID YOU WANT TO BE THE BEST PLAYER IN JAPAN.

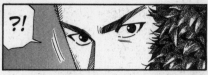

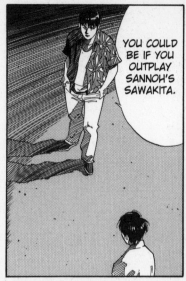

YOU COULD BE IF YOU OUTPLAY SANNOH'S SAWAKITA.

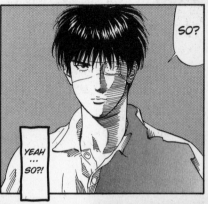

?!

SO?

YEAH ... SO?!

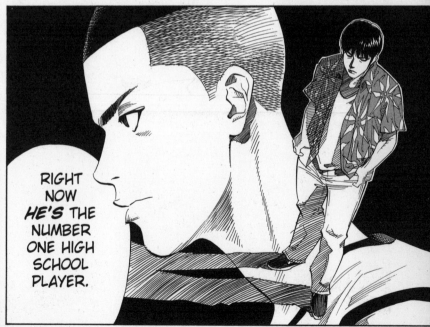

RIGHT NOW *HE'S* THE NUMBER ONE HIGH SCHOOL PLAYER.

READ THIS WAY

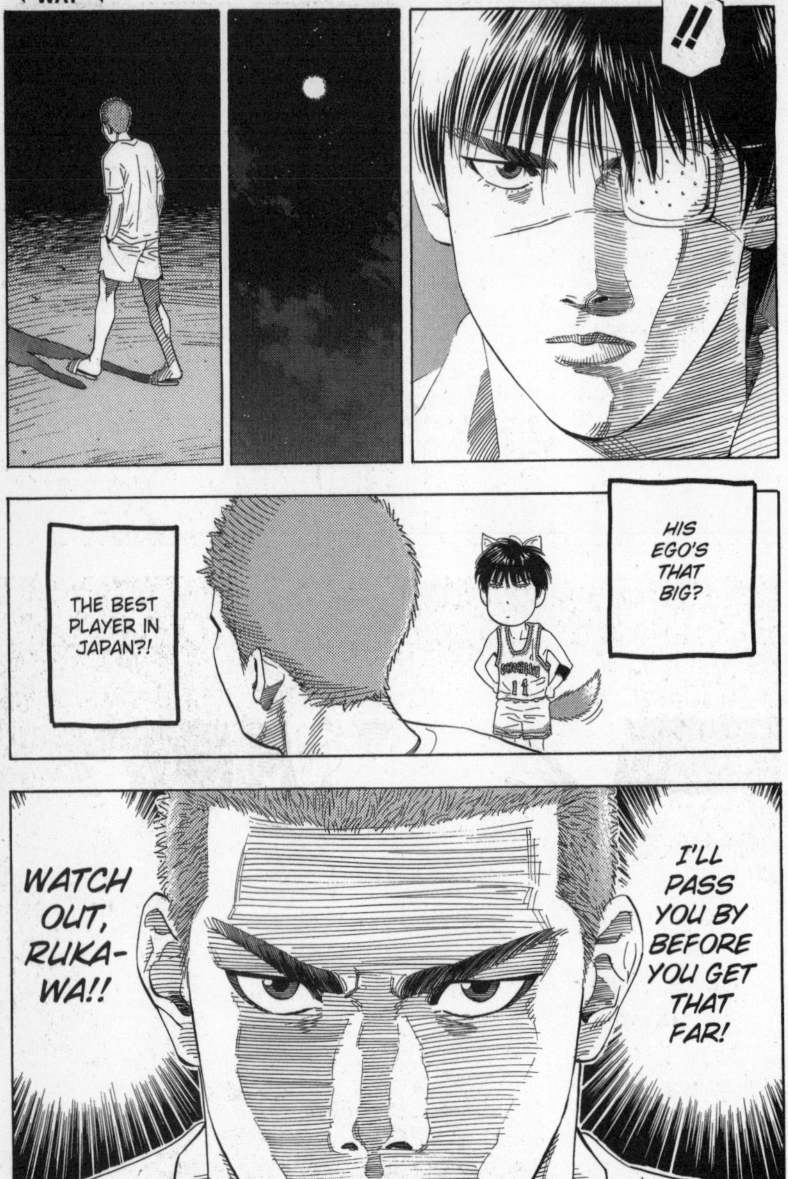
!!
HIS EGO'S THAT BIG?
THE BEST PLAYER IN JAPAN?!
I'LL PASS YOU BY BEFORE YOU GET THAT FAR!
WATCH OUT, RUKA-WA!!

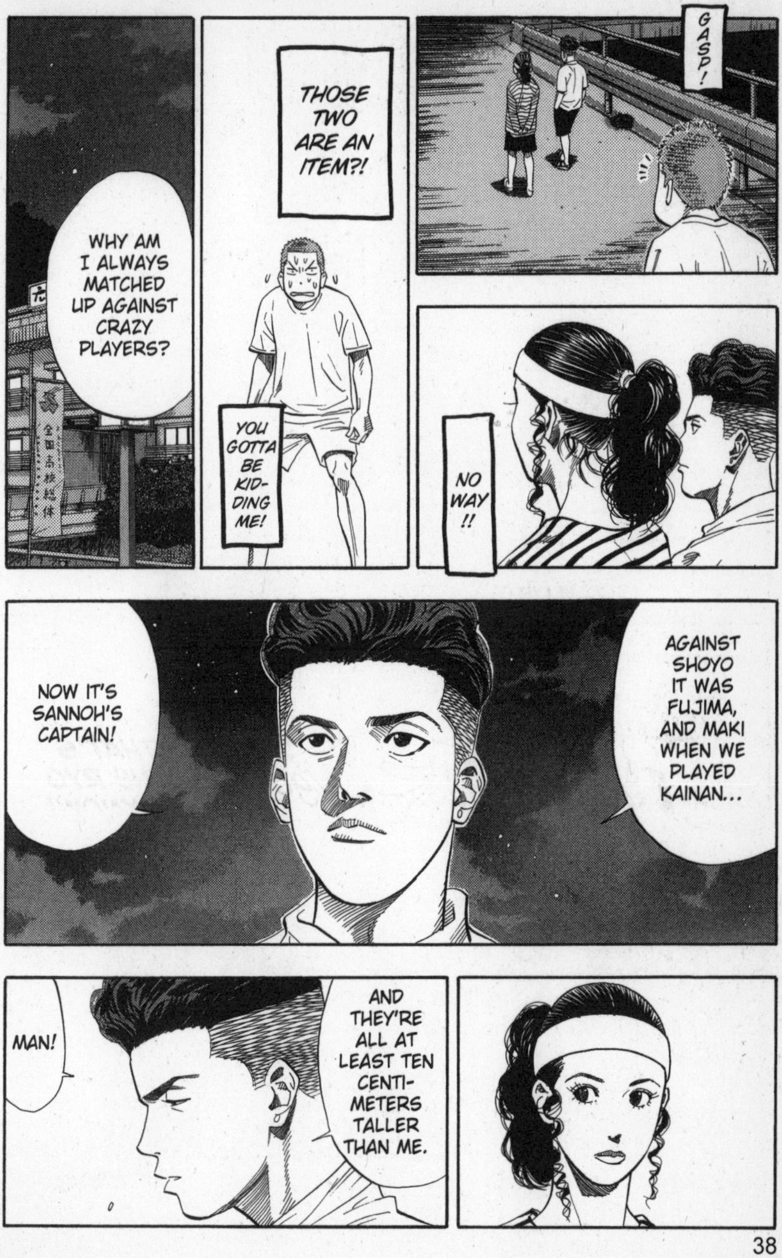
GASP!
NO WAY!!
THOSE TWO ARE AN ITEM?!
YOU GOTTA BE KID-DING ME!
WHY AM I ALWAYS MATCHED UP AGAINST CRAZY PLAYERS?
AGAINST SHOYO IT WAS FUJIMA, AND MAKI WHEN WE PLAYED KAINAN...
NOW IT'S SANNOH'S CAPTAIN!
AND THEY'RE ALL AT LEAST TEN CENTI-METERS TALLER THAN ME.
MAN!

READ THIS WAY

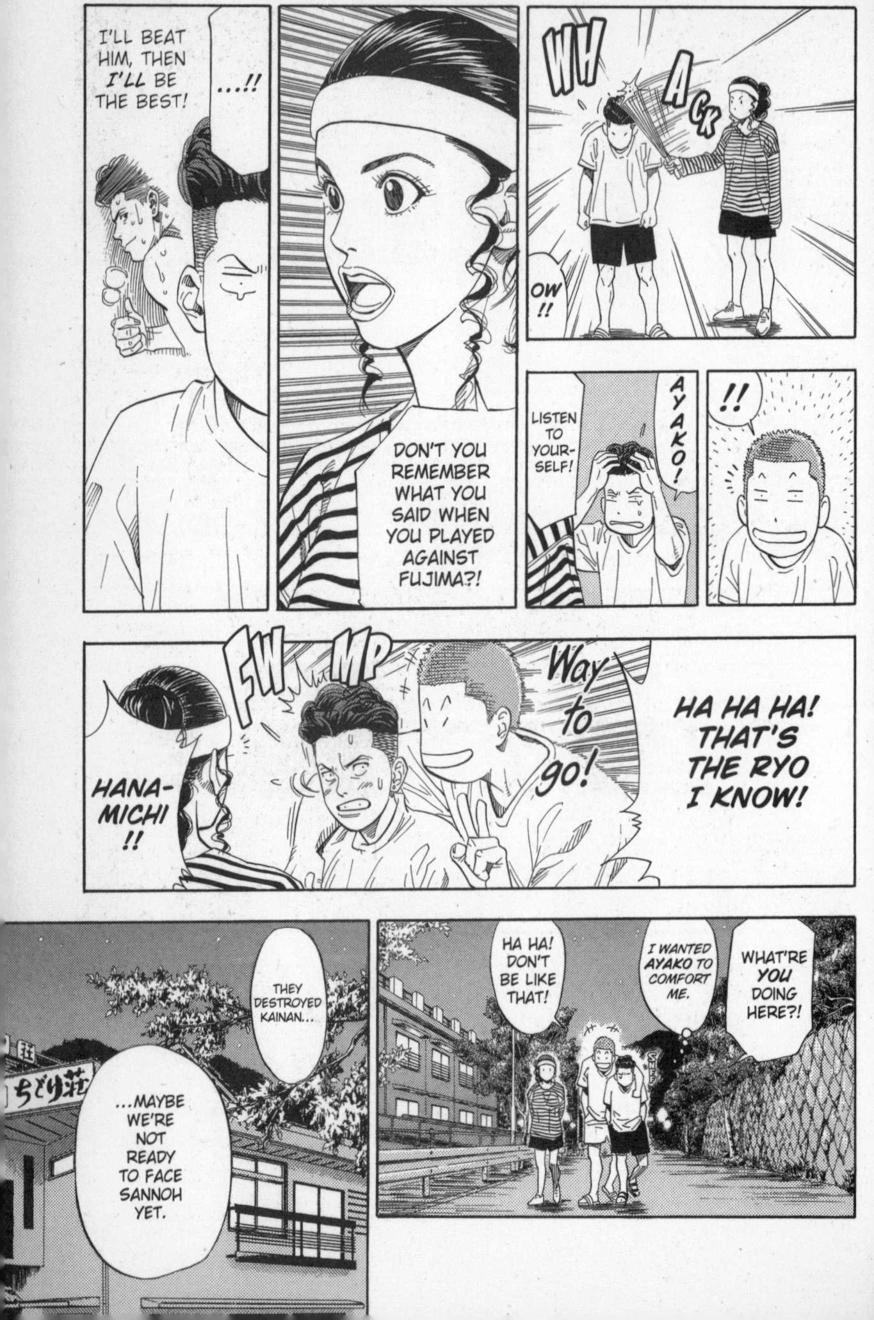
WHACK
OW!!
!!
AYAKO!
LISTEN TO YOURSELF!
DON'T YOU REMEMBER WHAT YOU SAID WHEN YOU PLAYED AGAINST FUJIMA?!
...!!
I'LL BEAT HIM, THEN *I'LL* BE THE BEST!
HA HA HA! THAT'S THE RYO I KNOW!
Way to go!
FWMP
HANAMICHI!!
WHAT'RE *YOU* DOING HERE?!
I WANTED AYAKO TO COMFORT ME.
HA HA! DON'T BE LIKE THAT!
THEY DESTROYED KAINAN...
...MAYBE WE'RE NOT READY TO FACE SANNOH YET.
ちどり荘

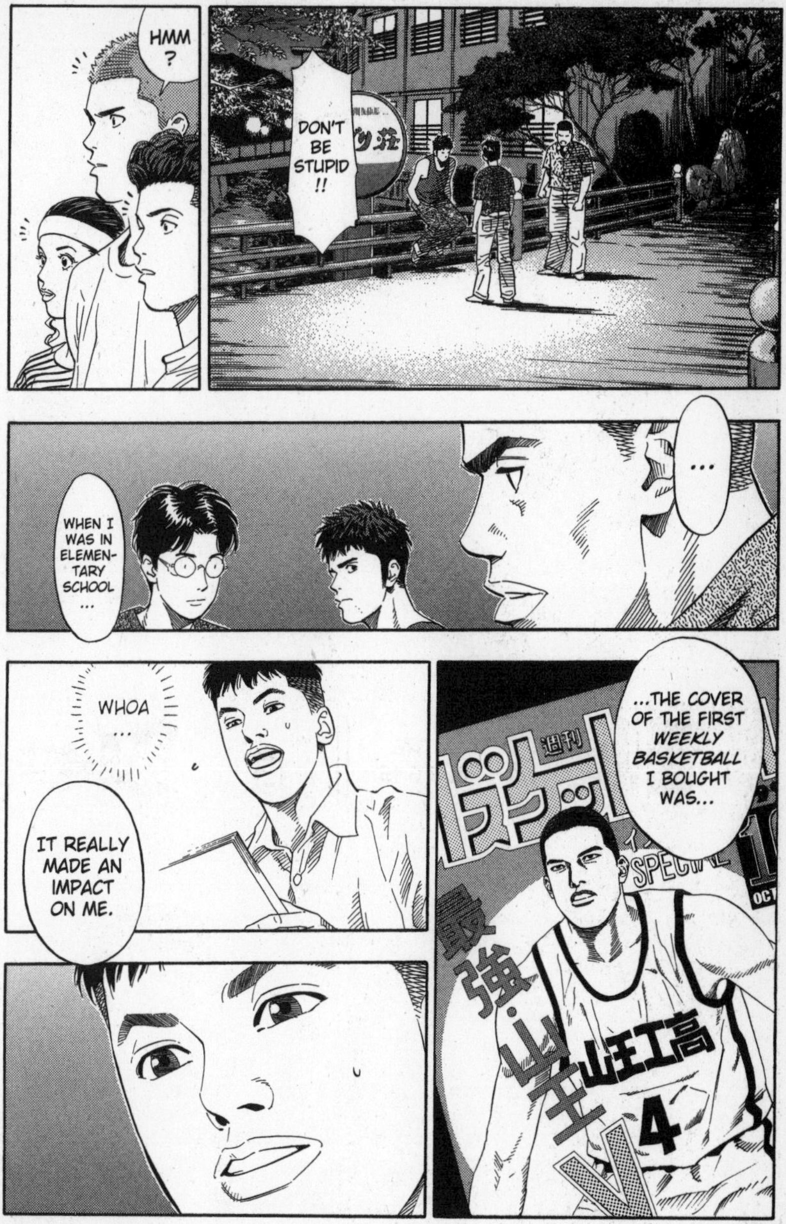
DON'T BE STUPID!!
HMM?
...
WHEN I WAS IN ELEMENTARY SCHOOL ...
...THE COVER OF THE FIRST WEEKLY BASKETBALL I BOUGHT WAS...
WHOA ...
IT REALLY MADE AN IMPACT ON ME.

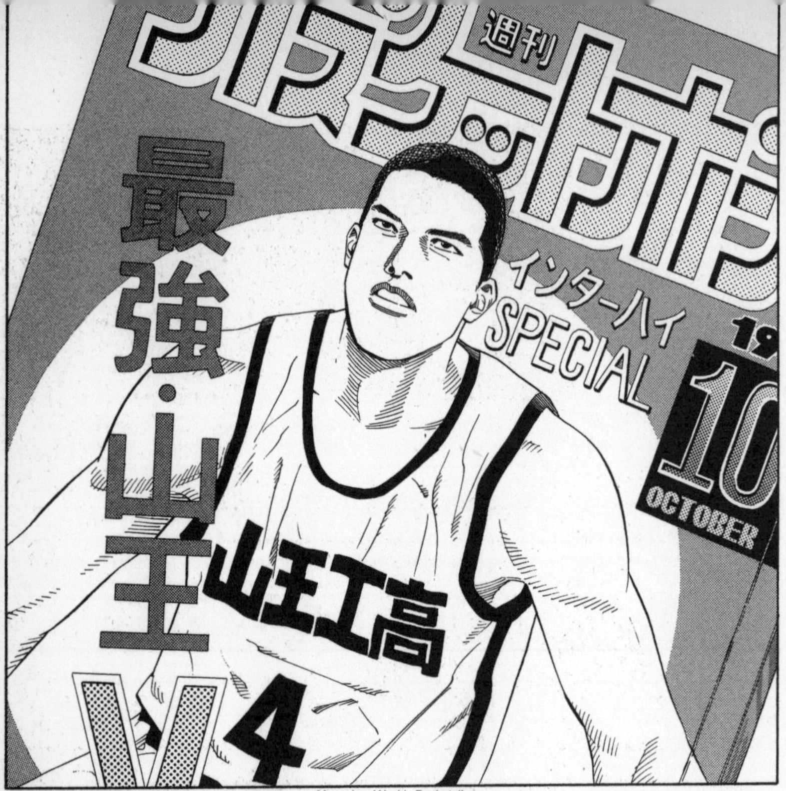
週刊
インターハイ
SPECIAL
19
10
OCTOBER
最強山王V
山王工高
4

Magazine: Weekly Basketall
Ultimate – Sannoh V

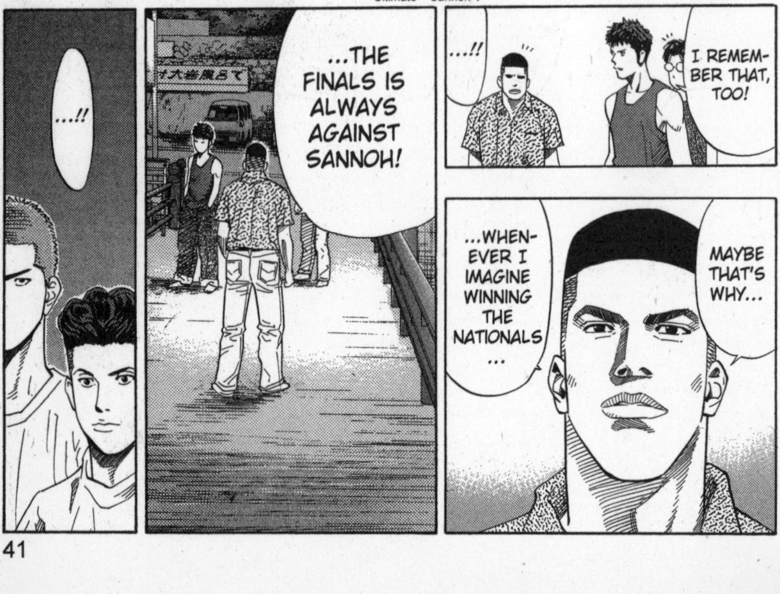
I REMEMBER THAT, TOO!
...!!
MAYBE THAT'S WHY...
...WHENEVER I IMAGINE WINNING THE NATIONALS...
...THE FINALS IS ALWAYS AGAINST SANNOH!
...!!

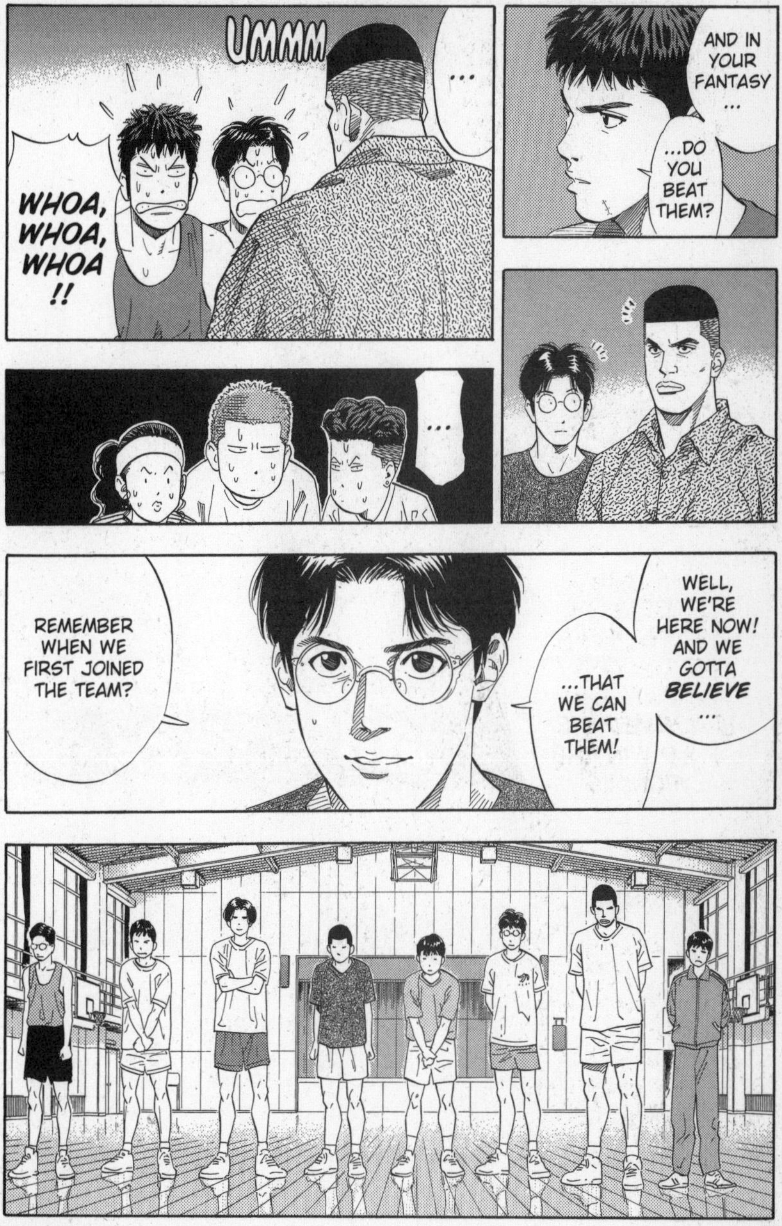
AND IN YOUR FANTASY ...
...DO YOU BEAT THEM?
...
UMMM
WHOA, WHOA, WHOA !!
...
WELL, WE'RE HERE NOW! AND WE GOTTA BELIEVE ...
...THAT WE CAN BEAT THEM!
REMEMBER WHEN WE FIRST JOINED THE TEAM?

READ THIS WAY

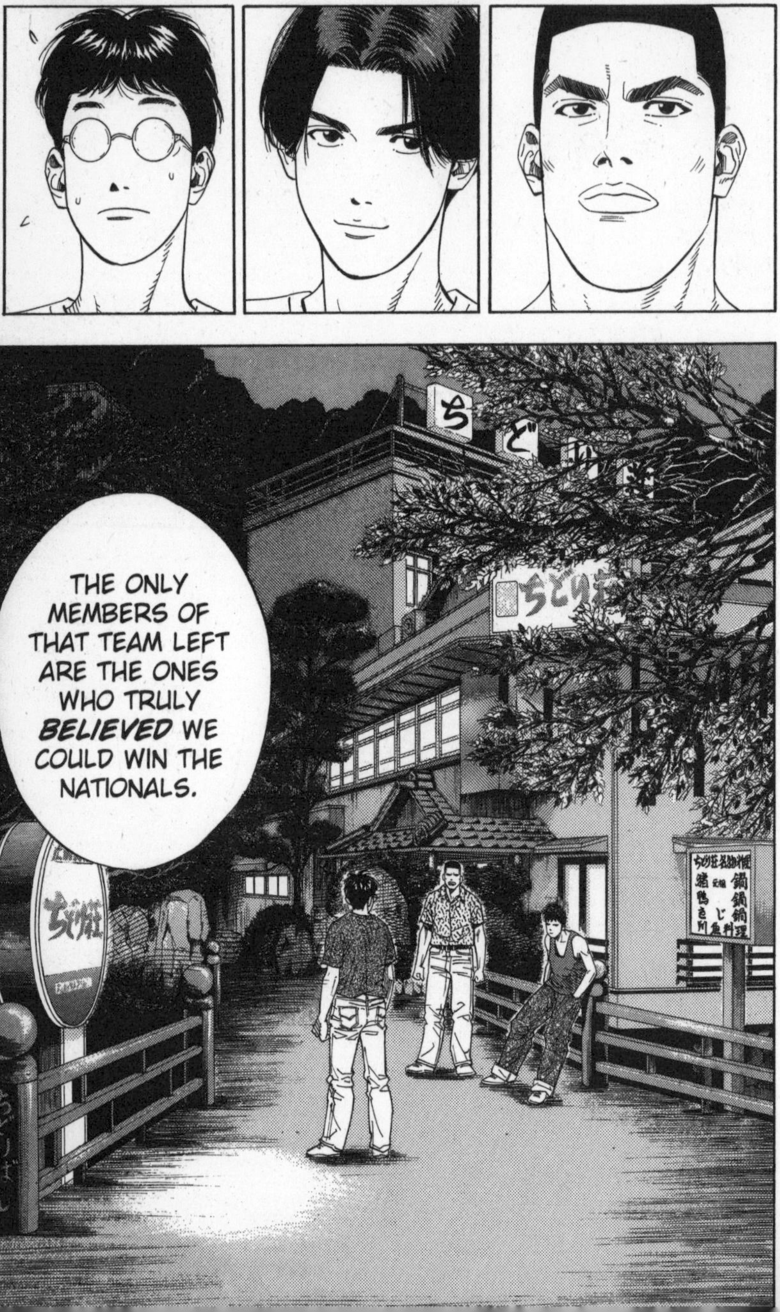
THE ONLY MEMBERS OF THAT TEAM LEFT ARE THE ONES WHO TRULY ***BELIEVED*** WE COULD WIN THE NATIONALS.
ちどりばし

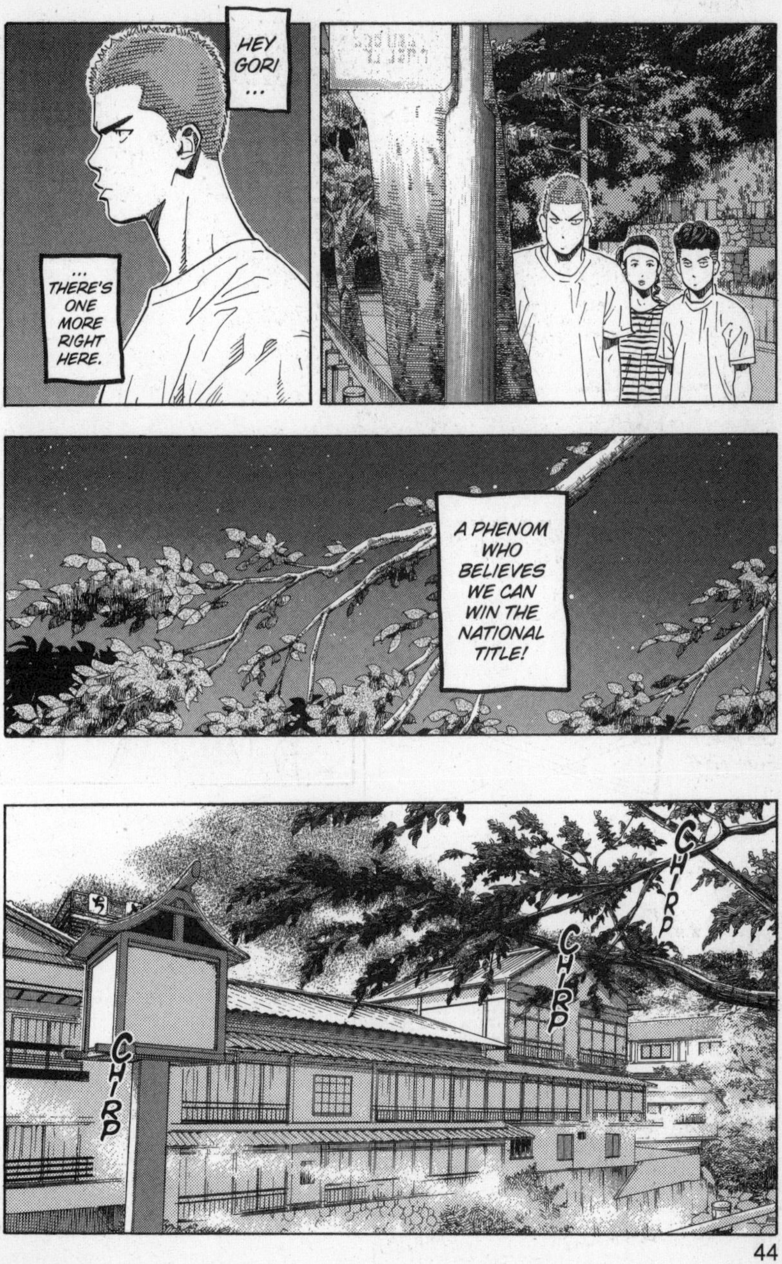
HEY GORI ...
... THERE'S ONE MORE RIGHT HERE.
A PHENOM WHO BELIEVES WE CAN WIN THE NATIONAL TITLE!
CHIRP
CHIRP
CHIRP
CHIRP

READ THIS WAY

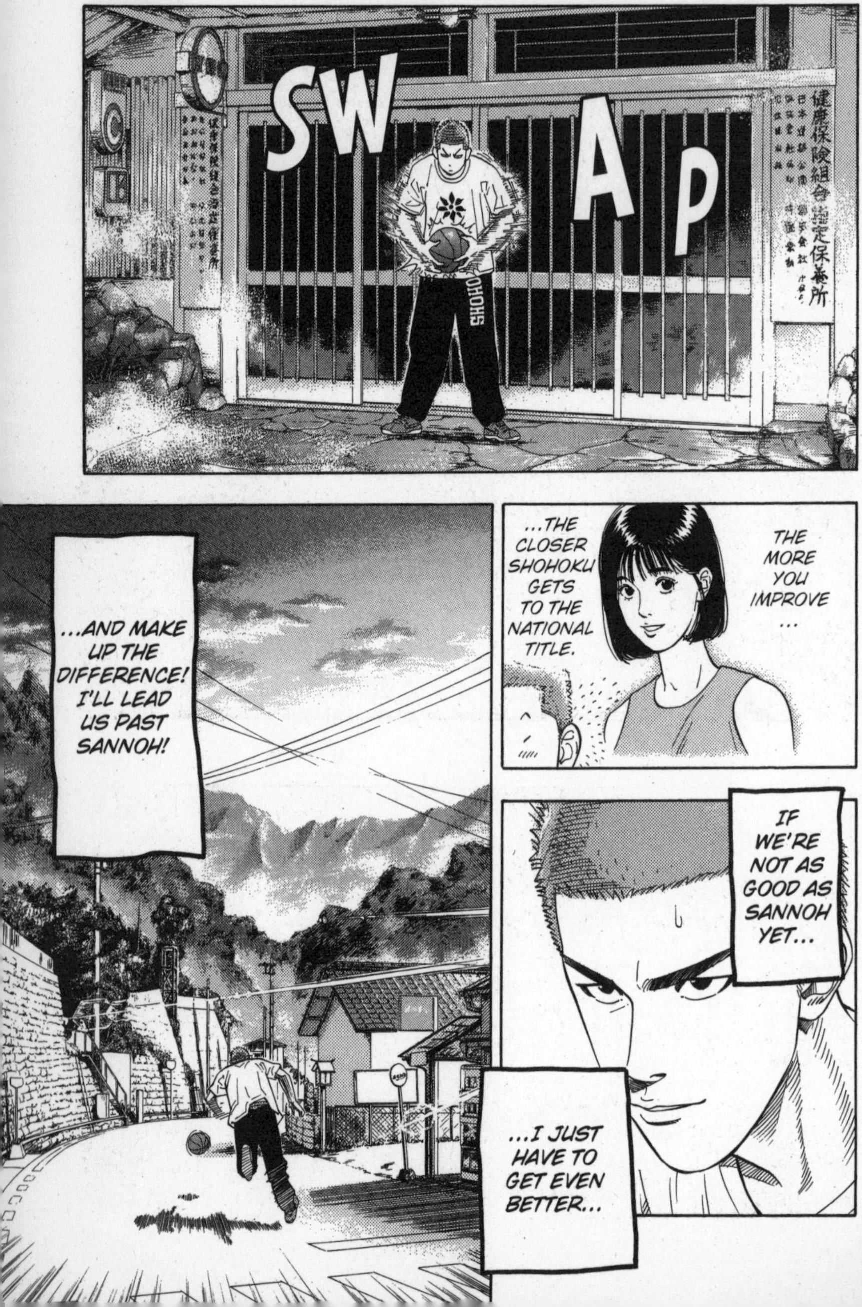
SWAP
健康保険組合指定保養所
THE MORE YOU IMPROVE...
...THE CLOSER SHOHOKU GETS TO THE NATIONAL TITLE.
IF WE'RE NOT AS GOOD AS SANNOH YET...
...I JUST HAVE TO GET EVEN BETTER...
...AND MAKE UP THE DIFFERENCE! I'LL LEAD US PAST SANNOH!

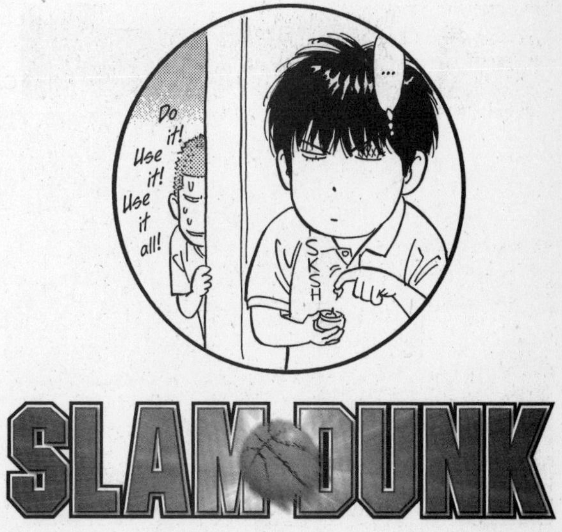
...
Do it! Use it! Use it all!
SKSH

SLAM DUNK

READ THIS WAY

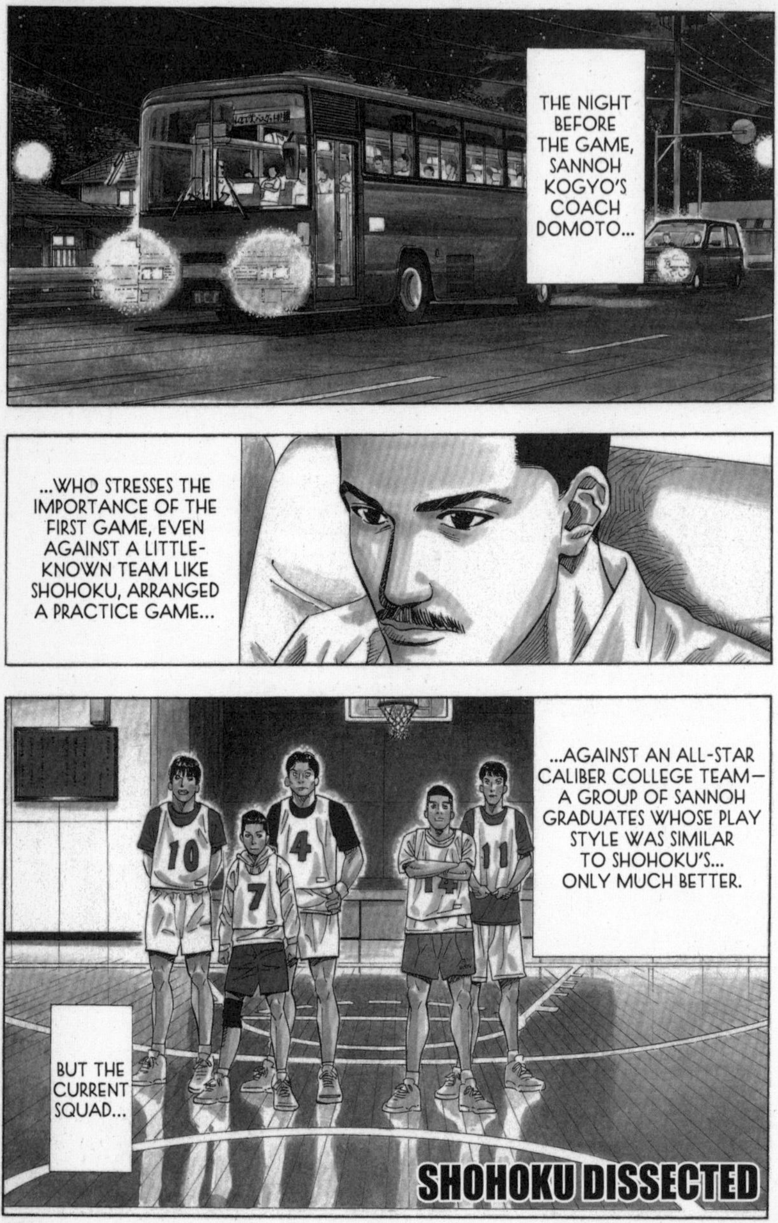
THE NIGHT BEFORE THE GAME, SANNOH KOGYO'S COACH DOMOTO...
...WHO STRESSES THE IMPORTANCE OF THE FIRST GAME, EVEN AGAINST A LITTLE-KNOWN TEAM LIKE SHOHOKU, ARRANGED A PRACTICE GAME...
...AGAINST AN ALL-STAR CALIBER COLLEGE TEAM—A GROUP OF SANNOH GRADUATES WHOSE PLAY STYLE WAS SIMILAR TO SHOHOKU'S... ONLY MUCH BETTER.
10
7
4
14
11
BUT THE CURRENT SQUAD...
SHOHOKU DISSECTED

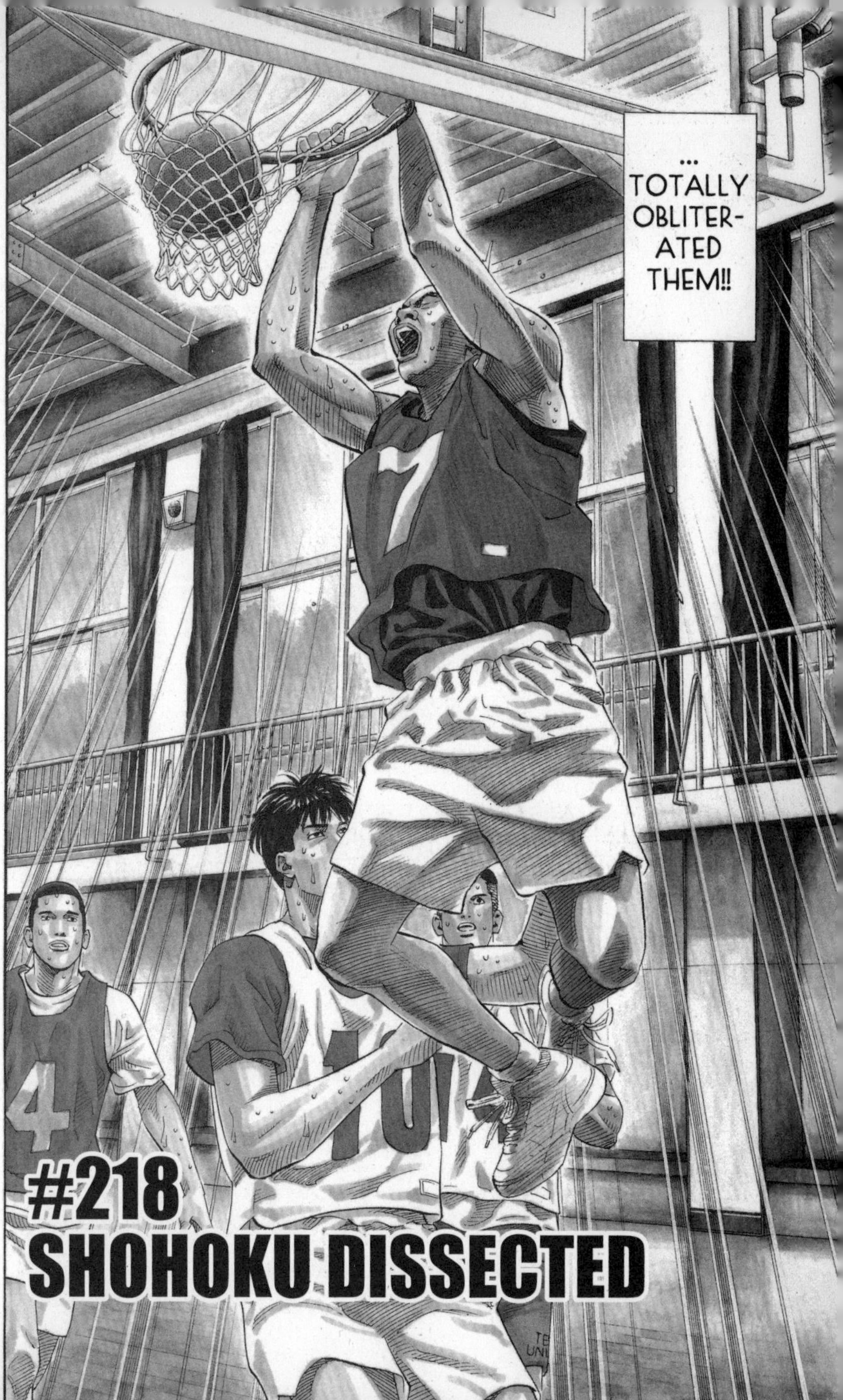

... TOTALLY OBLITER- ATED THEM!!
#218
SHOHOKU DISSECTED

READ THIS WAY

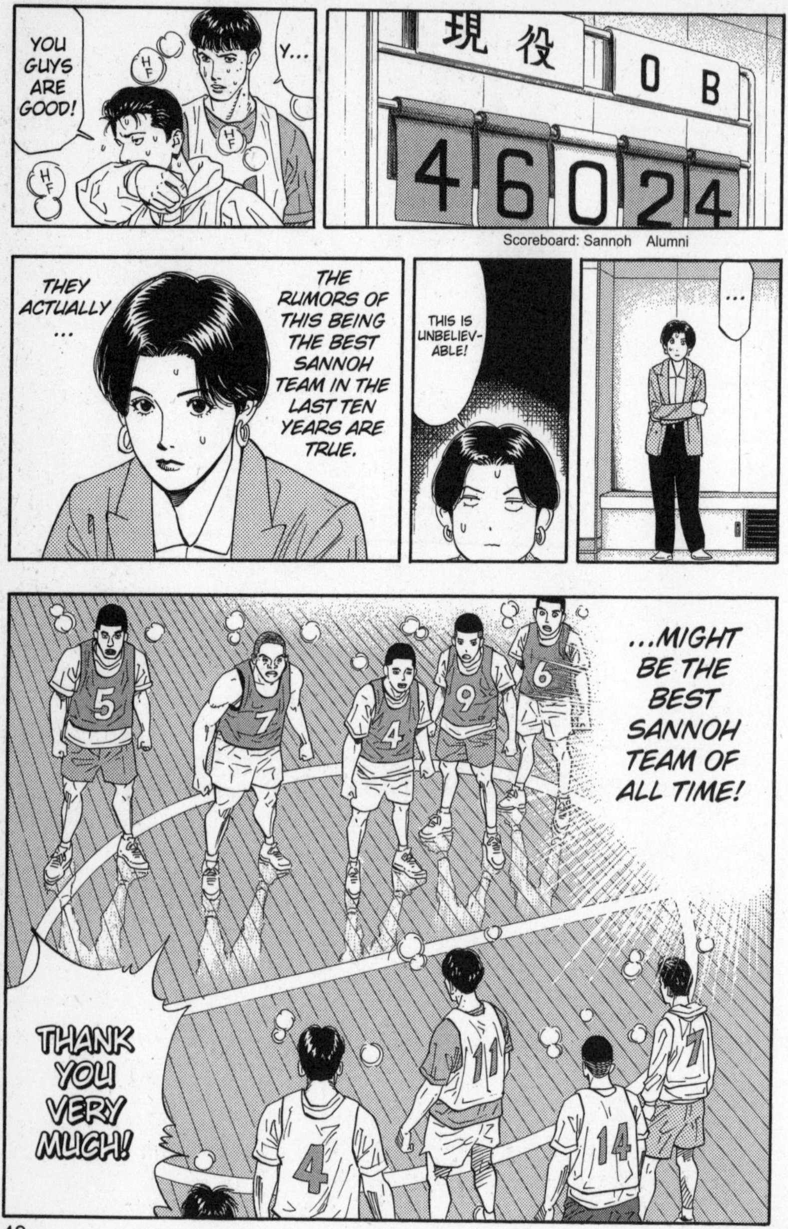

現役
OB
46024
Scoreboard: Sannoh Alumni
Y...
YOU GUYS ARE GOOD!
HF
HF
HF
...
THIS IS UNBELIEVABLE!
THE RUMORS OF THIS BEING THE BEST SANNOH TEAM IN THE LAST TEN YEARS ARE TRUE.
THEY ACTUALLY ...
...MIGHT BE THE BEST SANNOH TEAM OF ALL TIME!
THANK YOU VERY MUCH!

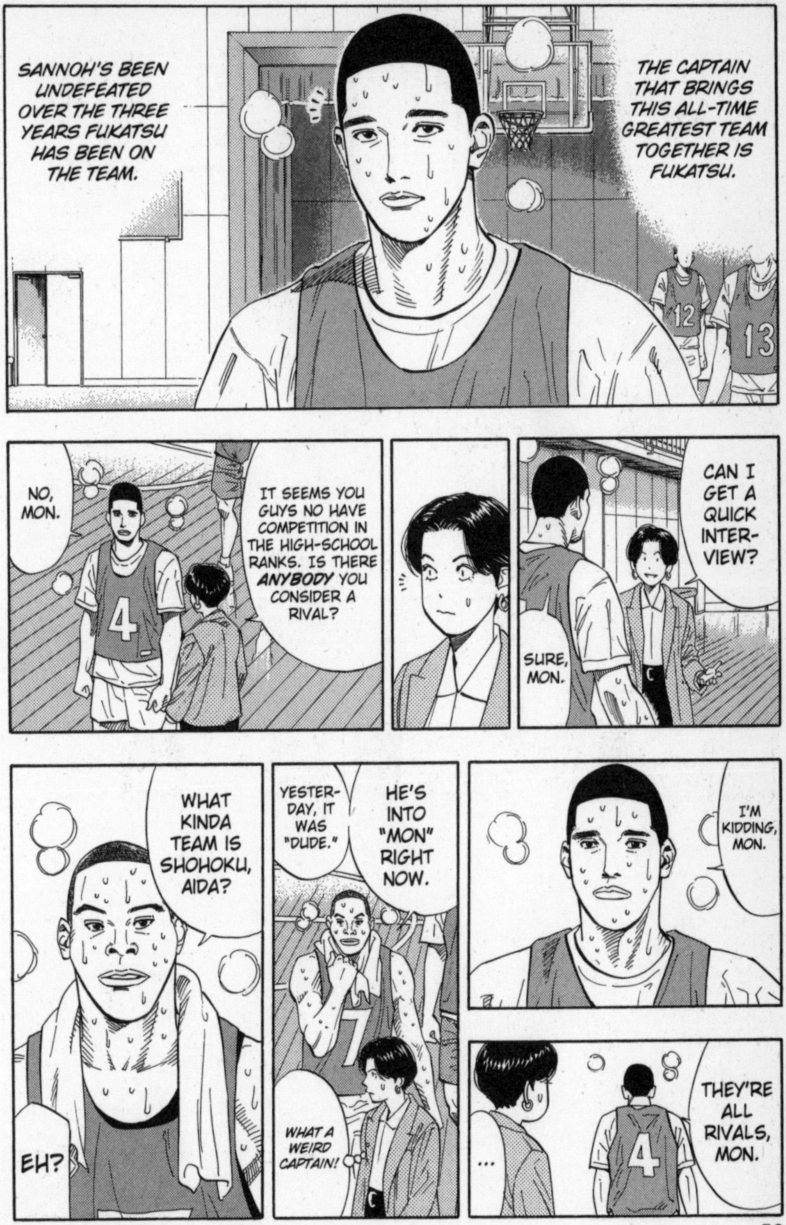
THE CAPTAIN THAT BRINGS THIS ALL-TIME GREATEST TEAM TOGETHER IS FUKATSU.
SANNOH'S BEEN UNDEFEATED OVER THE THREE YEARS FUKATSU HAS BEEN ON THE TEAM.
CAN I GET A QUICK INTERVIEW?
SURE, MON.
IT SEEMS YOU GUYS NO HAVE COMPETITION IN THE HIGH-SCHOOL RANKS. IS THERE ANYBODY YOU CONSIDER A RIVAL?
NO, MON.
I'M KIDDING, MON.
THEY'RE ALL RIVALS, MON.
...
HE'S INTO "MON" RIGHT NOW.
YESTERDAY, IT WAS "DUDE."
WHAT A WEIRD CAPTAIN!
WHAT KINDA TEAM IS SHOHOKU, AIDA?
EH?

READ THIS WAY

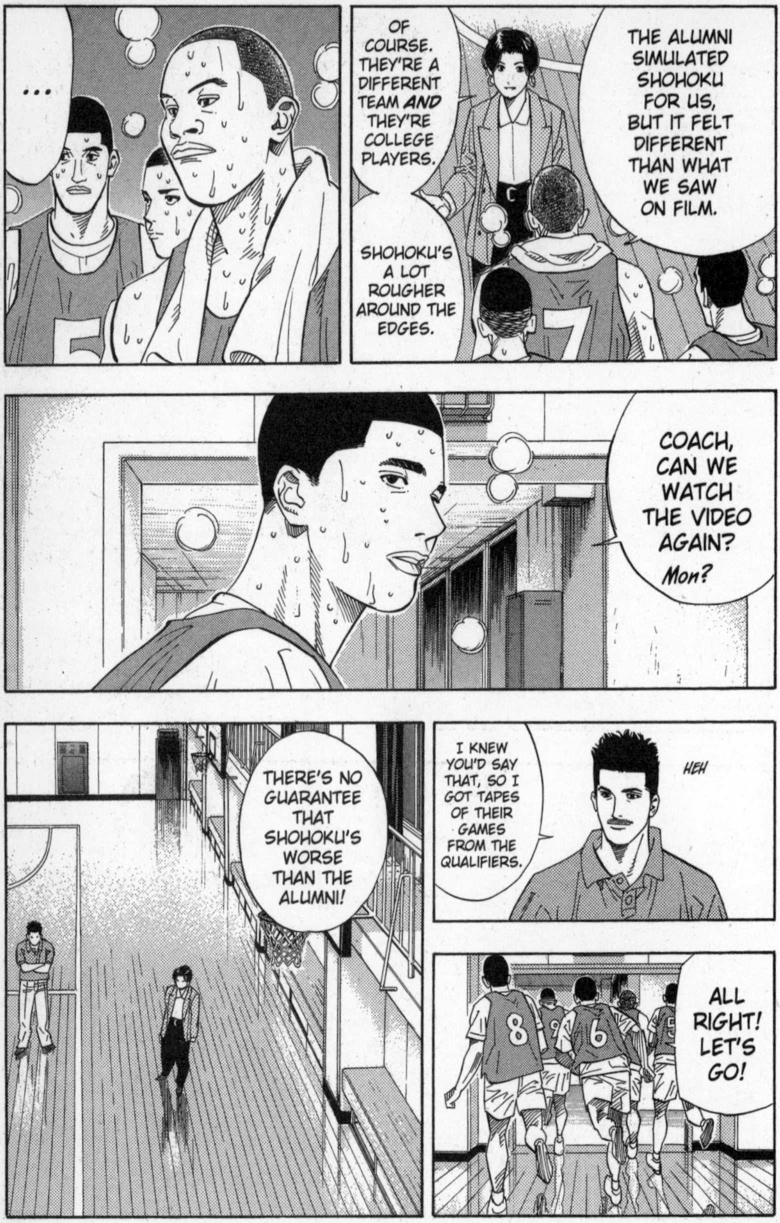
THE ALUMNI SIMULATED SHOHOKU FOR US, BUT IT FELT DIFFERENT THAN WHAT WE SAW ON FILM.
OF COURSE. THEY'RE A DIFFERENT TEAM *AND* THEY'RE COLLEGE PLAYERS.
SHOHOKU'S A LOT ROUGHER AROUND THE EDGES.
...
COACH, CAN WE WATCH THE VIDEO AGAIN?
Mon?
HEH
I KNEW YOU'D SAY THAT, SO I GOT TAPES OF THEIR GAMES FROM THE QUALIFIERS.
ALL RIGHT! LET'S GO!
THERE'S NO GUARANTEE THAT SHOHOKU'S WORSE THAN THE ALUMNI!

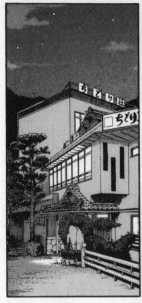

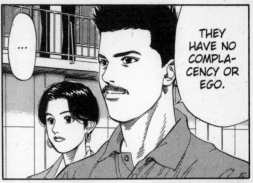
...

THEY HAVE NO COMPLACENCY OR EGO.

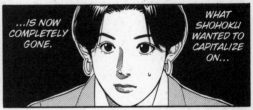
...IS NOW COMPLETELY GONE.

WHAT SHOHOKU WANTED TO CAPITALIZE ON...

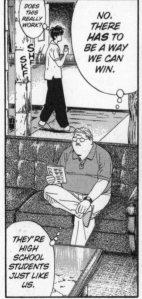
DOES THIS REALLY WORK?

NO. THERE HAS TO BE A WAY WE CAN WIN.

SHK F

THEY'RE HIGH SCHOOL STUDENTS JUST LIKE US.

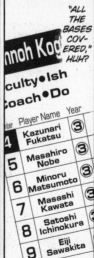
"ALL THE BASES COVERED," HUH?

nnoh Ko
culty●lsh
coach●Do

Number	Player Name	Year
4	Kazunari Fukatsu	③
5	Masahiro Nobe	③
6	Minoru Matsumoto	③
7	Masashi Kawata	
8	Satoshi Ichinokura	
9	Eiji Sawakita	

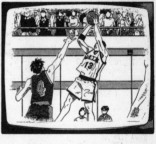
13

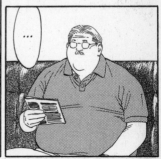
...

52

READ THIS WAY

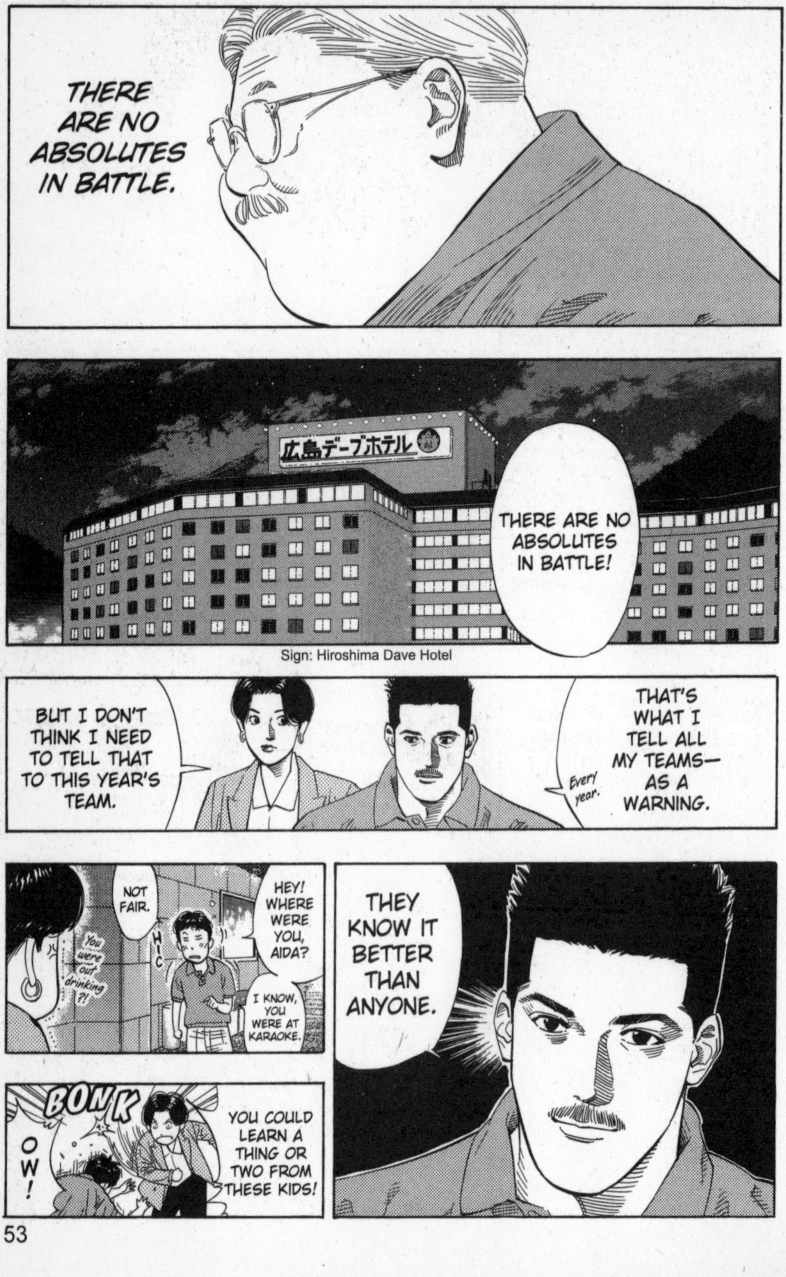
THERE ARE NO ABSOLUTES IN BATTLE.
広島デーブホテル
THERE ARE NO ABSOLUTES IN BATTLE!
Sign: Hiroshima Dave Hotel
THAT'S WHAT I TELL ALL MY TEAMS— AS A WARNING.
Every year.
BUT I DON'T THINK I NEED TO TELL THAT TO THIS YEAR'S TEAM.
THEY KNOW IT BETTER THAN ANYONE.
HEY! WHERE WERE YOU, AIDA?
I KNOW, YOU WERE AT KARAOKE.
NOT FAIR.
HIC
You were out drinking?!
YOU COULD LEARN A THING OR TWO FROM THESE KIDS!
BONK
OW!

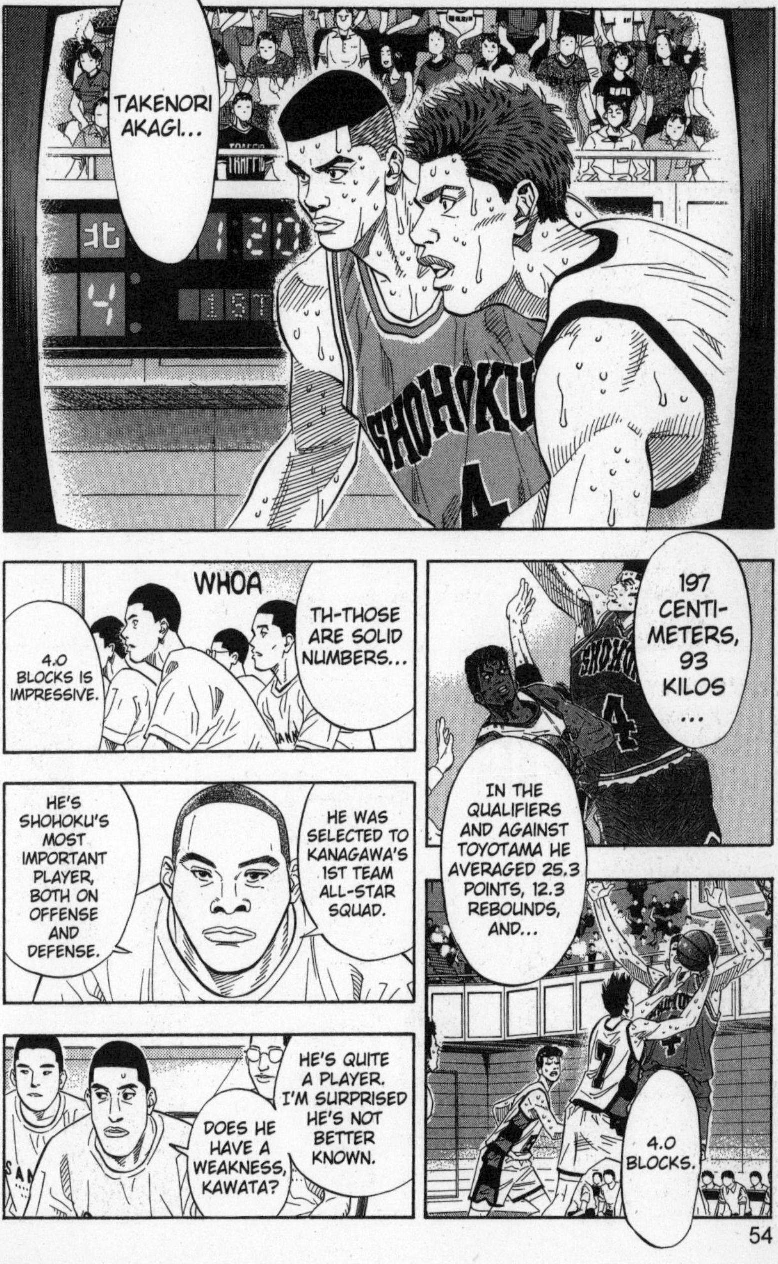
TAKENORI AKAGI...
197 CENTI-METERS, 93 KILOS ...
IN THE QUALIFIERS AND AGAINST TOYOTAMA HE AVERAGED 25.3 POINTS, 12.3 REBOUNDS, AND...
4.0 BLOCKS.
WHOA
TH-THOSE ARE SOLID NUMBERS...
4.0 BLOCKS IS IMPRESSIVE.
HE WAS SELECTED TO KANAGAWA'S 1ST TEAM ALL-STAR SQUAD.
HE'S SHOHOKU'S MOST IMPORTANT PLAYER, BOTH ON OFFENSE AND DEFENSE.
HE'S QUITE A PLAYER. I'M SURPRISED HE'S NOT BETTER KNOWN.
DOES HE HAVE A WEAKNESS, KAWATA?

READ THIS WAY

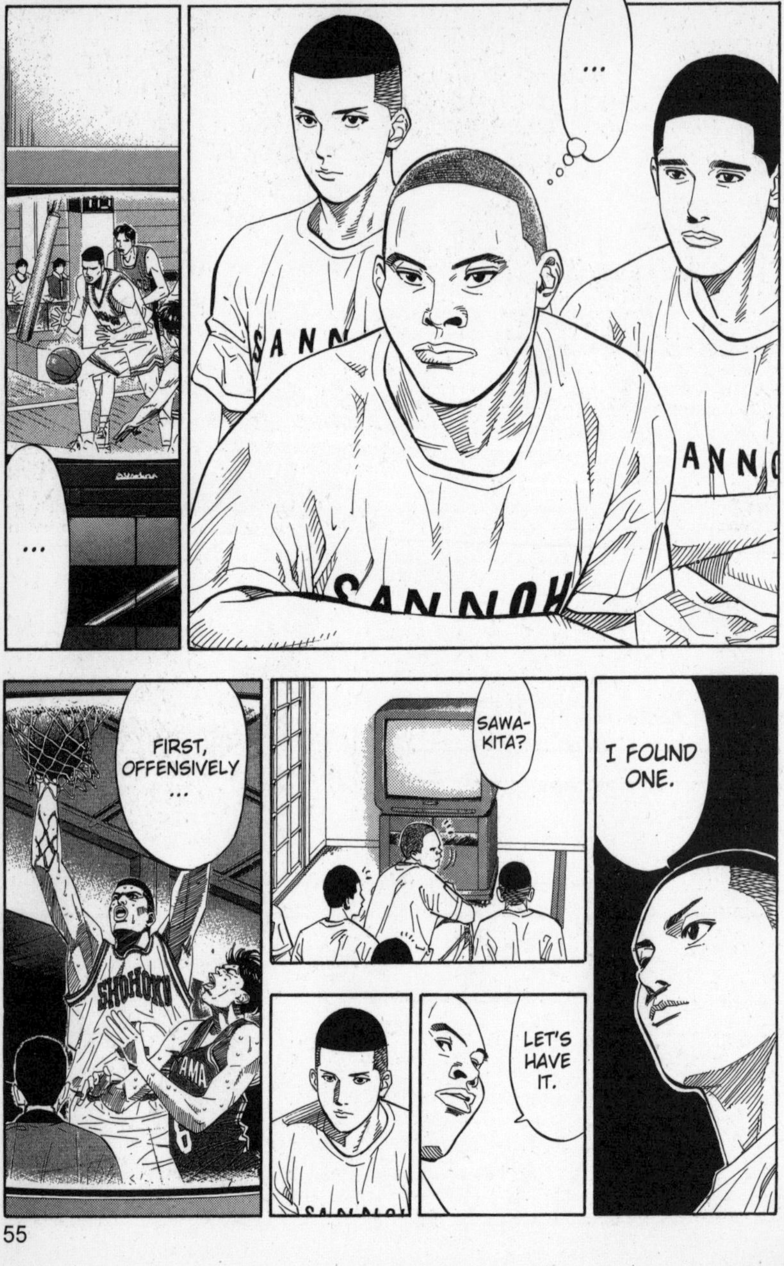

...
...
I FOUND ONE.
SAWA-KITA?
LET'S HAVE IT.
FIRST, OFFENSIVELY ...

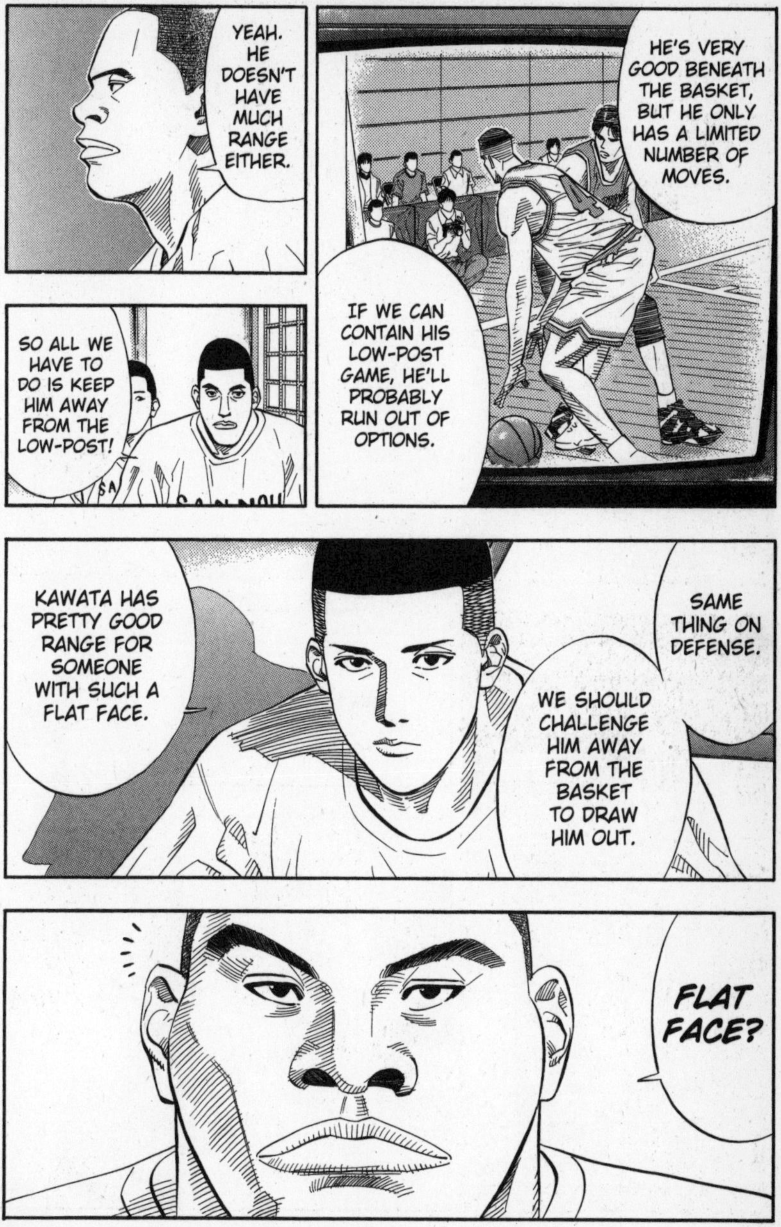

HE'S VERY GOOD BENEATH THE BASKET, BUT HE ONLY HAS A LIMITED NUMBER OF MOVES.
IF WE CAN CONTAIN HIS LOW-POST GAME, HE'LL PROBABLY RUN OUT OF OPTIONS.
YEAH. HE DOESN'T HAVE MUCH RANGE EITHER.
SO ALL WE HAVE TO DO IS KEEP HIM AWAY FROM THE LOW-POST!
SAME THING ON DEFENSE.
WE SHOULD CHALLENGE HIM AWAY FROM THE BASKET TO DRAW HIM OUT.
KAWATA HAS PRETTY GOOD RANGE FOR SOMEONE WITH SUCH A FLAT FACE.
FLAT FACE?

READ THIS WAY

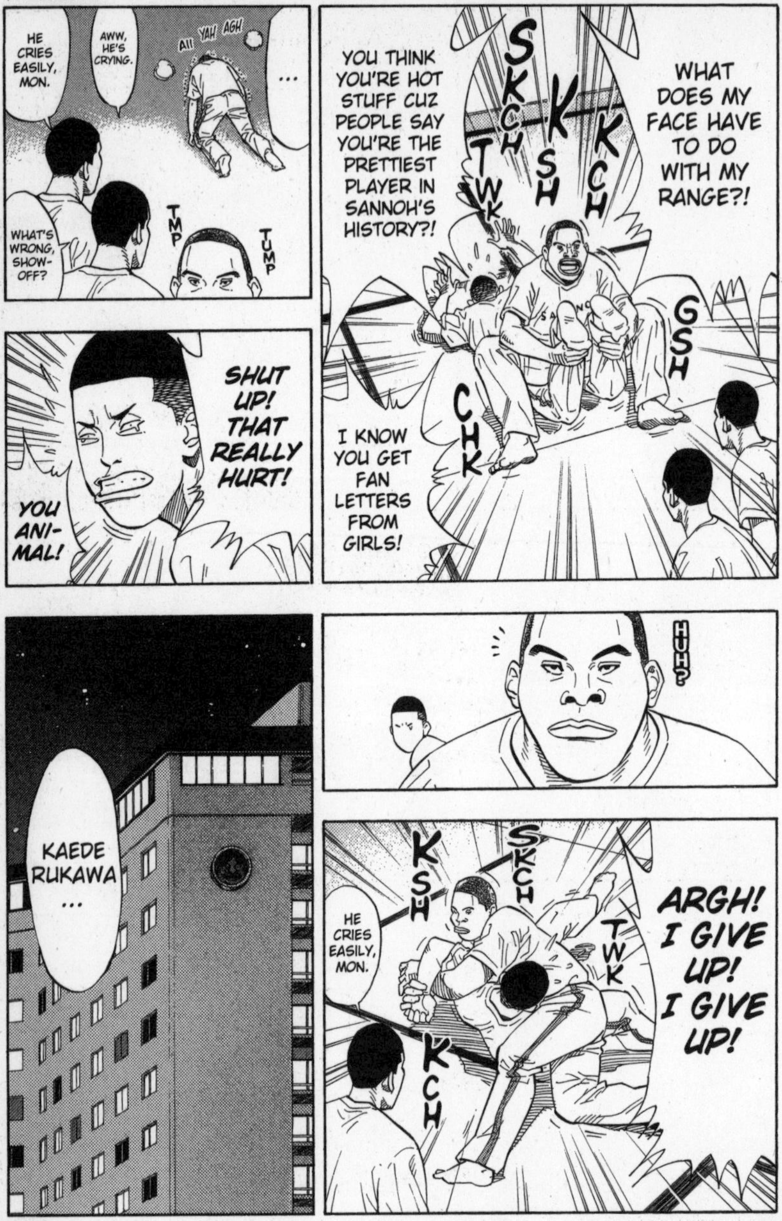
WHAT DOES MY FACE HAVE TO DO WITH MY RANGE?!
SKCH
KSH
KCH
TWK
YOU THINK YOU'RE HOT STUFF CUZ PEOPLE SAY YOU'RE THE PRETTIEST PLAYER IN SANNOH'S HISTORY?!
GSH
CHK
I KNOW YOU GET FAN LETTERS FROM GIRLS!
...
AII YAH AGH
AWW, HE'S CRYING.
HE CRIES EASILY, MON.
TUMP
TMP
WHAT'S WRONG, SHOW-OFF?
SHUT UP! THAT REALLY HURT!
YOU ANIMAL!
HUH?
ARGH! I GIVE UP! I GIVE UP!
TWK
SKCH
KSH
HE CRIES EASILY, MON.
KCH
KAEDE RUKAWA ...

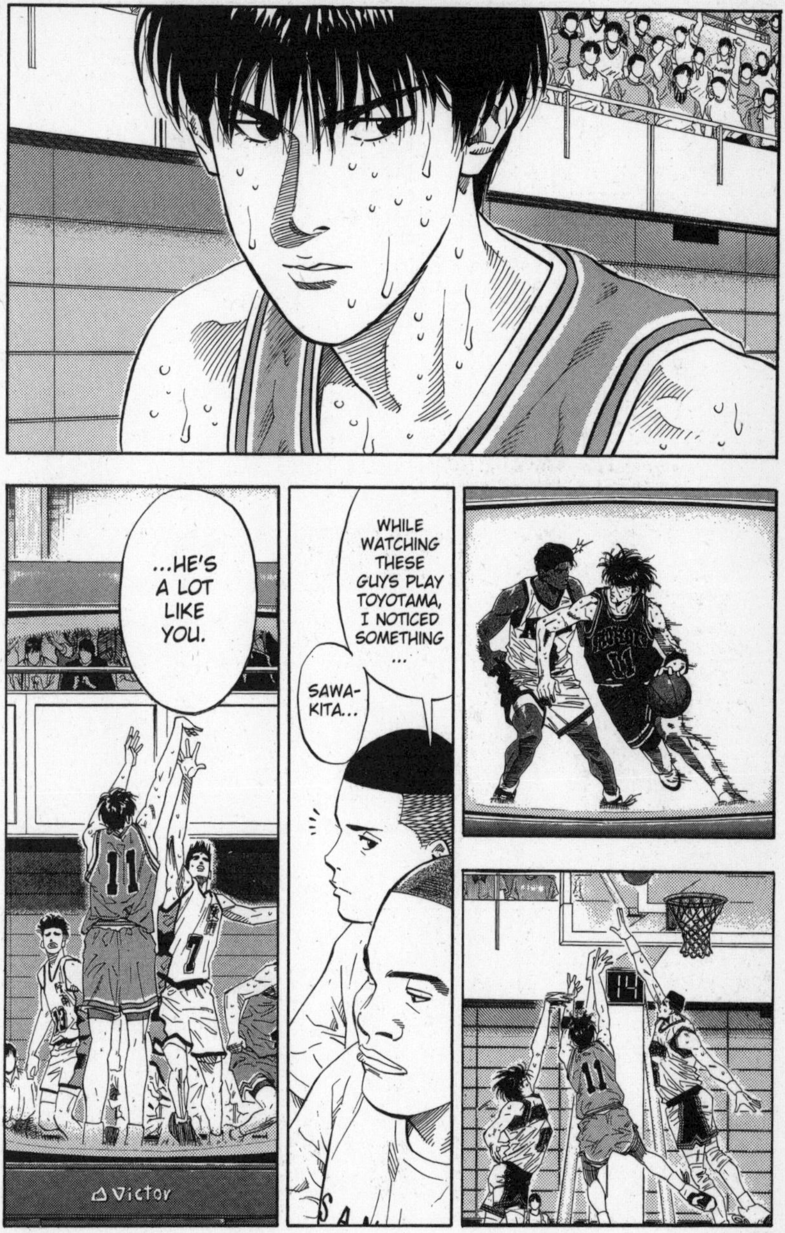
WHILE WATCHING THESE GUYS PLAY TOYOTAMA, I NOTICED SOMETHING ...
SAWA-KITA...
...HE'S A LOT LIKE YOU.
Victor

READ THIS WAY

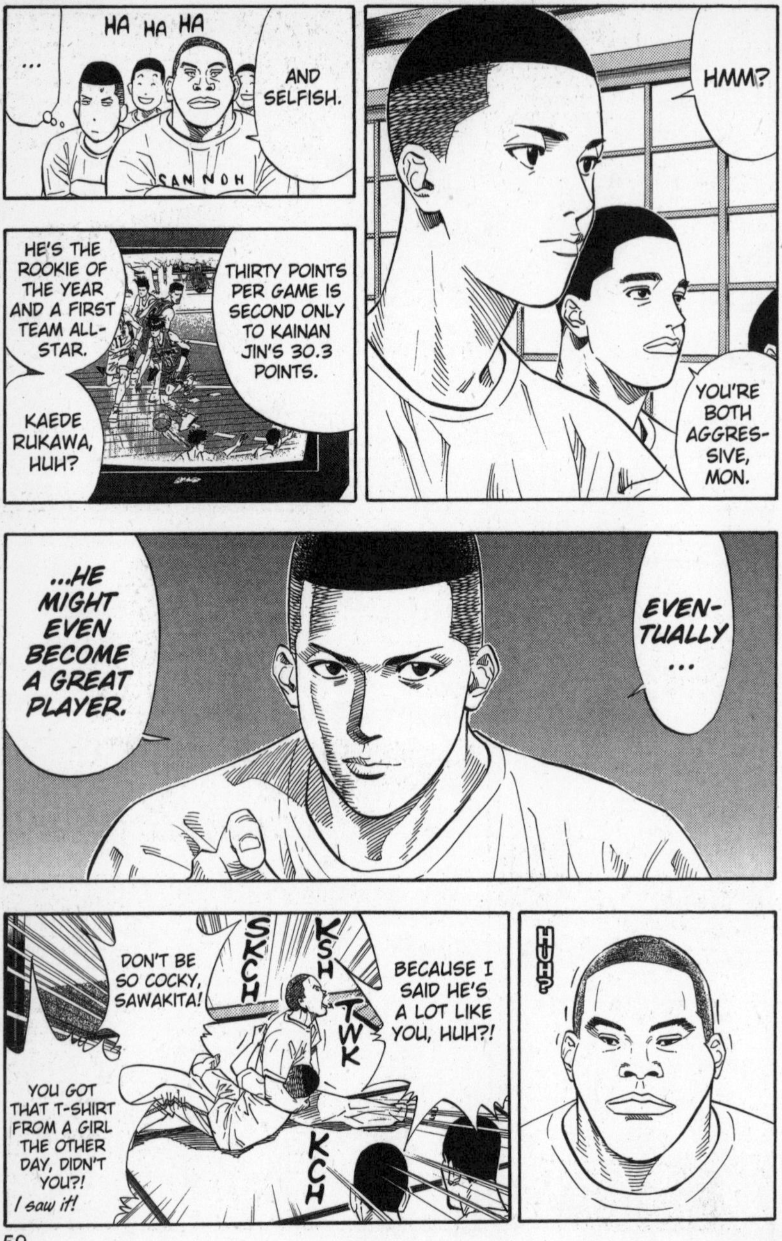
HMM?
YOU'RE BOTH AGGRES-SIVE, MON.
AND SELFISH.
HA HA HA
...
THIRTY POINTS PER GAME IS SECOND ONLY TO KAINAN JIN'S 30.3 POINTS.
HE'S THE ROOKIE OF THE YEAR AND A FIRST TEAM ALL-STAR.
KAEDE RUKAWA, HUH?
EVEN-TUALLY...
...HE MIGHT EVEN BECOME A GREAT PLAYER.
HUH?
BECAUSE I SAID HE'S A LOT LIKE YOU, HUH?!
KSH
SKCH
DON'T BE SO COCKY, SAWAKITA!
TWK
YOU GOT THAT T-SHIRT FROM A GIRL THE OTHER DAY, DIDN'T YOU?!
I saw it!
KCH

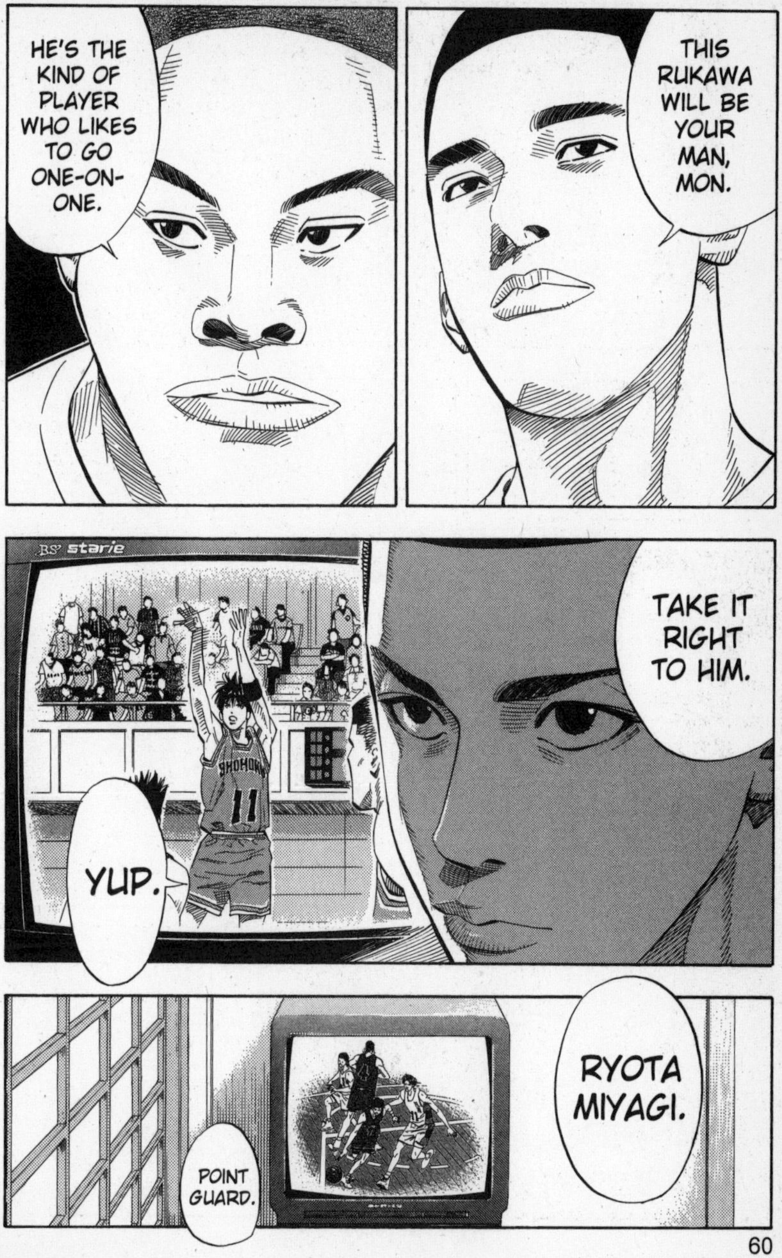
THIS RUKAWA WILL BE YOUR MAN, MON.
HE'S THE KIND OF PLAYER WHO LIKES TO GO ONE-ON-ONE.
TAKE IT RIGHT TO HIM.
YUP.
RYOTA MIYAGI.
POINT GUARD.

READ THIS WAY

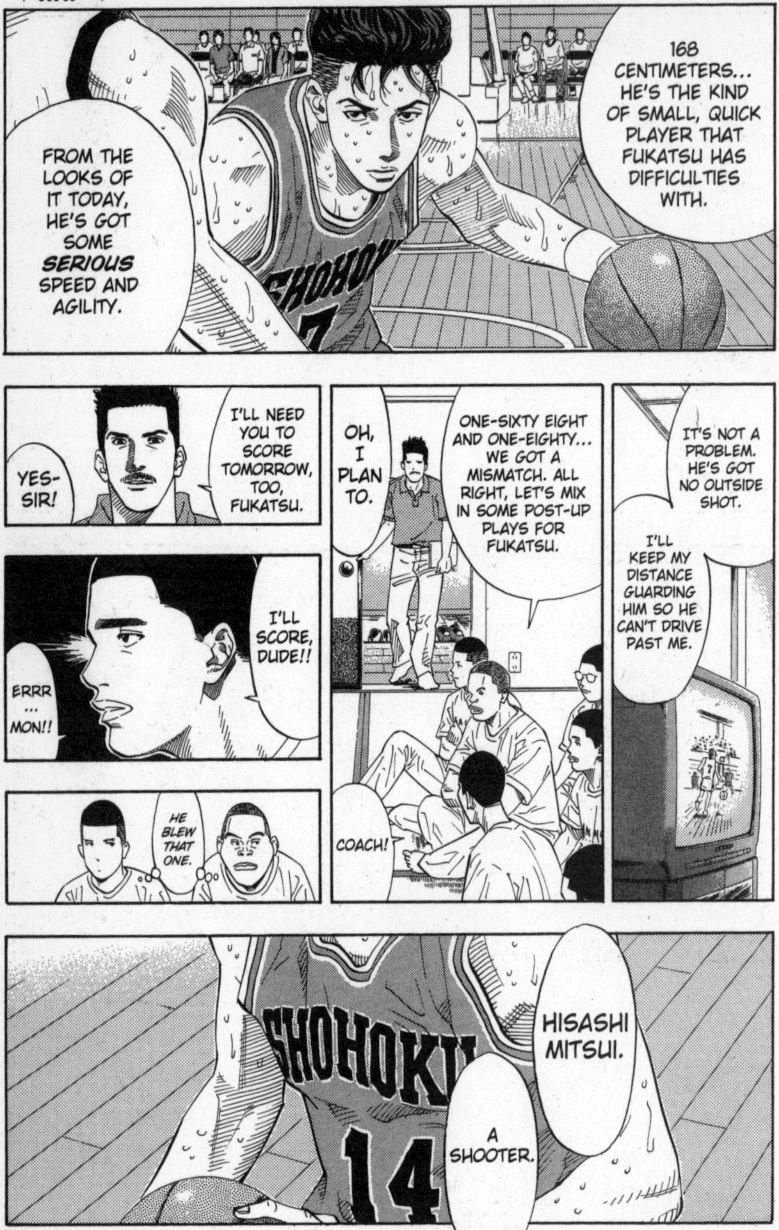

168 CENTIMETERS... HE'S THE KIND OF SMALL, QUICK PLAYER THAT FUKATSU HAS DIFFICULTIES WITH.
FROM THE LOOKS OF IT TODAY, HE'S GOT SOME *SERIOUS* SPEED AND AGILITY.
IT'S NOT A PROBLEM. HE'S GOT NO OUTSIDE SHOT.
I'LL KEEP MY DISTANCE GUARDING HIM SO HE CAN'T DRIVE PAST ME.
ONE-SIXTY EIGHT AND ONE-EIGHTY... WE GOT A MISMATCH. ALL RIGHT, LET'S MIX IN SOME POST-UP PLAYS FOR FUKATSU.
OH, I PLAN TO.
COACH!
I'LL NEED YOU TO SCORE TOMORROW, TOO, FUKATSU.
YES-SIR!
I'LL SCORE, DUDE!!
ERRR... MON!!
HE BLEW THAT ONE.
HISASHI MITSUI.
A SHOOTER.

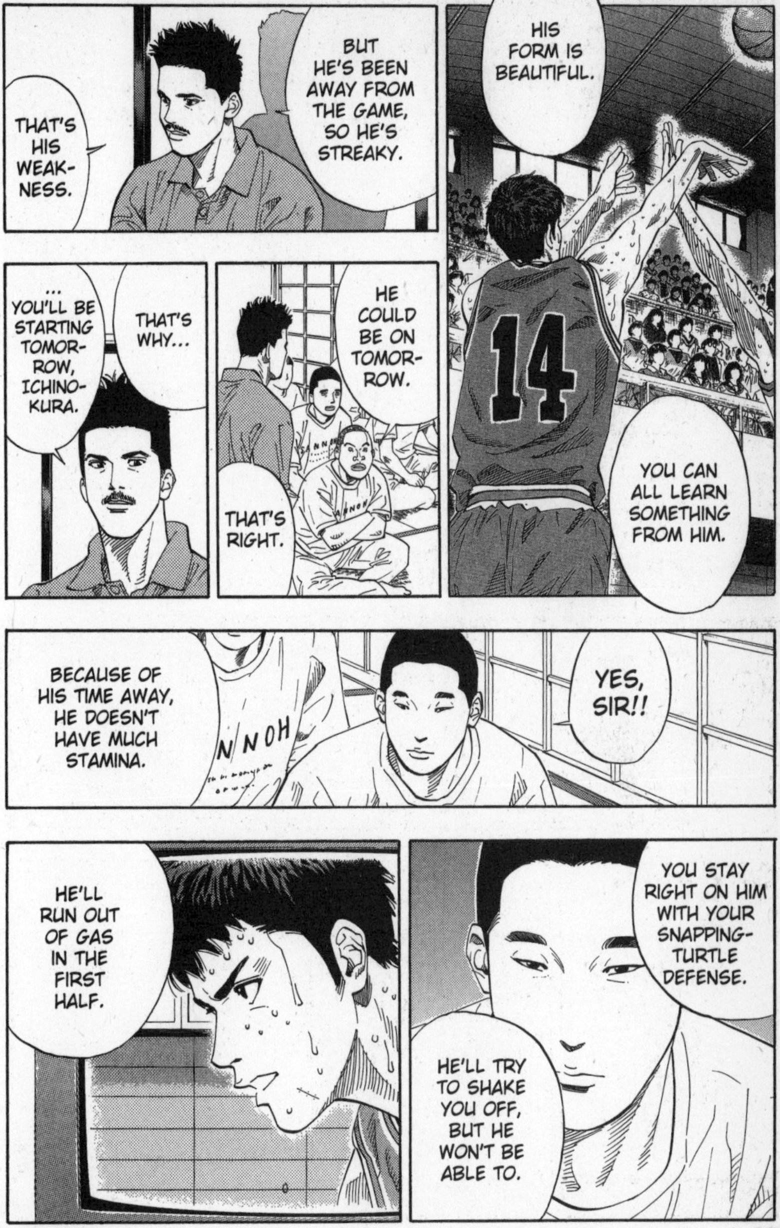
HIS FORM IS BEAUTIFUL.
YOU CAN ALL LEARN SOMETHING FROM HIM.
BUT HE'S BEEN AWAY FROM THE GAME, SO HE'S STREAKY.
THAT'S HIS WEAK-NESS.
HE COULD BE ON TOMOR-ROW.
THAT'S RIGHT.
THAT'S WHY...
... YOU'LL BE STARTING TOMOR-ROW, ICHINO-KURA.
YES, SIR!!
BECAUSE OF HIS TIME AWAY, HE DOESN'T HAVE MUCH STAMINA.
YOU STAY RIGHT ON HIM WITH YOUR SNAPPING-TURTLE DEFENSE.
HE'LL TRY TO SHAKE YOU OFF, BUT HE WON'T BE ABLE TO.
HE'LL RUN OUT OF GAS IN THE FIRST HALF.

READ THIS WAY

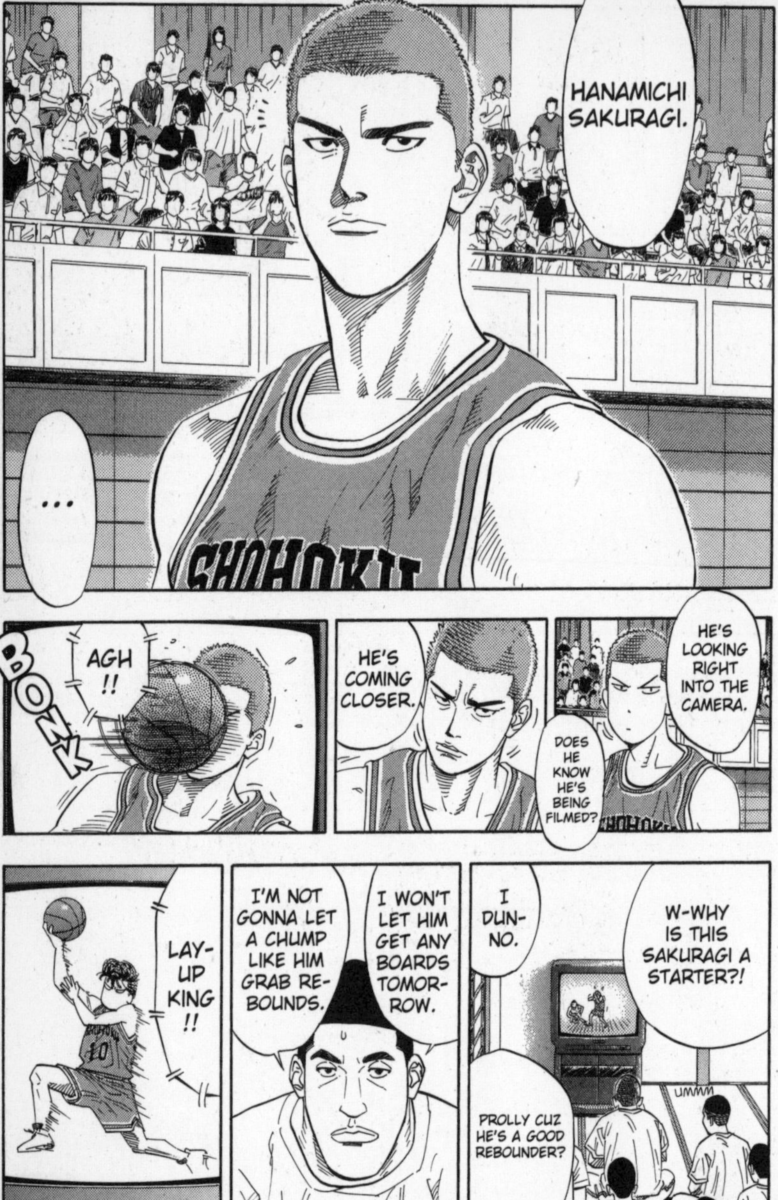
HANAMICHI SAKURAGI.
...
HE'S LOOKING RIGHT INTO THE CAMERA.
DOES HE KNOW HE'S BEING FILMED?
HE'S COMING CLOSER.
BONK
AGH!!
W-WHY IS THIS SAKURAGI A STARTER?!
I DUN-NO.
PROLLY CUZ HE'S A GOOD REBOUNDER?
UMMM
I WON'T LET HIM GET ANY BOARDS TOMOR-ROW.
I'M NOT GONNA LET A CHUMP LIKE HIM GRAB RE-BOUNDS.
LAY-UP KING!!

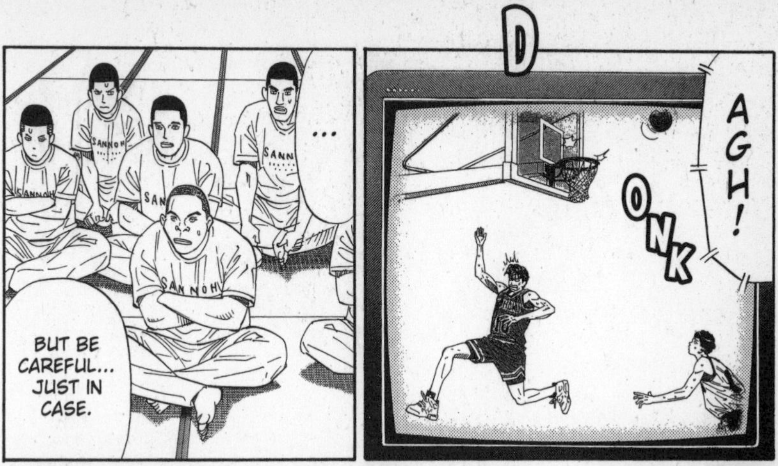
DONK
AGH!
...
BUT BE CAREFUL... JUST IN CASE.

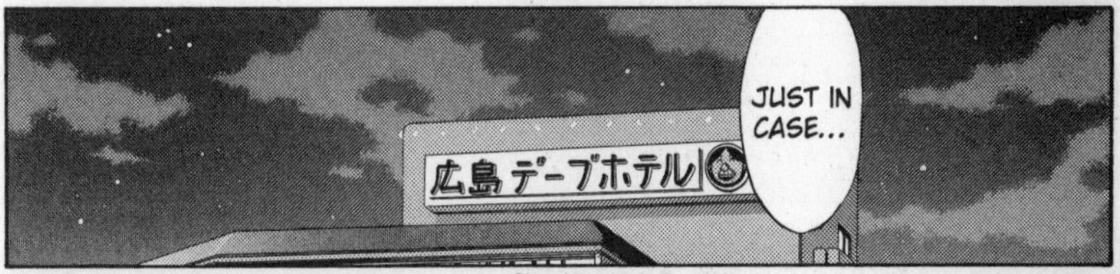
JUST IN CASE...
広島デーブホテル

Sign: Hiroshima Dave Hotel

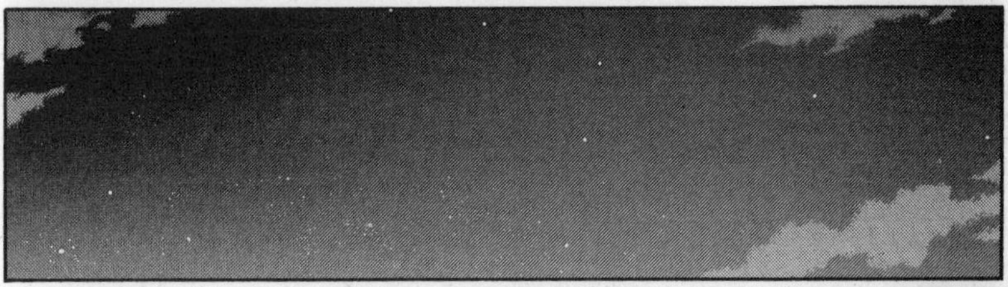

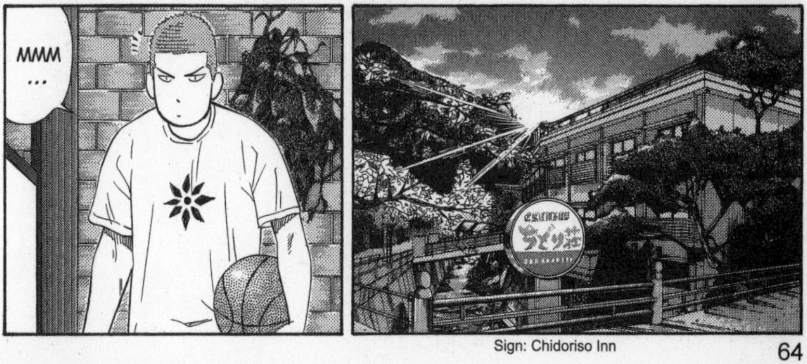
MMM...

Sign: Chidoriso Inn

READ THIS WAY

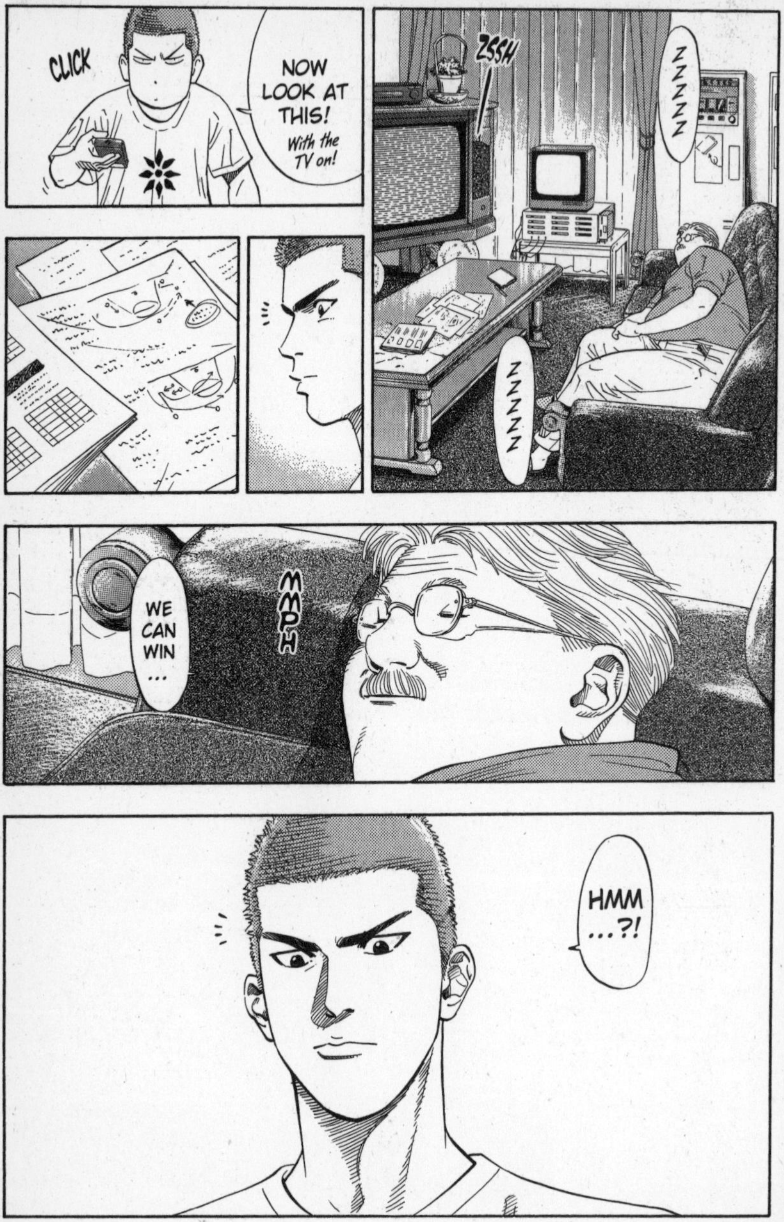
ZSSH
ZZZZZ
ZZZZZ
CLICK
NOW LOOK AT THIS! With the TV on!
WE CAN WIN ...
MMPH
HMM ...?!

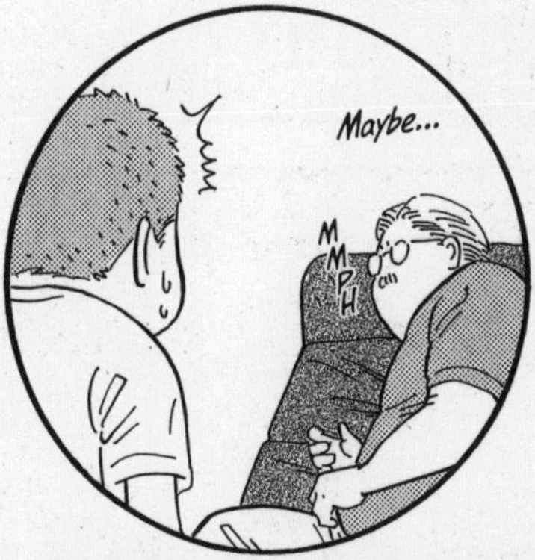
Maybe...
MMPH

SLAM DUNK

READ THIS WAY

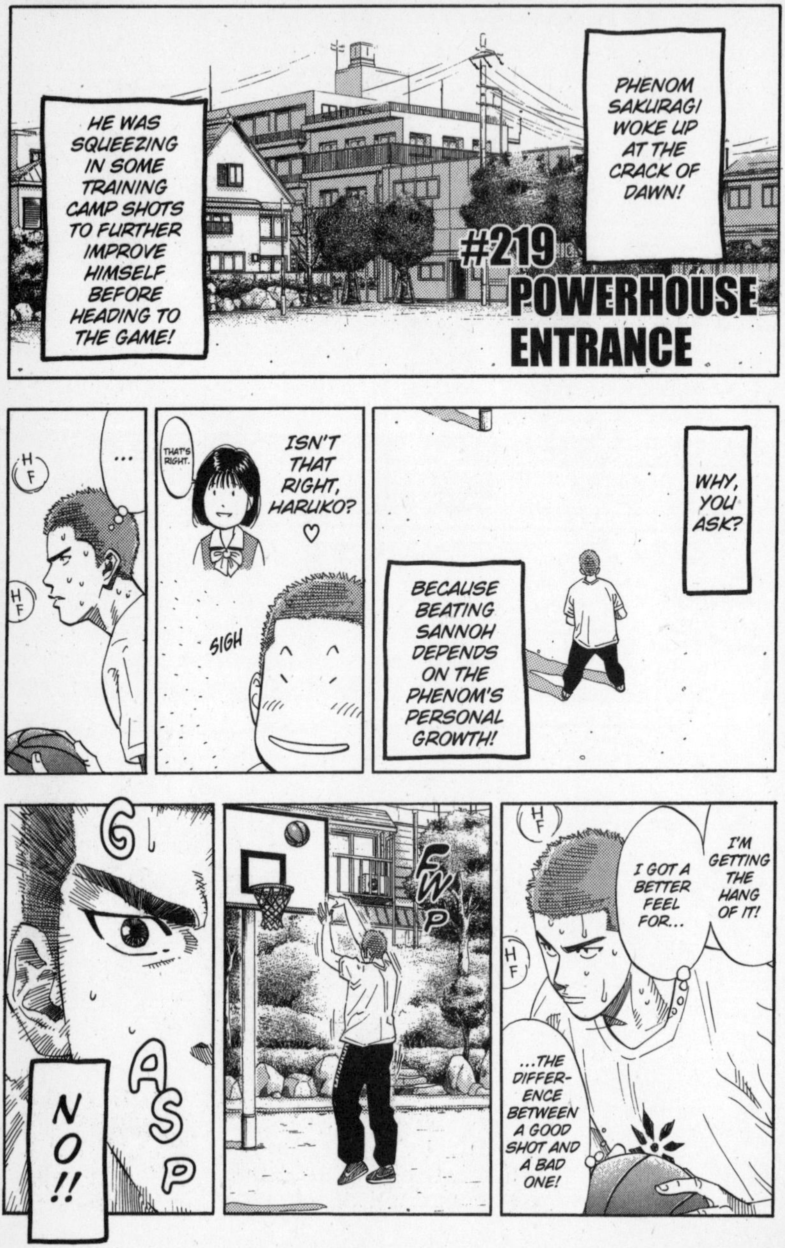
PHENOM SAKURAGI WOKE UP AT THE CRACK OF DAWN!
#219 POWERHOUSE ENTRANCE
HE WAS SQUEEZING IN SOME TRAINING CAMP SHOTS TO FURTHER IMPROVE HIMSELF BEFORE HEADING TO THE GAME!
WHY, YOU ASK?
BECAUSE BEATING SANNOH DEPENDS ON THE PHENOM'S PERSONAL GROWTH!
ISN'T THAT RIGHT, HARUKO? ♡
THAT'S RIGHT.
SIGH
HF
...
HF
HF
I'M GETTING THE HANG OF IT!
I GOT A BETTER FEEL FOR...
...THE DIFFER-ENCE BETWEEN A GOOD SHOT AND A BAD ONE!
HF
FWP
GASP
NO!!

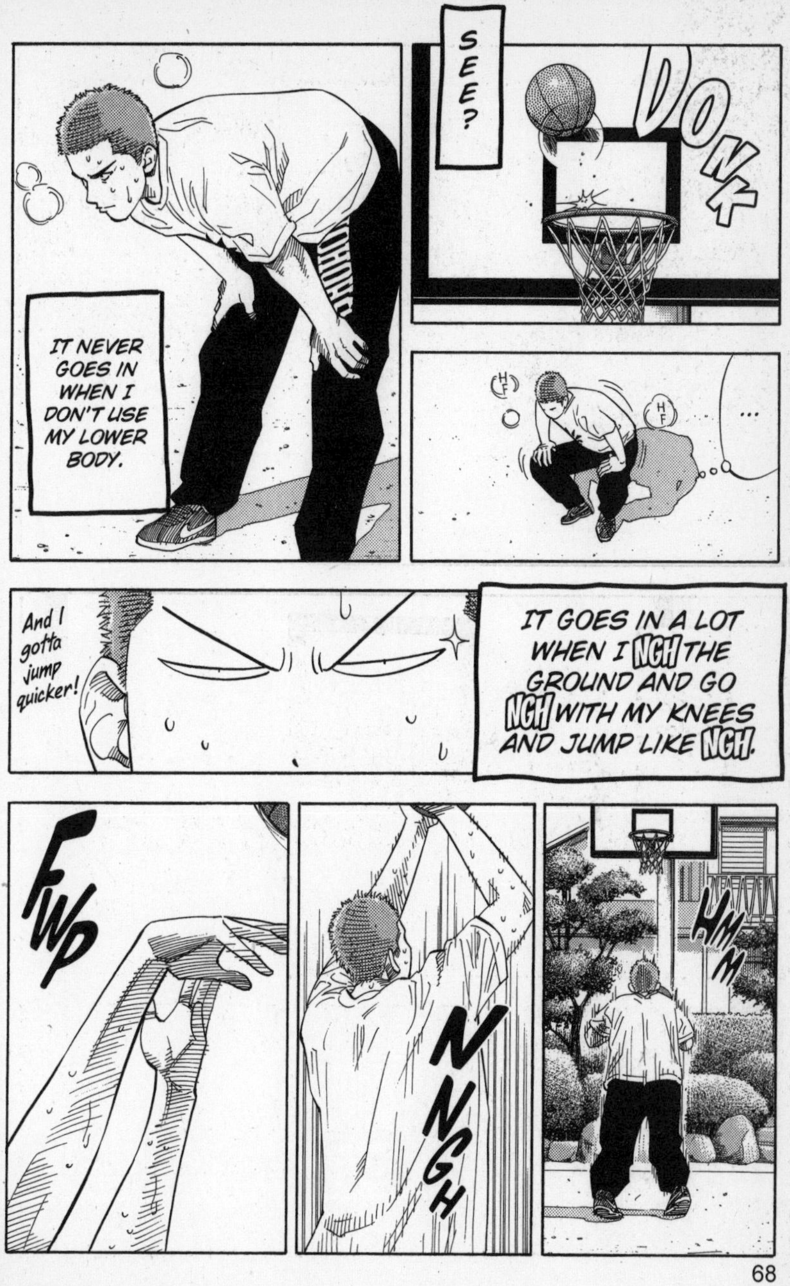
SEE?
DONK
HF
HF
...
IT NEVER GOES IN WHEN I DON'T USE MY LOWER BODY.
IT GOES IN A LOT WHEN I NGH THE GROUND AND GO NGH WITH MY KNEES AND JUMP LIKE NGH.
And I gotta jump quicker!
HMMM
NNGH
FWP

READ THIS WAY

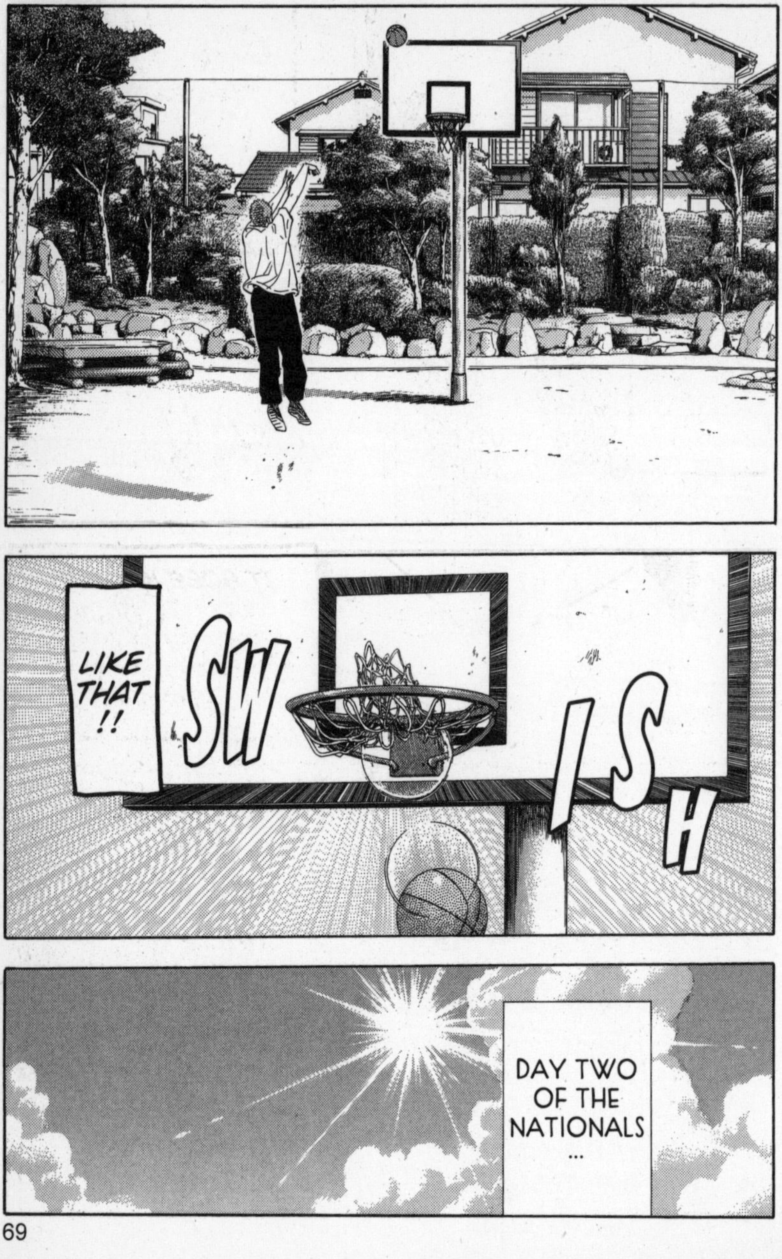
SWISH
LIKE THAT!!
DAY TWO OF THE NATIONALS ...

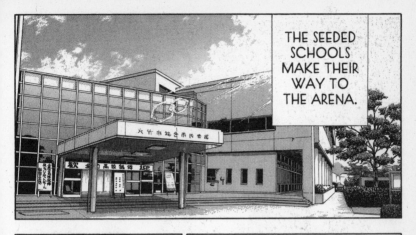

THE SEEDED SCHOOLS MAKE THEIR WAY TO THE ARENA.

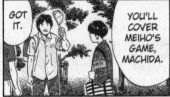

GOT IT.

YOU'LL COVER MEIHO'S GAME, MACHIDA.

TODAY'S GAMES

9 : 30	MEIHO KOGYO (AICHI)	
	vs.	
	JOSEI (SHIZUOKA)	
11 : 00	HIGASHISAKURA (TOKYO)	
	vs.	

R A A H

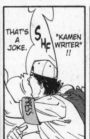

THAT'S A JOKE.

"KAMEN WRITER" !!

SHF

I'M MACHIDA. I'M A WRITER.

Hi there.

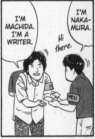

I'M NAKA- MURA.

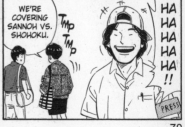

WE'RE COVERING SANNOH VS. SHOHOKU.

TMP TMP

HA HA HA HA HA !!

PRESS

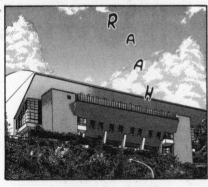

TODAY'S GAMES

10 : 00	KAINAN-DAI FUZOKU (KANAGAWA)	
	vs.	
	MAMIYA NISHI (IWATE)	
11 : 30	SANNOH KOGYO (AKITA)	
	vs.	
	SHOHOKU (KANAGAWA)	
13 : 00	KANEYAMA SHOGYO (NIIGATA)	
	vs.	

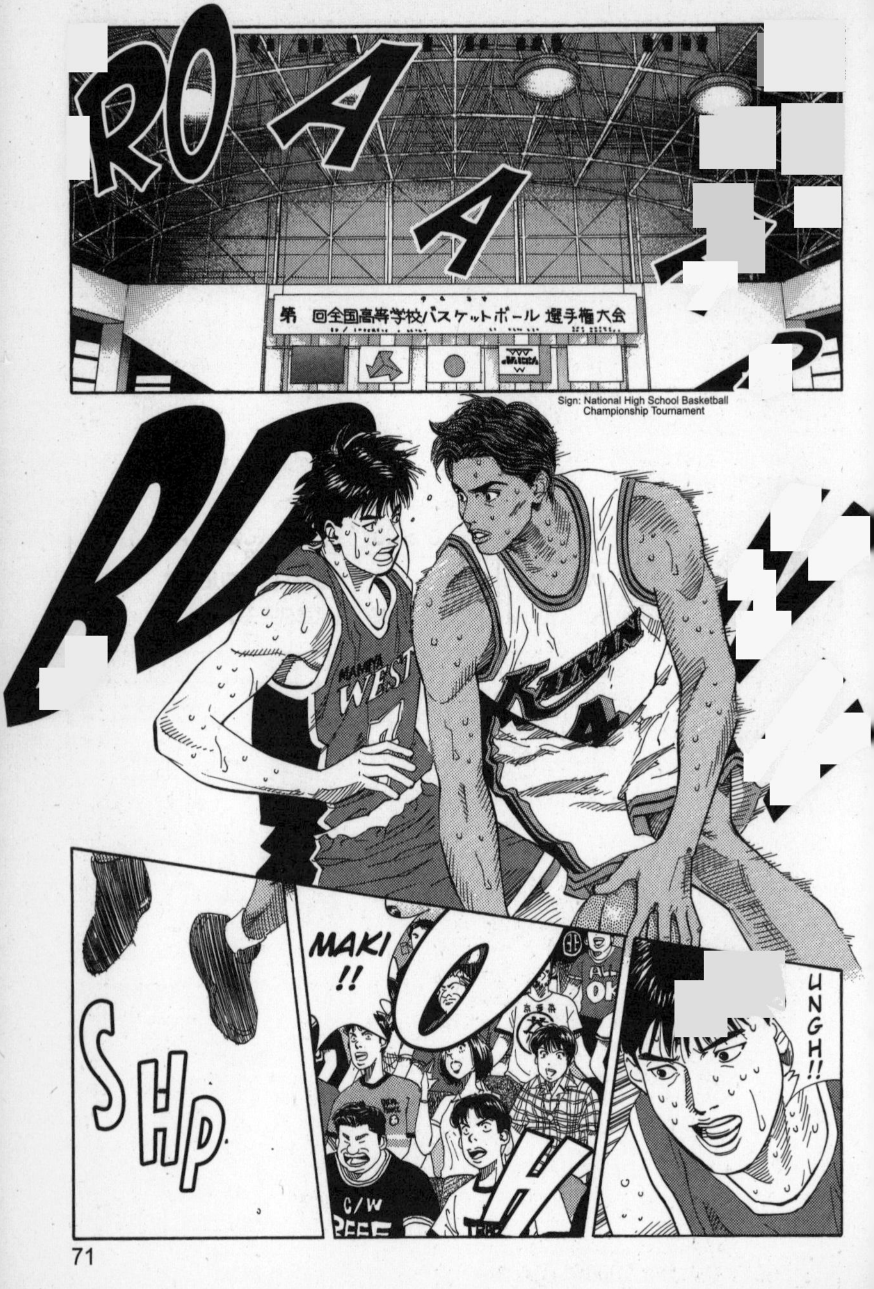

RO
A
A
第 回全国高等学校バスケットボール 選手権大会
Sign: National High School Basketball Championship Tournament
KAINAN
4
WEST
UNGH!!
MAKI!!
O
H
SHP

!!
SWAP

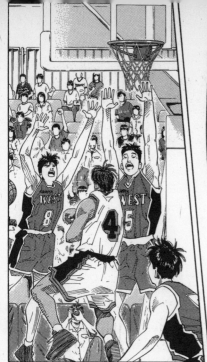

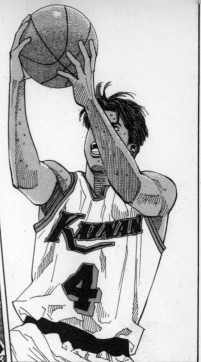

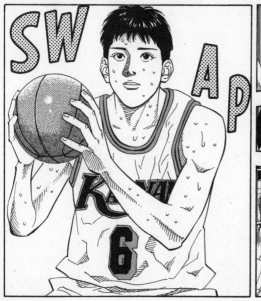

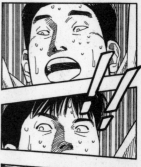

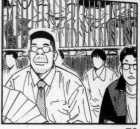

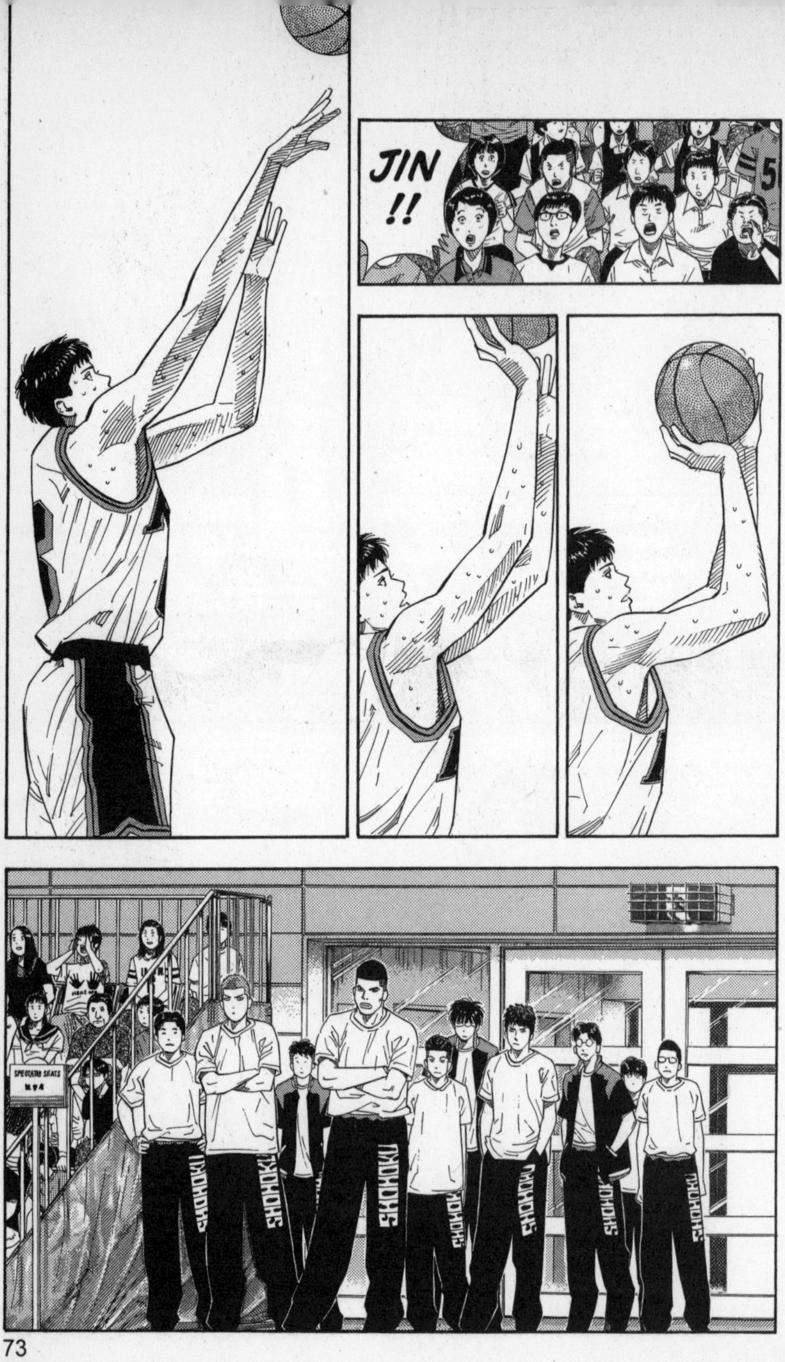
JIN !!
SHOHOKU

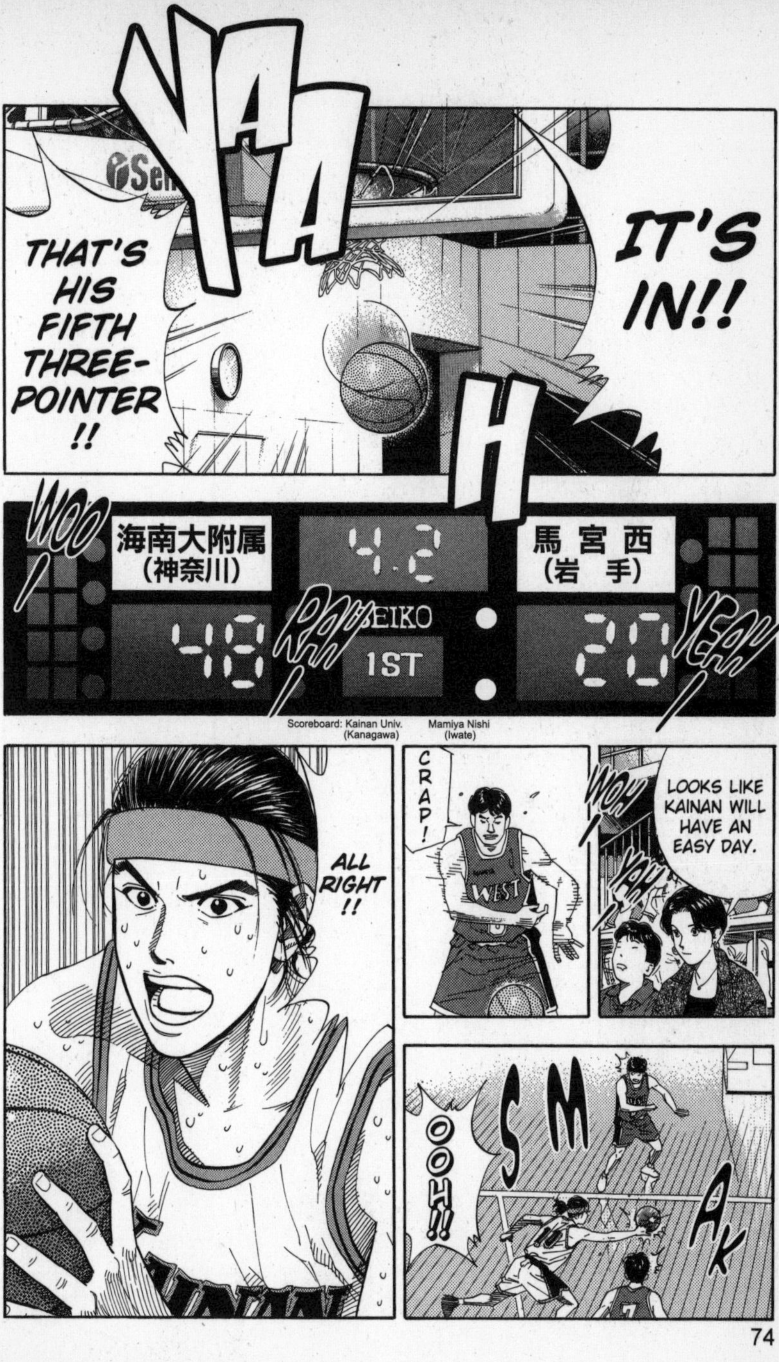
IT'S IN!!
YAAH
THAT'S HIS FIFTH THREE-POINTER!!
YEAH!
RAH!
WOO!
海南大附属
(神奈川)
4.2
馬 宮 西
(岩 手)
SEIKO
48
1ST
20
Scoreboard: Kainan Univ. (Kanagawa) Mamiya Nishi (Iwate)
LOOKS LIKE KAINAN WILL HAVE AN EASY DAY.
WOH!
YAH!
CRAP!
SMACK
OOOH!!
ALL RIGHT!!

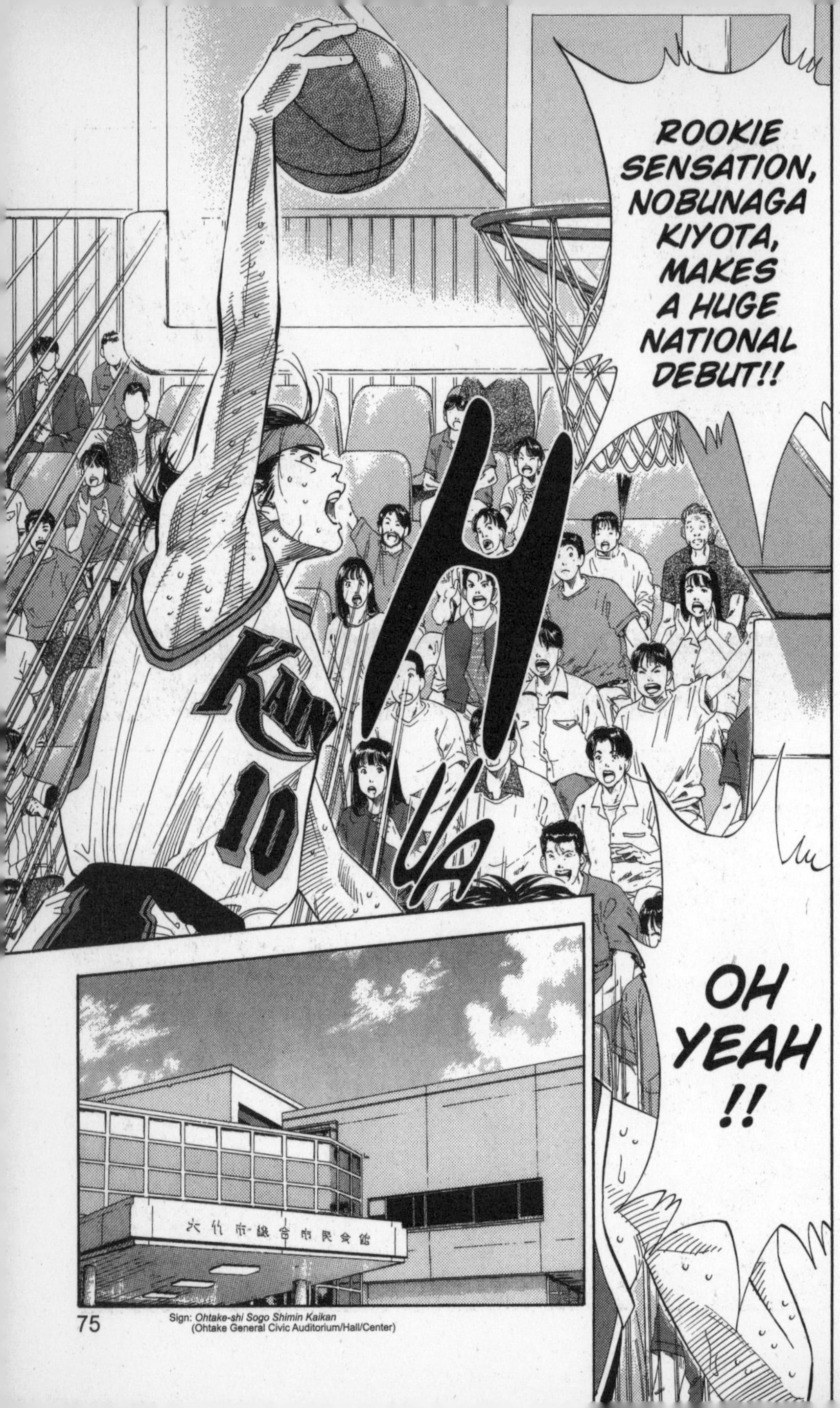
ROOKIE SENSATION, NOBUNAGA KIYOTA, MAKES A HUGE NATIONAL DEBUT!!
HUA
OH YEAH !!
大竹市総合市民会館

Sign: *Ohtake-shi Sogo Shimin Kaikan*
(Ohtake General Civic Auditorium/Hall/Center)

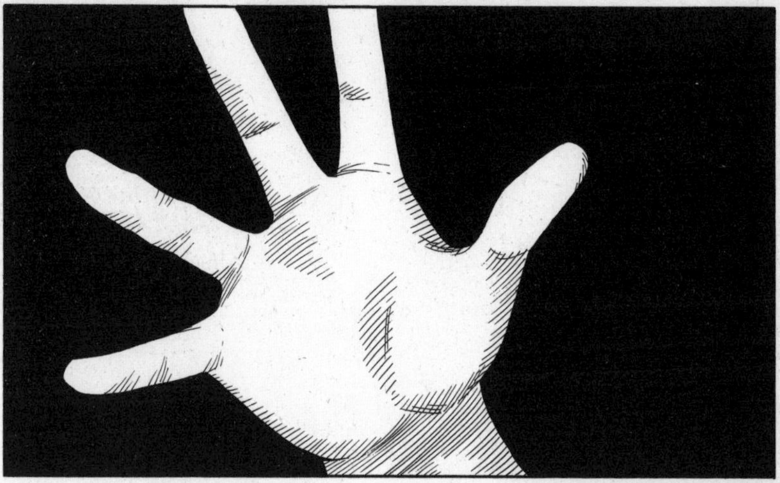

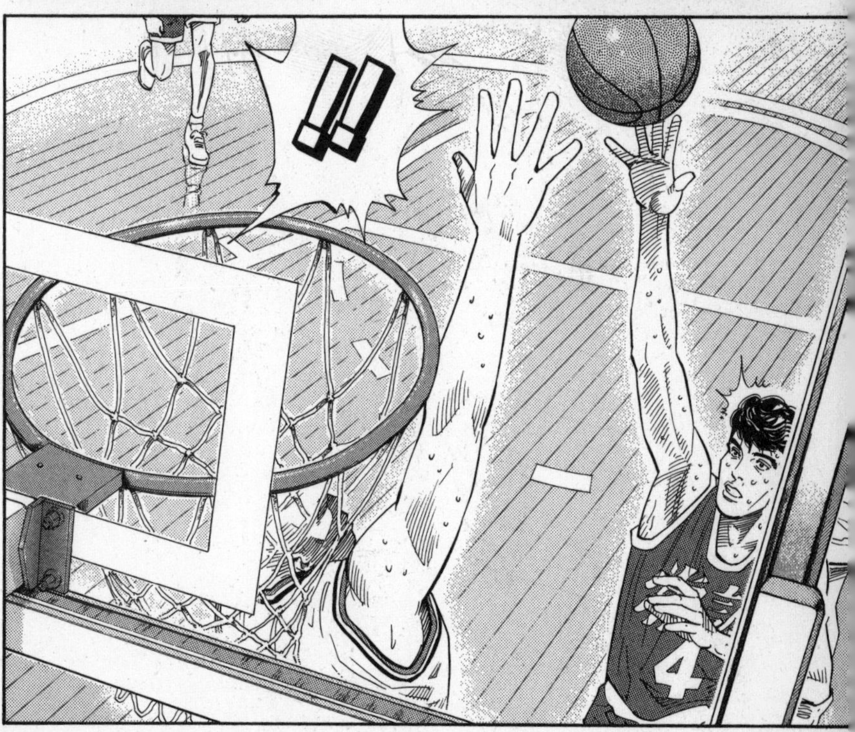
!!

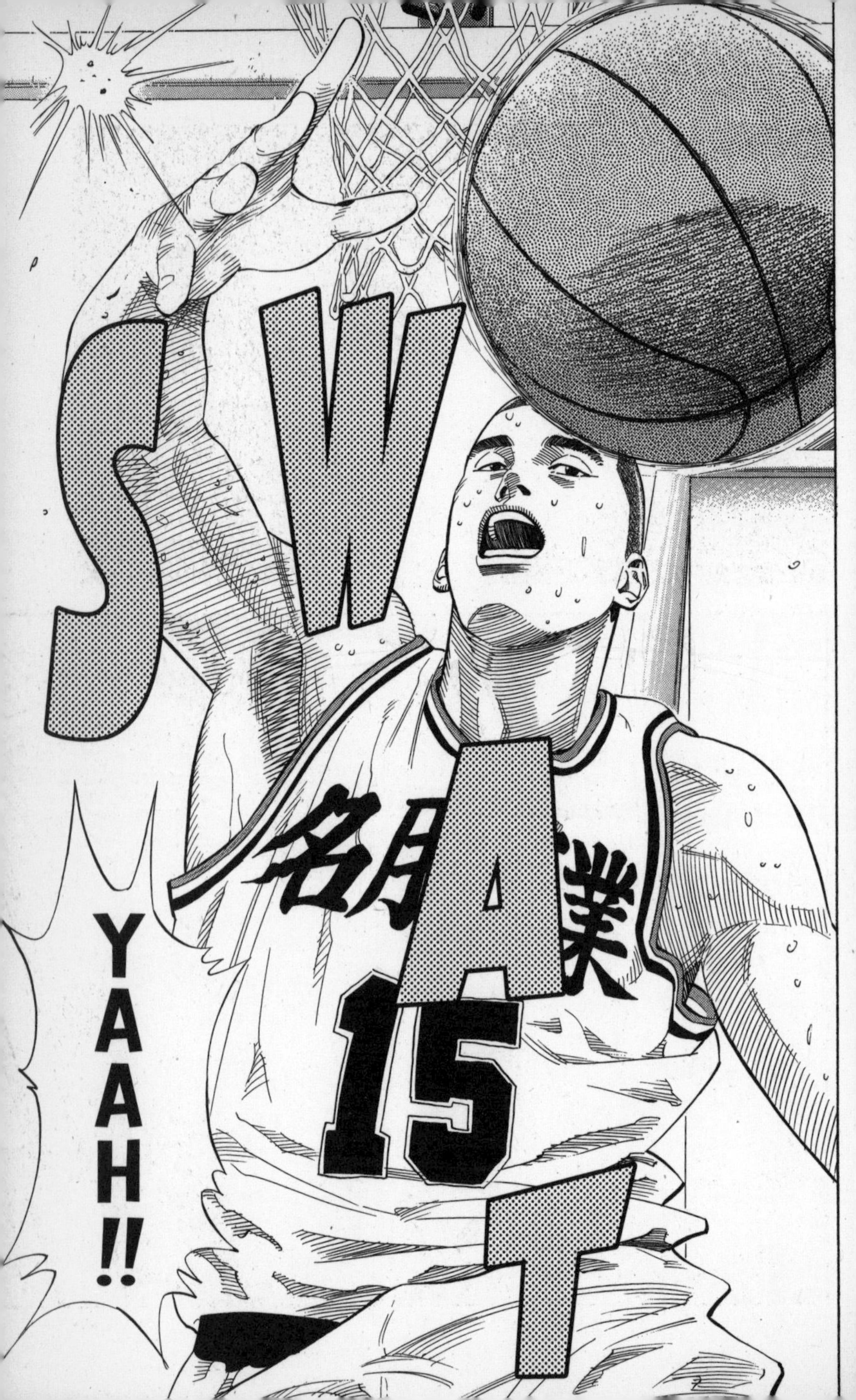
SWAT
YAAH!!

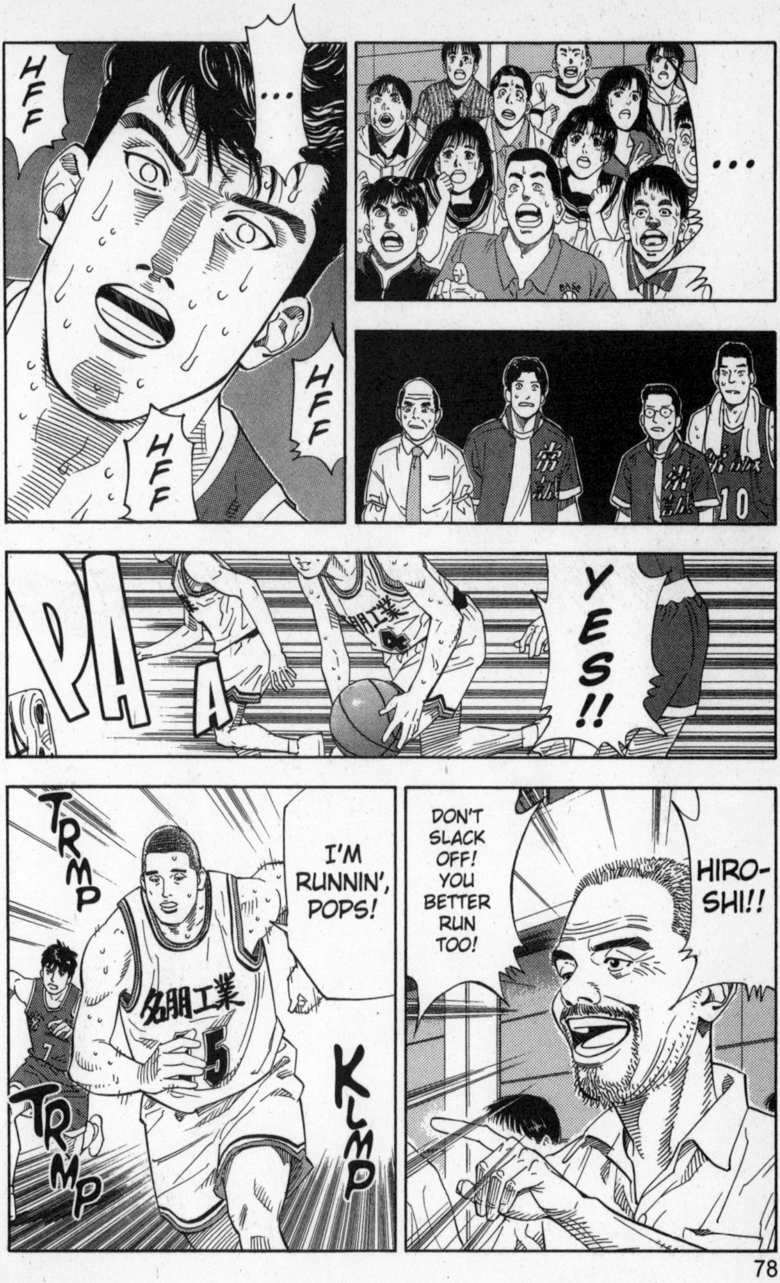
...
...
HFF
HFF
HFF
YES!!
PAA
HIRO-SHI!!
DON'T SLACK OFF! YOU BETTER RUN TOO!
I'M RUNNIN', POPS!
TRMP
KLMP
TRMP

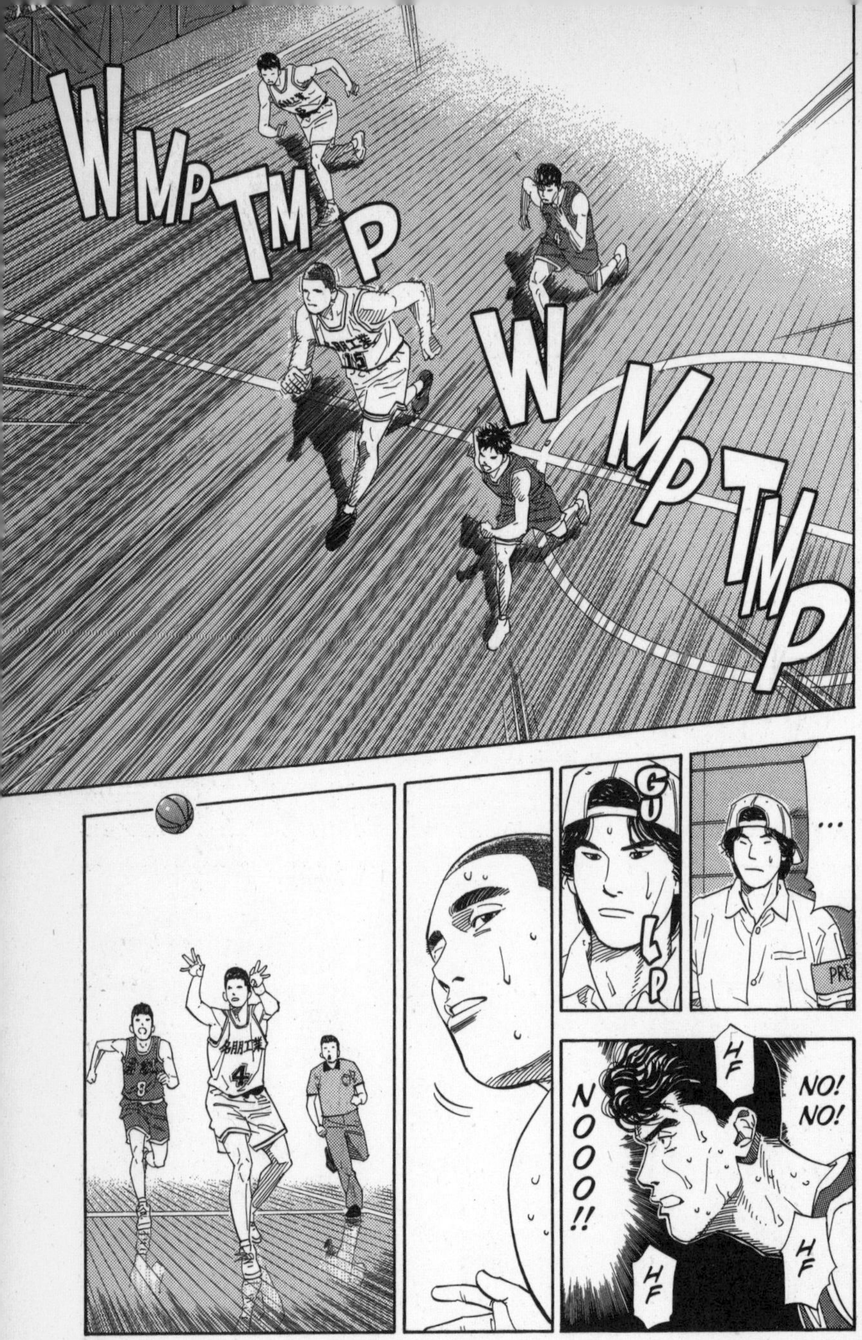
WMPTMP
WMPTMP
...
GULP
NO! NO!
HF
NOOOO!!
HF
HF

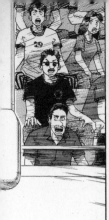

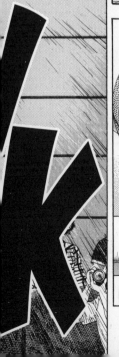

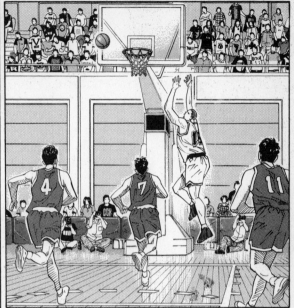

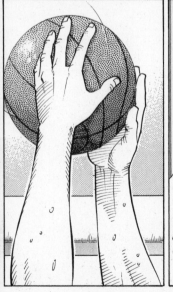

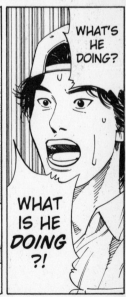

WHAT'S HE DOING?

WHAT IS HE *DOING*?!

80

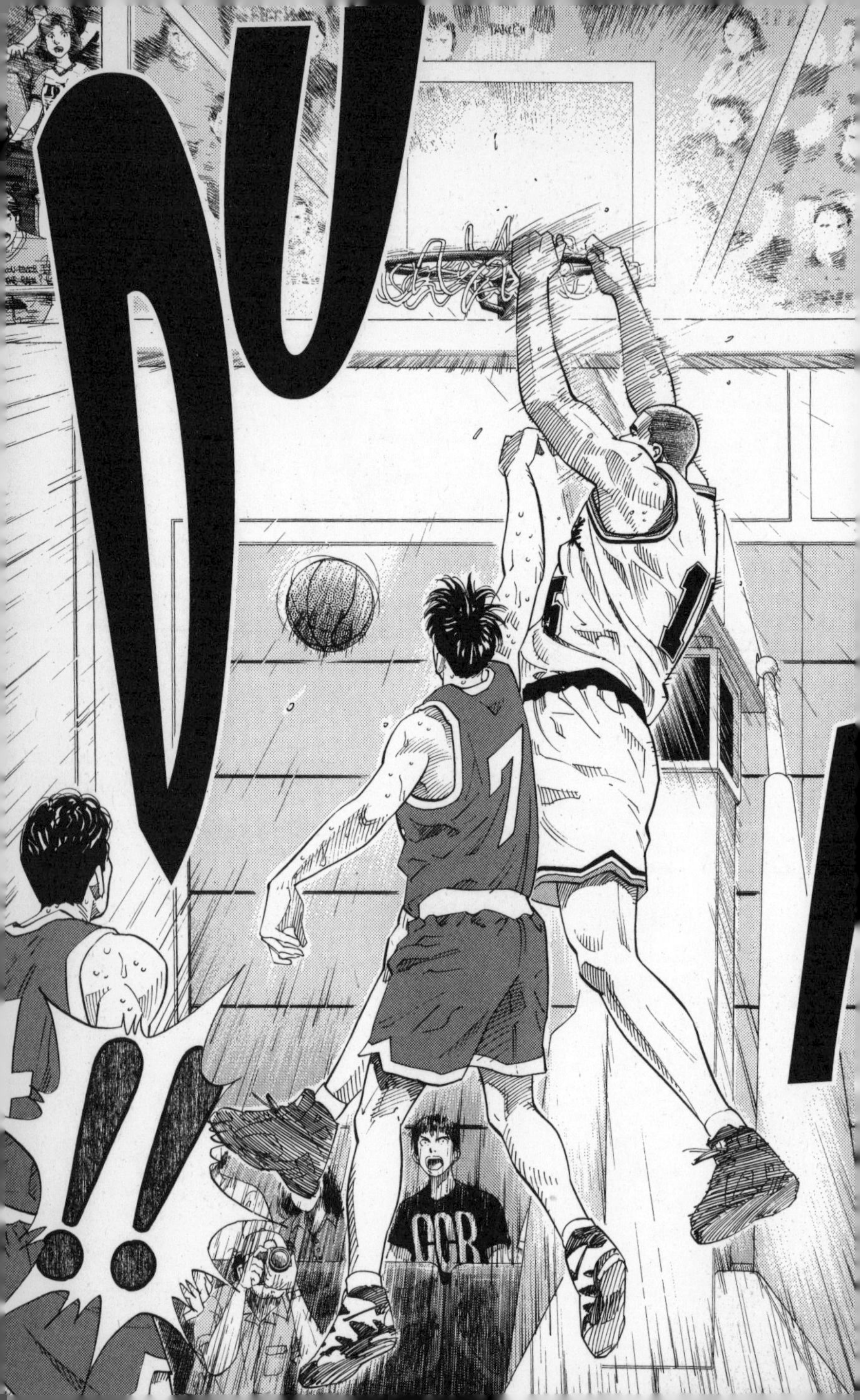
DU
!!
CGR

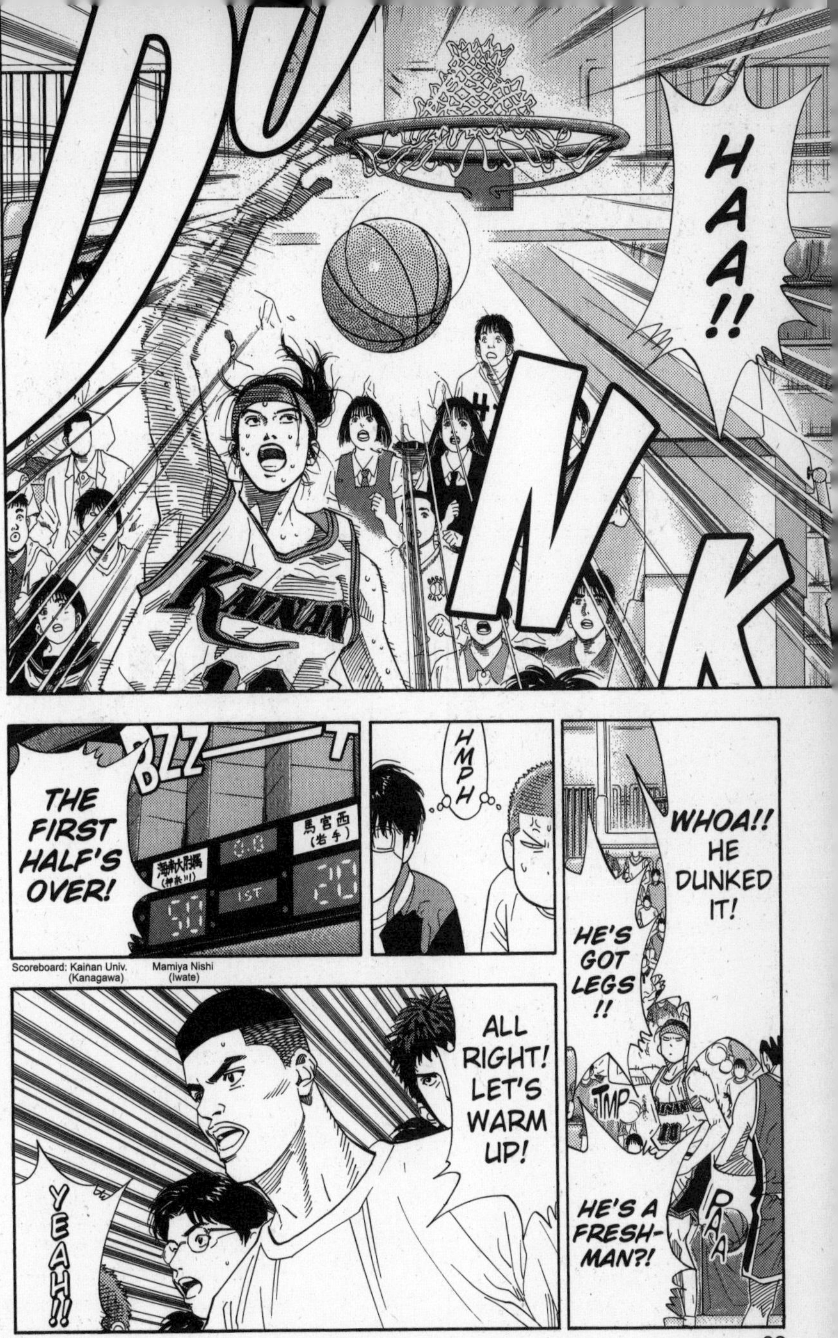
DUNK
HAA!!
WHOA!! HE DUNKED IT!
HE'S GOT LEGS!!
TMP
PAA
HE'S A FRESHMAN?!
HMPH
BZZ—T
THE FIRST HALF'S OVER!
ALL RIGHT! LET'S WARM UP!
YEAH!!

Scoreboard: Kainan Univ. (Kanagawa) Mamiya Nishi (Iwate)

READ THIS WAY

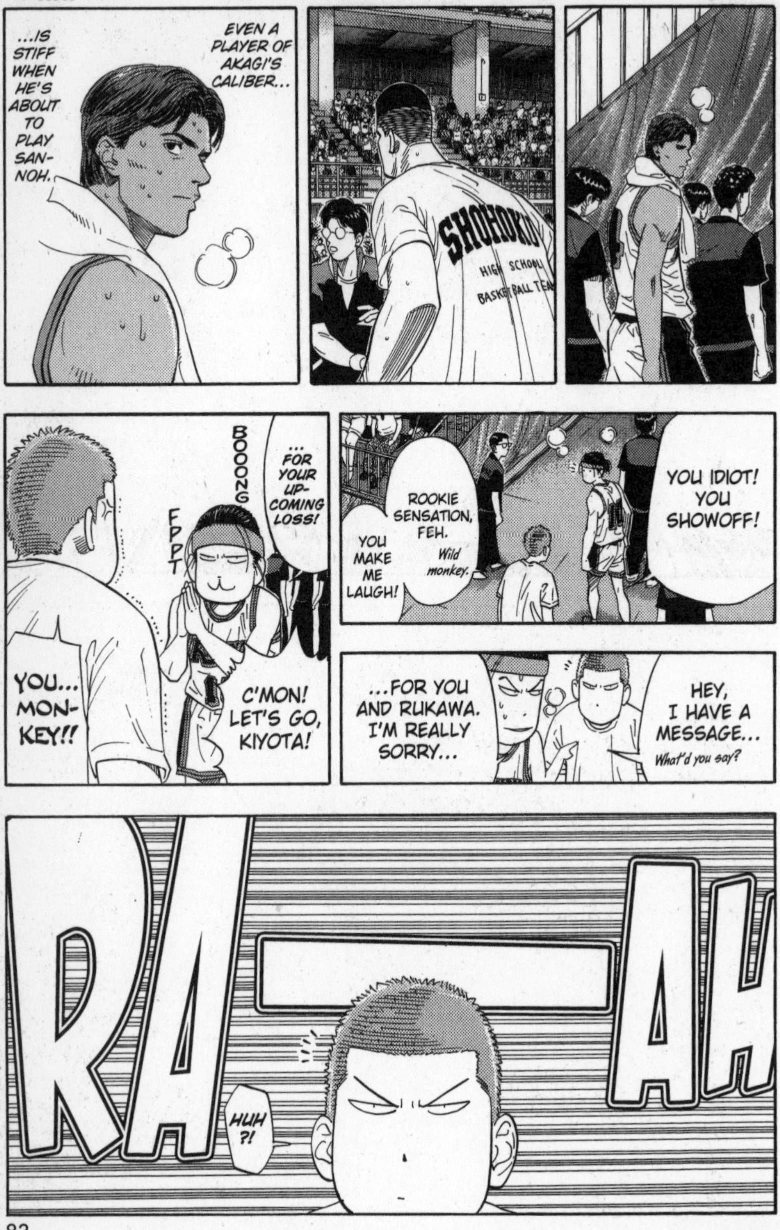
EVEN A PLAYER OF AKAGI'S CALIBER...
...IS STIFF WHEN HE'S ABOUT TO PLAY SAN-NOH.
YOU IDIOT! YOU SHOWOFF!
ROOKIE SENSATION, FEH.
Wild monkey.
YOU MAKE ME LAUGH!
HEY, I HAVE A MESSAGE...
What'd you say?
...FOR YOU AND RUKAWA. I'M REALLY SORRY...
...FOR YOUR UP-COMING LOSS!
BOOOONG
FPPT
C'MON! LET'S GO, KIYOTA!
YOU... MON-KEY!!
RA—AH
HUH?!

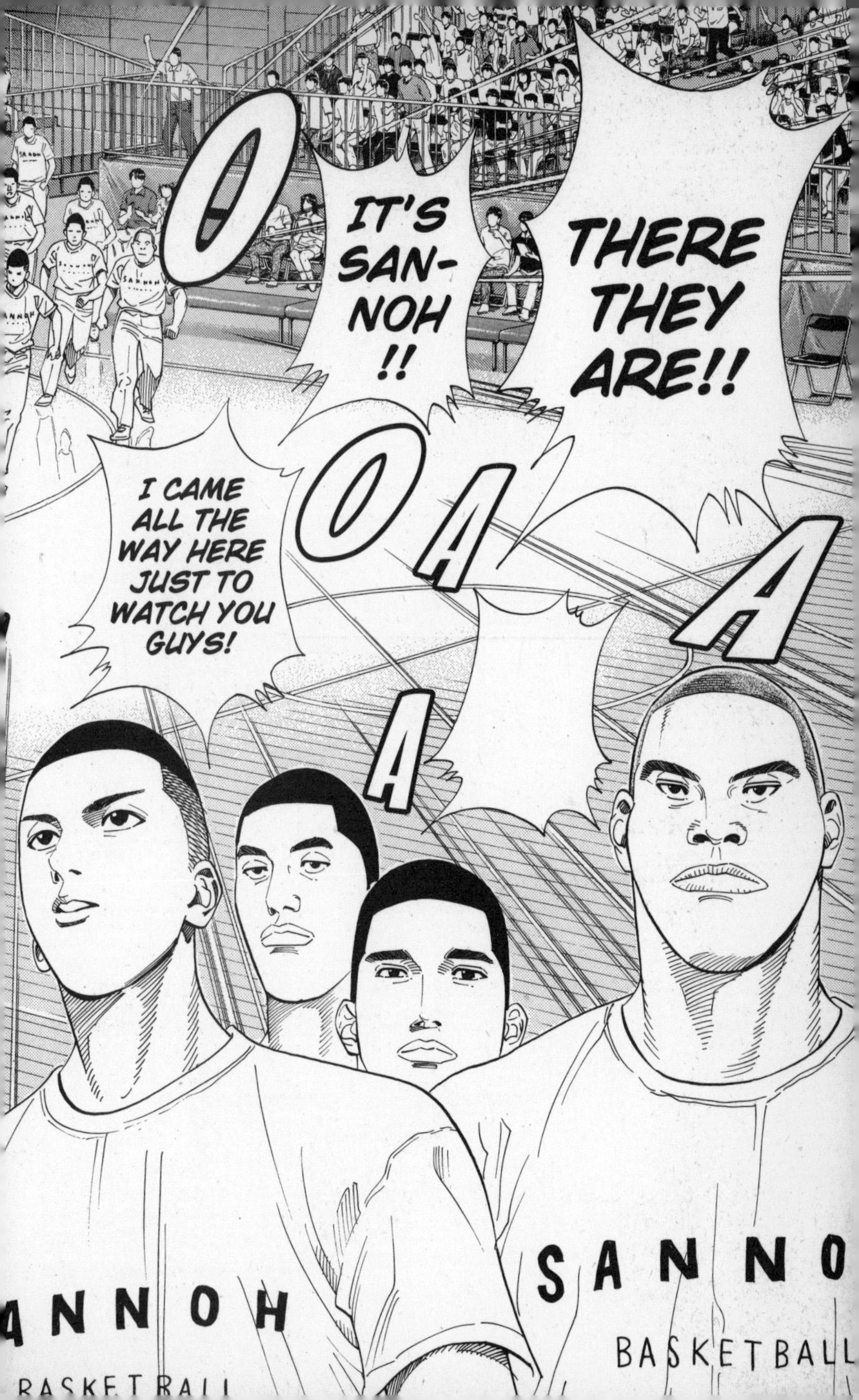
THERE THEY ARE!!
IT'S SAN-NOH!!
OOAAA
I CAME ALL THE WAY HERE JUST TO WATCH YOU GUYS!
SANNO
BASKETBALL
ANNOH

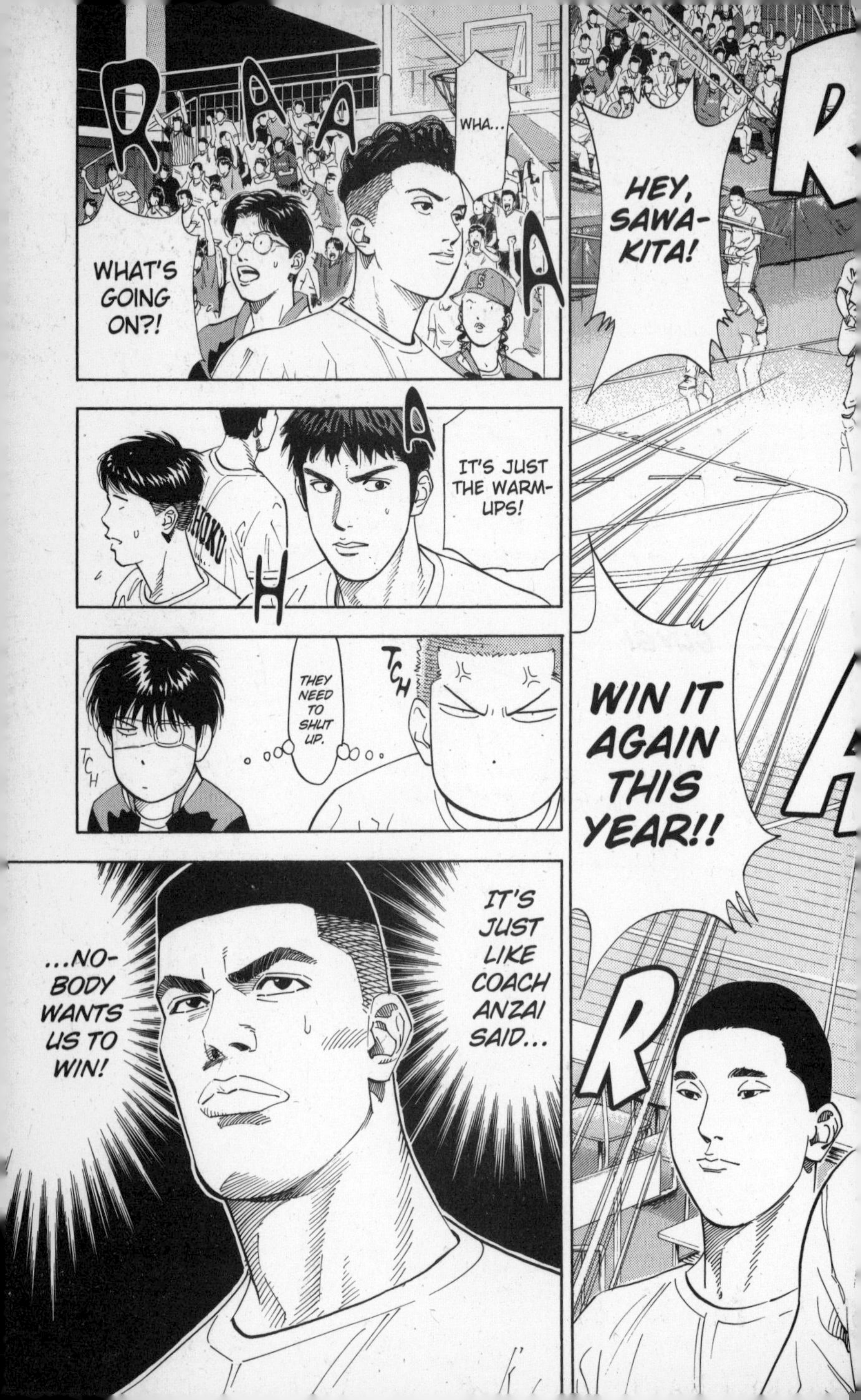
R
HEY, SAWA-KITA!
A
WIN IT AGAIN THIS YEAR!!
R
RAAAA
WHA...
WHAT'S GOING ON?!
A
IT'S JUST THE WARM-UPS!
H
TCH
THEY NEED TO SHUT UP.
TCH
IT'S JUST LIKE COACH ANZAI SAID...
...NO-BODY WANTS US TO WIN!

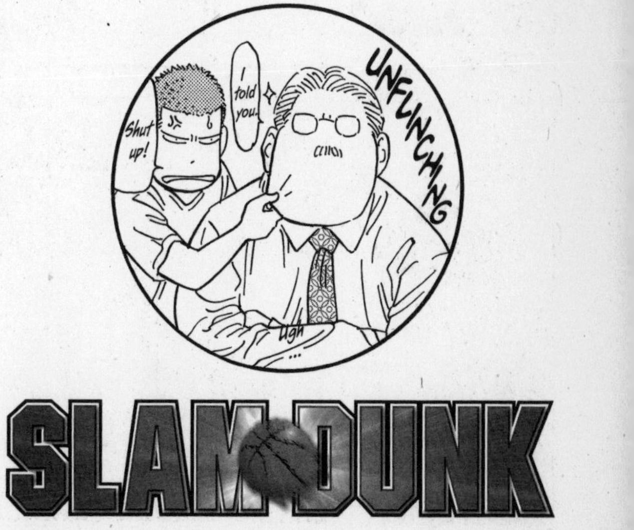
UNFLINCHING
I told you.
Shut up!
Ugh ...

SLAM DUNK

PRE-GAME

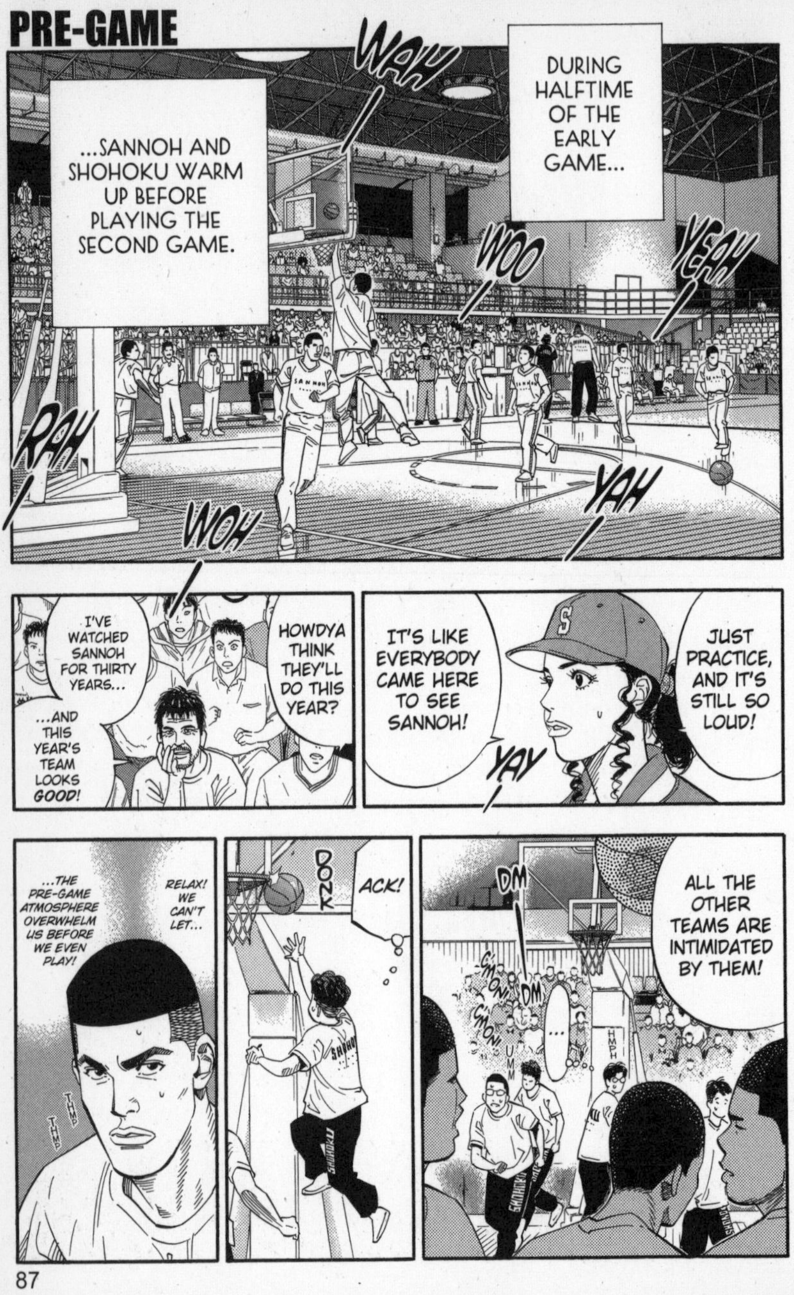
WAH
DURING HALFTIME OF THE EARLY GAME...
...SANNOH AND SHOHOKU WARM UP BEFORE PLAYING THE SECOND GAME.
YEAH
WOO
RAH
YAH
WOH
JUST PRACTICE, AND IT'S STILL SO LOUD!
IT'S LIKE EVERYBODY CAME HERE TO SEE SANNOH!
YAY
HOWDYA THINK THEY'LL DO THIS YEAR?
I'VE WATCHED SANNOH FOR THIRTY YEARS...
...AND THIS YEAR'S TEAM LOOKS GOOD!
ALL THE OTHER TEAMS ARE INTIMIDATED BY THEM!
DM
DM
C'MON! C'MON!
...
HMPH
UMM
DONK
ACK!
RELAX! WE CAN'T LET...
...THE PRE-GAME ATMOSPHERE OVERWHELM US BEFORE WE EVEN PLAY!
THMP THMP

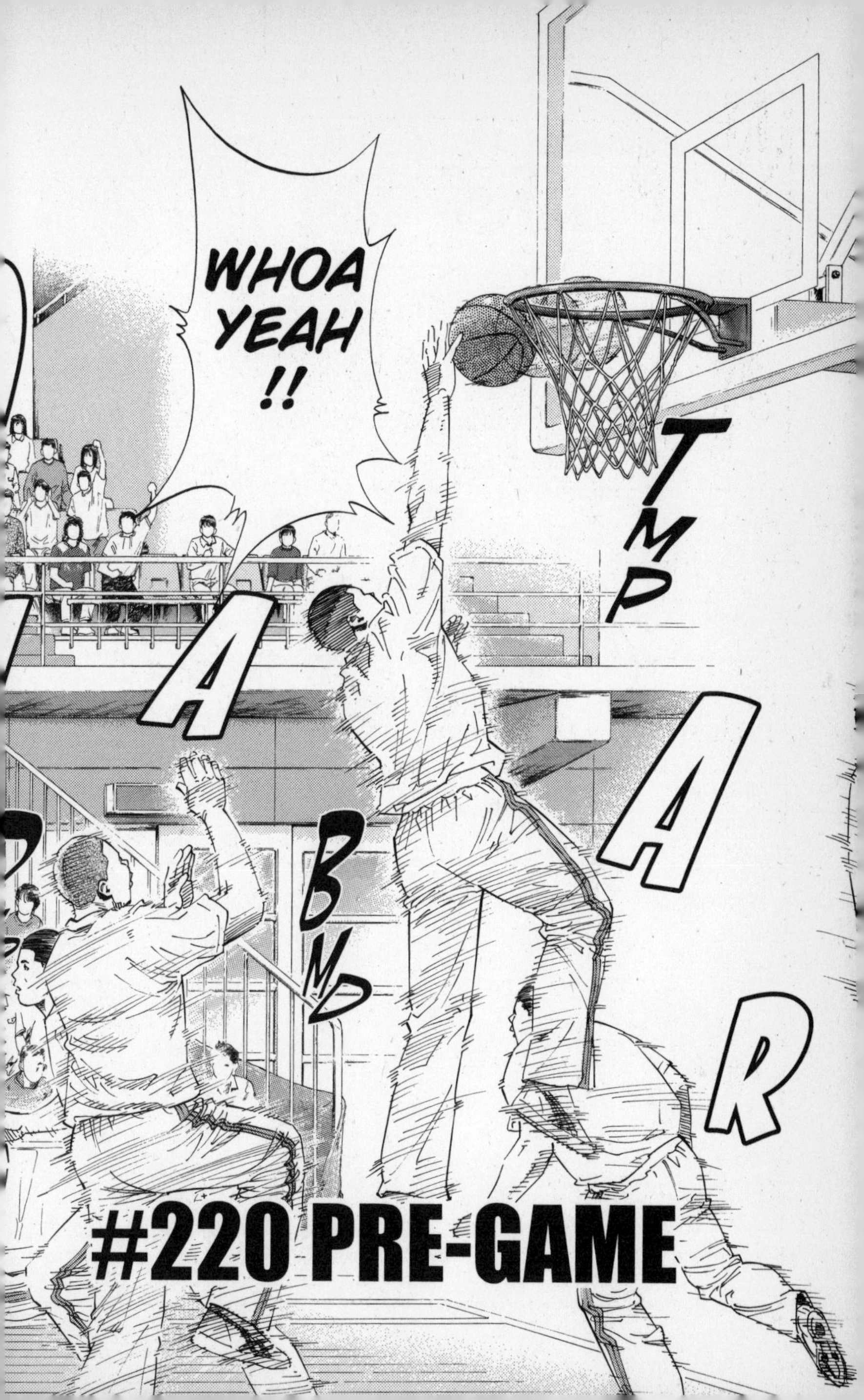
WHOA YEAH !!
TMP
BMD

#220 PRE-GAME

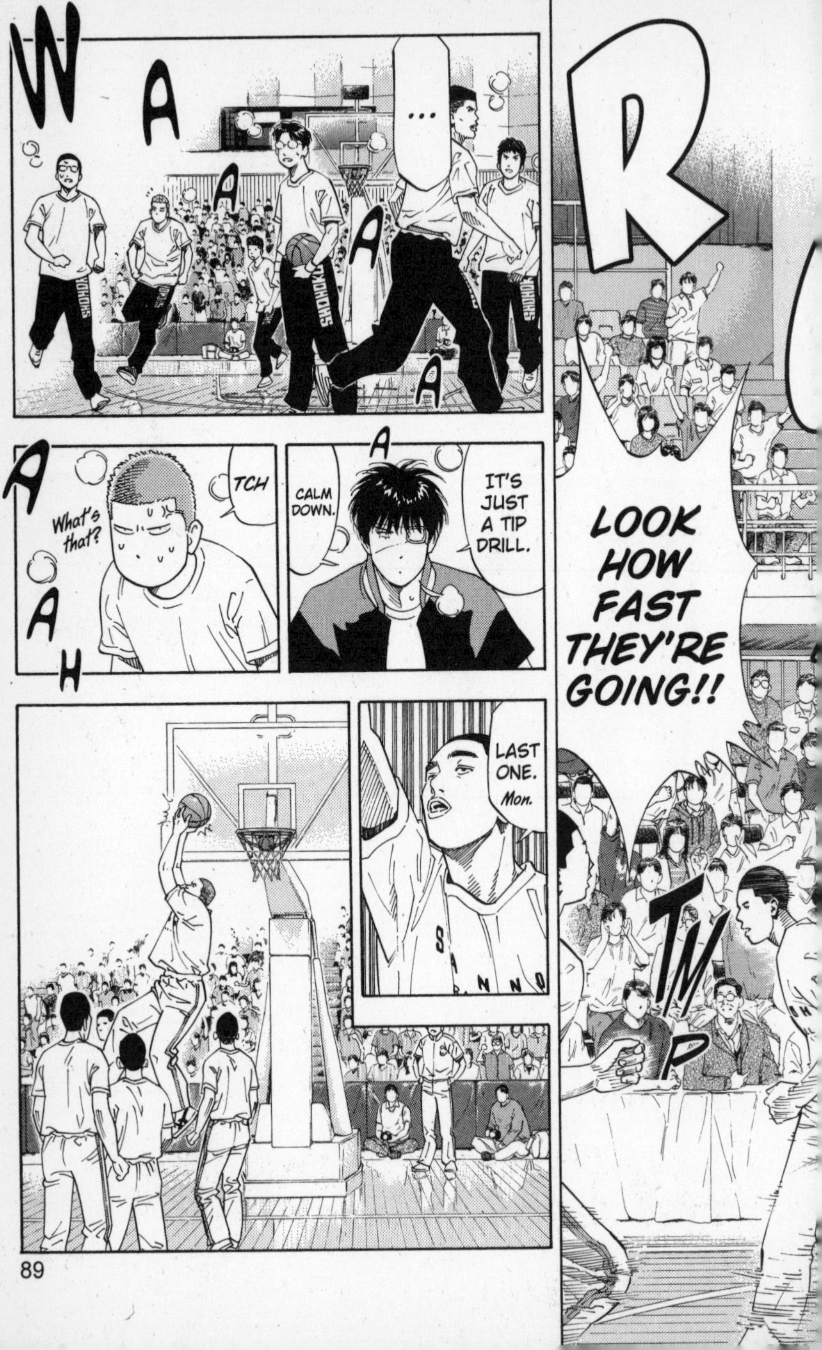
R
LOOK HOW FAST THEY'RE GOING!!
TMP
...
WAAAAAAAAAH
IT'S JUST A TIP DRILL.
CALM DOWN.
TCH
What's that?
LAST ONE.
Mon.

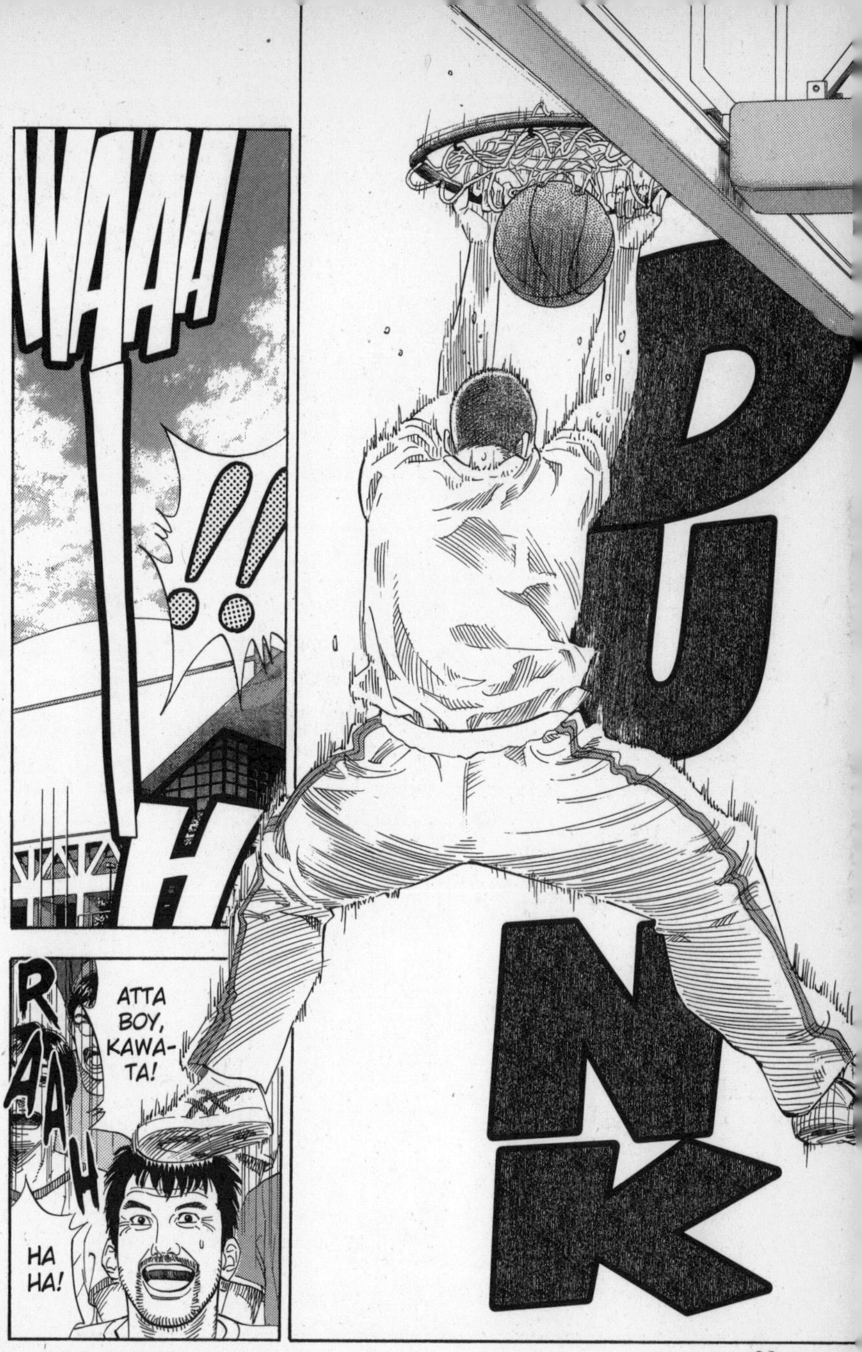
DUNK
WAAAAH
!!
RAAAH
ATTA BOY, KAWATA!
HA HA!

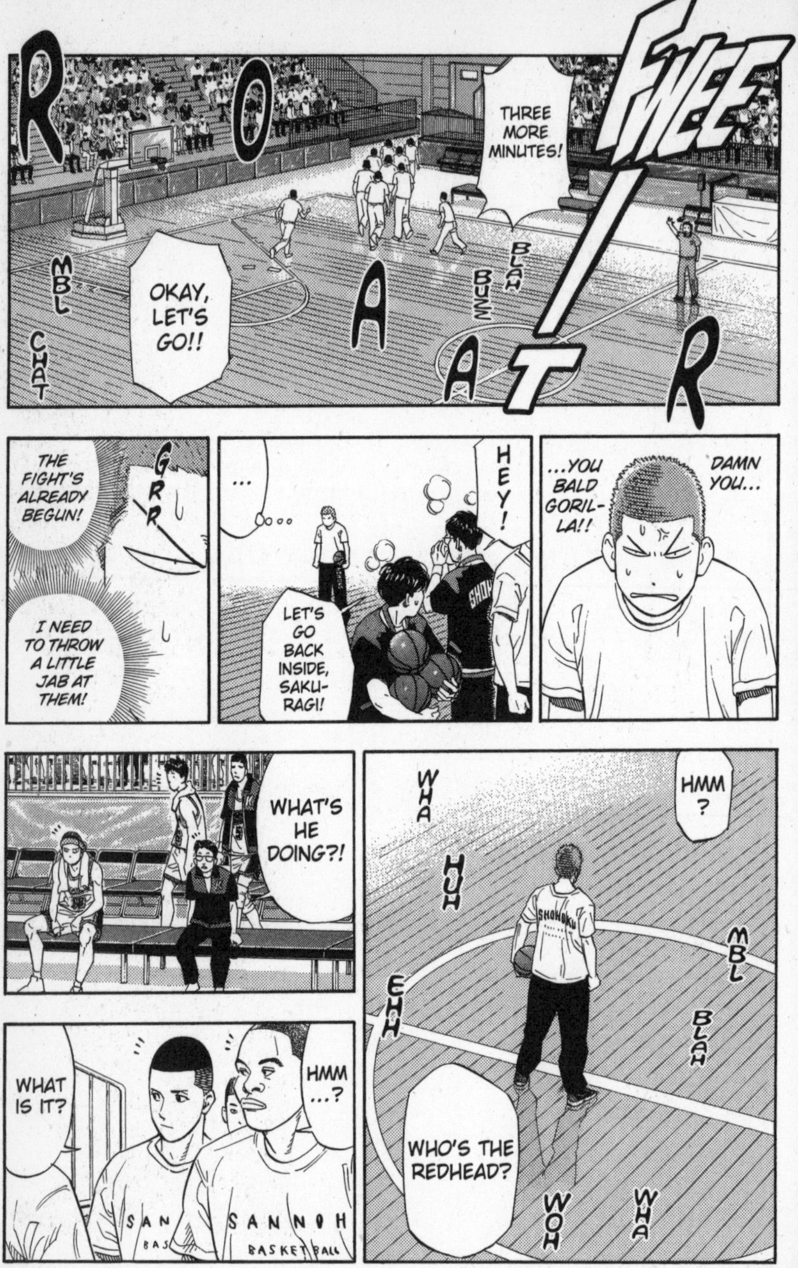
FWEE
THREE MORE MINUTES!
ROAR
BLAH
BUZZ
OKAY, LET'S GO!!
MBL
CHAT
DAMN YOU...
...YOU BALD GORIL-LA!!
HEY!
...
LET'S GO BACK INSIDE, SAKU-RAGI!
GRR
THE FIGHT'S ALREADY BEGUN!
I NEED TO THROW A LITTLE JAB AT THEM!
HMM?
WHA
HUH
MBL
BLAH
EHH
WHO'S THE REDHEAD?
WHA
WOH
WHAT'S HE DOING?!
HMM...?
WHAT IS IT?
SANNOH
BASKETBALL

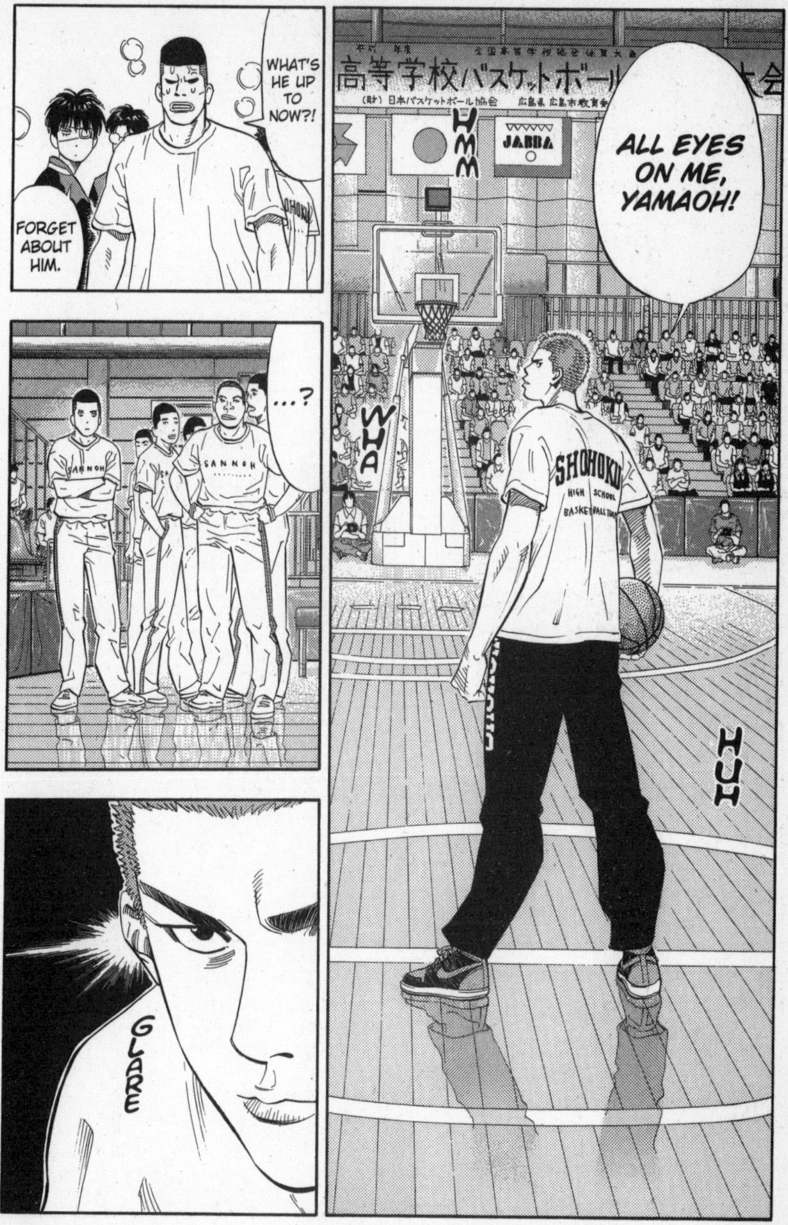
高等学校バスケットボール
大会
(財)日本バスケットボール協会
JABBA
HMM
ALL EYES ON ME, YAMAOH!
WHA
SHOHOKU
HUH
WHAT'S HE UP TO NOW?!
FORGET ABOUT HIM.
SANNOH
...?
GLARE

Sign: National High School Basketball Championship Tournament

READ THIS WAY

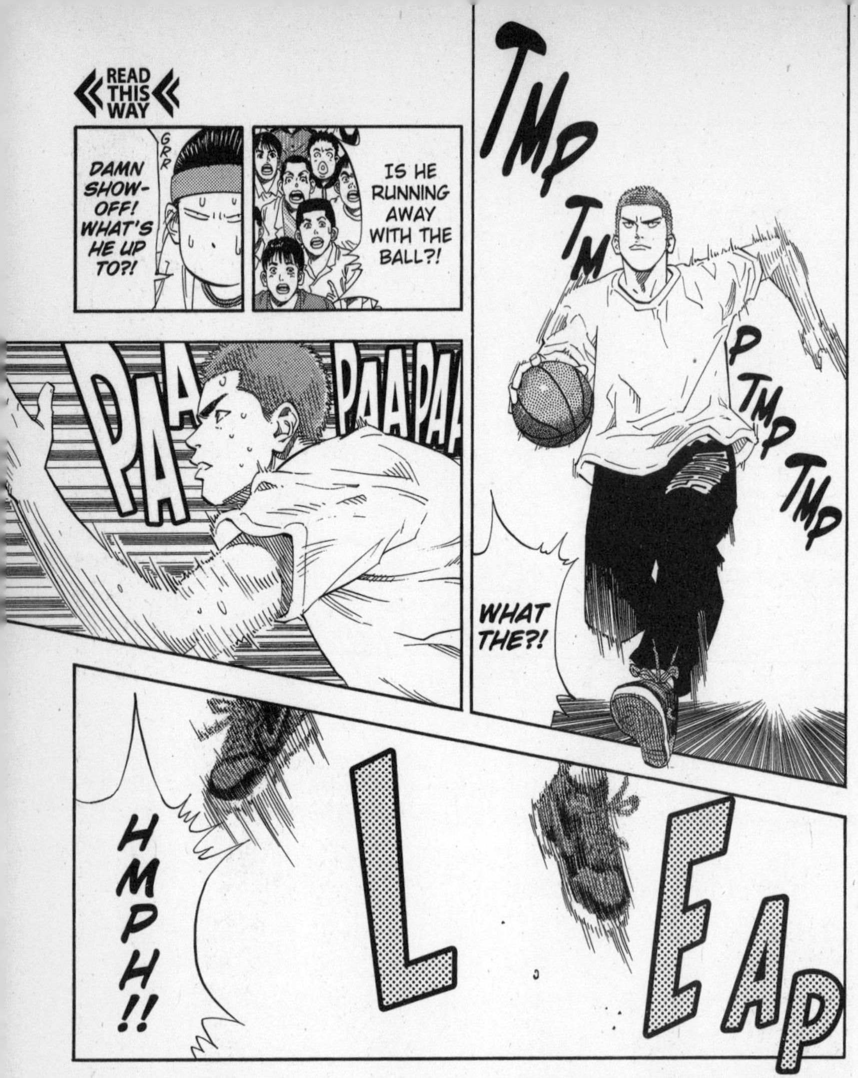

TMP TMP
TMP TMP TMP
WHAT THE?!
IS HE RUNNING AWAY WITH THE BALL?!
GRR
DAMN SHOW-OFF! WHAT'S HE UP TO?!
PAPAA
PAAPAA
LEAP
HMPH!!
GASP!!

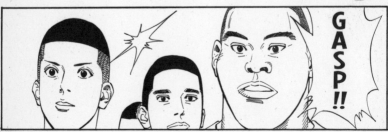

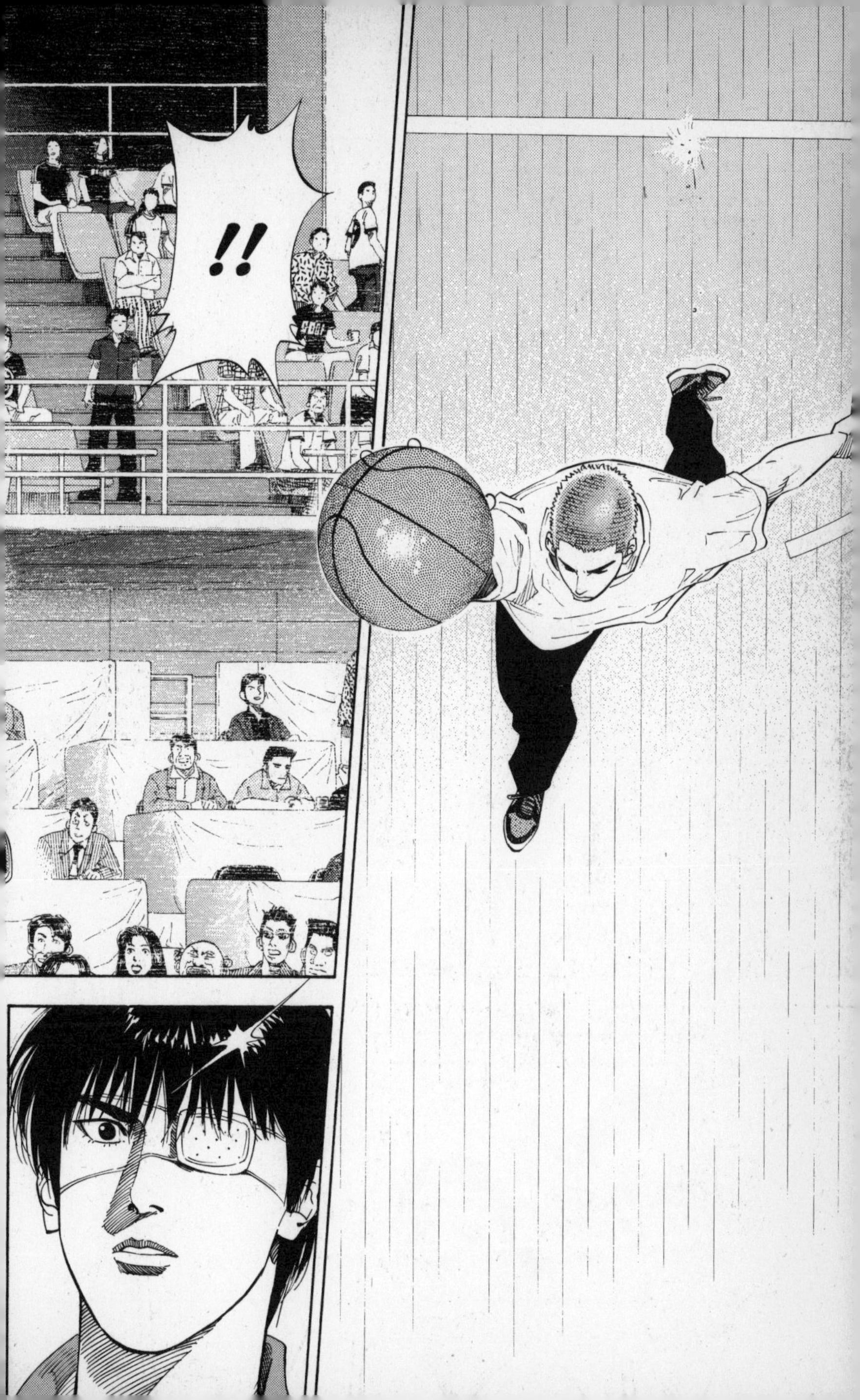
!!

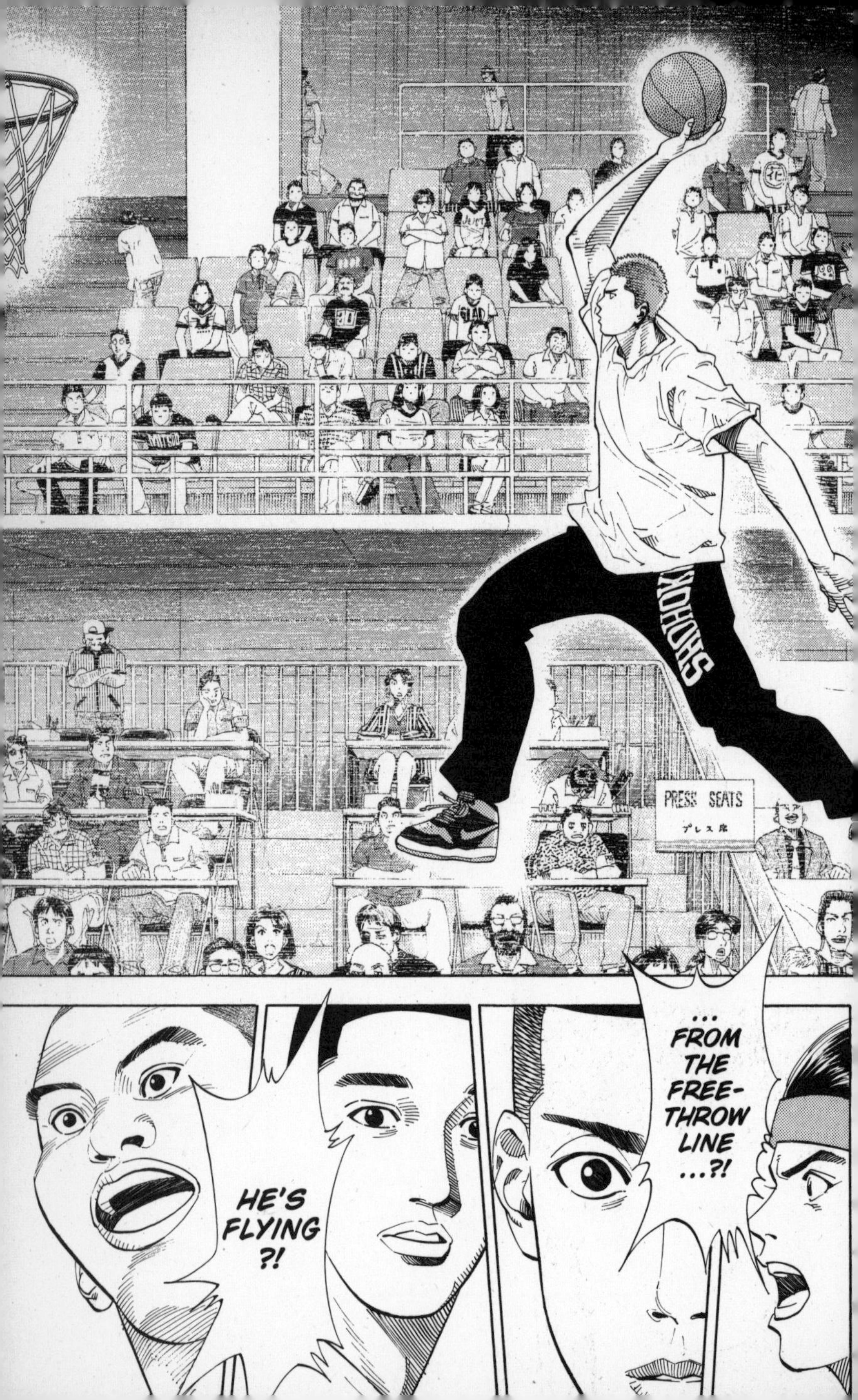
PRESS SEATS
プレス席
... FROM THE FREE-THROW LINE ...?!
HE'S FLYING ?!

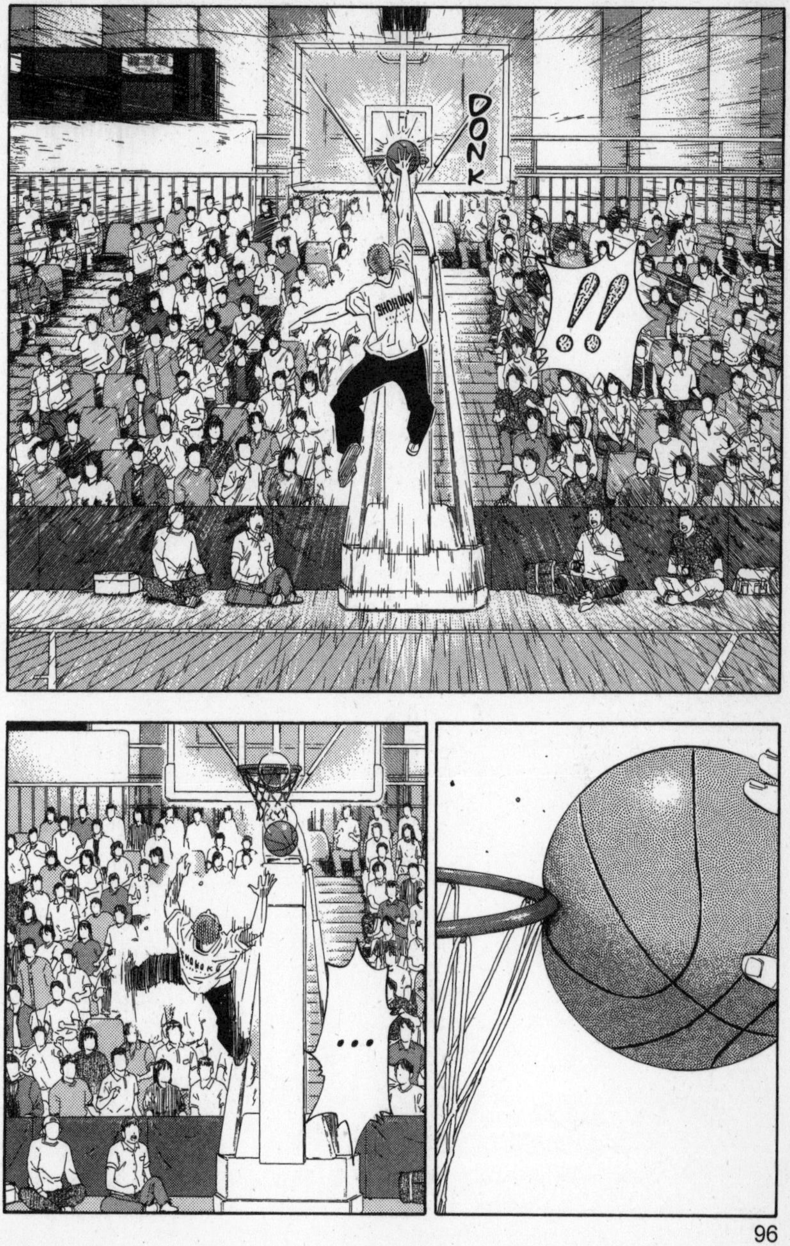
DONK
!!
SHOHOKU
SHOHOKU
...

READ THIS WAY

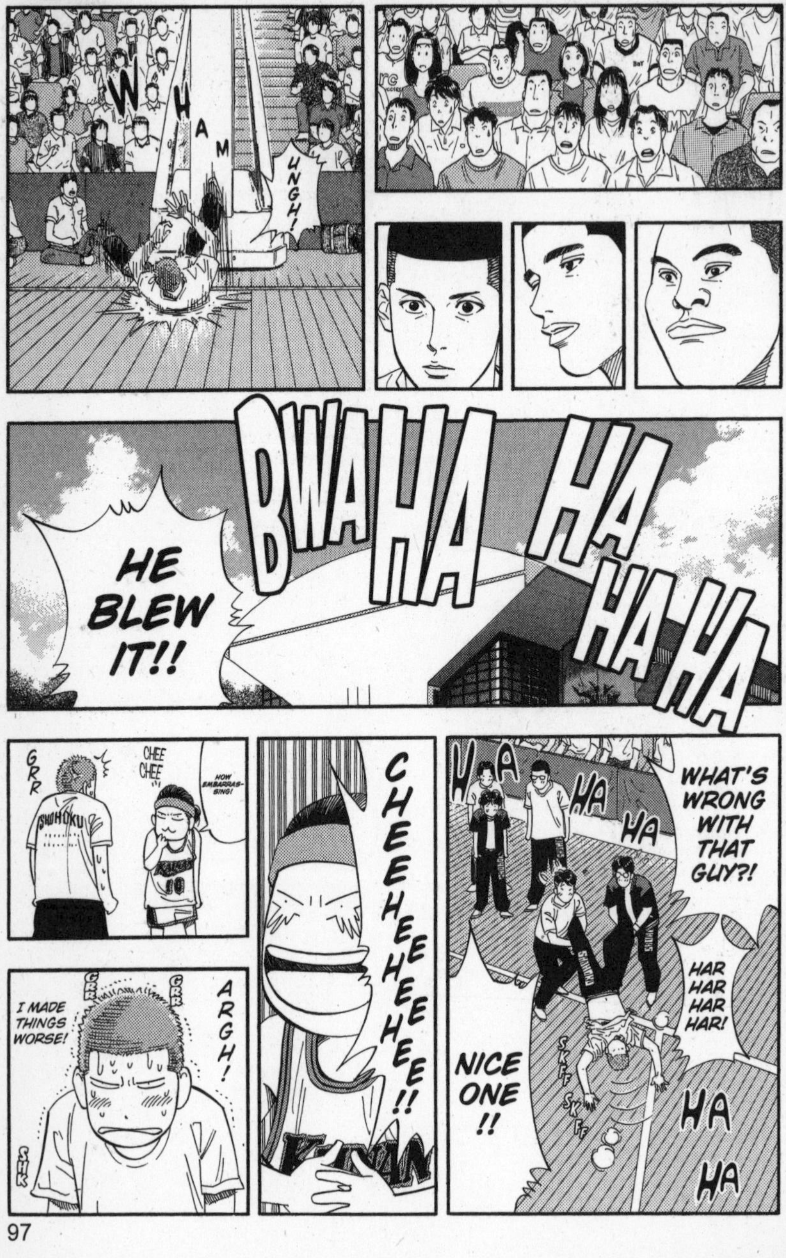
WHAM
UNGH!
BWAHA HA HA HA HA HA
HE BLEW IT!!
WHAT'S WRONG WITH THAT GUY?!
HA HA HA HA
HAR HAR HAR HAR!
HA HA
NICE ONE!!
SKFF SKFF
CHEEHEHEHEHEE!!
GRR
CHEE CHEE
HOW EMBARRASSING!
ARGH!
GRR GRR
I MADE THINGS WORSE!
SHK

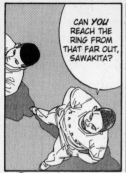

CAN *YOU* REACH THE RING FROM THAT FAR OUT, SAWAKITA?

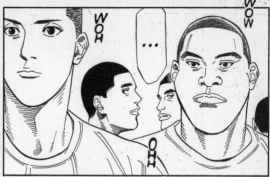

WOH

...

WOW

WOW

OH

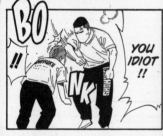

BO

!!

NK

YOU IDIOT !!

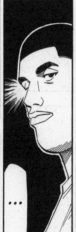

...

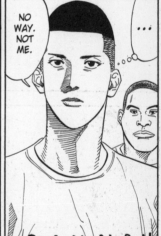

NO WAY. NOT ME.

...

...

...

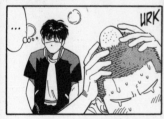

...

URK

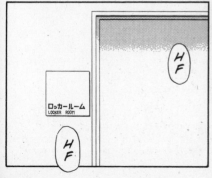

HF

ロッカールーム
LOCKER ROOM

HF

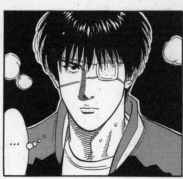

...

READ THIS WAY

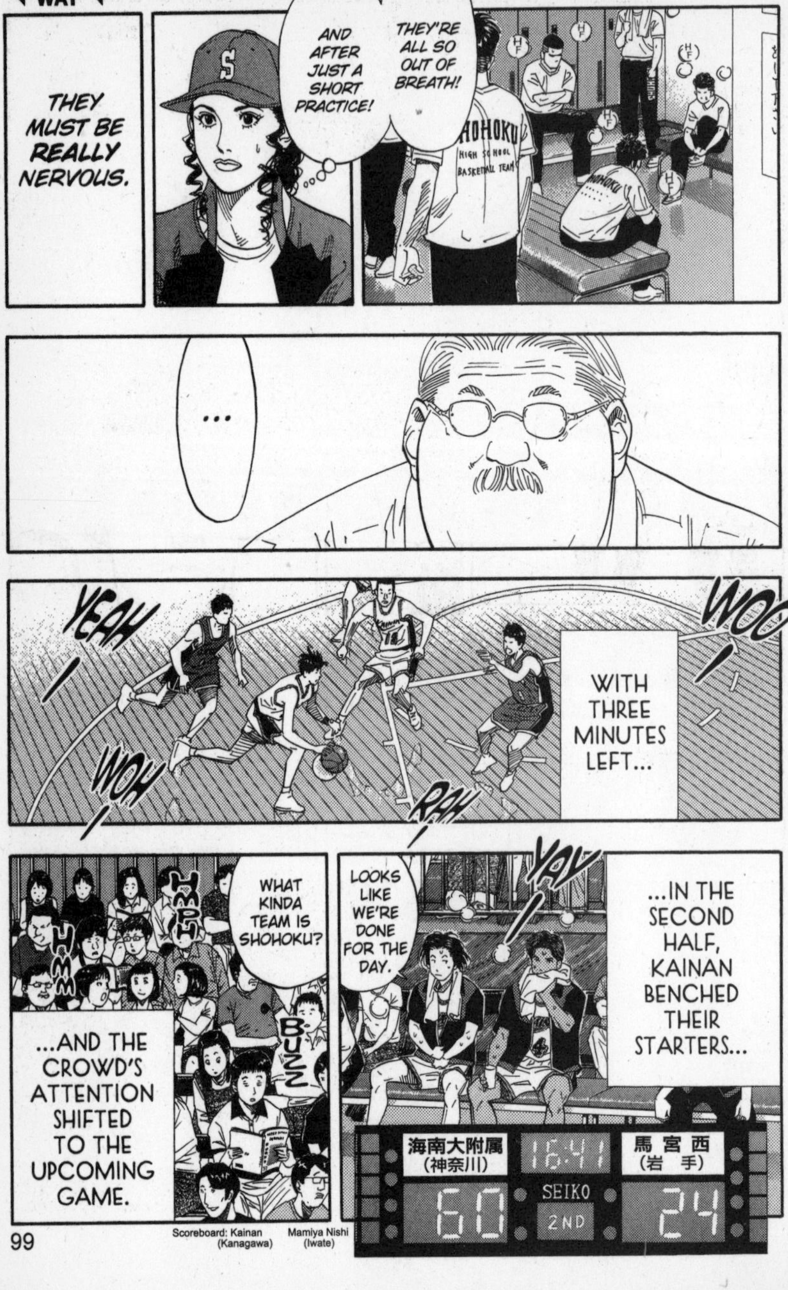
THEY'RE ALL SO OUT OF BREATH!
AND AFTER JUST A SHORT PRACTICE!
THEY MUST BE REALLY NERVOUS.
...
WOO
WITH THREE MINUTES LEFT...
YEAH
WOH
RAH
...IN THE SECOND HALF, KAINAN BENCHED THEIR STARTERS...
YAY
LOOKS LIKE WE'RE DONE FOR THE DAY.
海南大附属 (神奈川)
16:41
馬宮西 (岩手)
60
SEIKO
2ND
24
WHAT KINDA TEAM IS SHOHOKU?
HMPH
HMM
BUZZ
...AND THE CROWD'S ATTENTION SHIFTED TO THE UPCOMING GAME.

Scoreboard: Kainan (Kanagawa) Mamiya Nishi (Iwate)

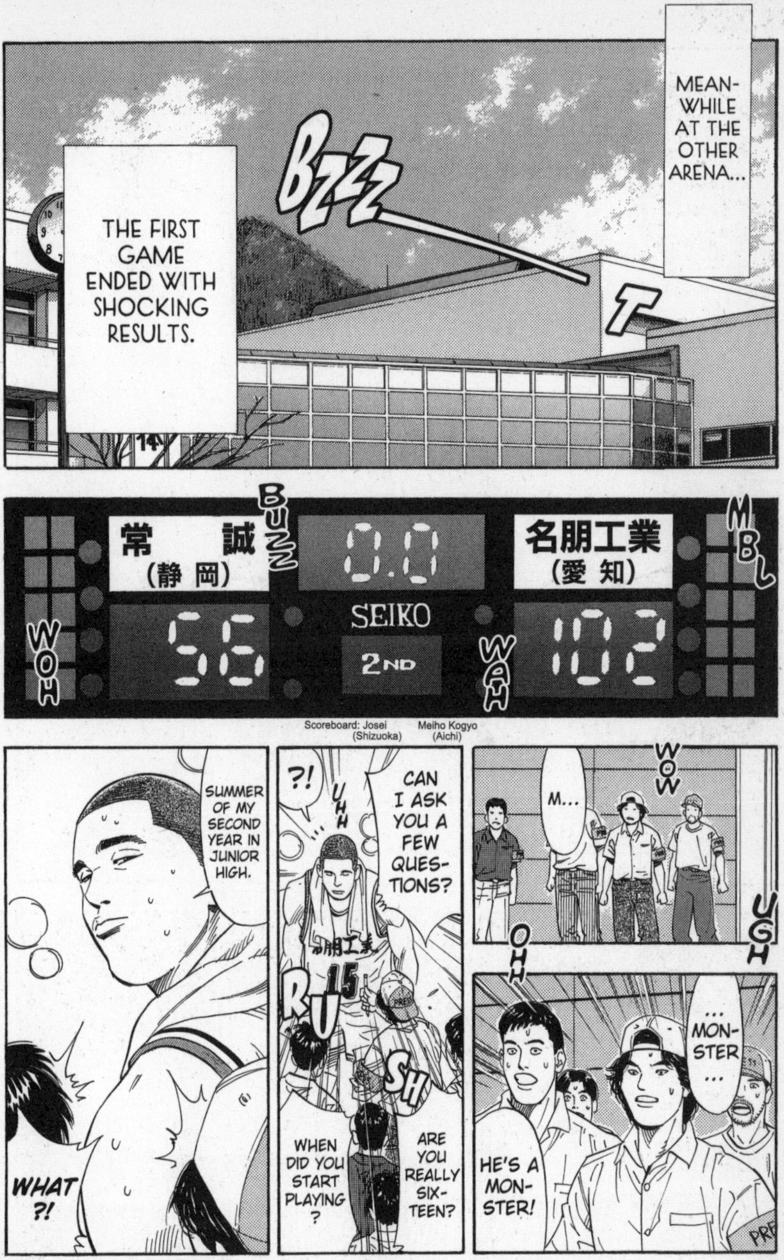

MEAN-WHILE AT THE OTHER ARENA...
BZZZT
THE FIRST GAME ENDED WITH SHOCKING RESULTS.
MBL
名朋工業
(愛知)
0.0
BUZZ
常誠
(静岡)
SEIKO
2ND
WAH
102
56
WOH
Scoreboard: Josei (Shizuoka) Meiho Kogyo (Aichi)
WOW
M...
UGH
OHH
... MONSTER ...
HE'S A MONSTER!
CAN I ASK YOU A FEW QUESTIONS?
?!
UHH
ARE YOU REALLY SIXTEEN?
WHEN DID YOU START PLAYING?
RUSH
SUMMER OF MY SECOND YEAR IN JUNIOR HIGH.
WHAT?!

READ THIS WAY

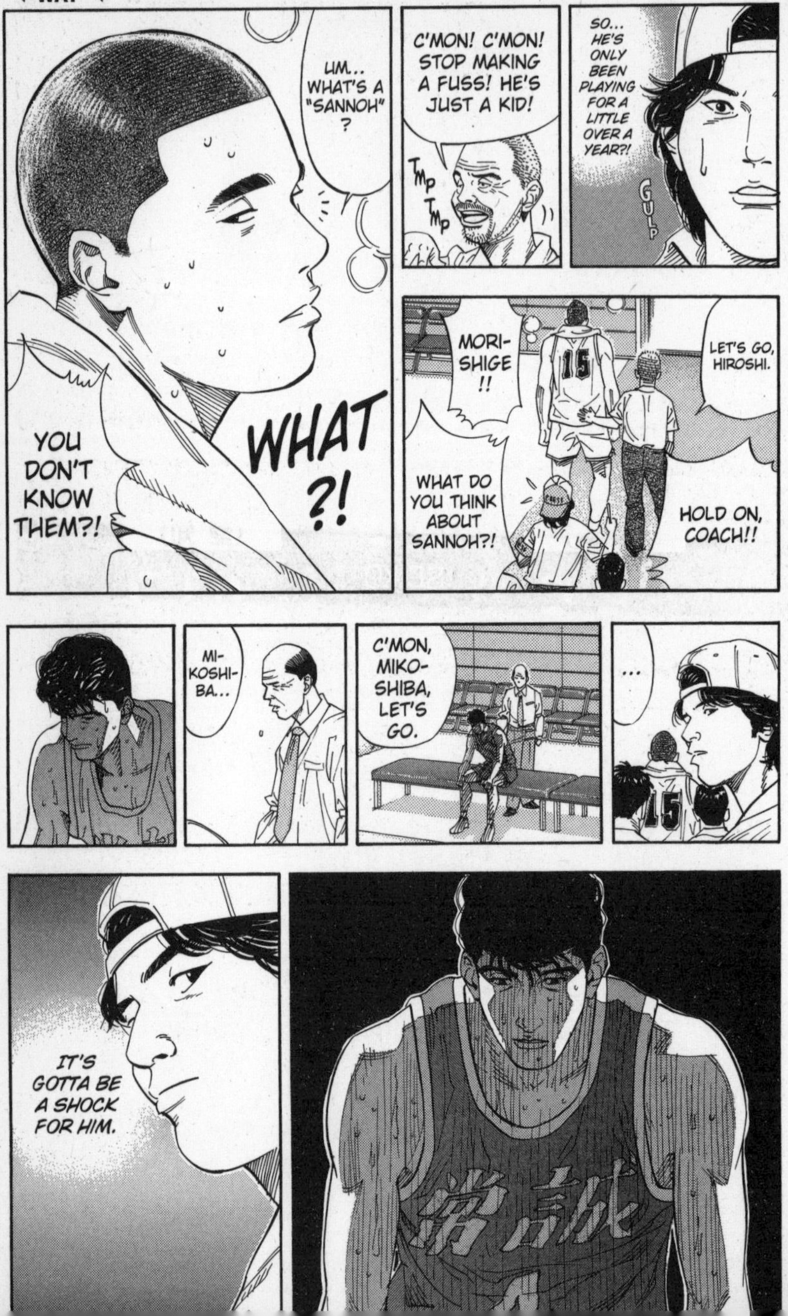
SO... HE'S ONLY BEEN PLAYING FOR A LITTLE OVER A YEAR?!
GULP
C'MON! C'MON! STOP MAKING A FUSS! HE'S JUST A KID!
TMP TMP
LET'S GO, HIROSHI.
MORI-SHIGE!!
HOLD ON, COACH!!
WHAT DO YOU THINK ABOUT SANNOH?!
UM... WHAT'S A "SANNOH"?
WHAT?!
YOU DON'T KNOW THEM?!
...
C'MON, MIKO-SHIBA, LET'S GO.
MI-KOSHIBA...
IT'S GOTTA BE A SHOCK FOR HIM.

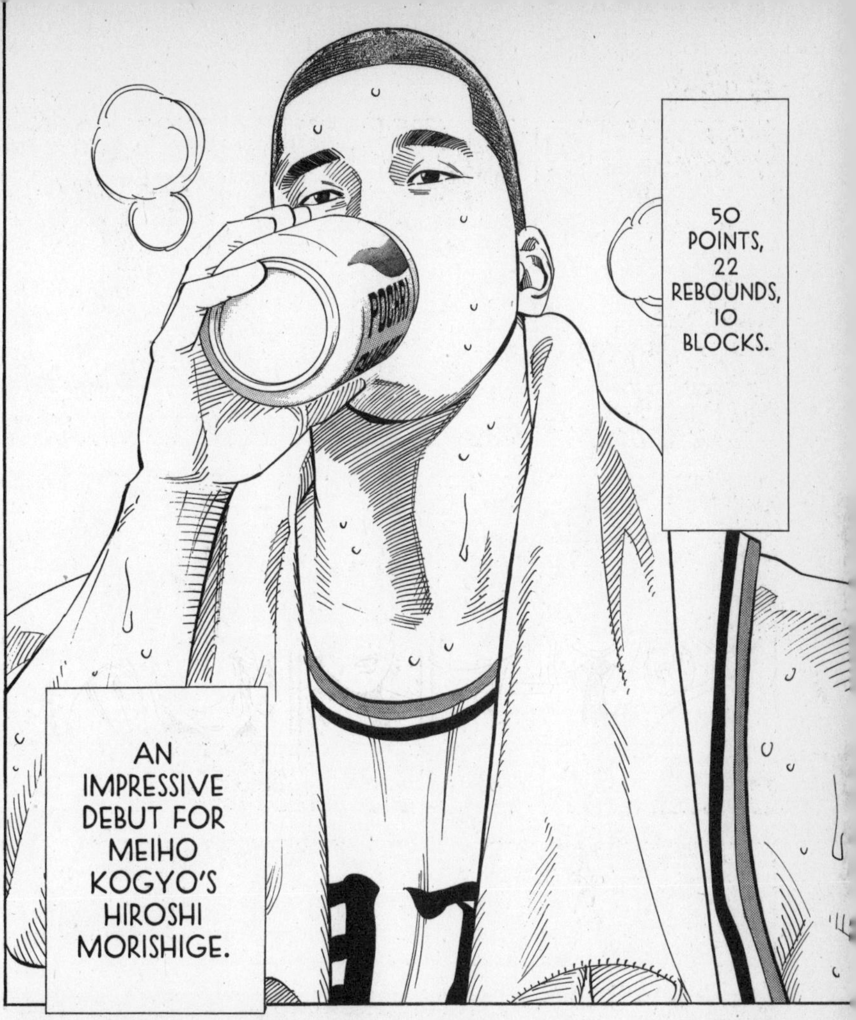
50 POINTS, 22 REBOUNDS, 10 BLOCKS.
AN IMPRESSIVE DEBUT FOR MEIHO KOGYO'S HIROSHI MORISHIGE.

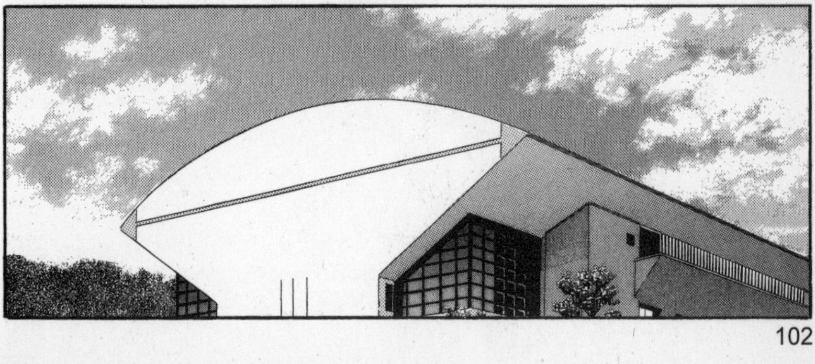

READ THIS WAY

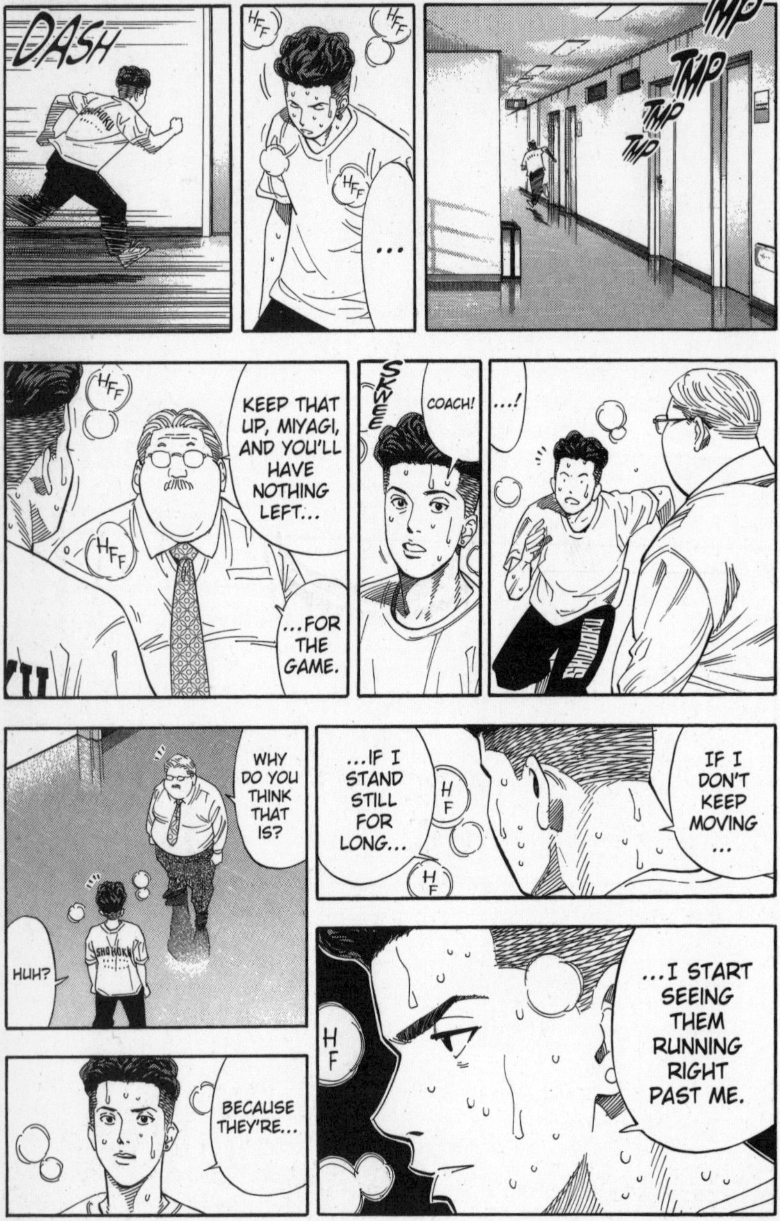
TMP TMP TMP TMP
HFF
HFF
HFF
...
DASH
...!
SKWEE
COACH!
KEEP THAT UP, MIYAGI, AND YOU'LL HAVE NOTHING LEFT...
HFF
HFF
...FOR THE GAME.
WHY DO YOU THINK THAT IS?
HUH?
BECAUSE THEY'RE...
IF I DON'T KEEP MOVING ...
...IF I STAND STILL FOR LONG...
HF
HF
...I START SEEING THEM RUNNING RIGHT PAST ME.
HF

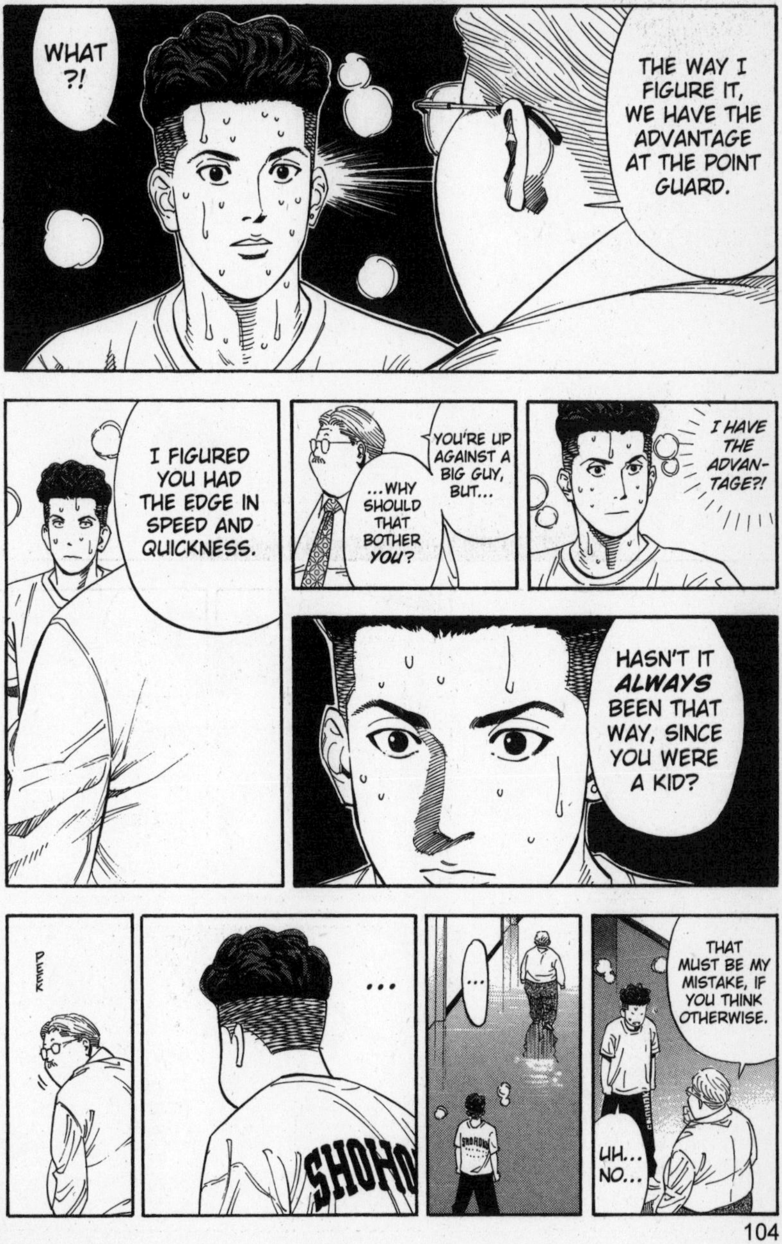
THE WAY I FIGURE IT, WE HAVE THE ADVANTAGE AT THE POINT GUARD.
WHAT ?!
I HAVE THE ADVANTAGE?!
YOU'RE UP AGAINST A BIG GUY, BUT...
...WHY SHOULD THAT BOTHER YOU?
HASN'T IT ALWAYS BEEN THAT WAY, SINCE YOU WERE A KID?
I FIGURED YOU HAD THE EDGE IN SPEED AND QUICKNESS.
THAT MUST BE MY MISTAKE, IF YOU THINK OTHERWISE.
UH... NO...
...
...
PEEK

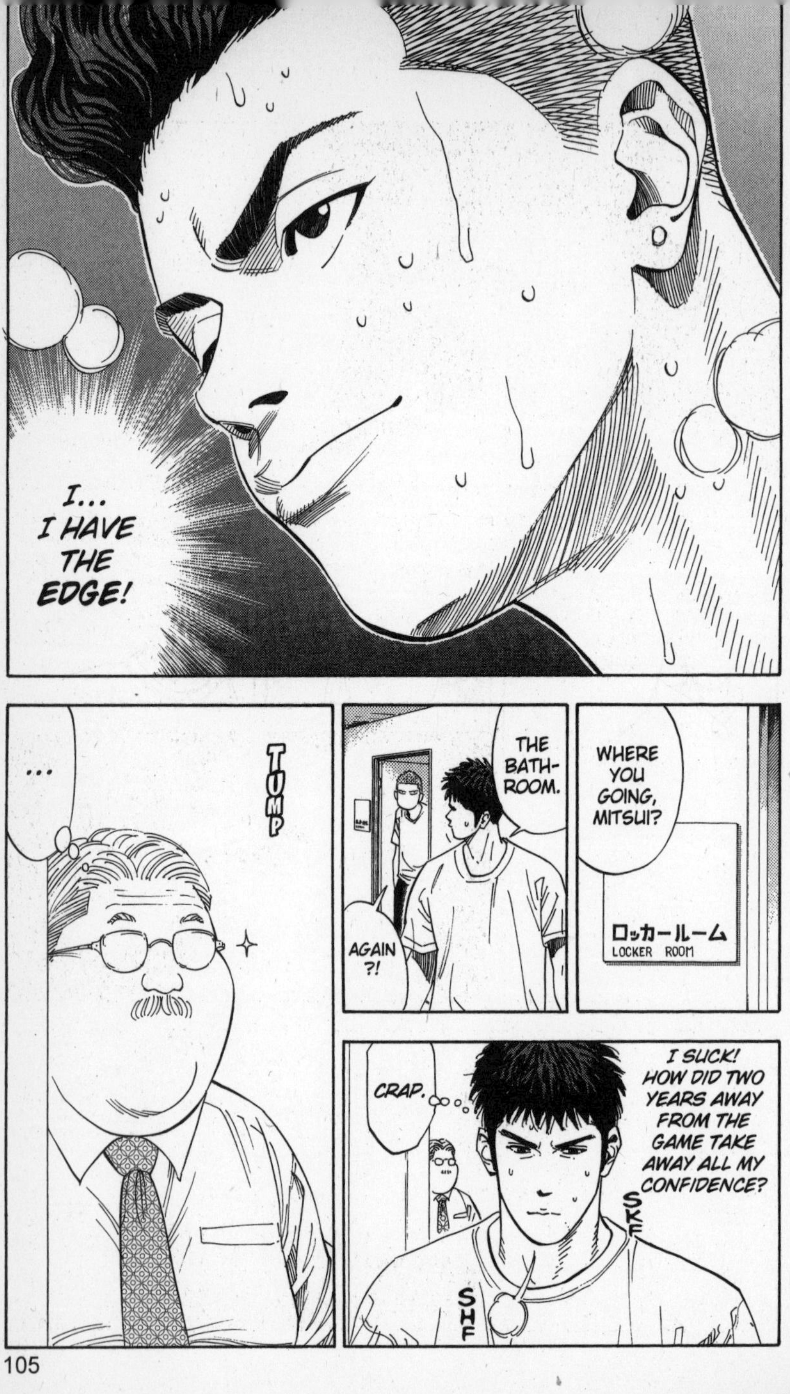
I...
I HAVE THE EDGE!
WHERE YOU GOING, MITSUI?
ロッカールーム
LOCKER ROOM
THE BATH-ROOM.
AGAIN?!
I SUCK! HOW DID TWO YEARS AWAY FROM THE GAME TAKE AWAY ALL MY CONFIDENCE?
CRAP.
SKF
SHF
TUMP
...

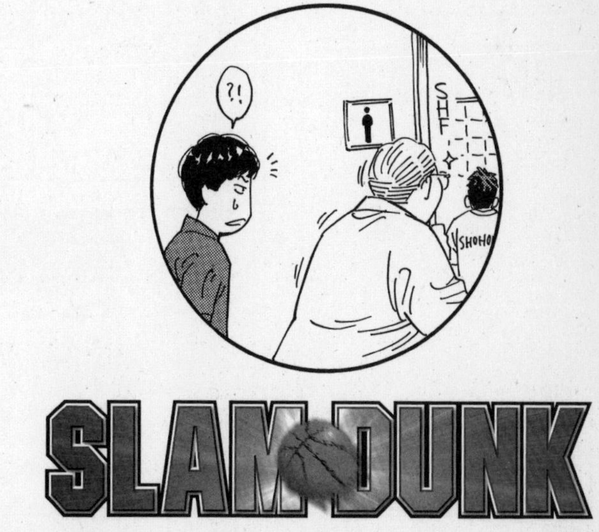
?!

SLAM DUNK

CAN'T WAIT TO SEE SANNOH

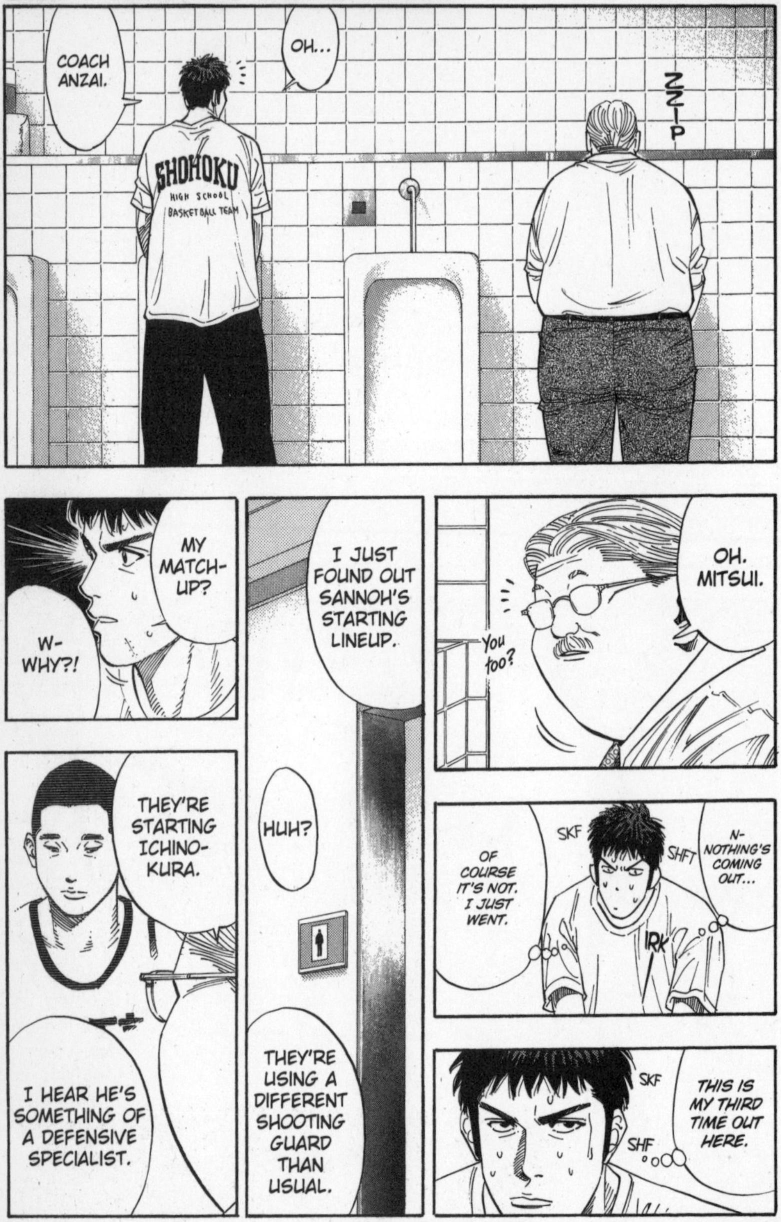
ZZIP
OH...
COACH ANZAI.
OH. MITSUI.
You too?
N-NOTHING'S COMING OUT...
SHFT
SKF
OF COURSE IT'S NOT. I JUST WENT.
IRK
THIS IS MY THIRD TIME OUT HERE.
SKF
SHF
I JUST FOUND OUT SANNOH'S STARTING LINEUP.
HUH?
THEY'RE USING A DIFFERENT SHOOTING GUARD THAN USUAL.
MY MATCH-UP?
W-WHY?!
THEY'RE STARTING ICHINOKURA.
I HEAR HE'S SOMETHING OF A DEFENSIVE SPECIALIST.

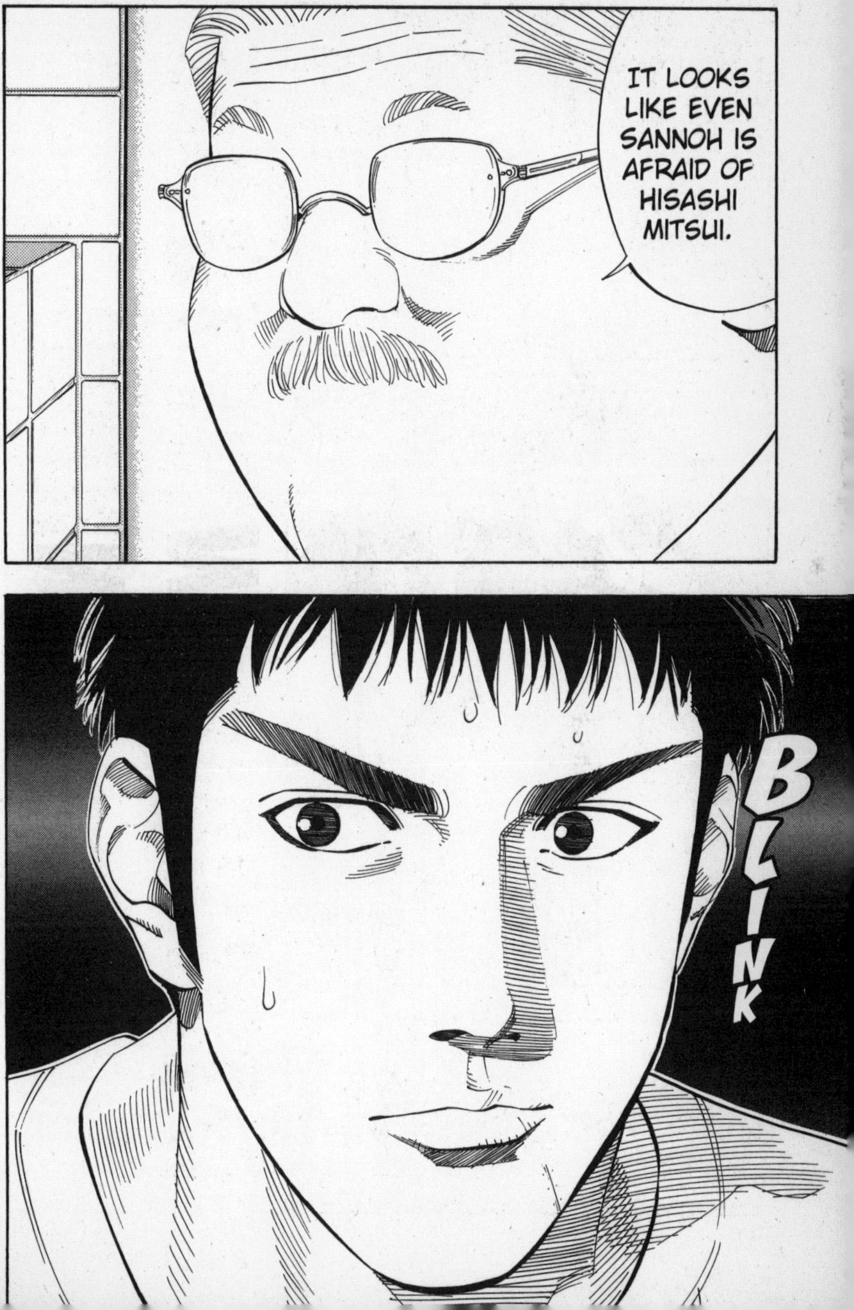
IT LOOKS LIKE EVEN SANNOH IS AFRAID OF HISASHI MITSUI.
BLINK

#221 CAN'T WAIT TO SEE SANNOH

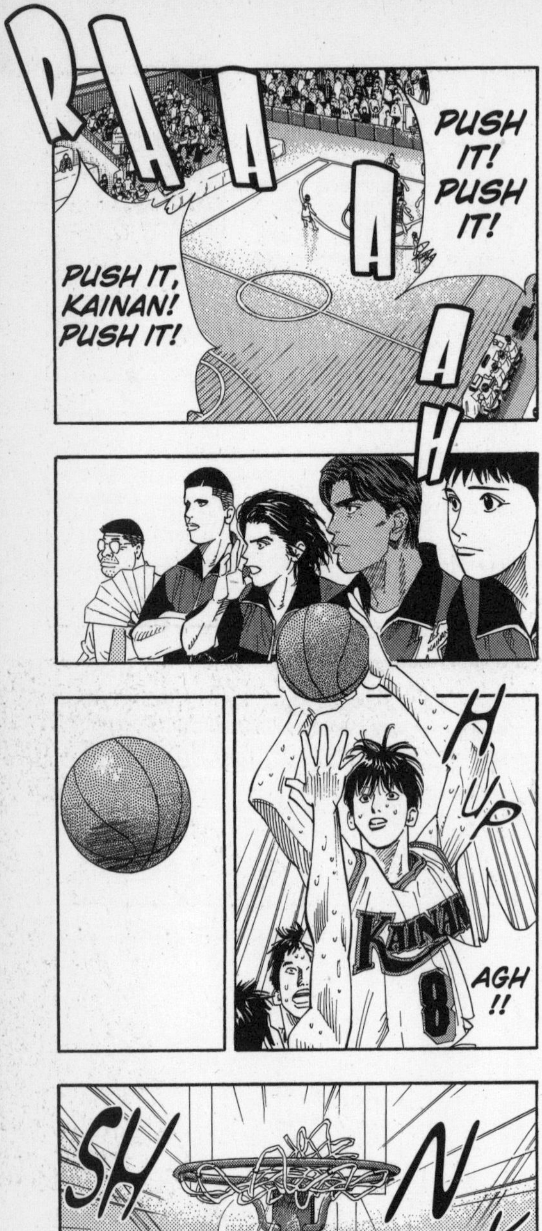

RAAAAH
PUSH IT! PUSH IT!
PUSH IT, KAINAN! PUSH IT!
HUP
AGH !!
SHNK

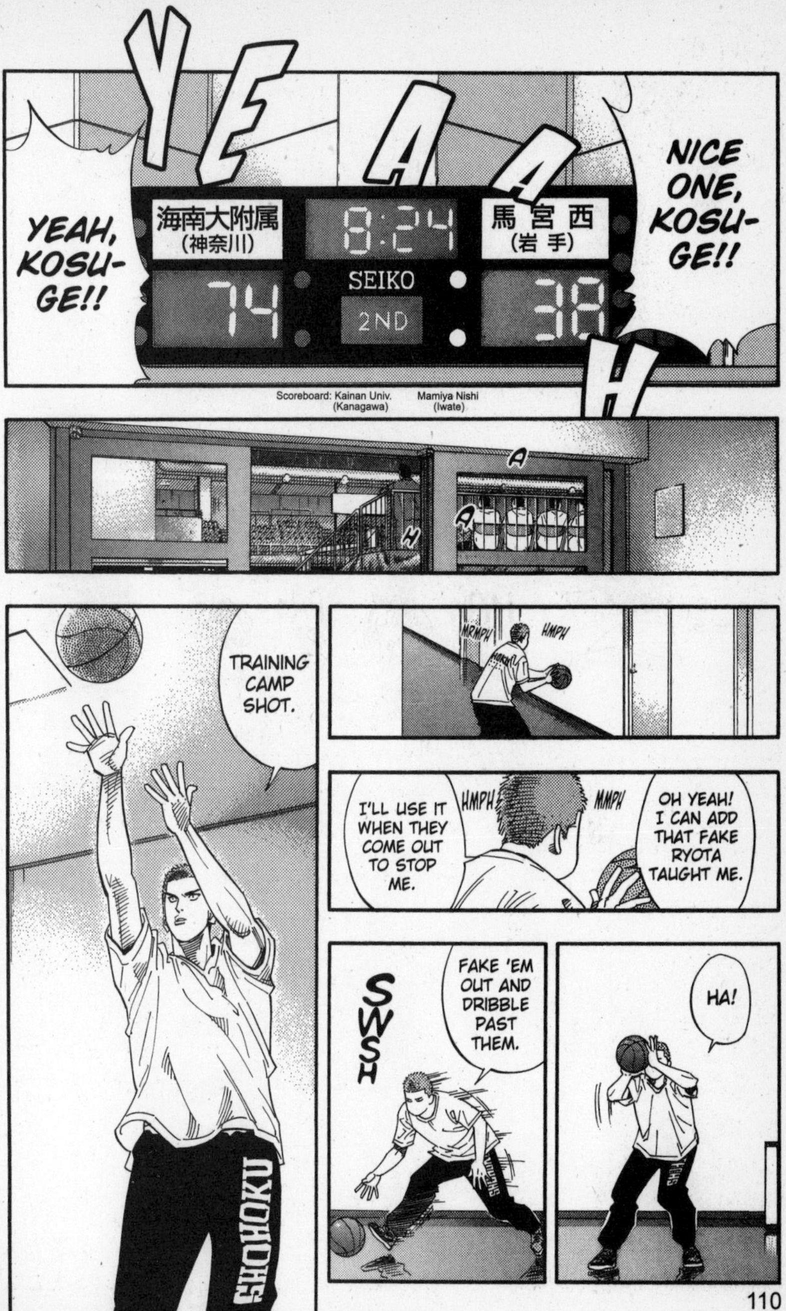

NICE ONE, KOSUGE!!
YEAAAH
海南大附属 (神奈川)
8:24
馬宮西 (岩手)
SEIKO
2ND
74
38
YEAH, KOSUGE!!
AAH
MRMPH
HMPH
OH YEAH! I CAN ADD THAT FAKE RYOTA TAUGHT ME.
MMPH
HMPH
I'LL USE IT WHEN THEY COME OUT TO STOP ME.
HA!
FAKE 'EM OUT AND DRIBBLE PAST THEM.
SWSH
TRAINING CAMP SHOT.
SHOHOKU

Scoreboard: Kainan Univ. (Kanagawa) Mamiya Nishi (Iwate)

READ THIS WAY

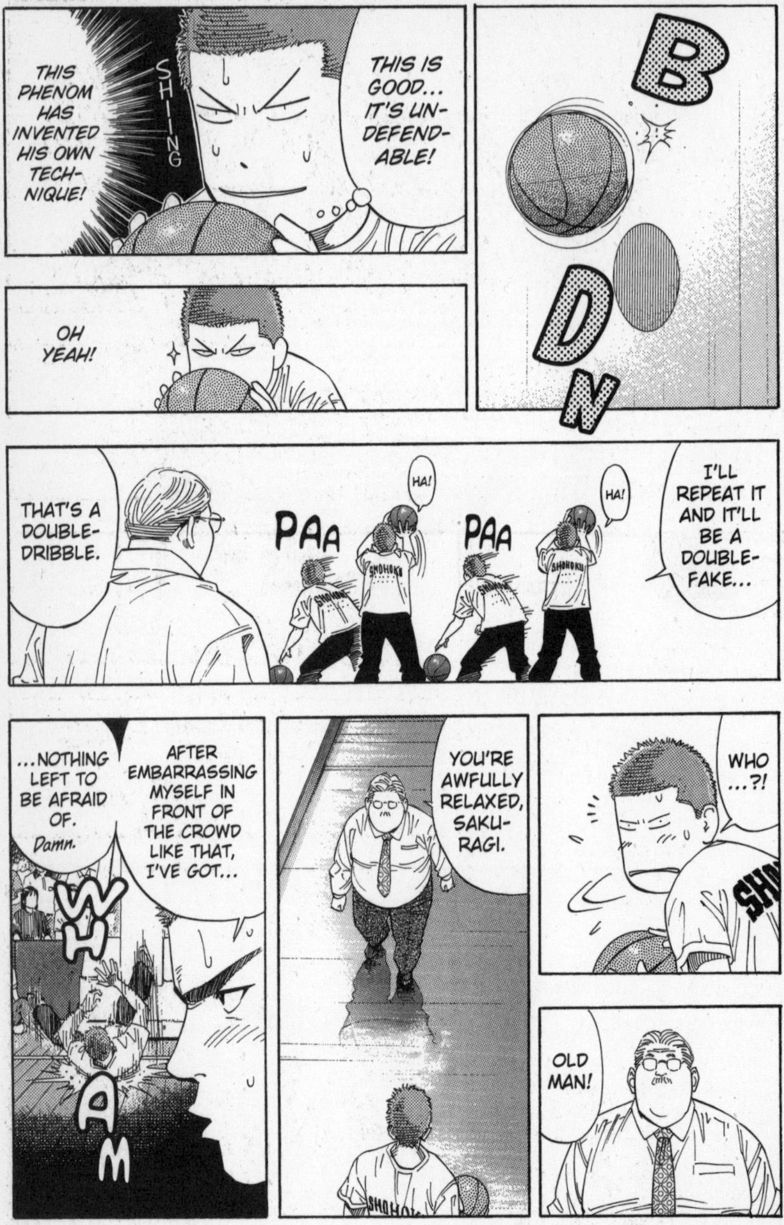
BDN
THIS IS GOOD... IT'S UN-DEFENDABLE!
SHIING
THIS PHENOM HAS INVENTED HIS OWN TECH-NIQUE!
OH YEAH!
I'LL REPEAT IT AND IT'LL BE A DOUBLE-FAKE...
HA!
PAA
HA!
PAA
THAT'S A DOUBLE-DRIBBLE.
WHO ...?!
OLD MAN!
YOU'RE AWFULLY RELAXED, SAKU-RAGI.
AFTER EMBARRASSING MYSELF IN FRONT OF THE CROWD LIKE THAT, I'VE GOT...
...NOTHING LEFT TO BE AFRAID OF.
Damn.
WHAM

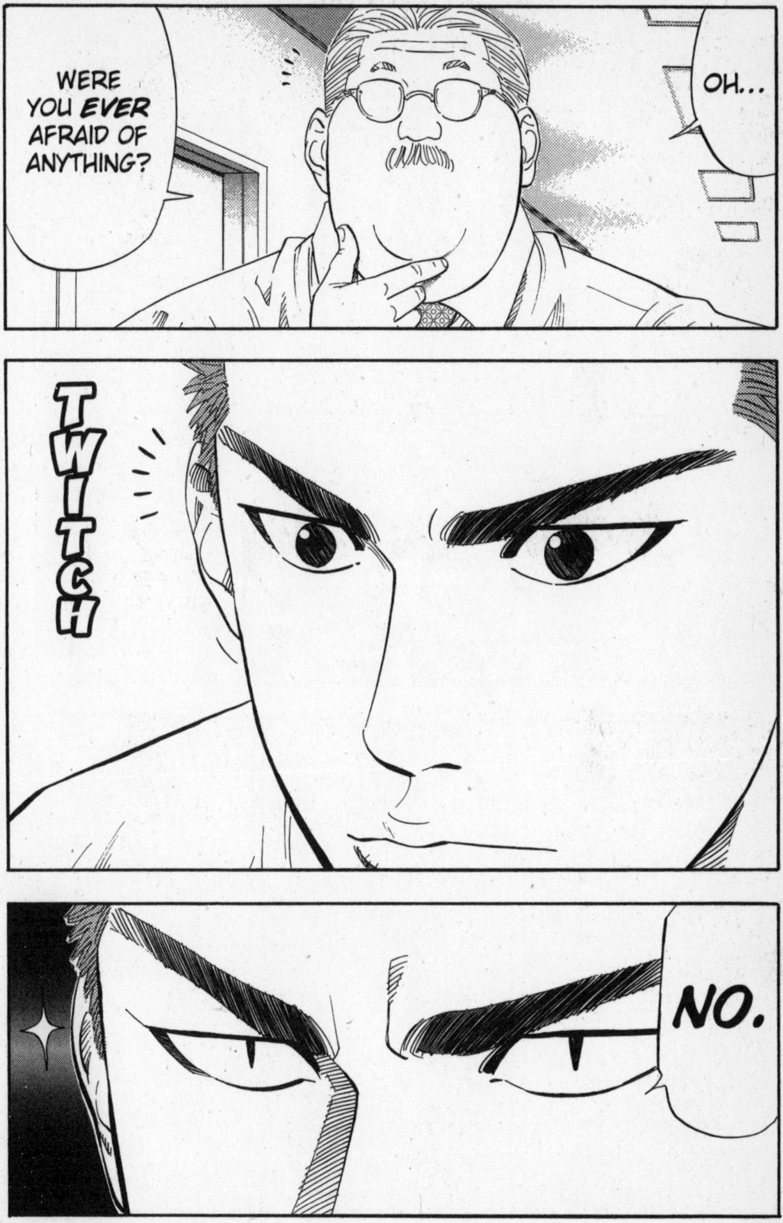
OH...
WERE YOU EVER AFRAID OF ANYTHING?
TWITCH
NO.

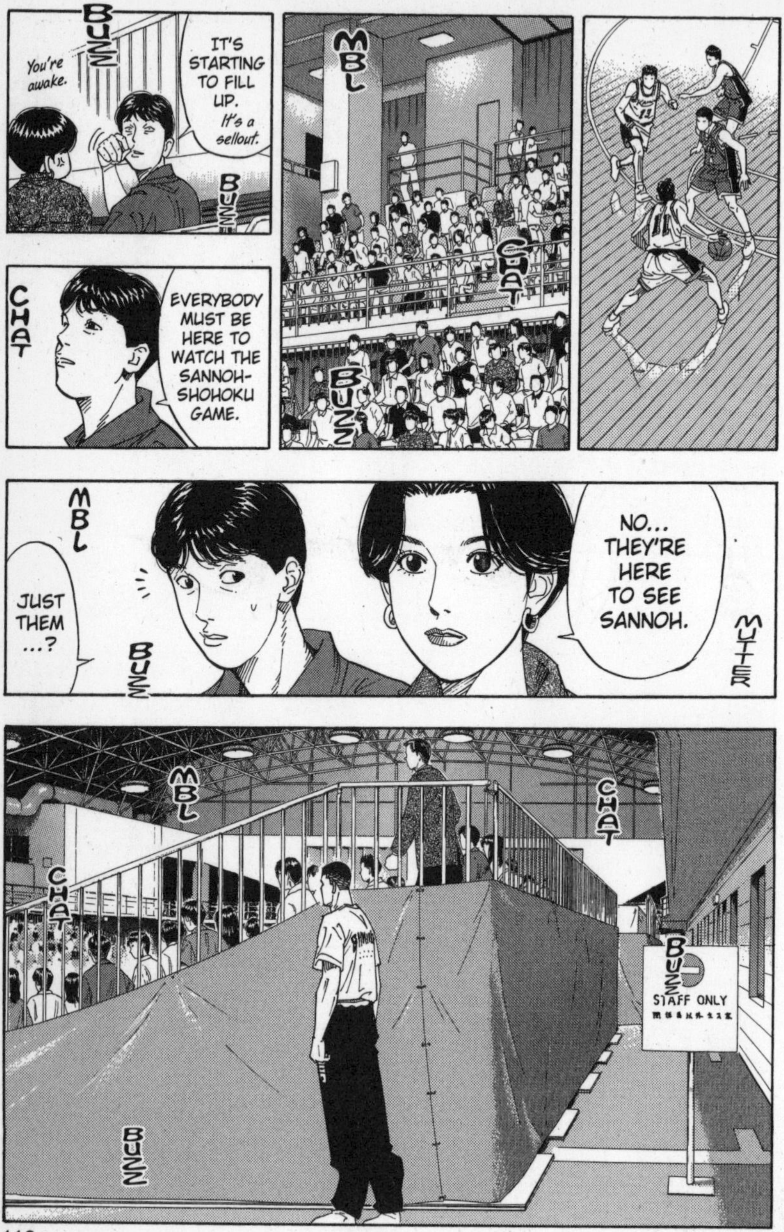
MBL
CHAT
BUZZ
BUZZ
IT'S STARTING TO FILL UP.
It's a sellout.
You're awake.
BUZZ
EVERYBODY MUST BE HERE TO WATCH THE SANNOH-SHOHOKU GAME.
CHAT
MUTTER
NO... THEY'RE HERE TO SEE SANNOH.
BUZZ
MBL
JUST THEM ...?
CHAT
MBL
CHAT
BUZZ
STAFF ONLY
BUZZ

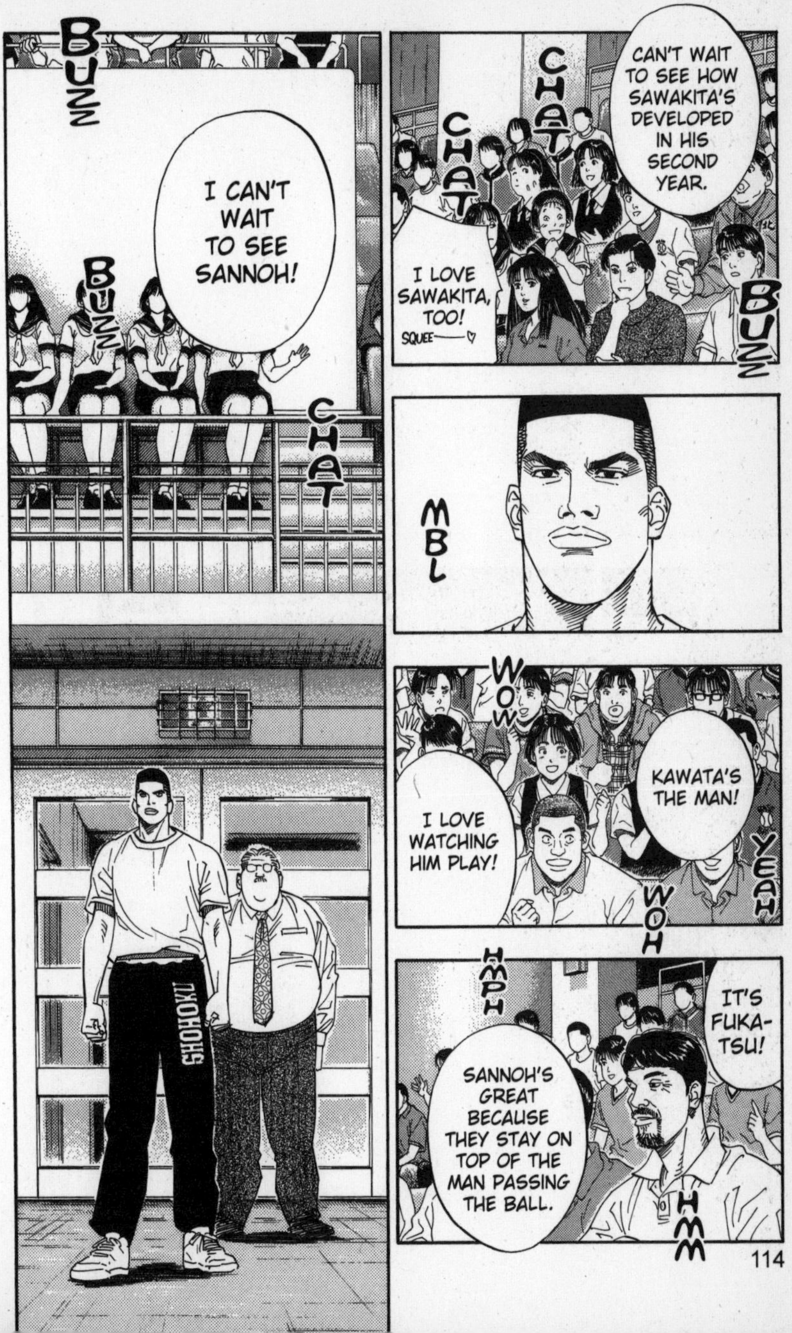
CHAT
CHAT
CAN'T WAIT TO SEE HOW SAWAKITA'S DEVELOPED IN HIS SECOND YEAR.
I LOVE SAWAKITA, TOO!
SQUEE
BUZZ
MBL
WOW
KAWATA'S THE MAN!
I LOVE WATCHING HIM PLAY!
YEAH
WOH
HMPH
IT'S FUKA-TSU!
SANNOH'S GREAT BECAUSE THEY STAY ON TOP OF THE MAN PASSING THE BALL.
HMM
BUZZ
I CAN'T WAIT TO SEE SANNOH!
BUZZ
CHAT
SHOHOKU

READ THIS WAY

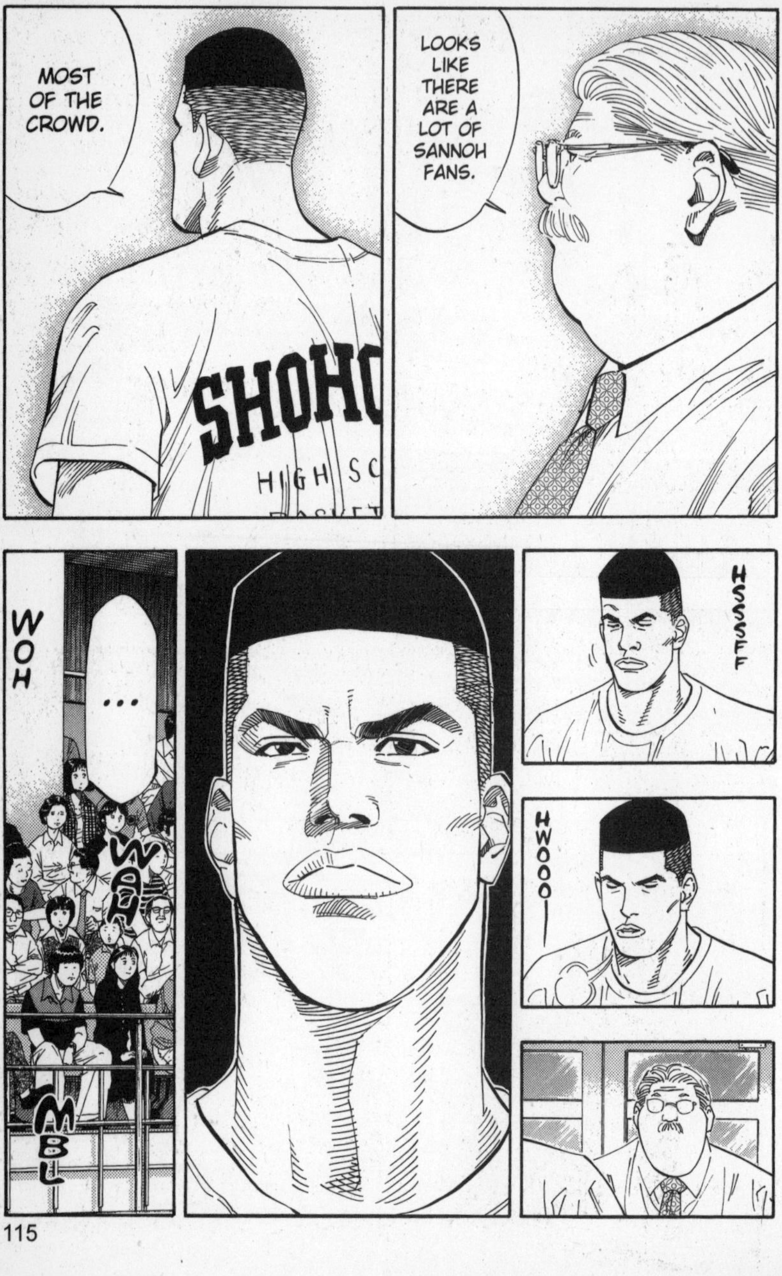

LOOKS LIKE THERE ARE A LOT OF SANNOH FANS.
MOST OF THE CROWD.
SHOHOKU HIGH SC
HSSSFF
HWOOO
...
WOH
WAH
MBL

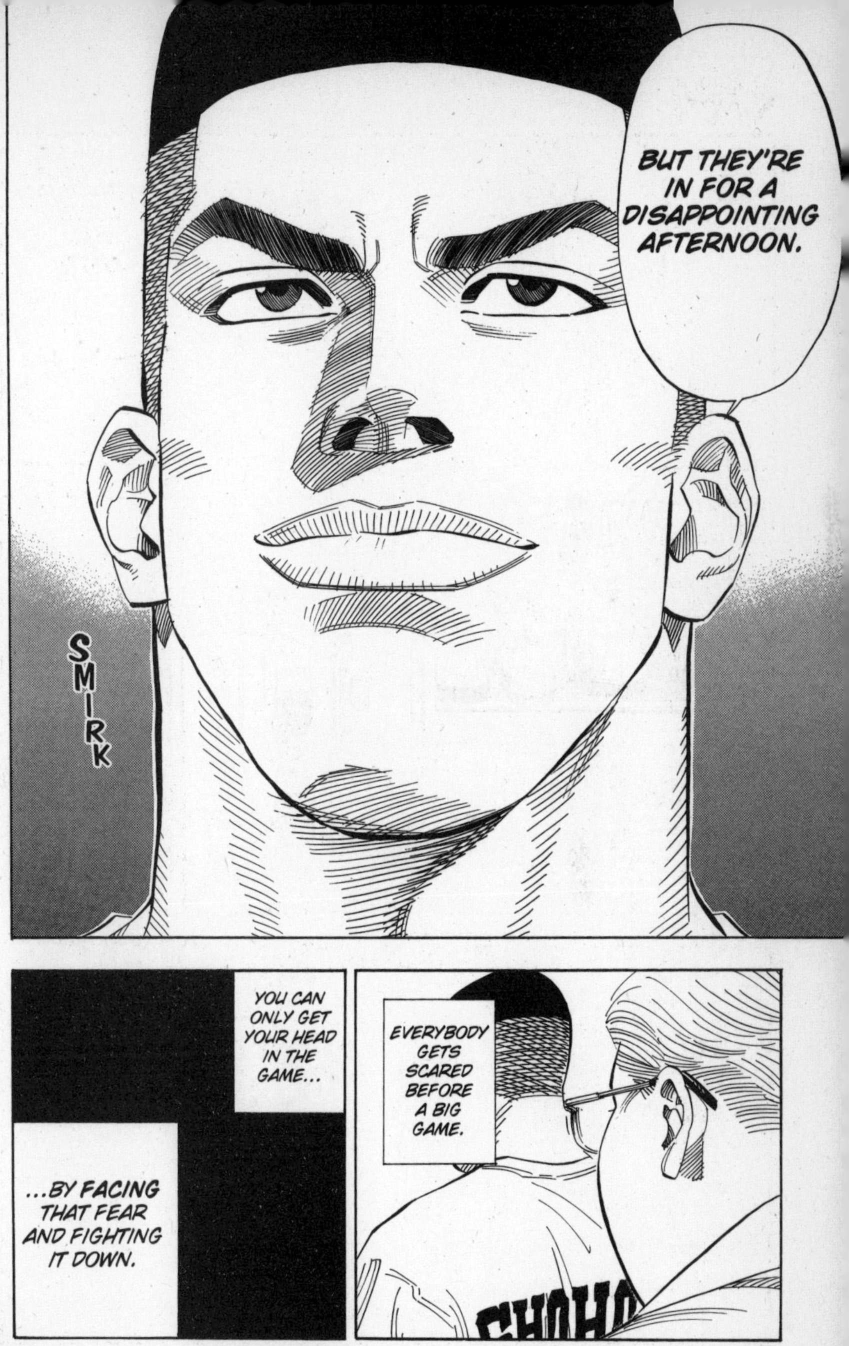
BUT THEY'RE IN FOR A DISAPPOINTING AFTERNOON.
SMIRK
EVERYBODY GETS SCARED BEFORE A BIG GAME.
YOU CAN ONLY GET YOUR HEAD IN THE GAME...
...BY FACING THAT FEAR AND FIGHTING IT DOWN.

READ THIS WAY

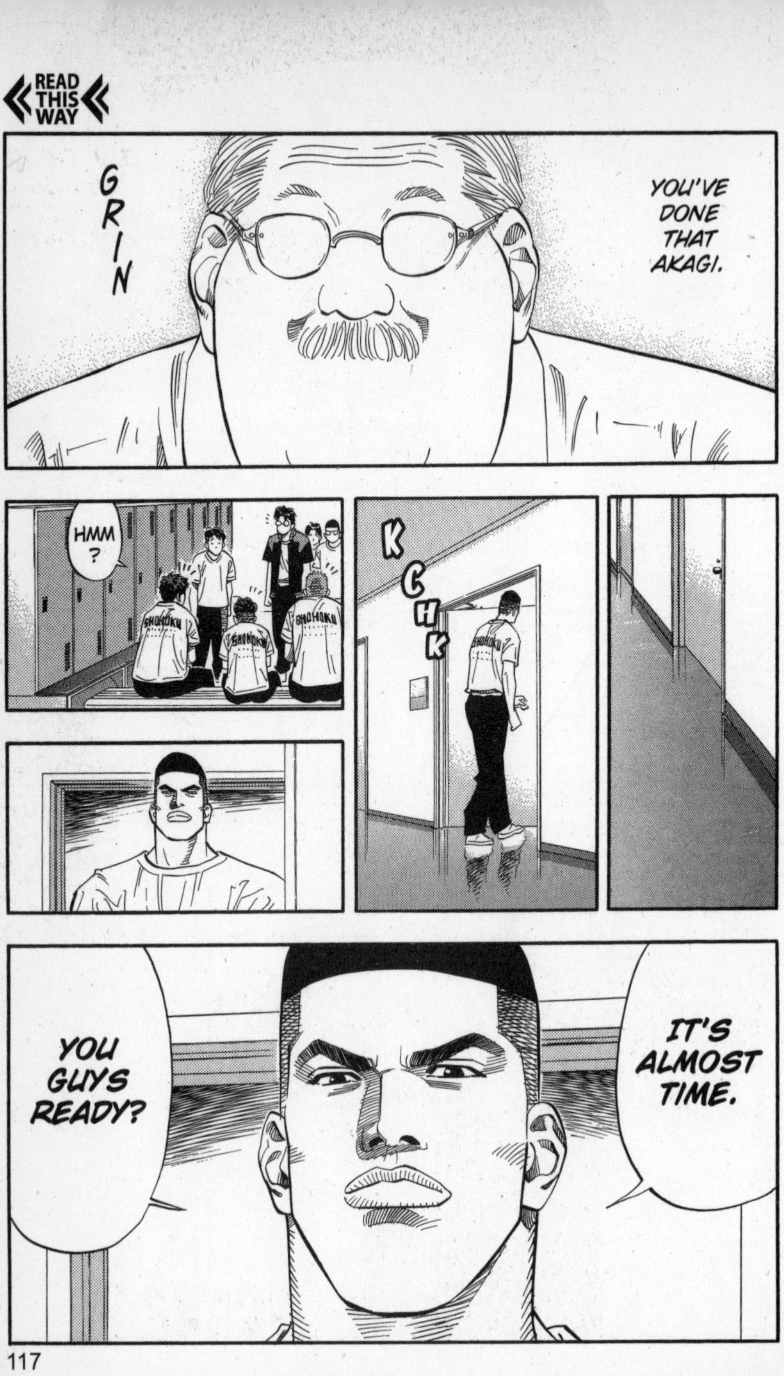
YOU'VE DONE THAT AKAGI.
GRIN
KCHK
HMM?
IT'S ALMOST TIME.
YOU GUYS READY?

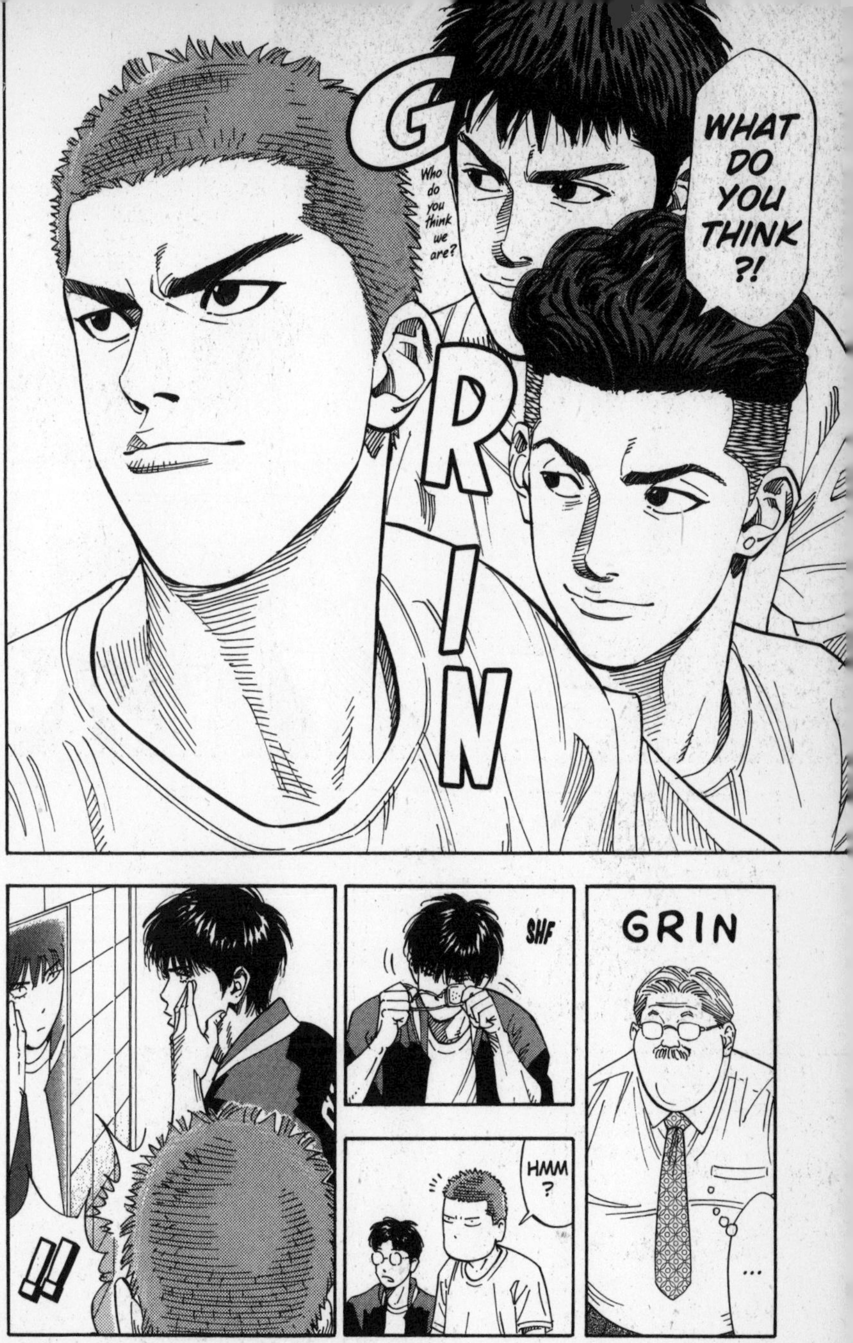
WHAT DO YOU THINK ?!
GRIN
Who do you think we are?
GRIN
...
SHF
HMM ?
!!

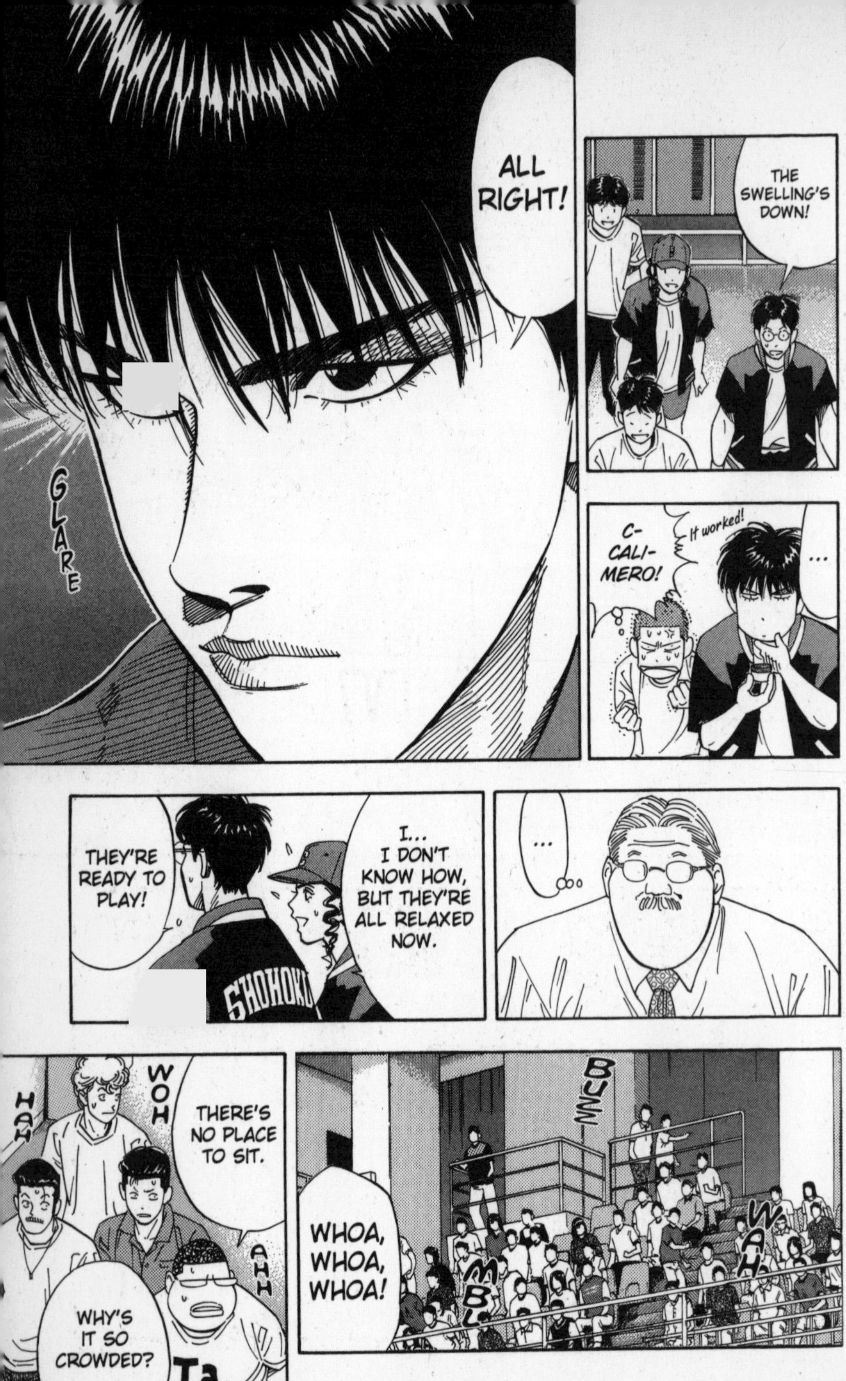
THE SWELLING'S DOWN!
...
It worked!
C-CALIMERO!
ALL RIGHT!
GLARE
...
I... I DON'T KNOW HOW, BUT THEY'RE ALL RELAXED NOW.
THEY'RE READY TO PLAY!
BUNN
WAH
WHOA, WHOA, WHOA!
MBL
WOH
THERE'S NO PLACE TO SIT.
HAH
AHH
WHY'S IT SO CROWDED?
Ta.

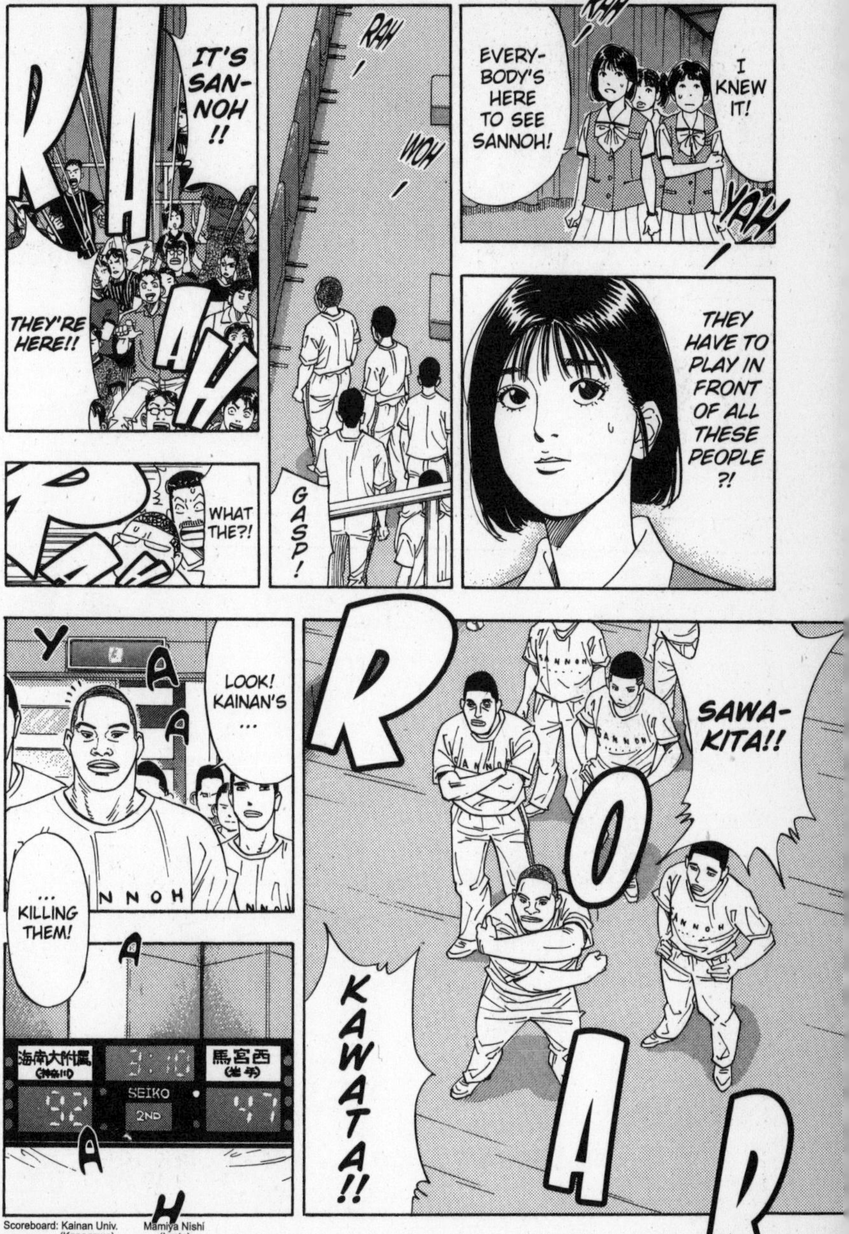
I KNEW IT!
RAH!
EVERY-BODY'S HERE TO SEE SANNOH!
YAH!
THEY HAVE TO PLAY IN FRONT OF ALL THESE PEOPLE?!
RAH!
WOH!
GASP!
IT'S SAN-NOH!!
RAAAH
THEY'RE HERE!!
WHAT THE?!
SAWA-KITA!!
ROAR
KAWATA!!
YAA
LOOK! KAINAN'S ...
SANNOH
... KILLING THEM!
海南大附属
(神奈川)
3:10
馬宮西
(岩手)
SEIKO
92
2ND
47
AAH

Scoreboard: Kainan Univ. (Kanagawa) Mamiya Nishi (Iwate)

READ THIS WAY

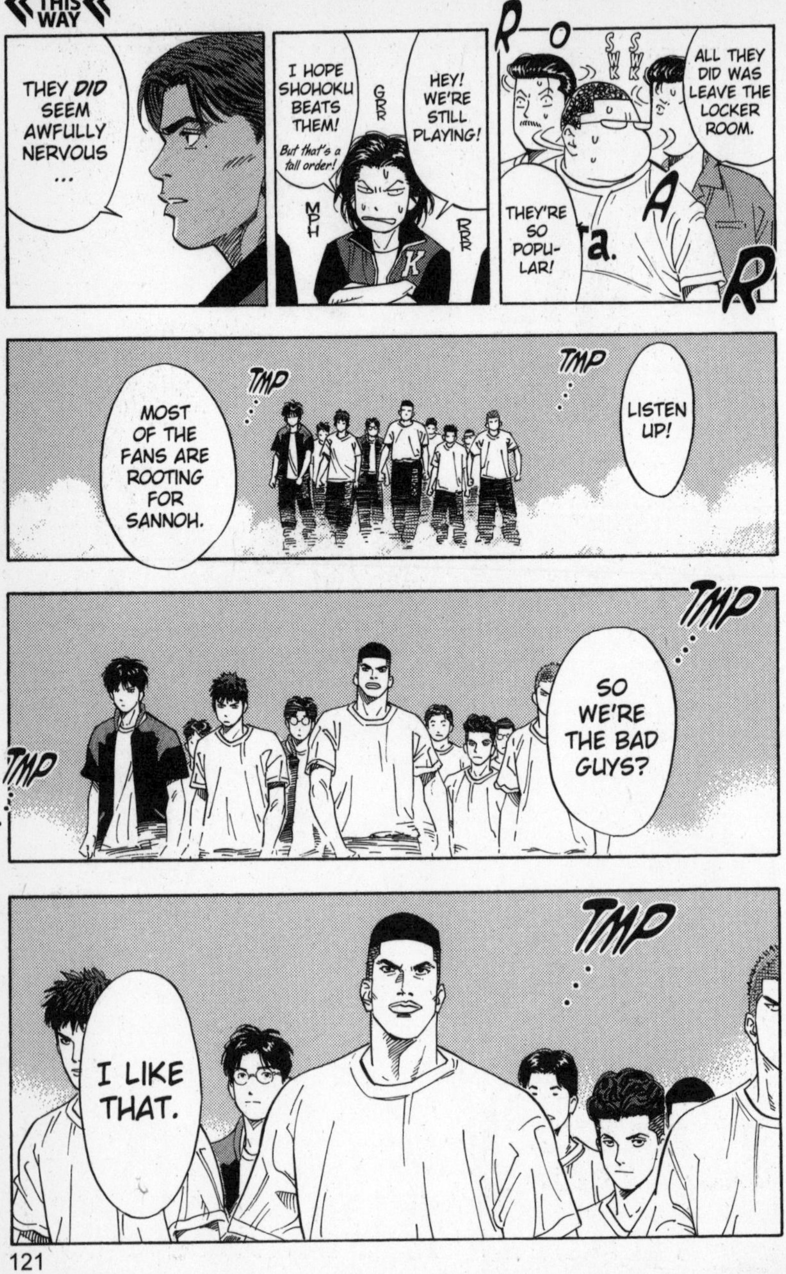
ROAR
ALL THEY DID WAS LEAVE THE LOCKER ROOM.
THEY'RE SO POPULAR!
HEY! WE'RE STILL PLAYING!
GRR
I HOPE SHOHOKU BEATS THEM!
But that's a tall order!
MPH
RRR
THEY DID SEEM AWFULLY NERVOUS ...
LISTEN UP!
TMP
TMP
MOST OF THE FANS ARE ROOTING FOR SANNOH.
TMP
SO WE'RE THE BAD GUYS?
TMP
TMP
I LIKE THAT.

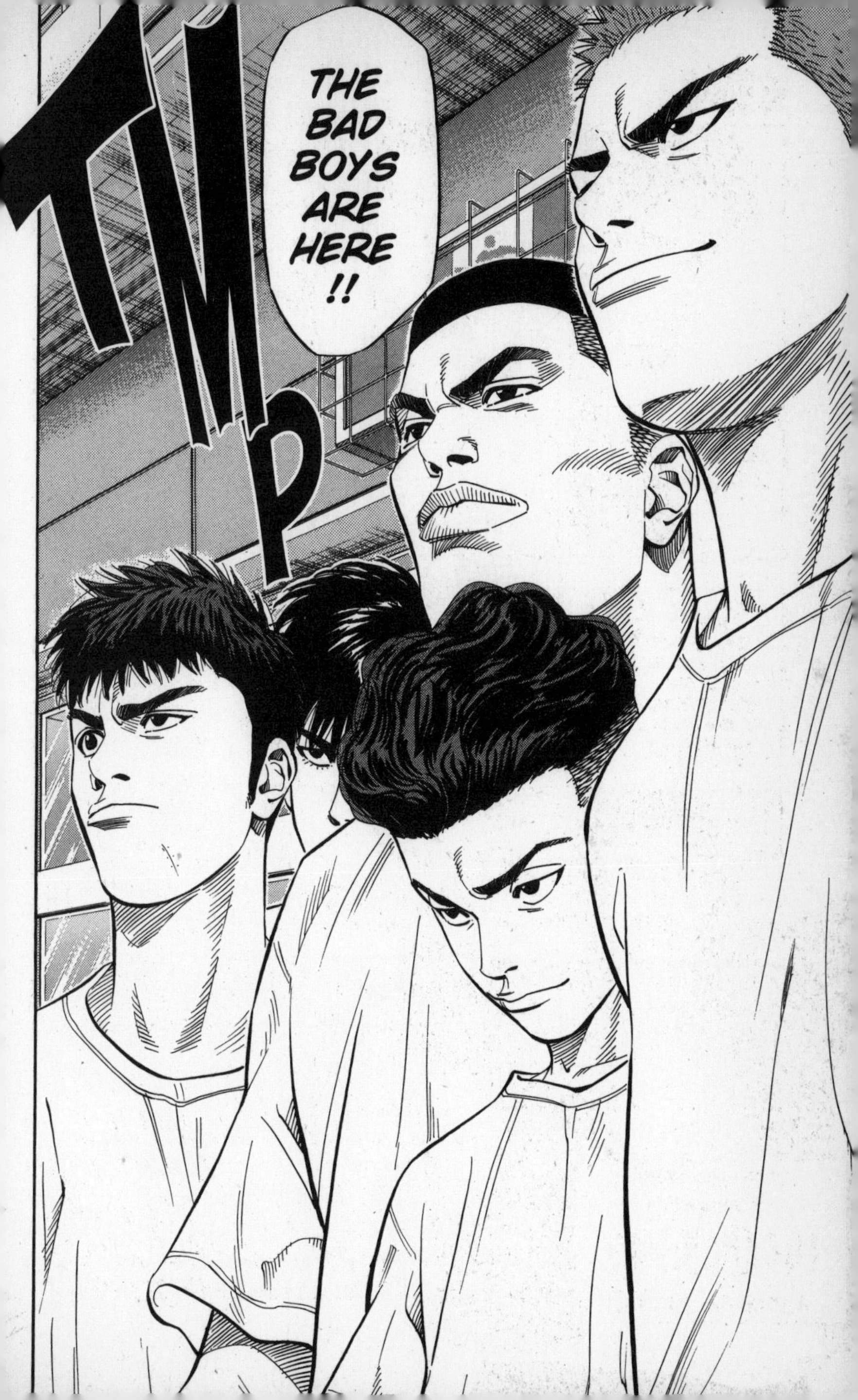
THE BAD BOYS ARE HERE!!
TMP

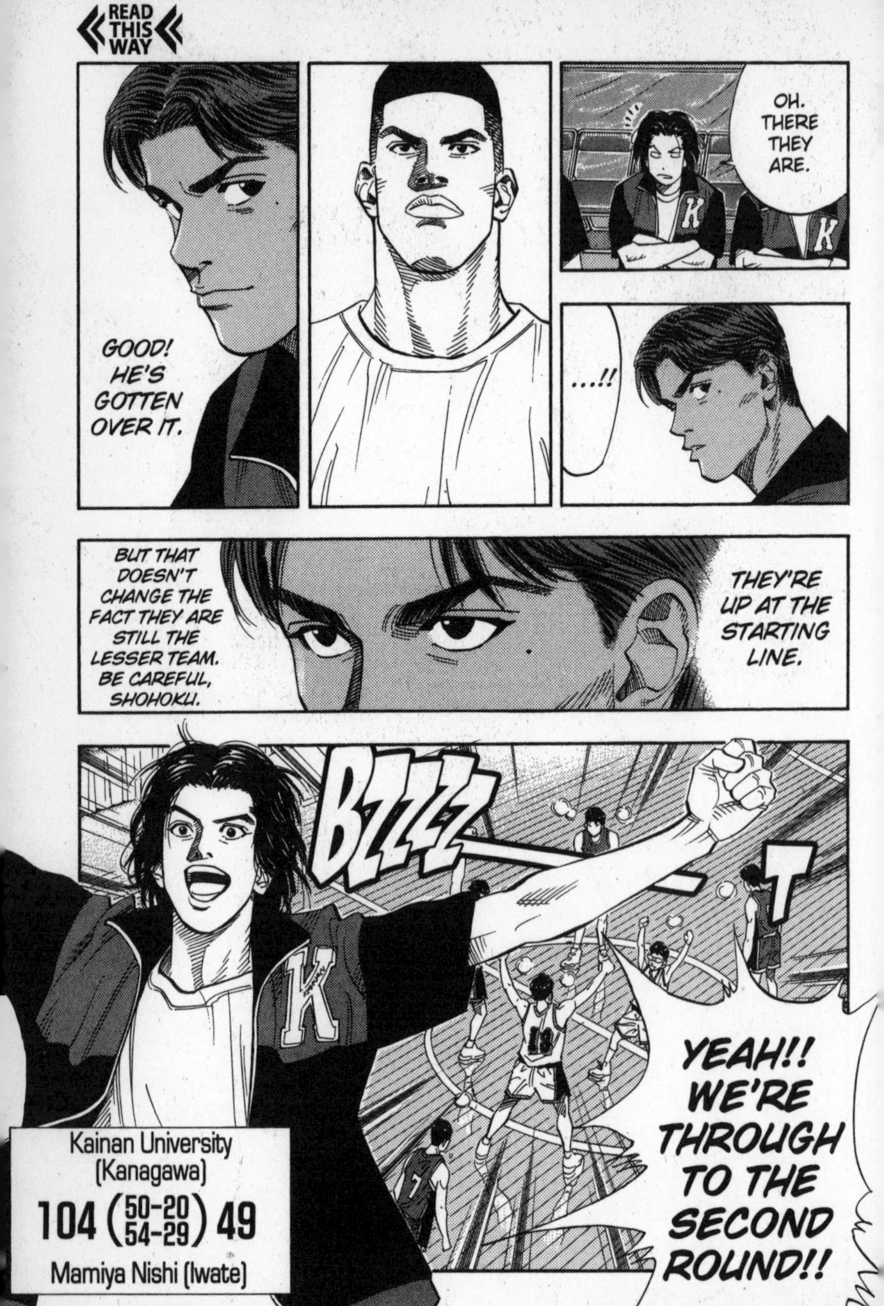
READ THIS WAY
OH. THERE THEY ARE.
...!!
GOOD! HE'S GOTTEN OVER IT.
THEY'RE UP AT THE STARTING LINE.
BUT THAT DOESN'T CHANGE THE FACT THEY ARE STILL THE LESSER TEAM. BE CAREFUL, SHOHOKU.
BZZZZT
YEAH!! WE'RE THROUGH TO THE SECOND ROUND!!
Kainan University (Kanagawa)
104 (50-20 / 54-29) 49
Mamiya Nishi (Iwate)

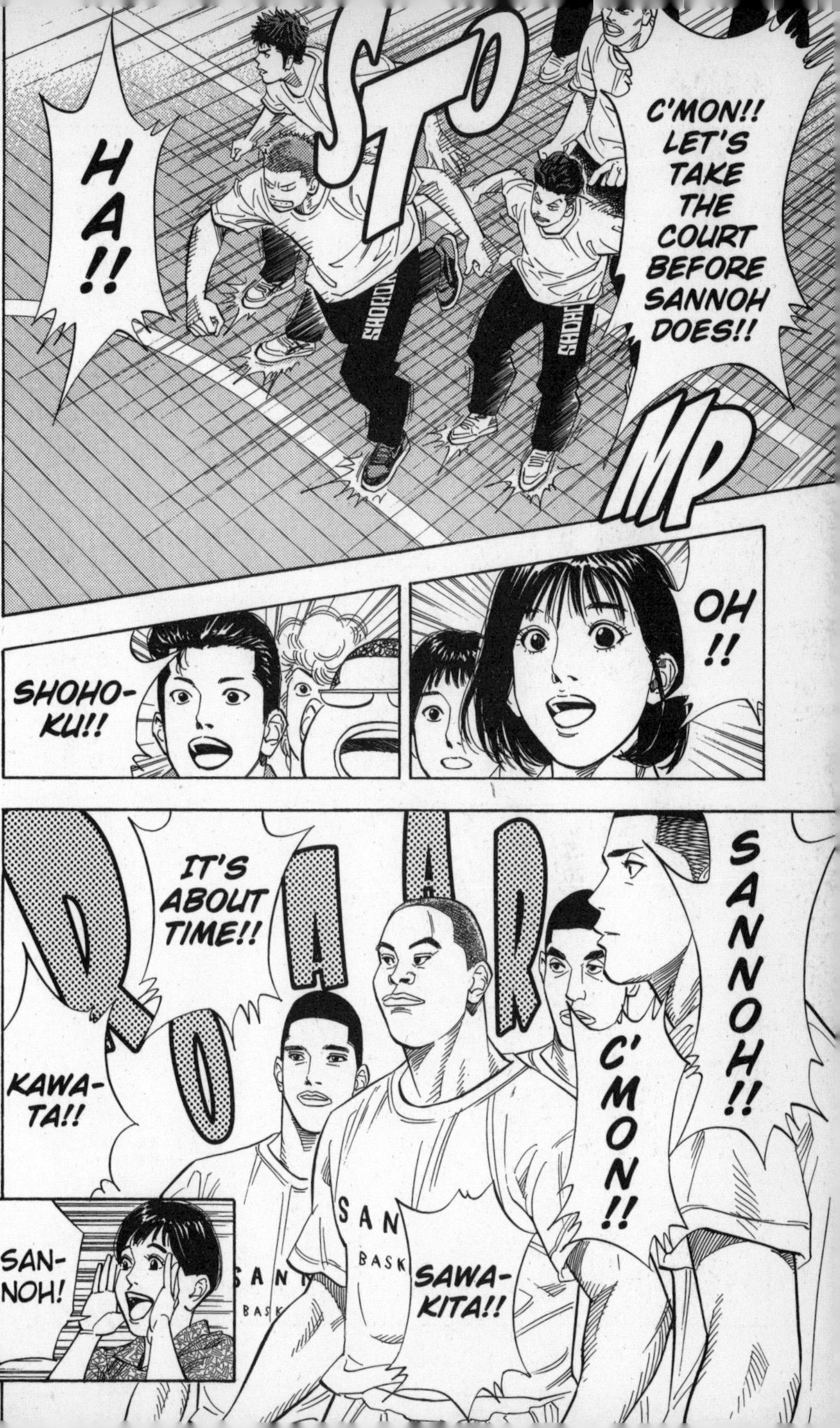
C'MON!! LET'S TAKE THE COURT BEFORE SANNOH DOES!!
STOMP
HA!!
OH!!
SHOHO-KU!!
SANNOH!!
C'MON!!
ROAR
IT'S ABOUT TIME!!
SAWA-KITA!!
KAWA-TA!!
SAN-NOH!

READ THIS WAY

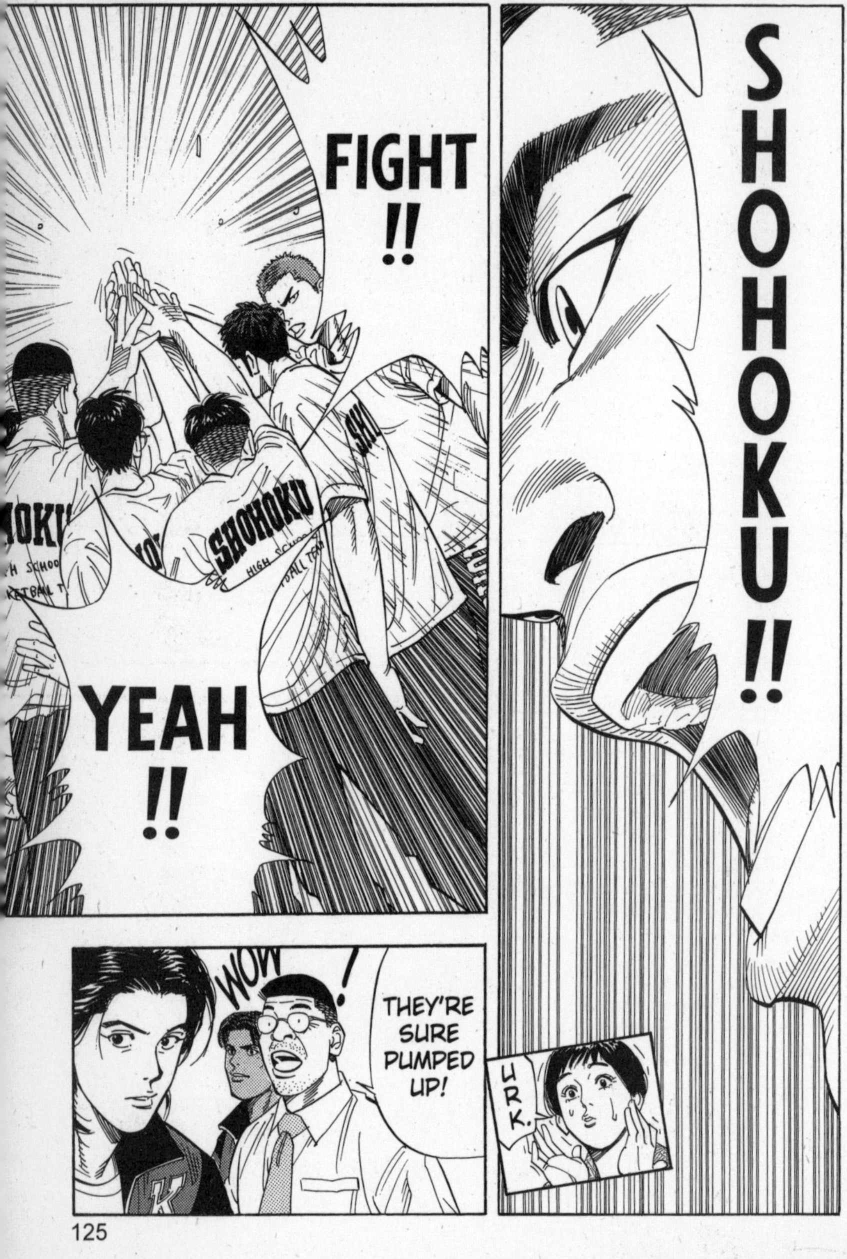
SHOHOKU!!
URK.
FIGHT!!
SHOHOKU
YEAH!!
WOW!
THEY'RE SURE PUMPED UP!

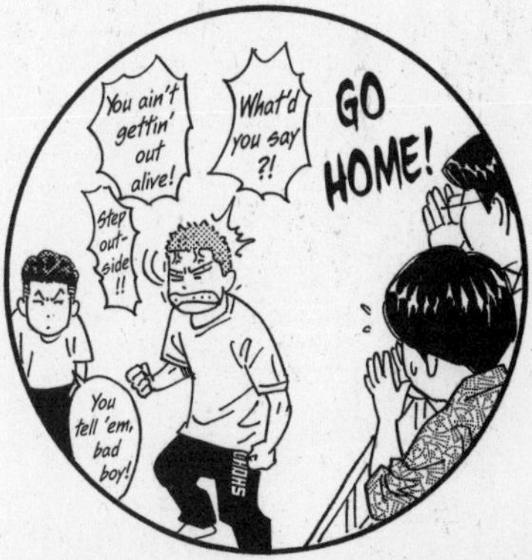
GO HOME!
What'd you say?!
You ain't gettin' out alive!
Step out-side!!
You tell 'em, bad boy!
SHOHOKU

SLAM DUNK

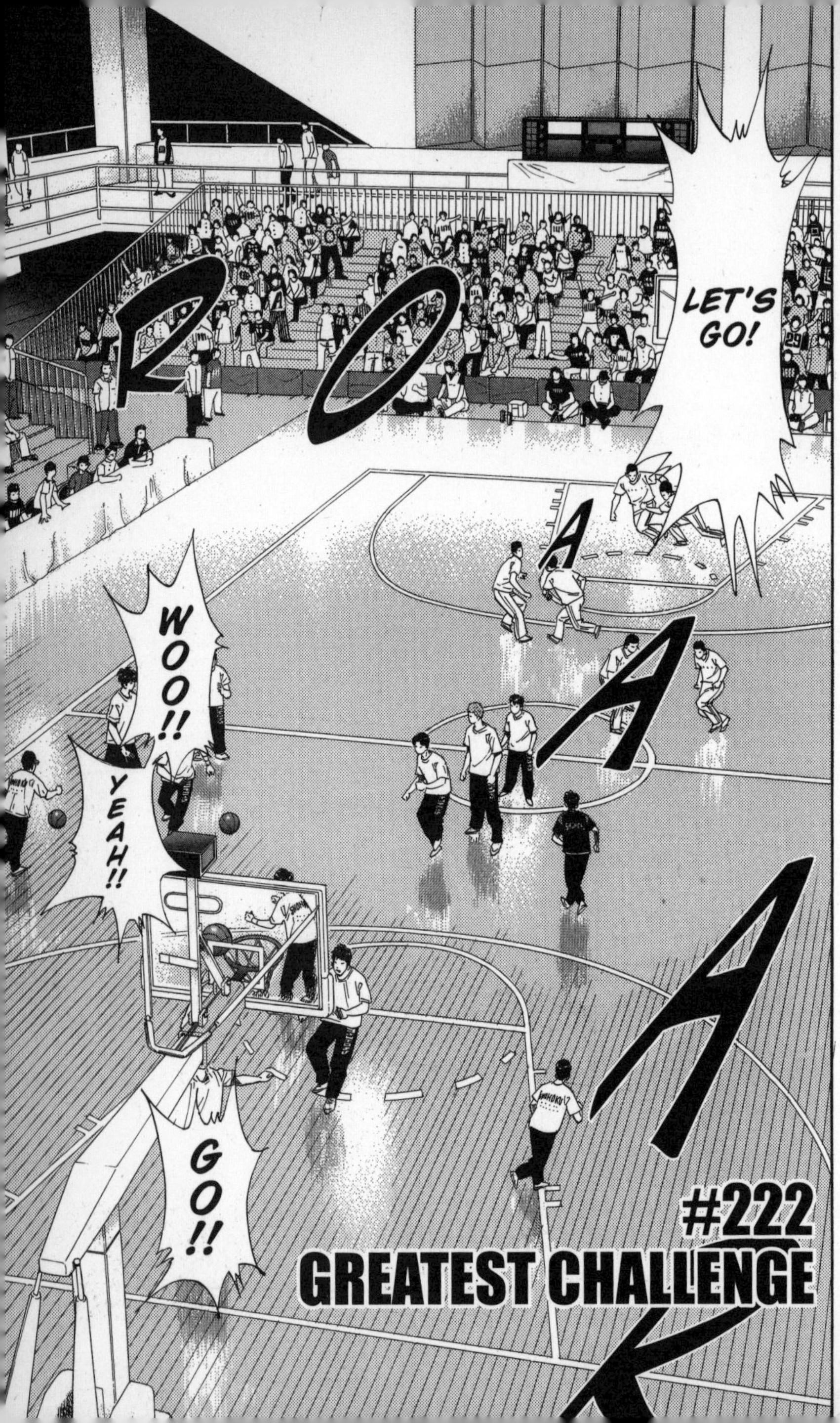
LET'S GO!
ROAAAR
WOOO!!
YEAH!!
GO!!

#222 GREATEST CHALLENGE

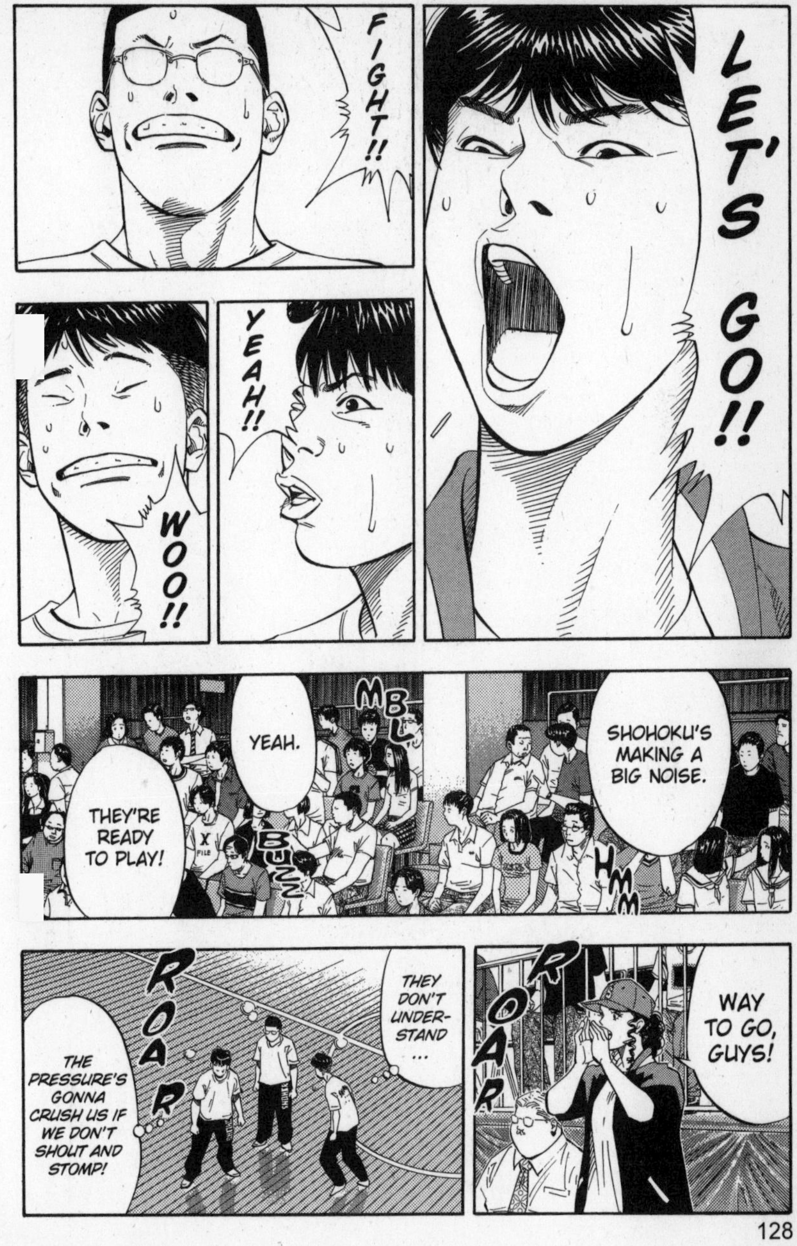
LET'S GO!!
FIGHT!!
YEAH!!
WOO!!
SHOHOKU'S MAKING A BIG NOISE.
HMM
MBL
YEAH.
BUZZ
THEY'RE READY TO PLAY!
ROAR
WAY TO GO, GUYS!
THEY DON'T UNDER-STAND...
ROAR
THE PRESSURE'S GONNA CRUSH US IF WE DON'T SHOUT AND STOMP!

READ THIS WAY

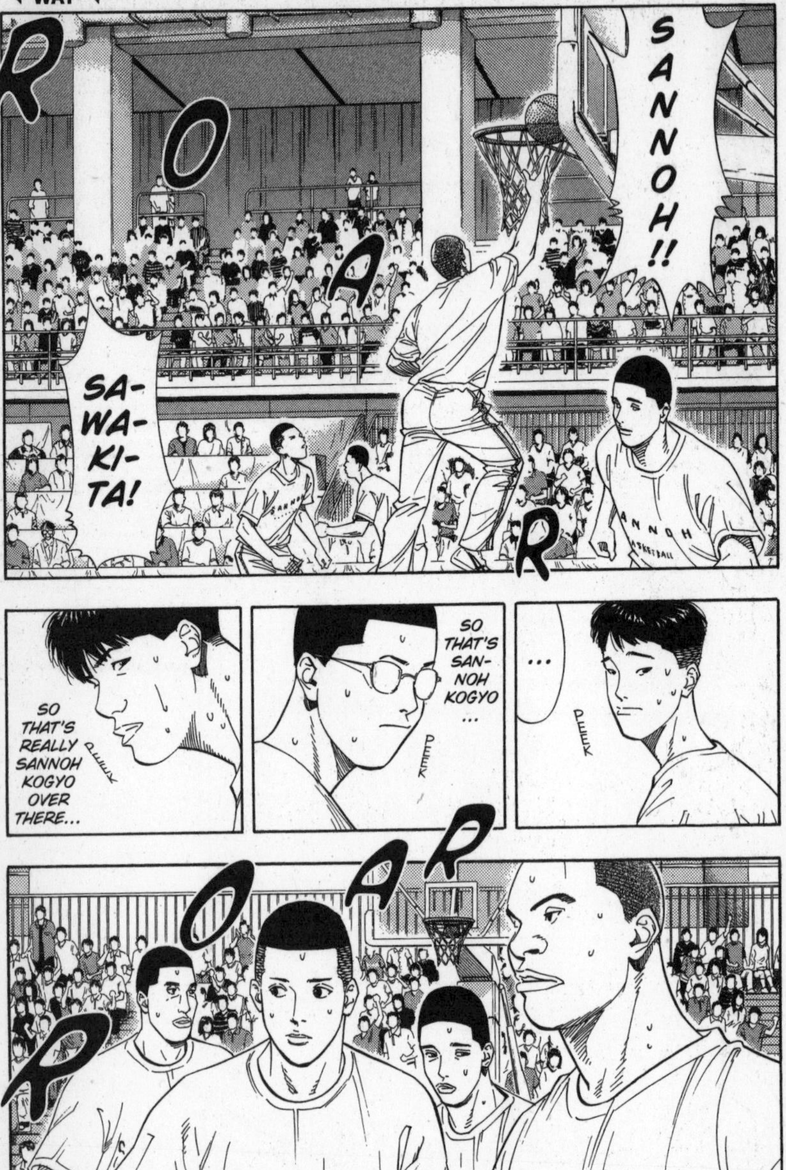
ROAR
SANNOH!!
SA-WA-KI-TA!
...
PEEK
SO THAT'S SAN-NOH KOGYO ...
PEEK
SO THAT'S REALLY SANNOH KOGYO OVER THERE...
ROAR
SANNOH

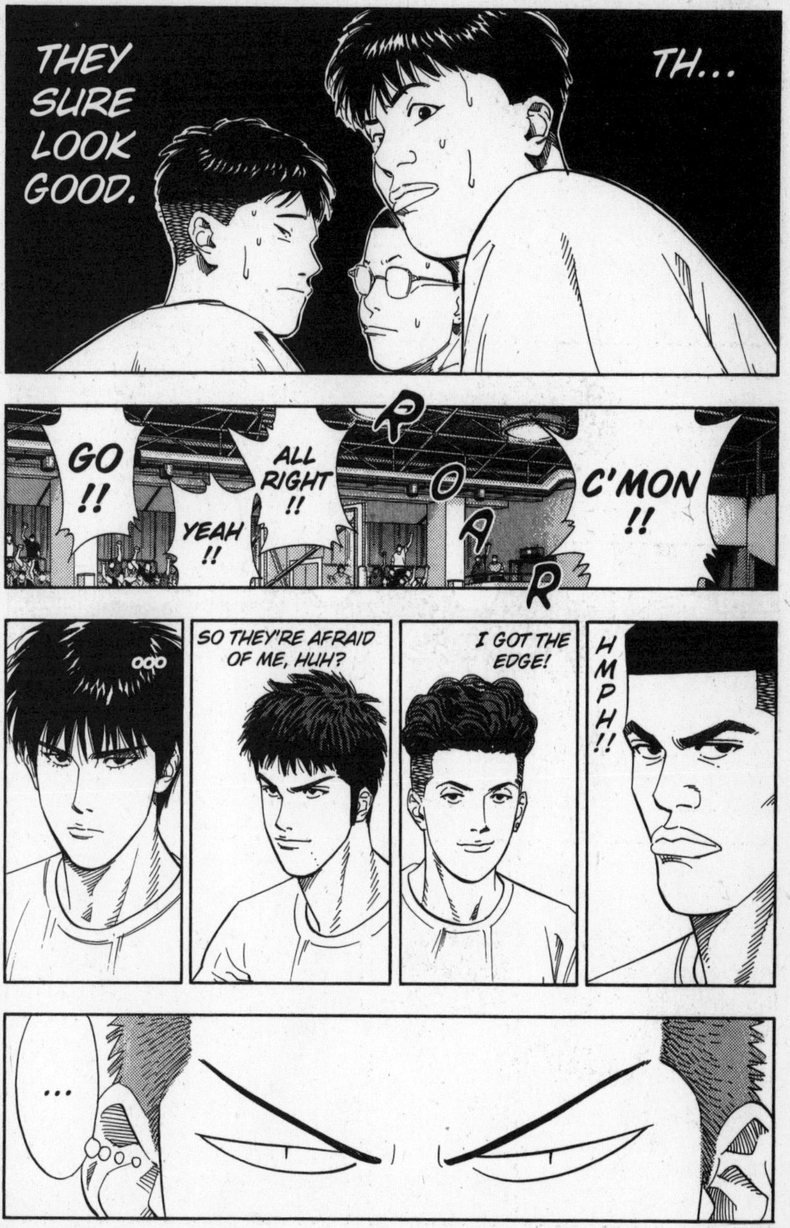
TH...
THEY SURE LOOK GOOD.
C'MON!!
ROAR
ALL RIGHT!!
YEAH!!
GO!!
HMPH!!
I GOT THE EDGE!
SO THEY'RE AFRAID OF ME, HUH?
...

« READ THIS WAY «

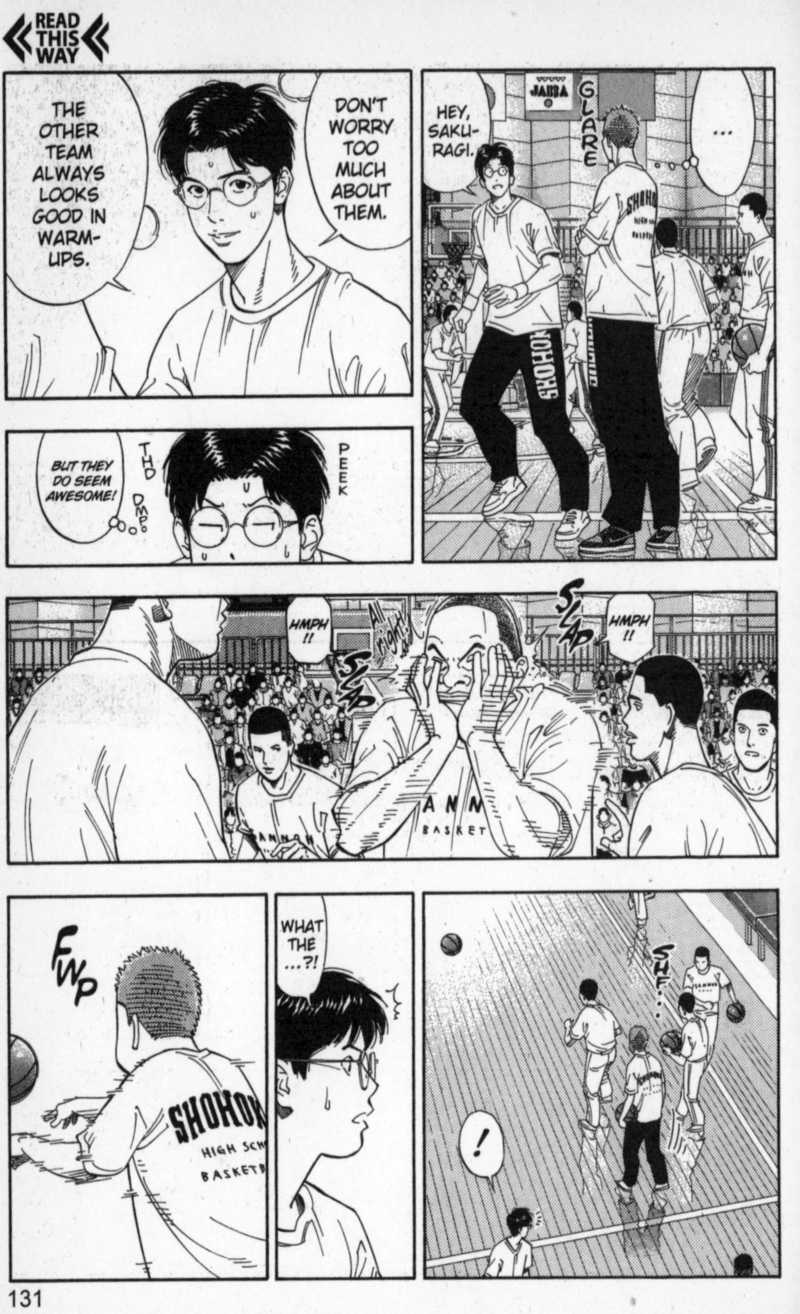
HEY, SAKU-RAGI.
GLARE
...
DON'T WORRY TOO MUCH ABOUT THEM.
THE OTHER TEAM ALWAYS LOOKS GOOD IN WARM-UPS.
PEEK
THD
DMP
BUT THEY DO SEEM AWESOME!
HMPH!!
SLAP
All right!
SLAP
HMPH!!
SHF...
!
WHAT THE ...?!
FWP

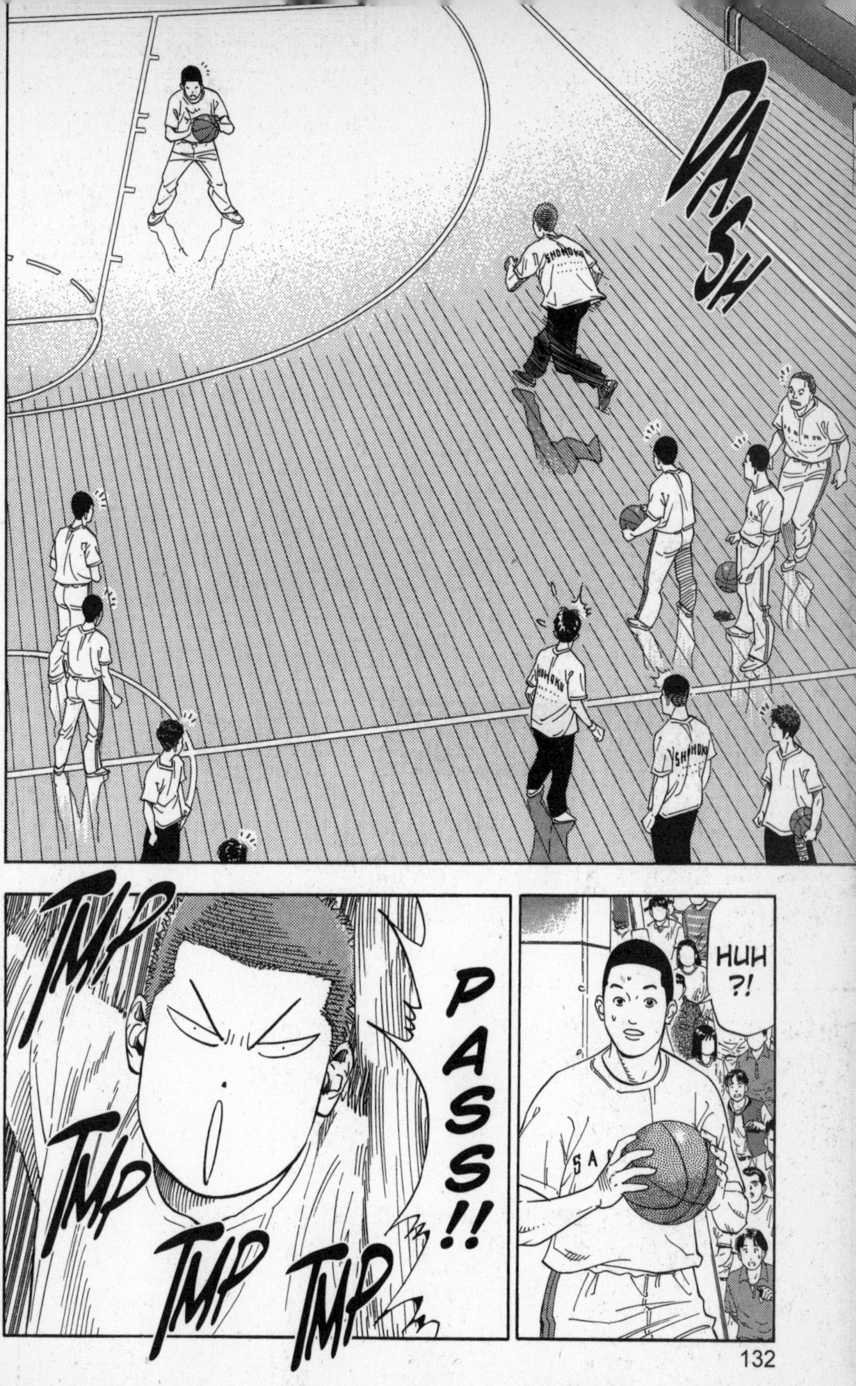
DASH
HUH?!
PASS!!
TMP TMP TMP TMP

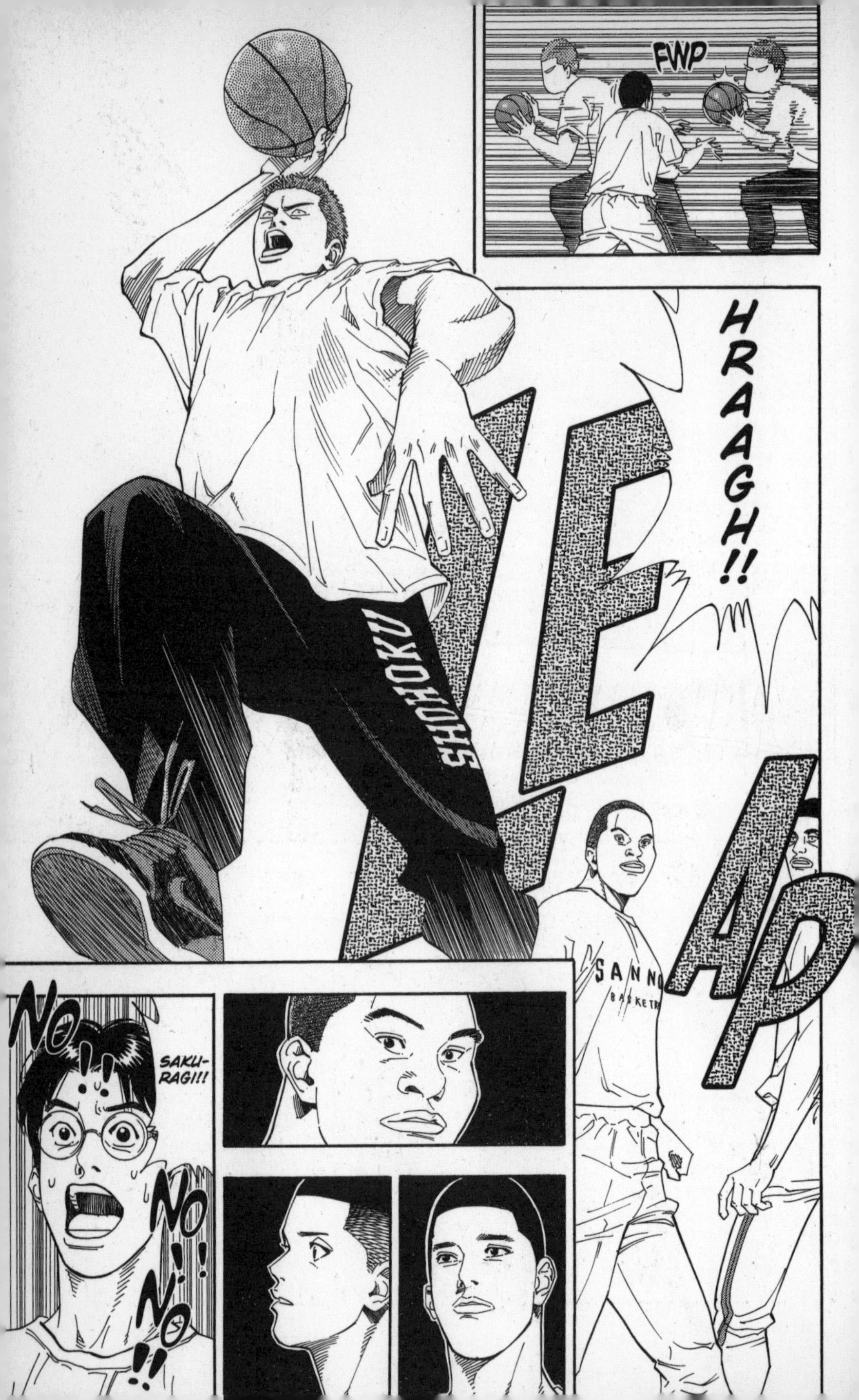
FWP
HRAAAGH!!
LEAP
SHOHOKU
SANNO
NO!!
SAKU-RAGI!!
NO!!
NO!!

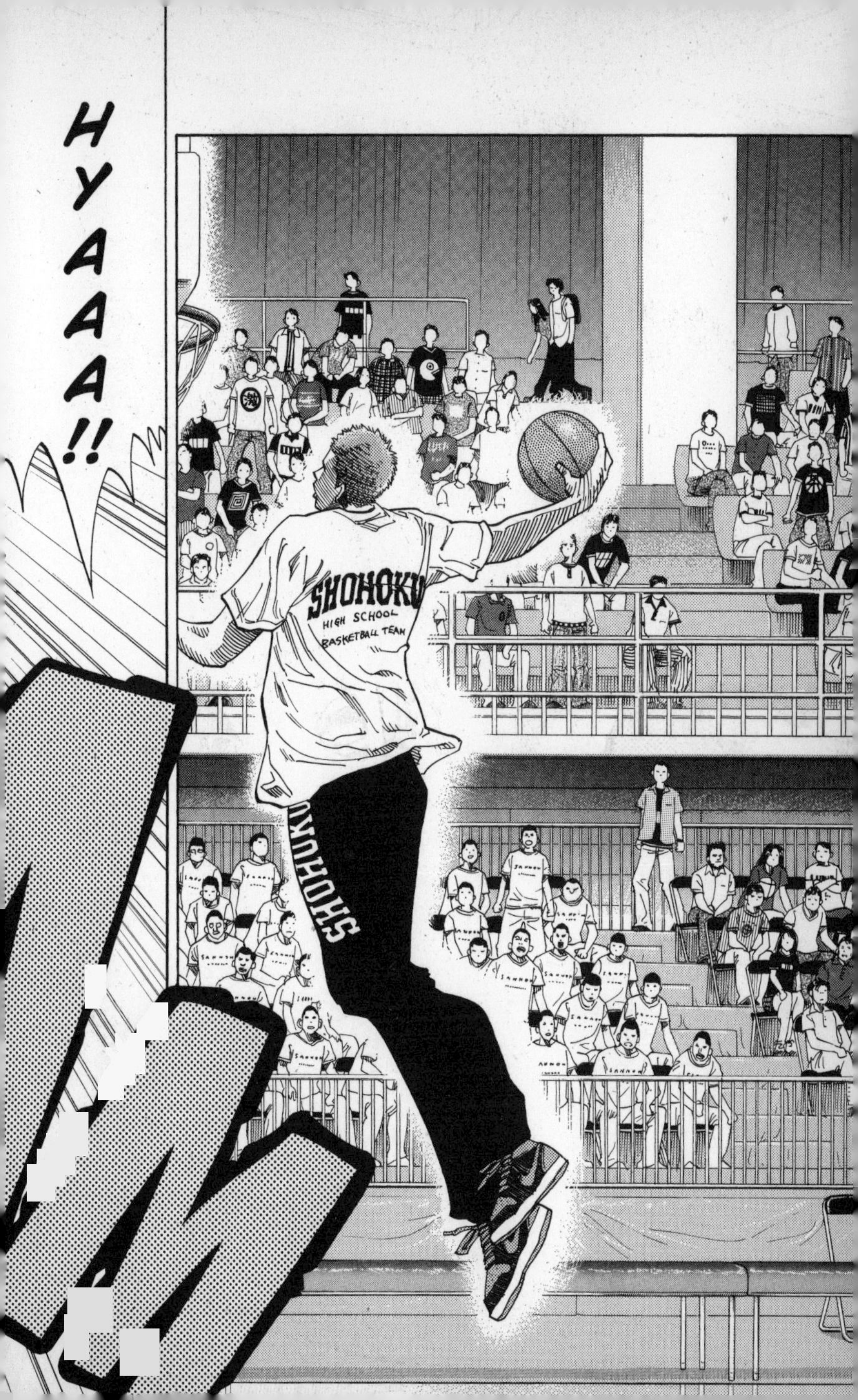
HYAAA!!
SHOHOKU
HIGH SCHOOL
BASKETBALL TEAM
SHOHOKU

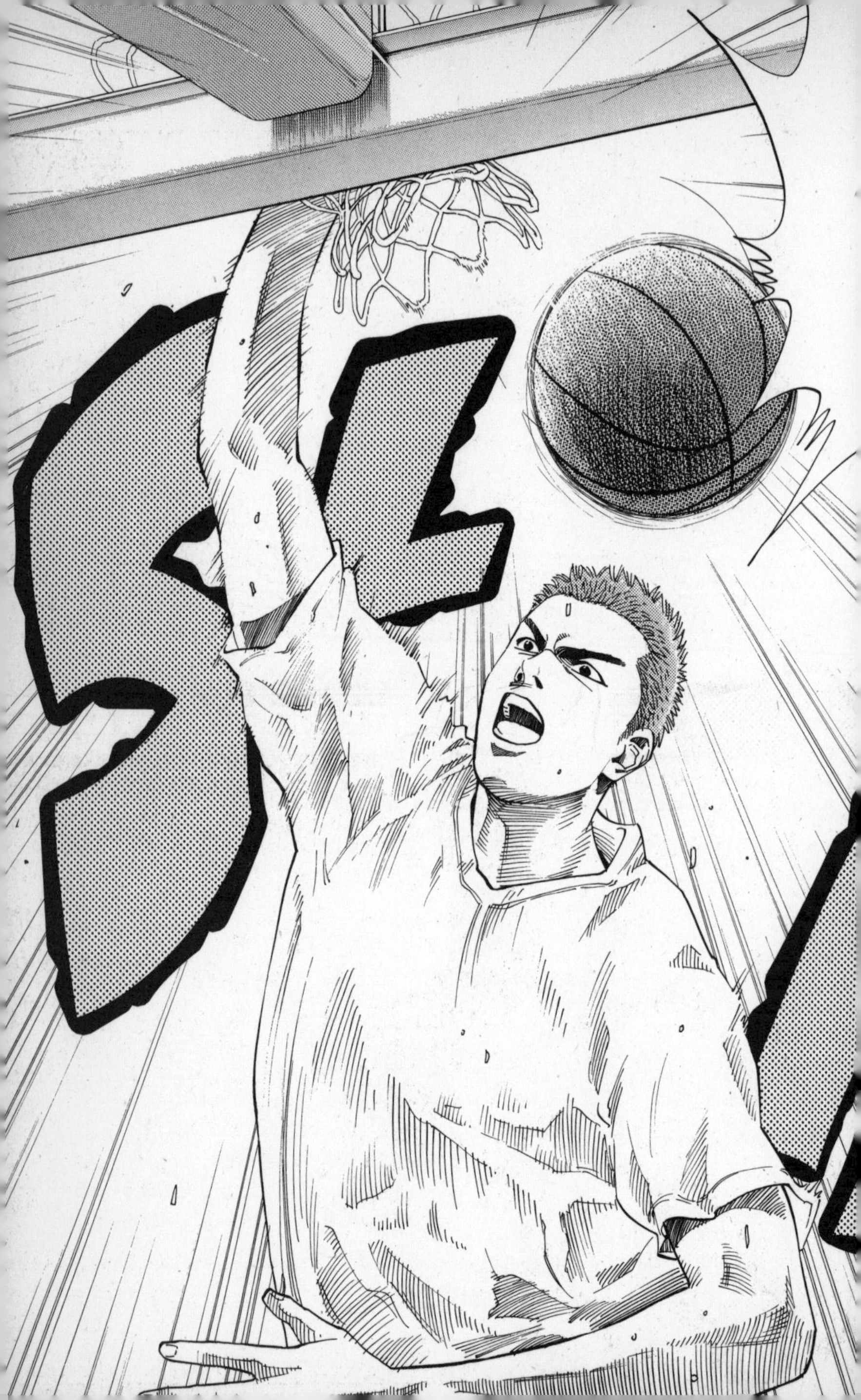

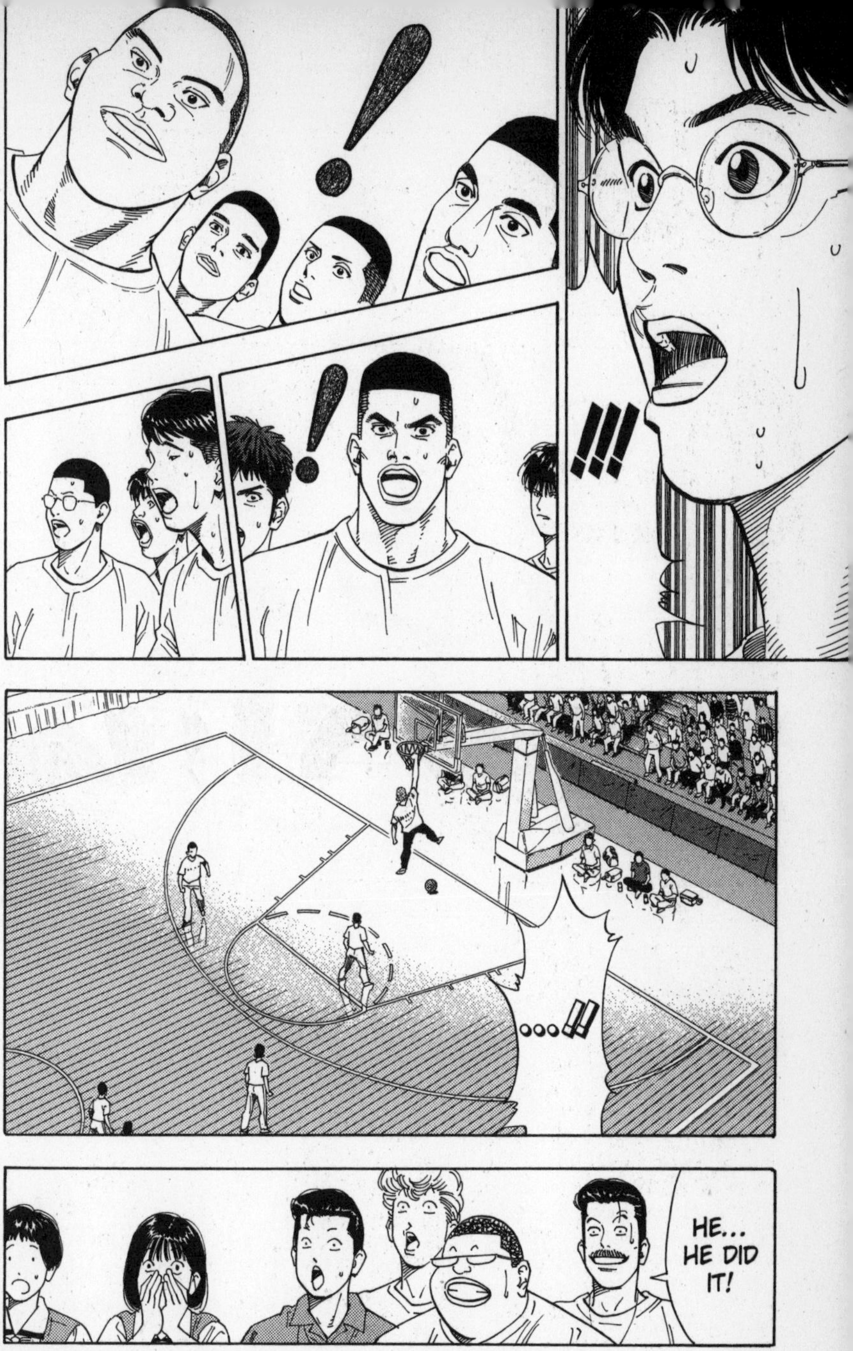
!!!!
!
!
...!!
HE... HE DID IT!

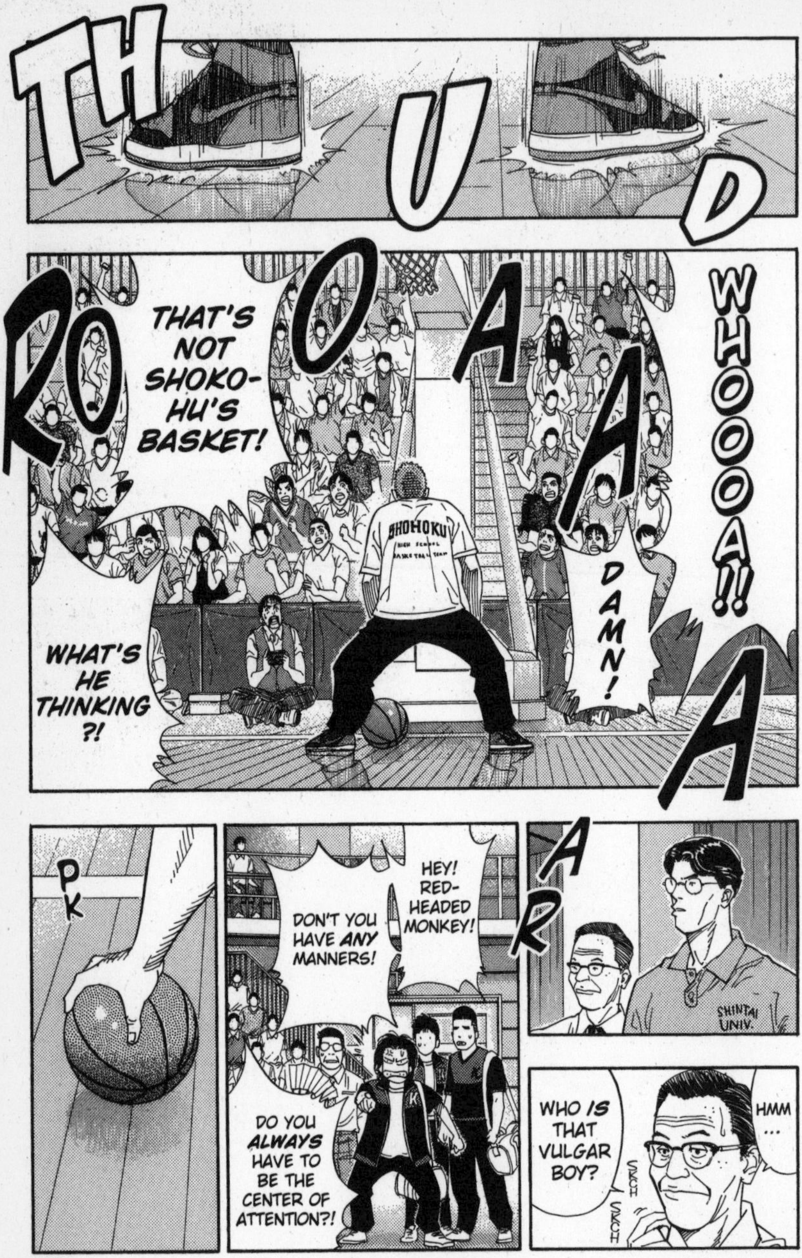
THUD
WHOOOOA!!
ROOAAAAR
THAT'S NOT SHOKOHU'S BASKET!
DAMN!
WHAT'S HE THINKING?!
SHINTAI UNIV.
HMM...
SKCH SKCH
WHO IS THAT VULGAR BOY?
HEY! RED-HEADED MONKEY!
DON'T YOU HAVE ANY MANNERS!
DO YOU ALWAYS HAVE TO BE THE CENTER OF ATTENTION?!
PK

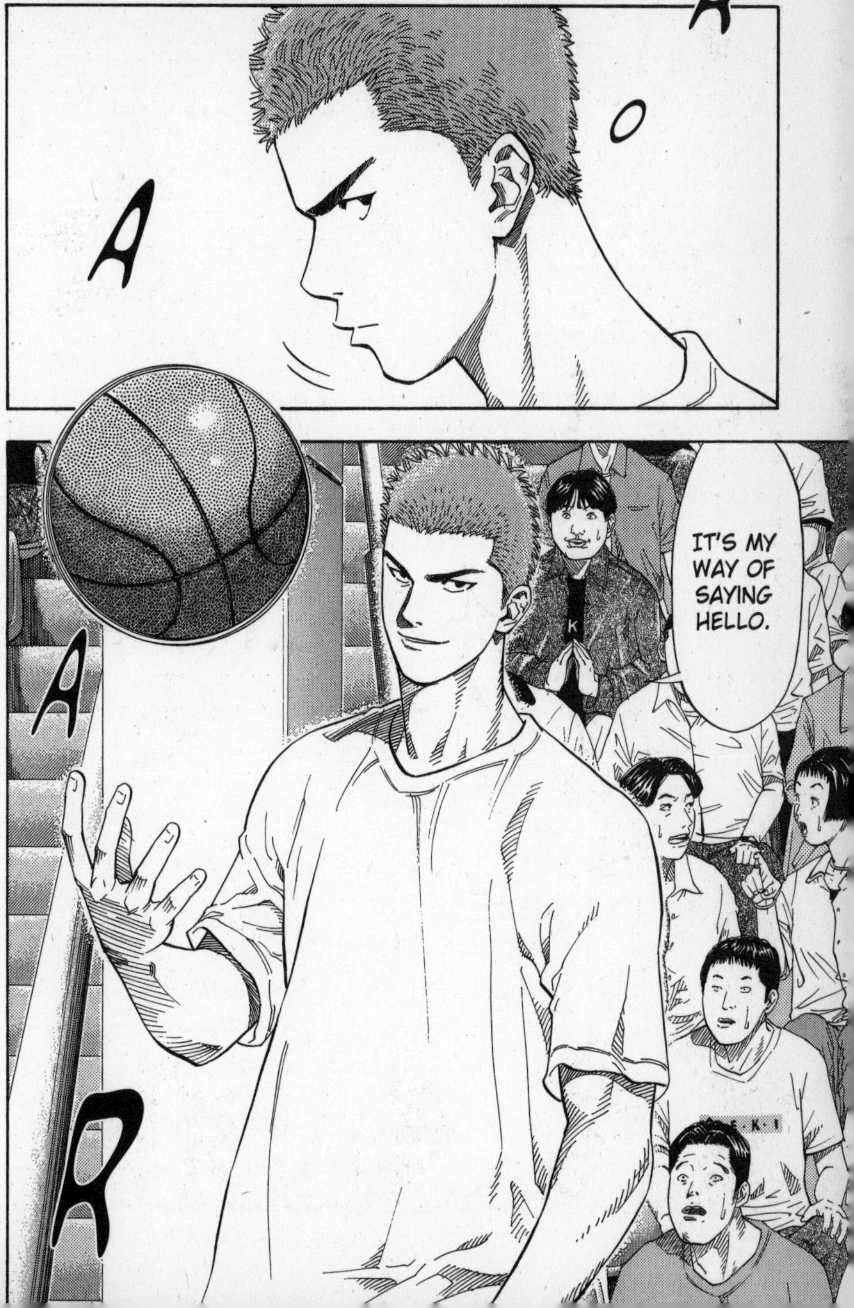
R
O
A
IT'S MY WAY OF SAYING HELLO.
A
R

READ THIS WAY

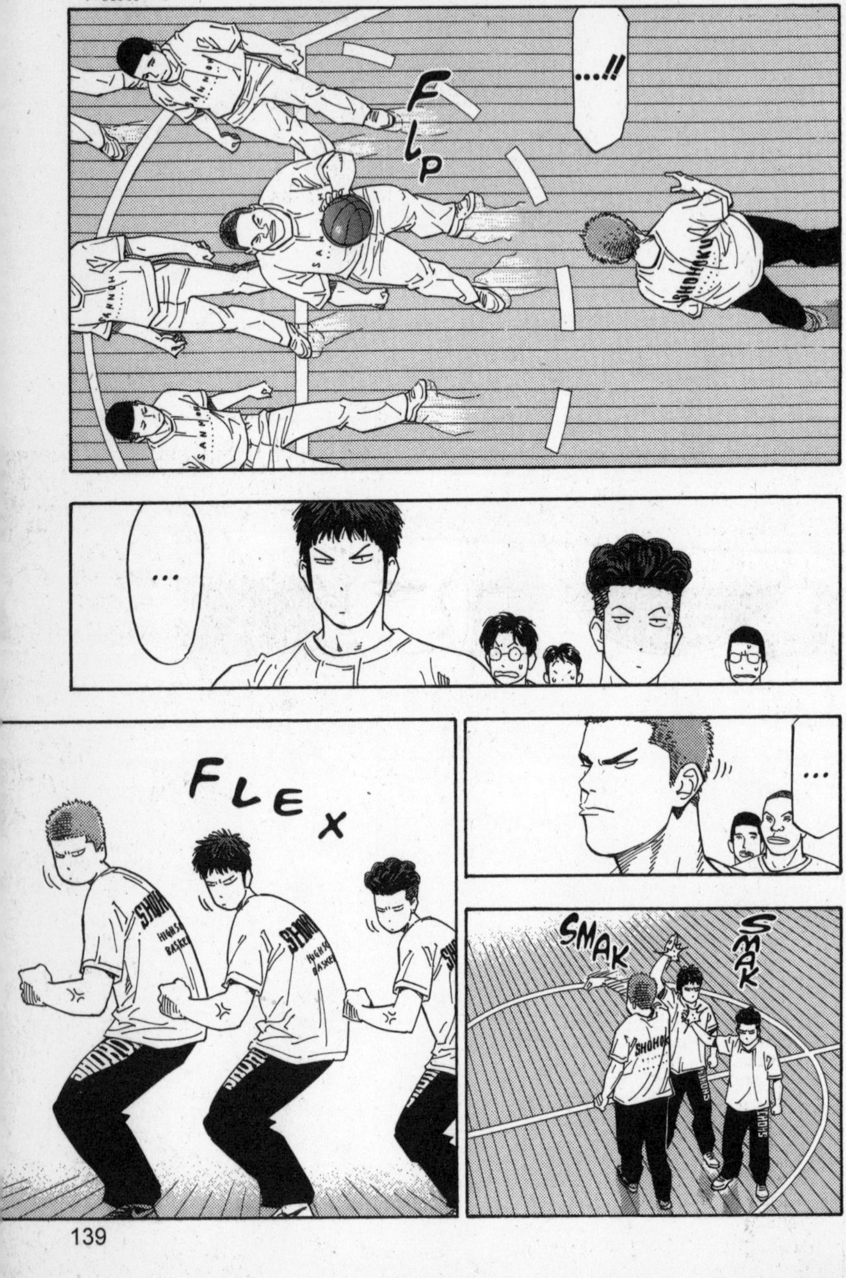
...!!
FLP
...
...
SMAK
SMAK
FLEX

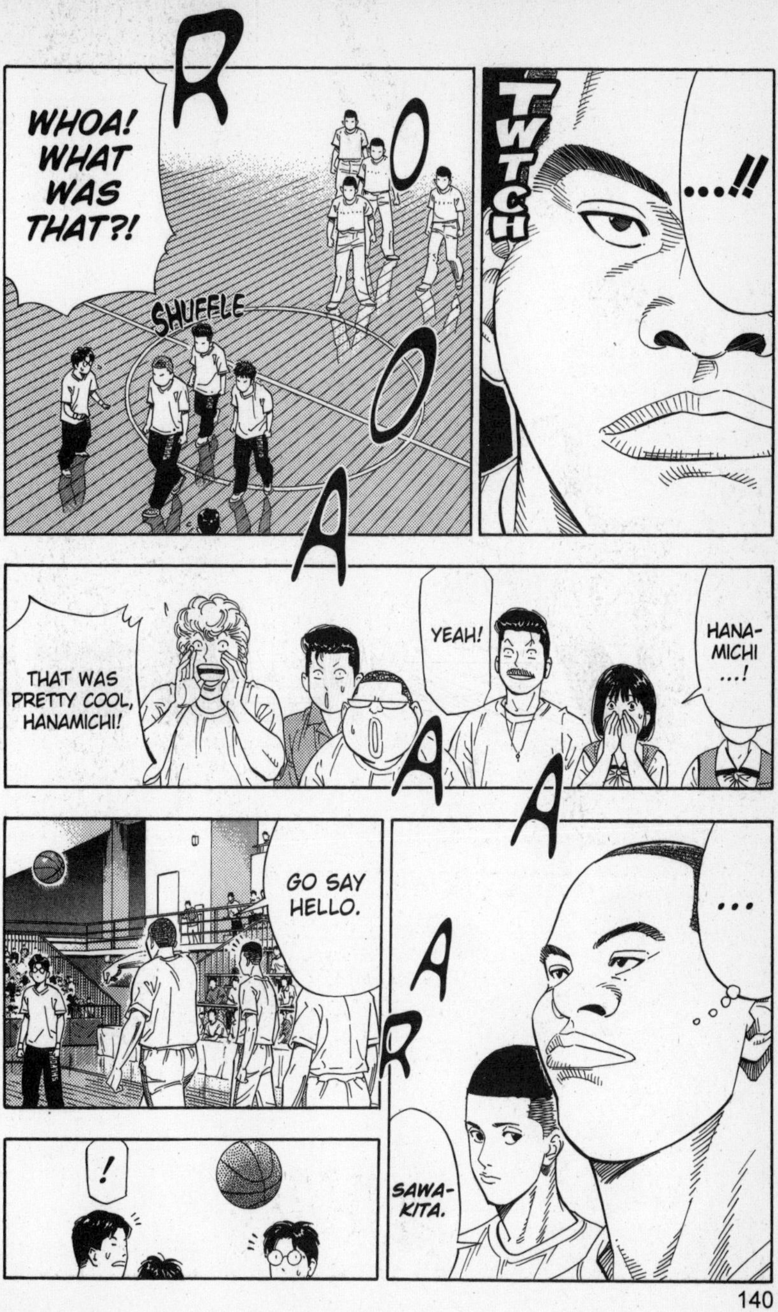
TWTCH
...!!
WHOA! WHAT WAS THAT?!
SHUFFLE
ROOAAAAR
HANA-MICHI ...!
YEAH!
THAT WAS PRETTY COOL, HANAMICHI!
...
SAWA-KITA.
GO SAY HELLO.
!

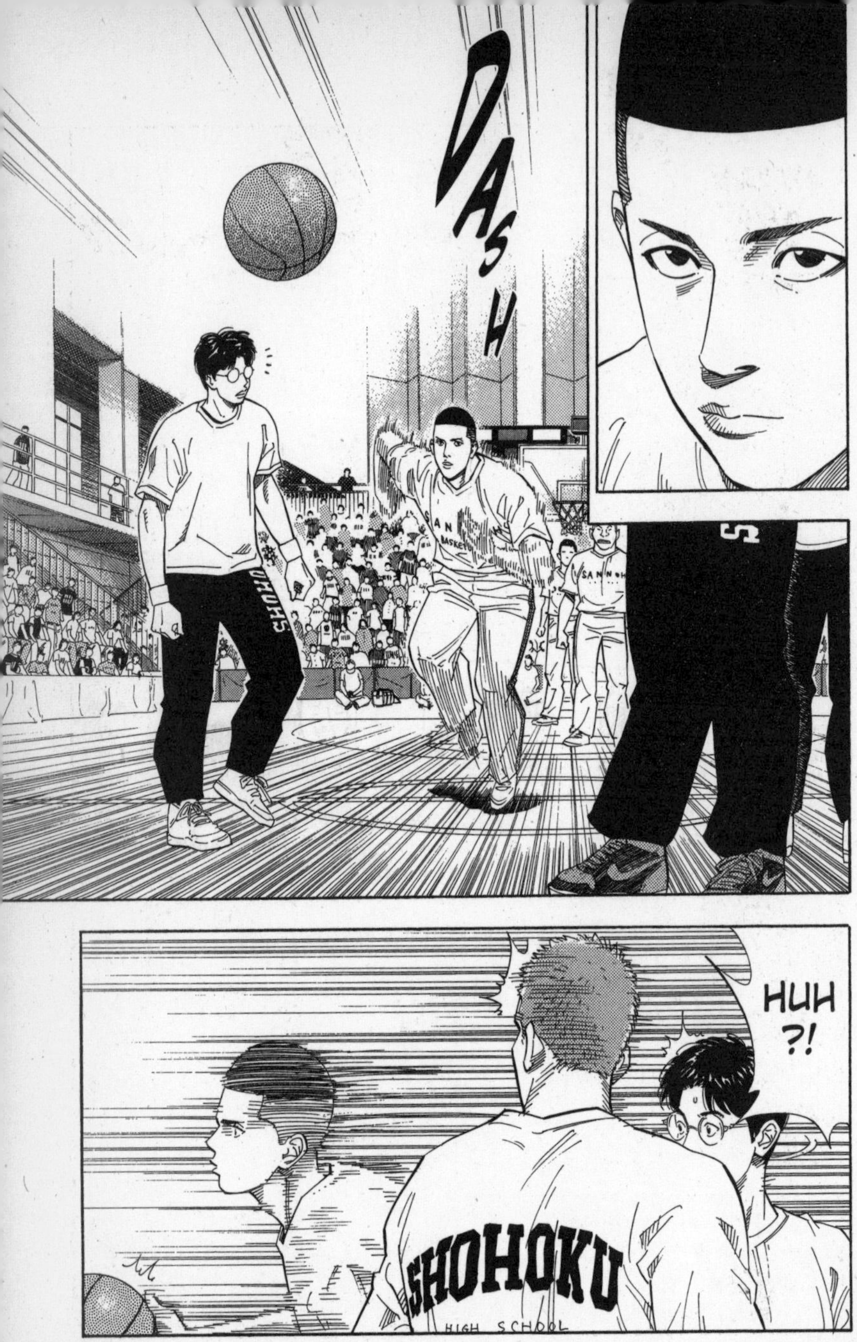
DASH
HUH ?!
SHOHOKU
HIGH SCHOOL

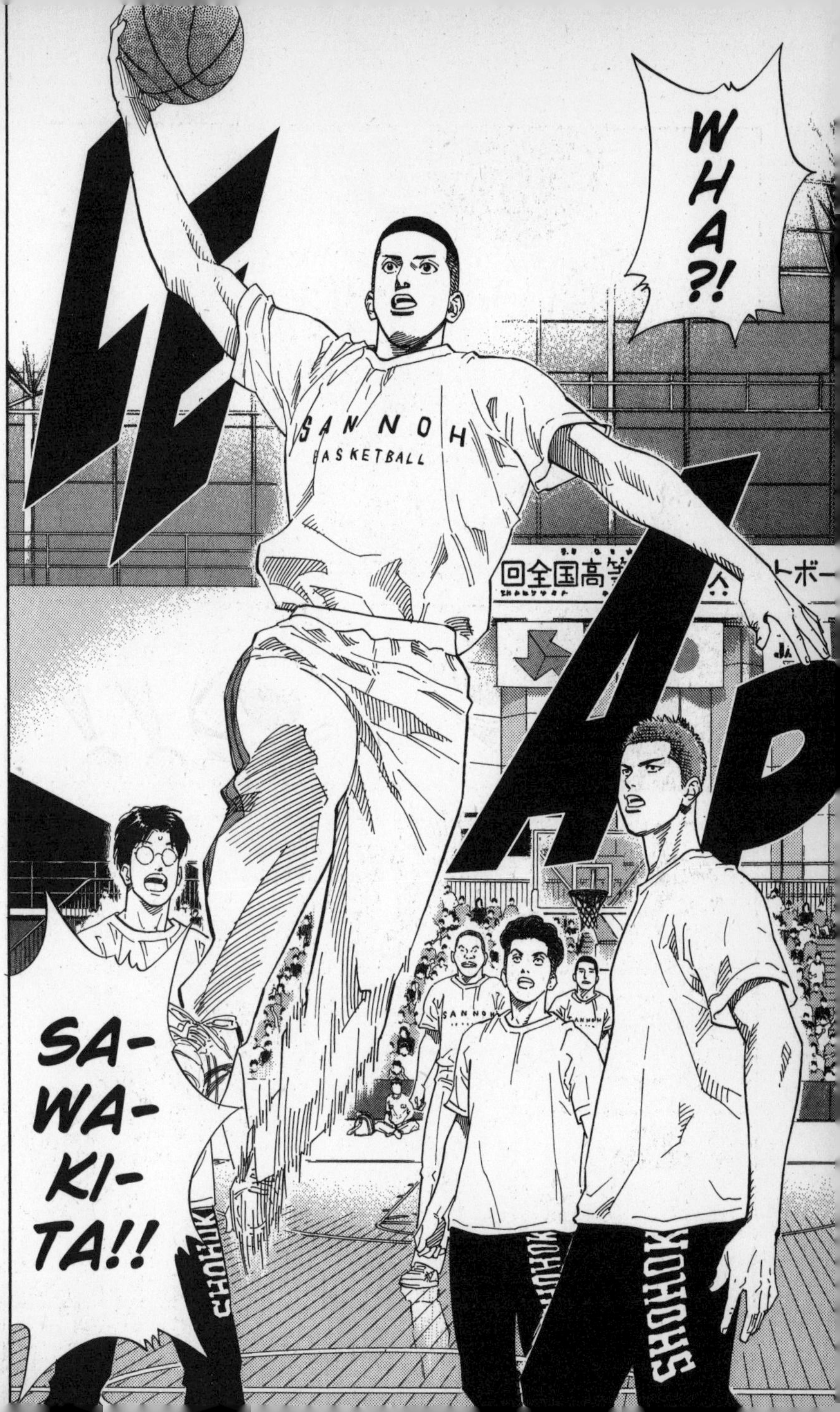
WHA?!
SANNOH
BASKETBALL
SA-
WA-
KI-
TA!!

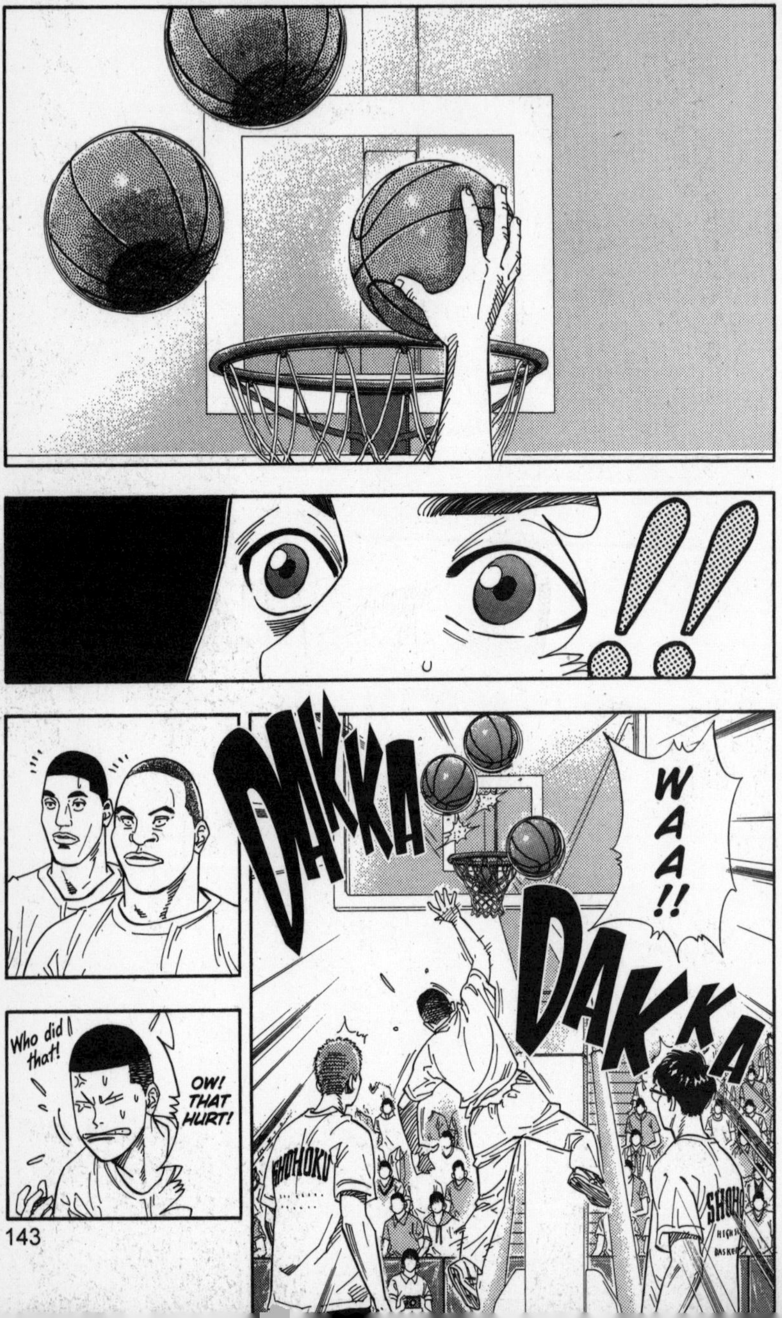
DAKKA
WAA!!
DAKKA
OW! THAT HURT!
Who did that!

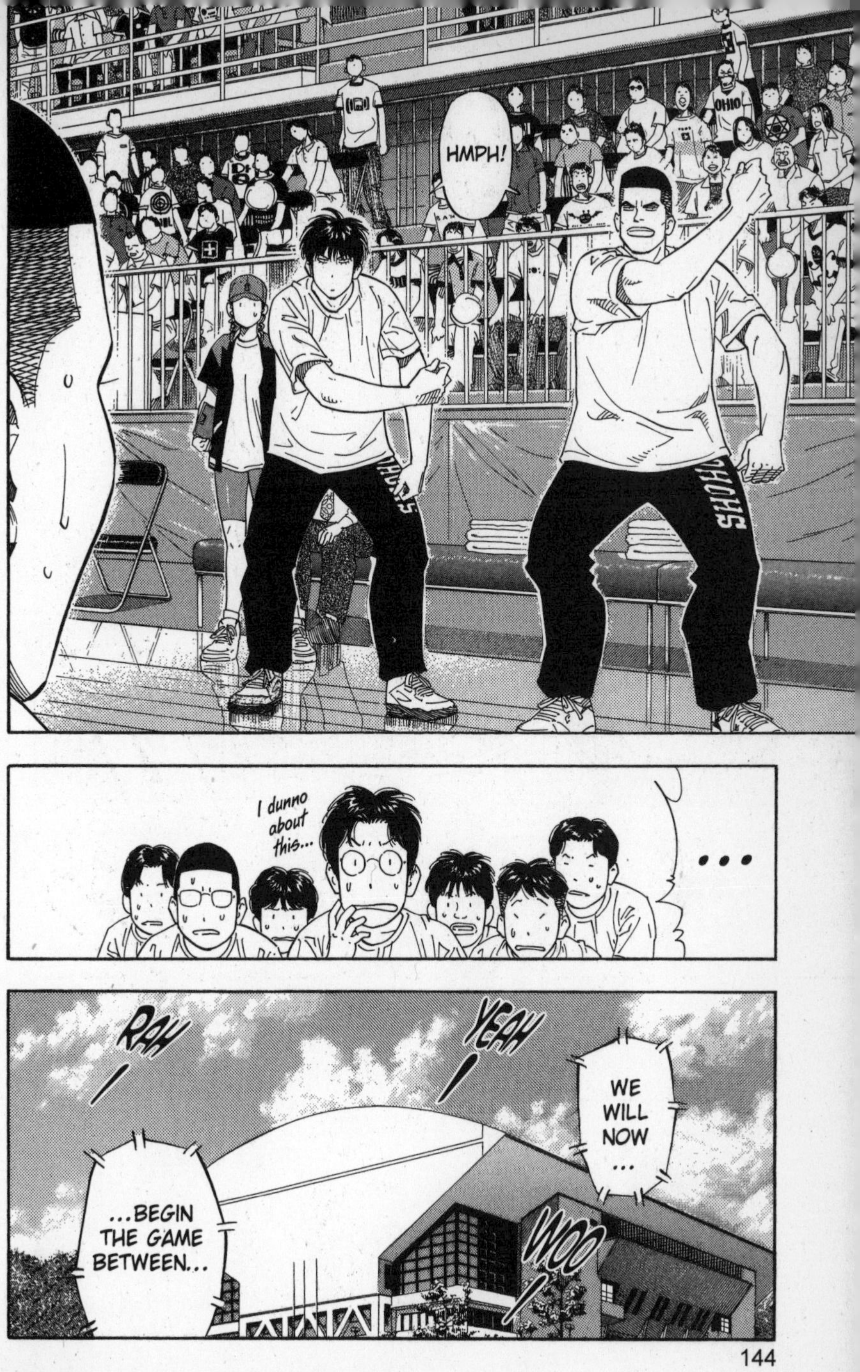
HMPH!
...
I dunno about this...
YEAH
RAH
WE WILL NOW ...
...BEGIN THE GAME BETWEEN...
WOO

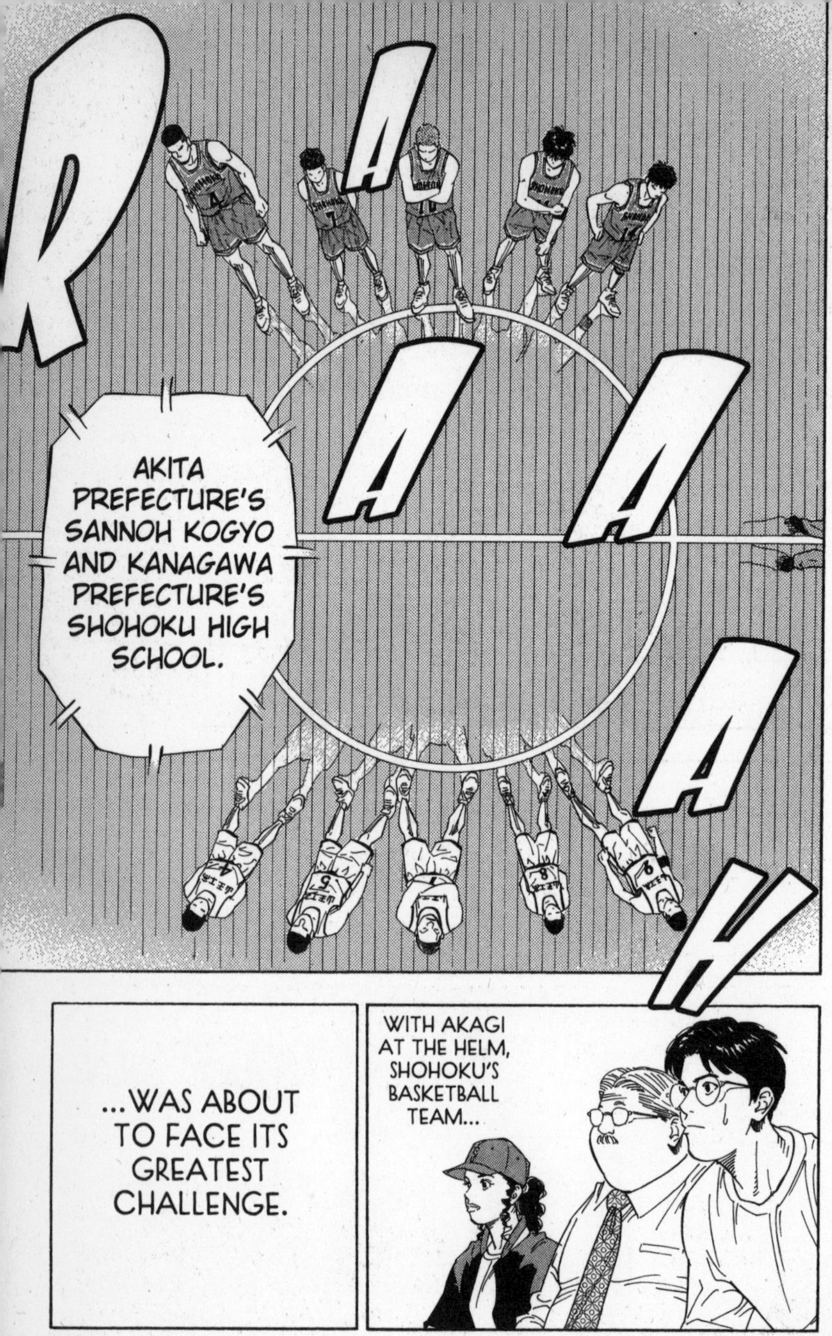
RAAAAH
AKITA PREFECTURE'S SANNOH KOGYO AND KANAGAWA PREFECTURE'S SHOHOKU HIGH SCHOOL.
WITH AKAGI AT THE HELM, SHOHOKU'S BASKETBALL TEAM...
...WAS ABOUT TO FACE ITS GREATEST CHALLENGE.

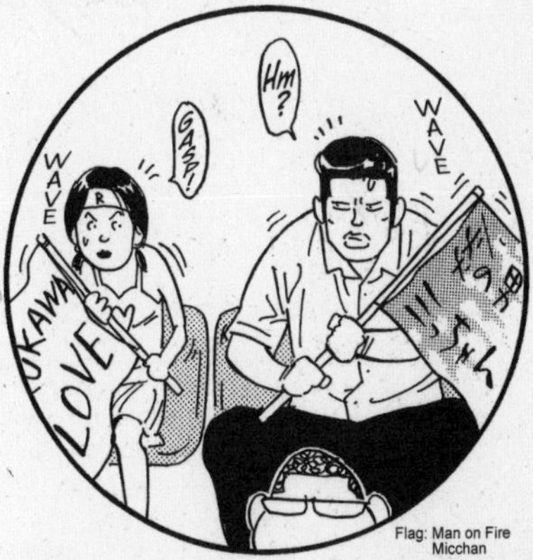
WAVE
Hm?
GASP!
WAVE
UKAWA
LOVE
Flag: Man on Fire
Micchan

SLAM DUNK

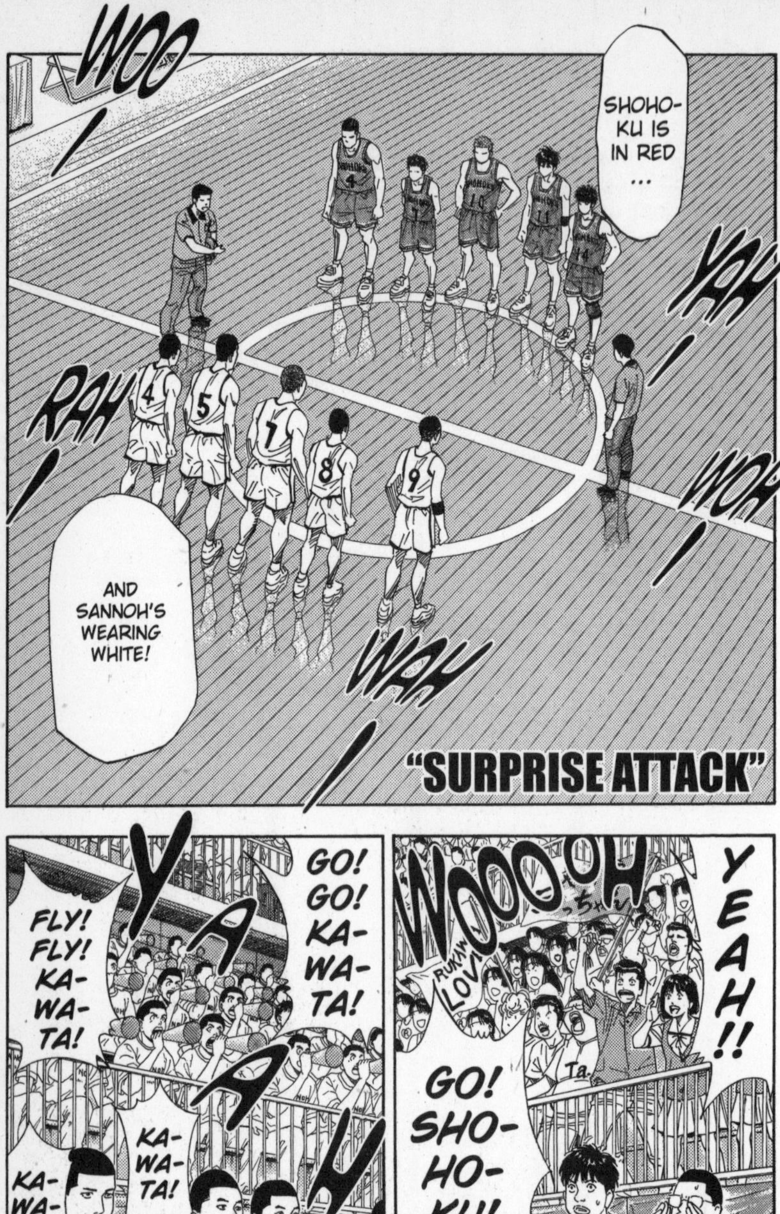

SHOHOKU IS IN RED...
YAH!
WOO!
WOH!
RAH!
AND SANNOH'S WEARING WHITE!
WAH!
"SURPRISE ATTACK"
YEAH!!
WOOOOH
GO! SHOHOKU!
Ta.
GO! GO! KAWATA!
YAAAH
FLY! FLY! KAWATA!
KAWATA!
KAWATA!

"SURPRISE ATTACK"

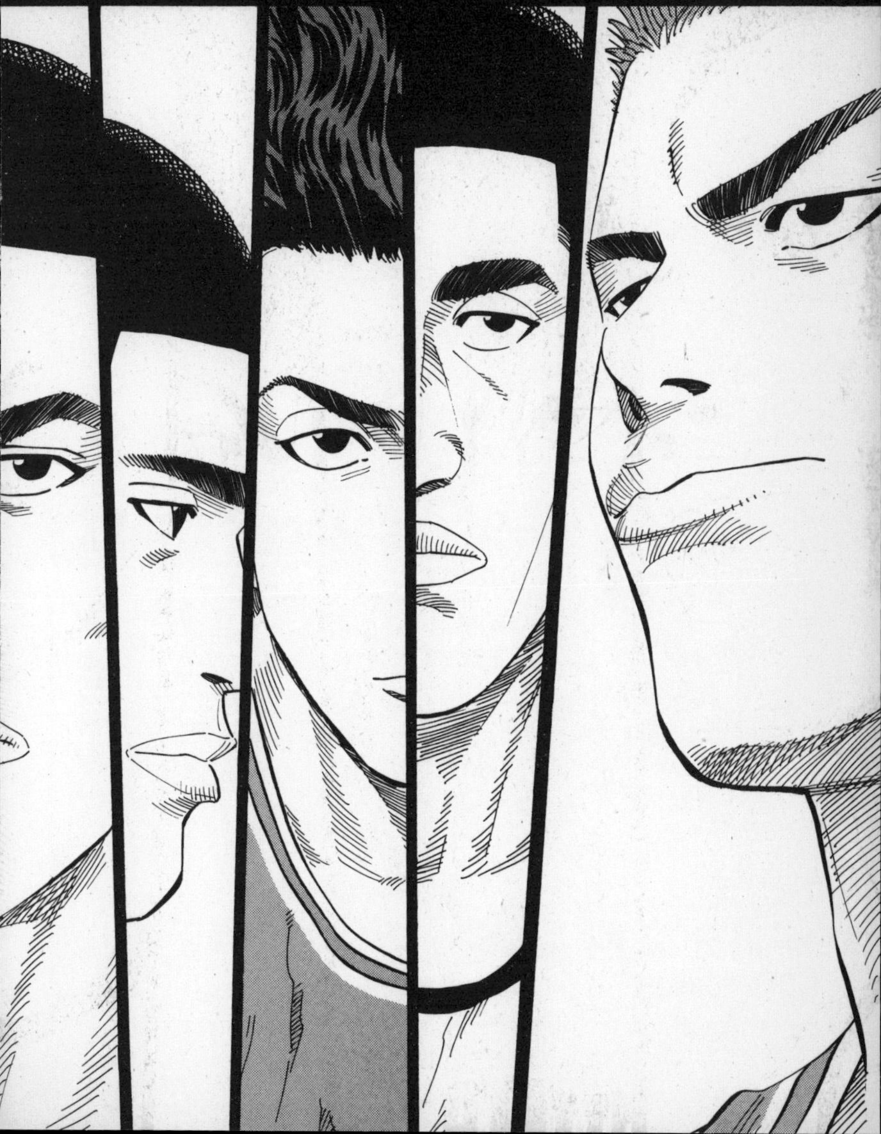

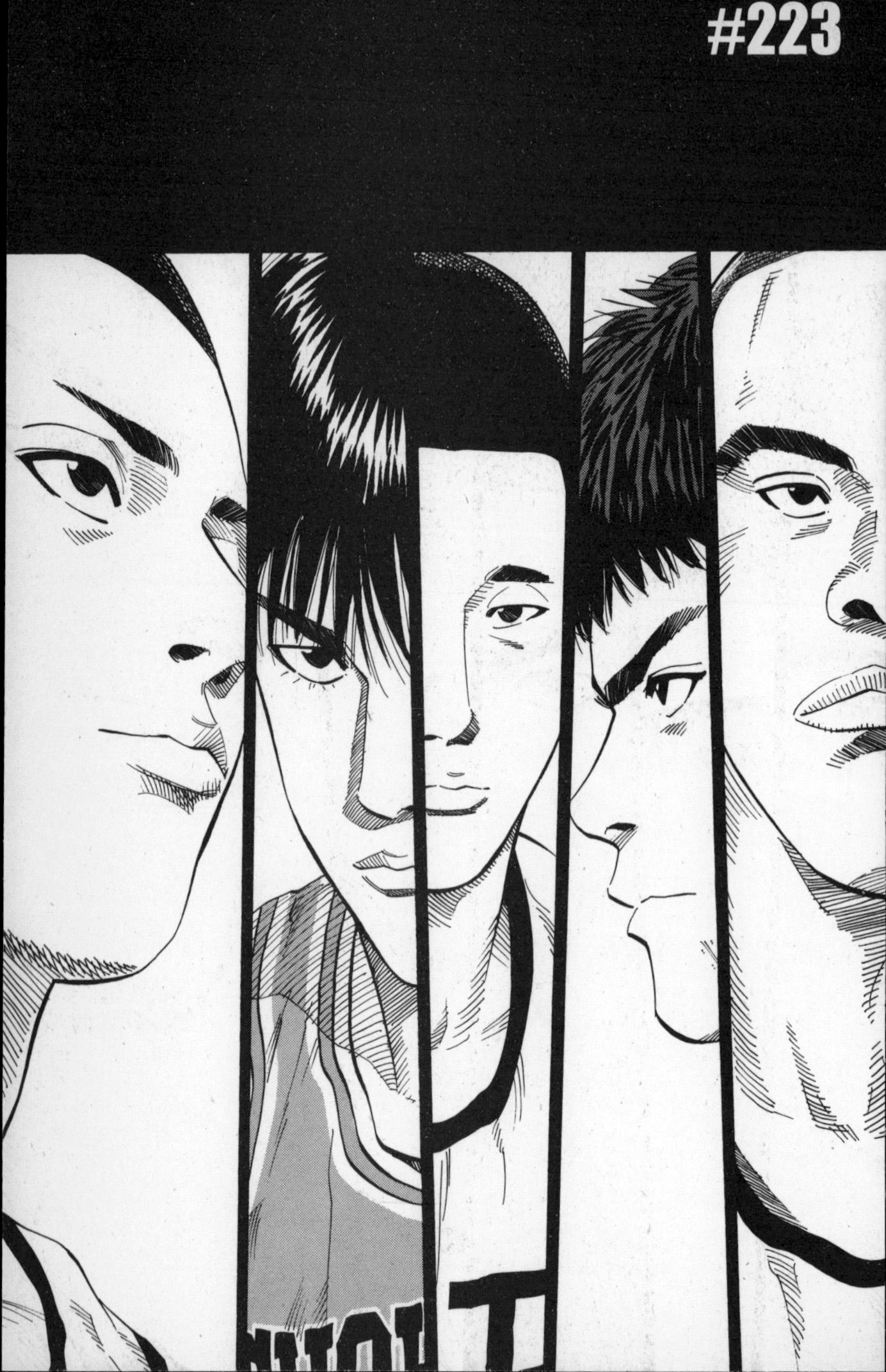
#223

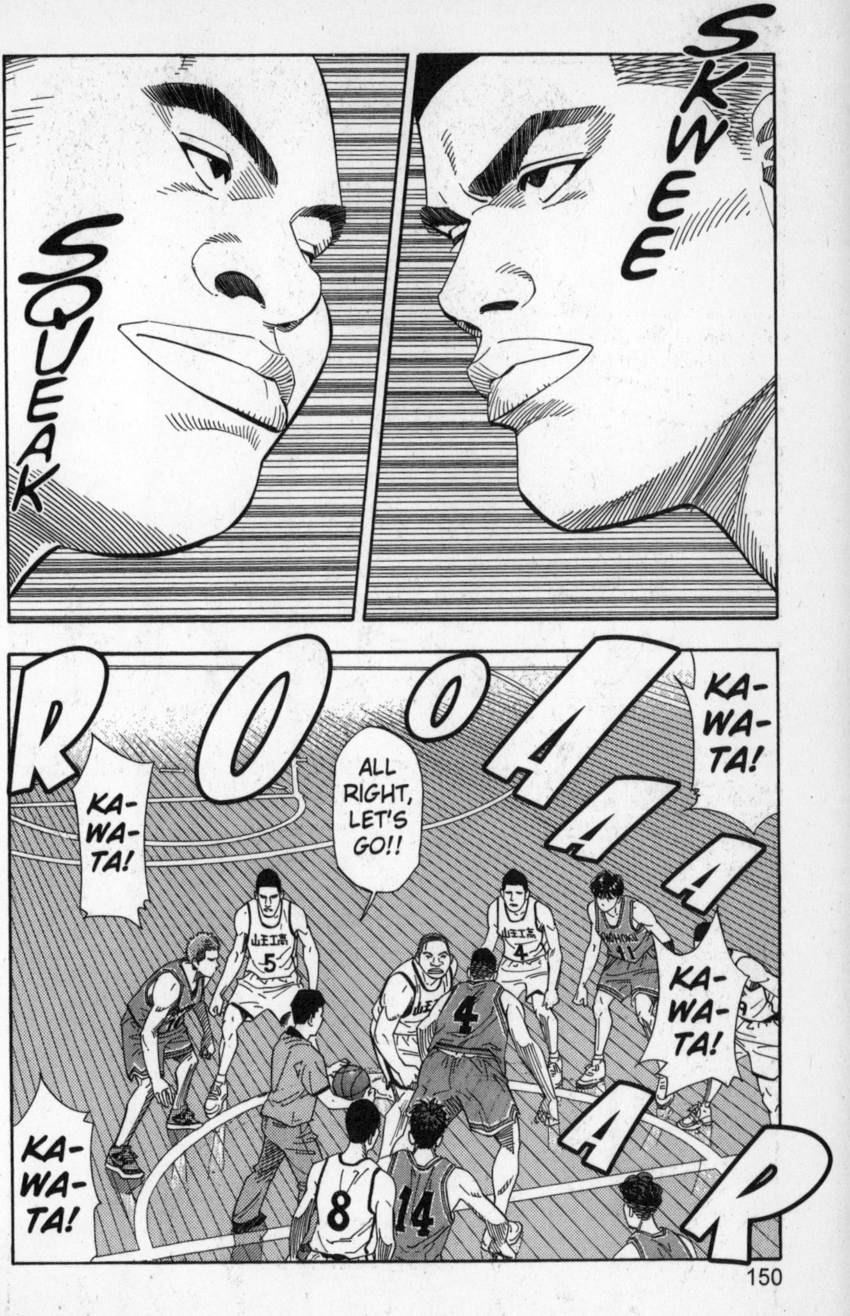
SKWEEE
SQUEAK
ROOAAAAAR
KA-WA-TA!
ALL RIGHT, LET'S GO!!
KA-WA-TA!
KA-WA-TA!
KA-WA-TA!

READ THIS WAY

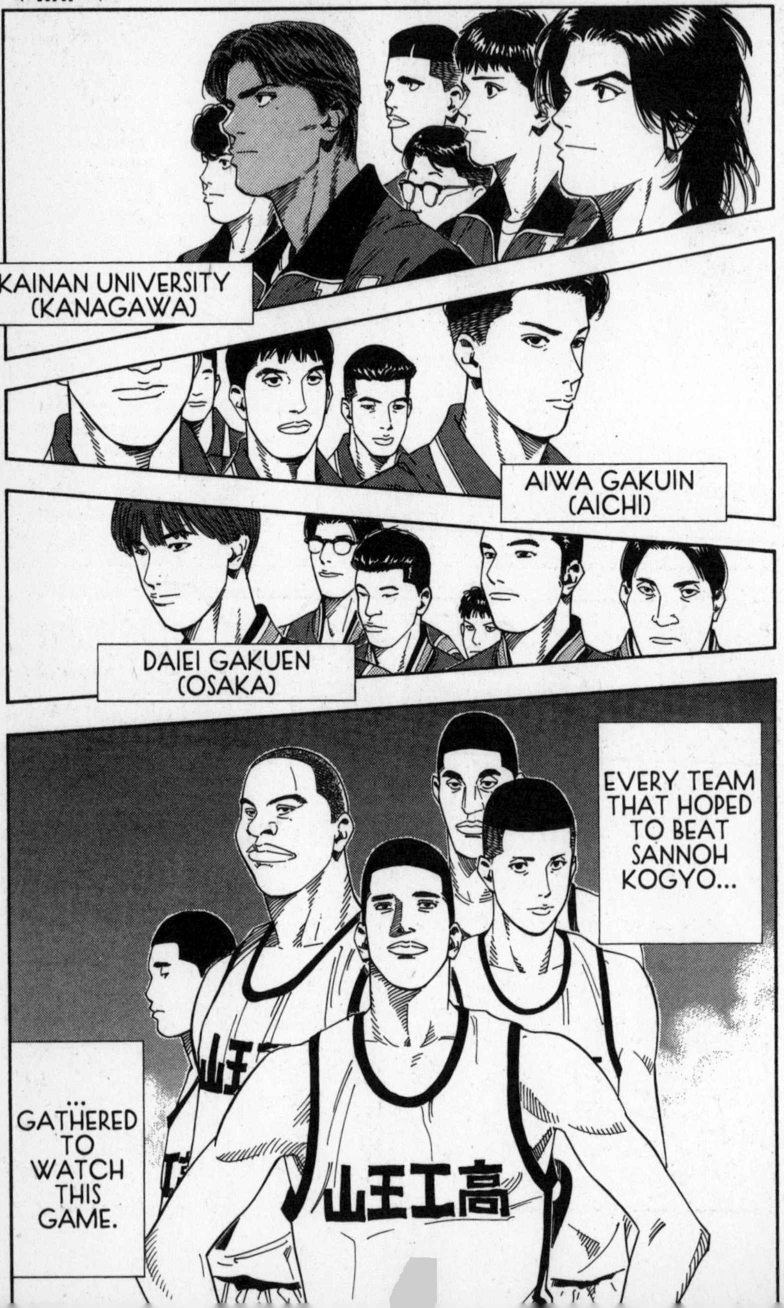
KAINAN UNIVERSITY (KANAGAWA)
AIWA GAKUIN (AICHI)
DAIEI GAKUEN (OSAKA)
EVERY TEAM THAT HOPED TO BEAT SANNOH KOGYO...
山王工高
...GATHERED TO WATCH THIS GAME.

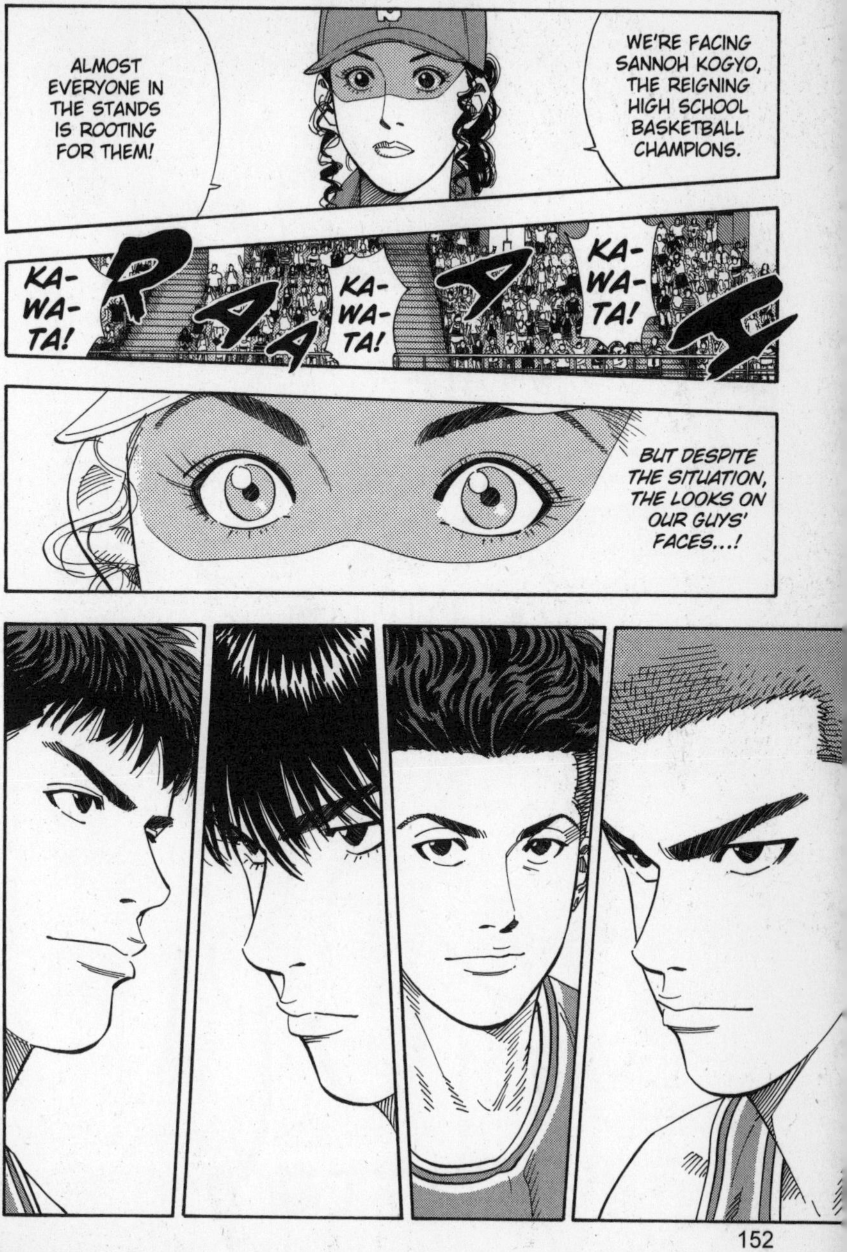
WE'RE FACING SANNOH KOGYO, THE REIGNING HIGH SCHOOL BASKETBALL CHAMPIONS.
ALMOST EVERYONE IN THE STANDS IS ROOTING FOR THEM!
KA-WA-TA!
KA-WA-TA!
KA-WA-TA!
RAAAAH
BUT DESPITE THE SITUATION, THE LOOKS ON OUR GUYS' FACES...!

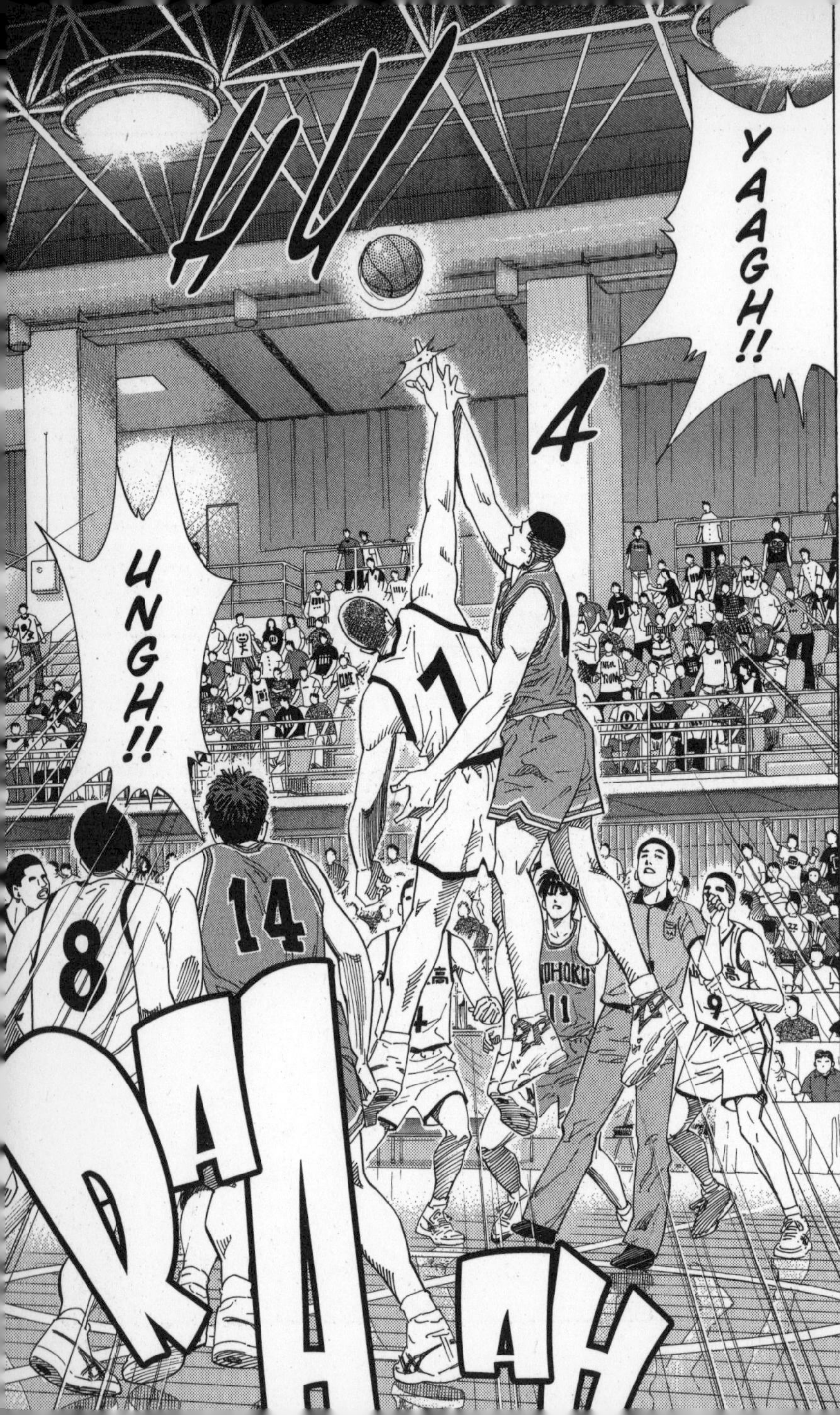
YAAGH!!
UNGH!!
RAAAH

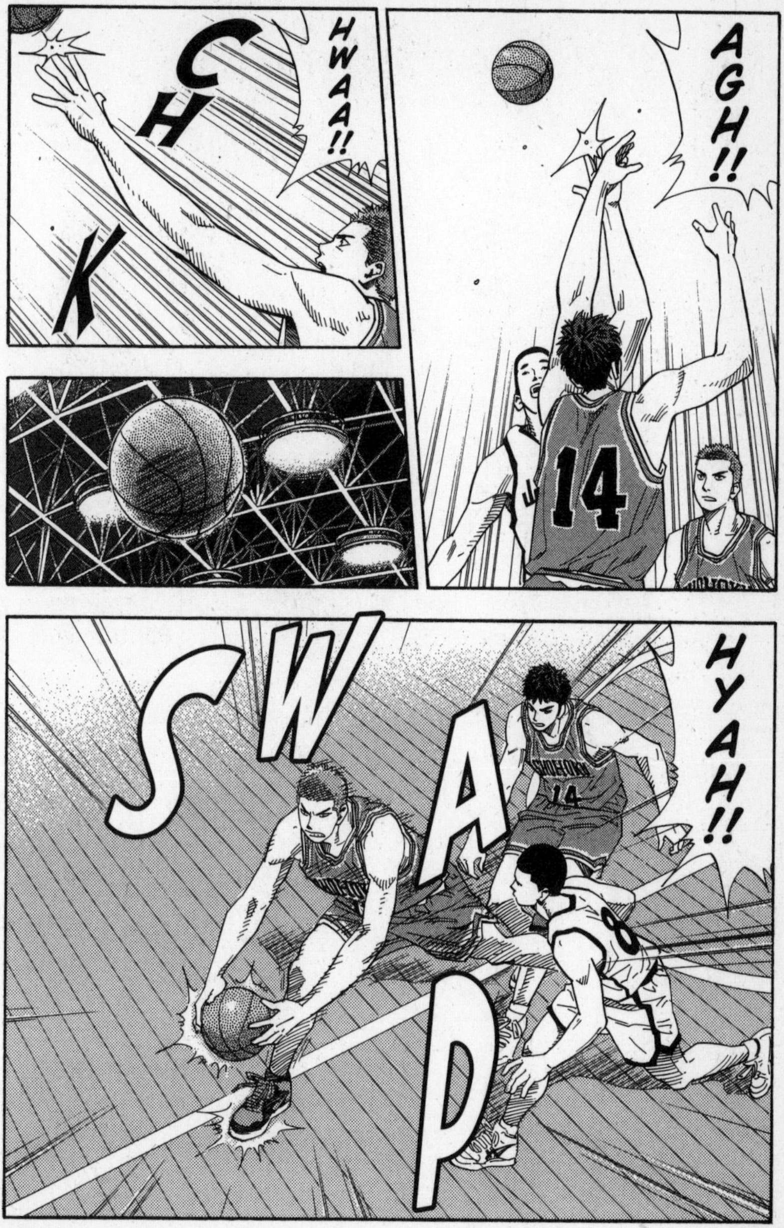
AGH!!
HWAAA!!
CHK
HYAH!!
SWAP

READ THIS WAY

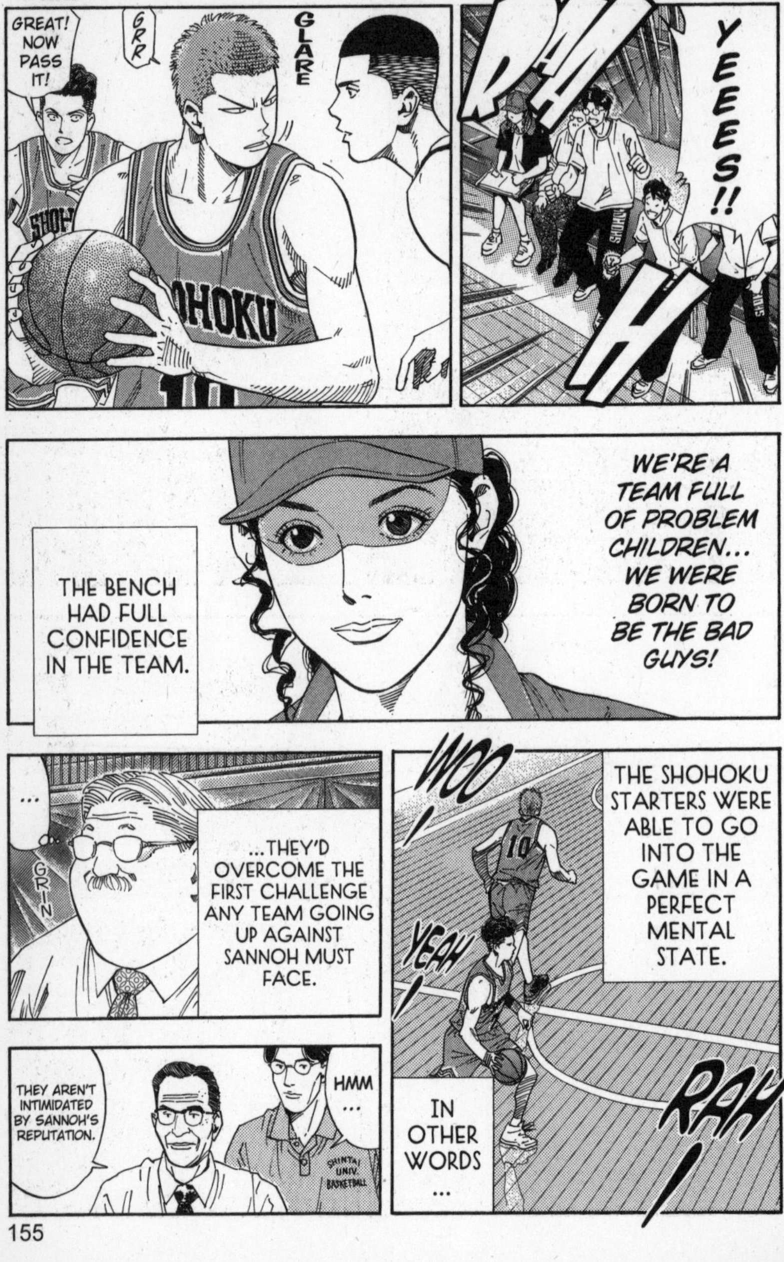
DAH
YEEEES!!
H
GREAT! NOW PASS IT!
GRR
GLARE
WE'RE A TEAM FULL OF PROBLEM CHILDREN... WE WERE BORN TO BE THE BAD GUYS!
THE BENCH HAD FULL CONFIDENCE IN THE TEAM.
WOO
THE SHOHOKU STARTERS WERE ABLE TO GO INTO THE GAME IN A PERFECT MENTAL STATE.
YEAH
RAH
IN OTHER WORDS ...
...
GRIN
...THEY'D OVERCOME THE FIRST CHALLENGE ANY TEAM GOING UP AGAINST SANNOH MUST FACE.
HMM ...
THEY AREN'T INTIMIDATED BY SANNOH'S REPUTATION.
SHINTAI UNIV. BASKETBALL

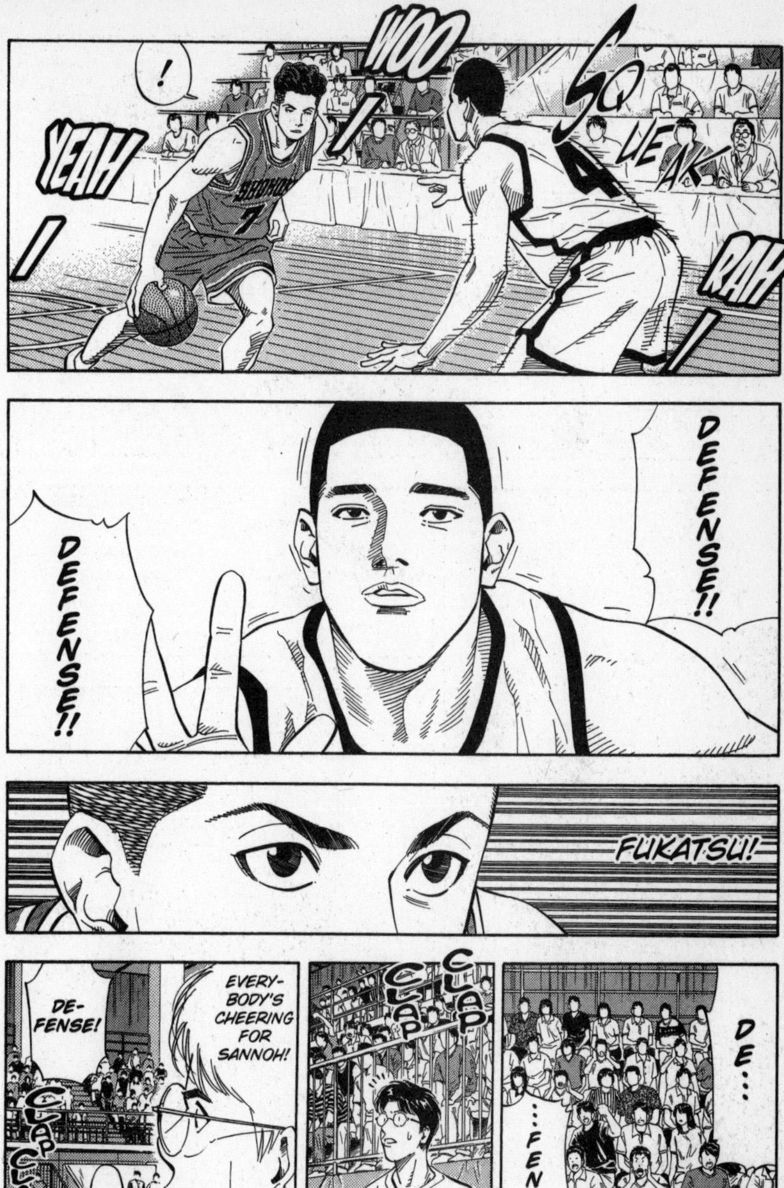
SQUEAK
RAH!
WOO!
!
YEAH!
DEFENSE!!
DEFENSE!!
FUKATSU!
DE...
...FENSE!
CLAP CLAP
EVERY-BODY'S CHEERING FOR SANNOH!
DE-FENSE!
CLAP CLAP
Damn...

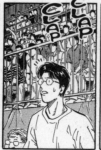

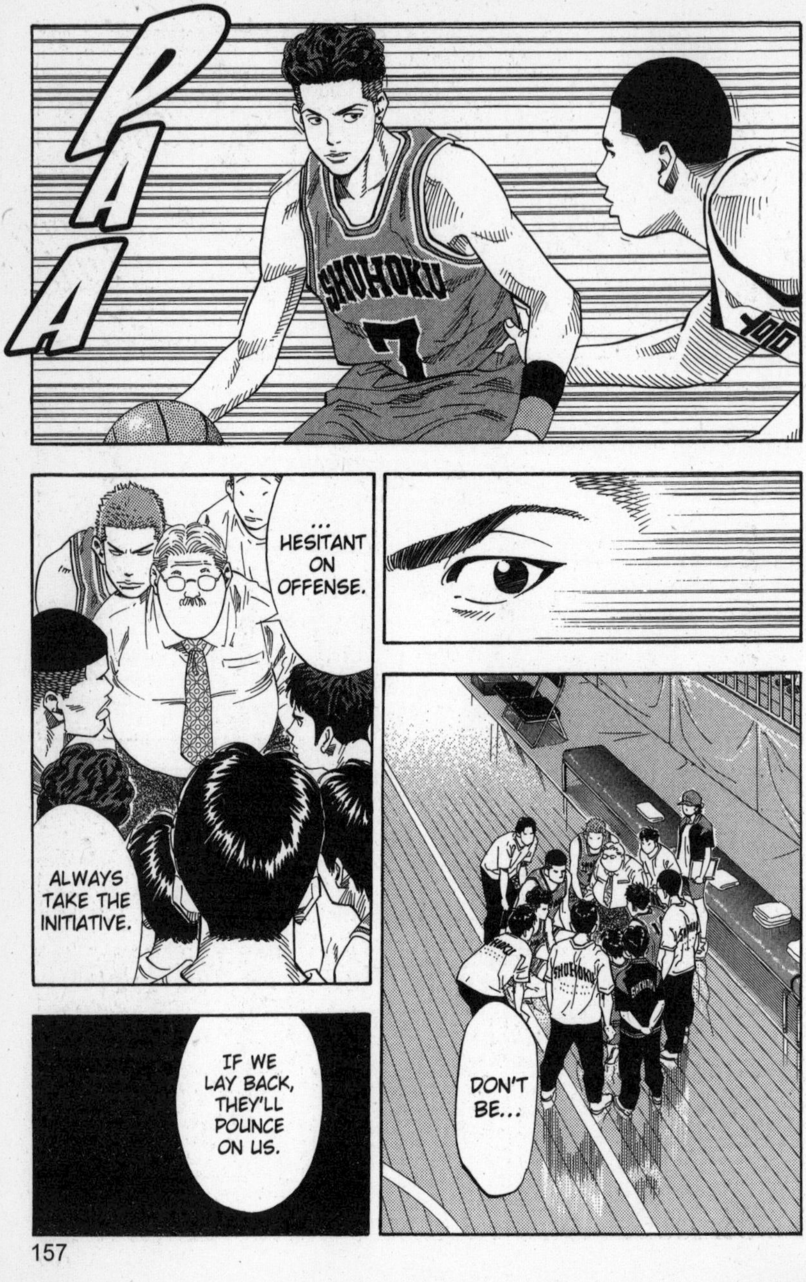
PAAA
DON'T BE...
...HESITANT ON OFFENSE.
ALWAYS TAKE THE INITIATIVE.
IF WE LAY BACK, THEY'LL POUNCE ON US.

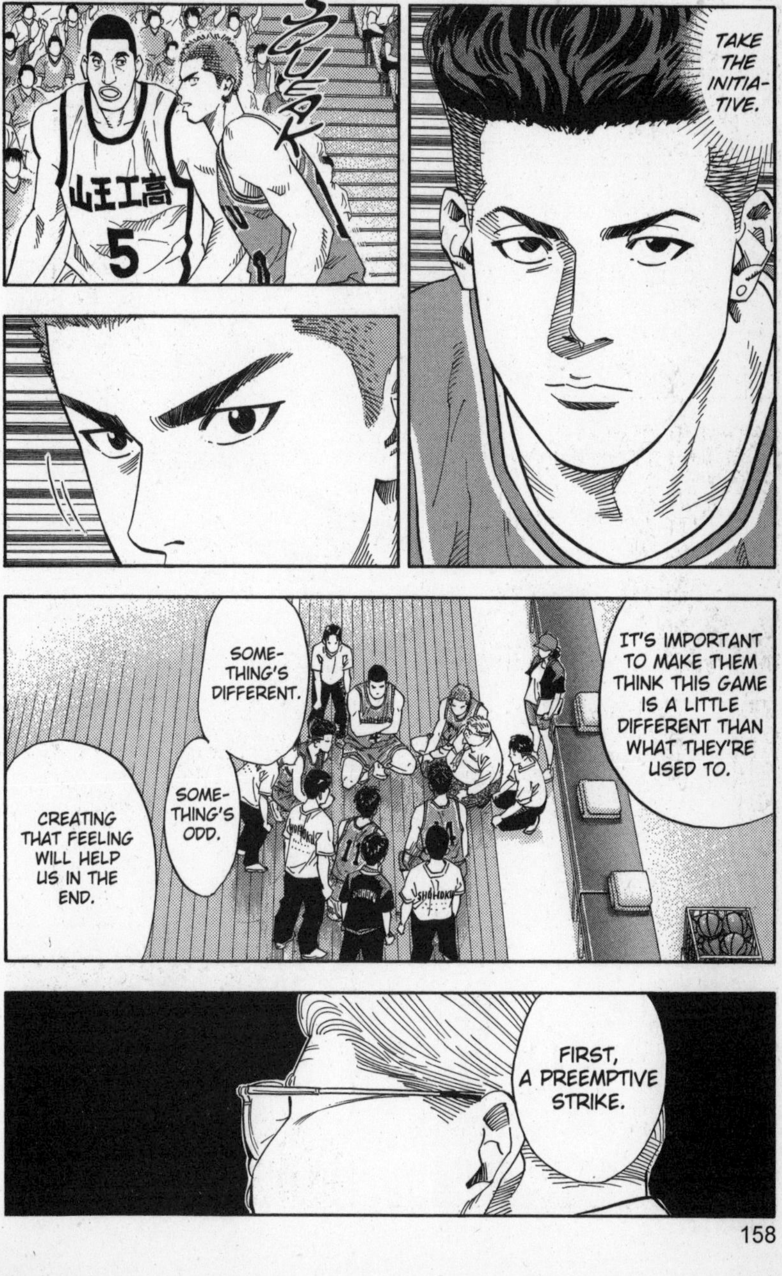
TAKE THE INITIA-TIVE.
SQUEAK
山王工高
5
IT'S IMPORTANT TO MAKE THEM THINK THIS GAME IS A LITTLE DIFFERENT THAN WHAT THEY'RE USED TO.
SOME-THING'S DIFFERENT.
SOME-THING'S ODD.
CREATING THAT FEELING WILL HELP US IN THE END.
FIRST, A PREEMPTIVE STRIKE.

READ THIS WAY

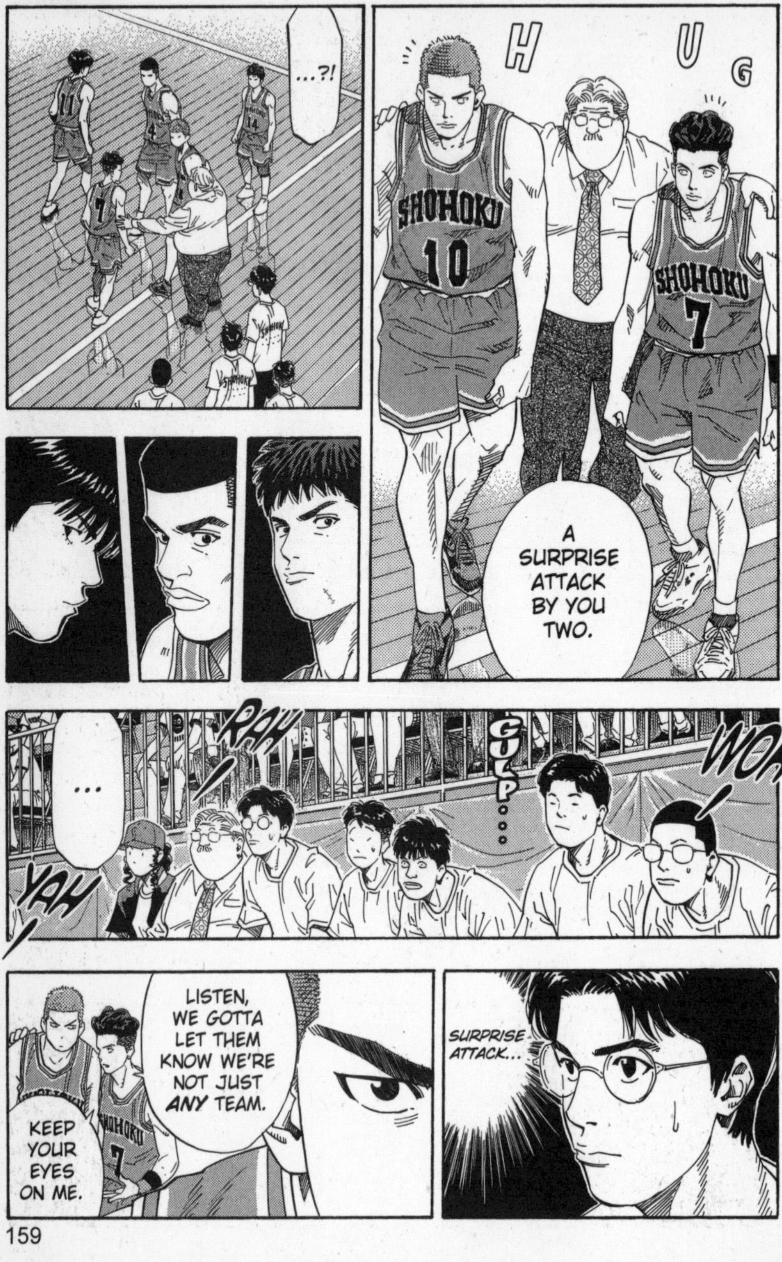

HUG
A SURPRISE ATTACK BY YOU TWO.
...?!
WOH
GULP...
RAH
...
YAH
SURPRISE ATTACK...
LISTEN, WE GOTTA LET THEM KNOW WE'RE NOT JUST *ANY* TEAM.
KEEP YOUR EYES ON ME.

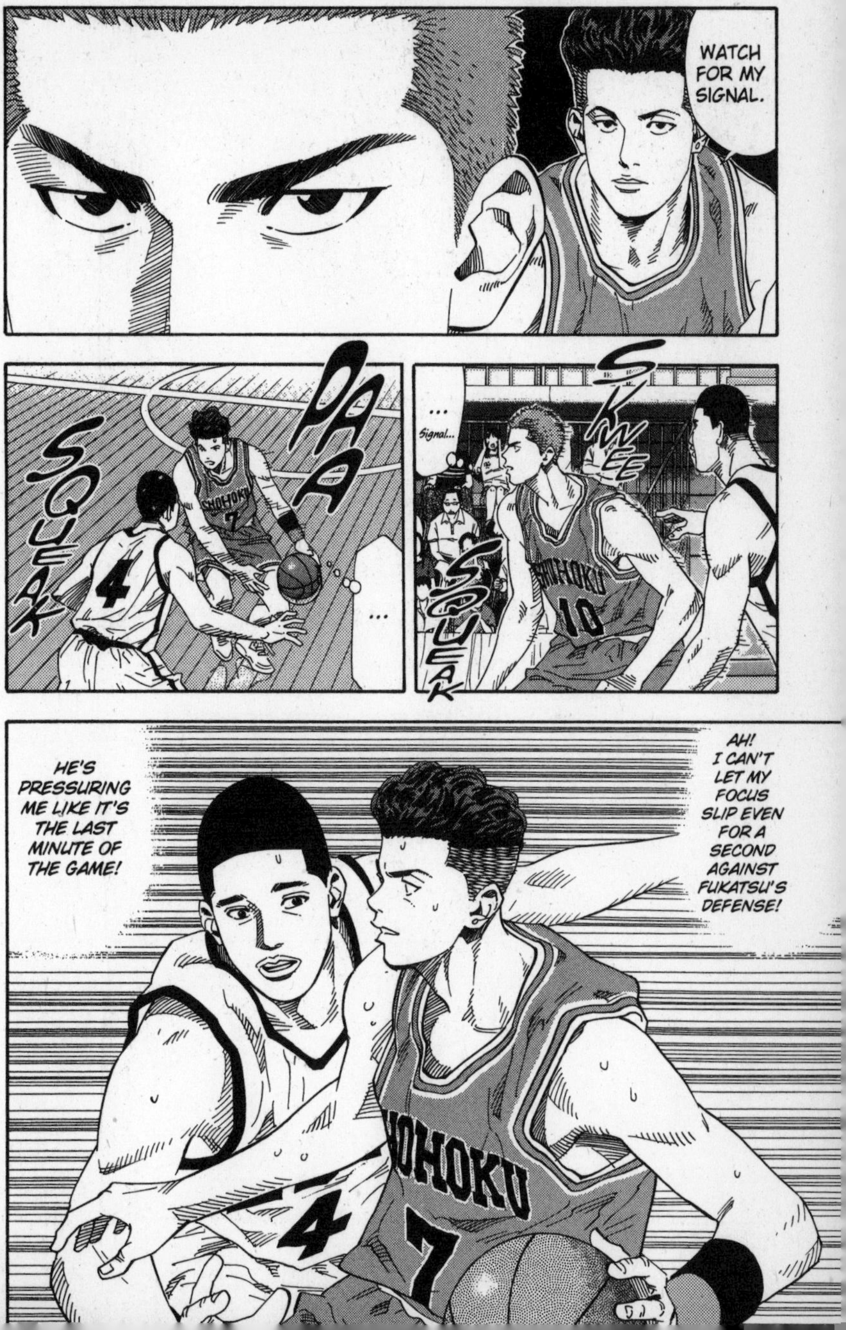
WATCH FOR MY SIGNAL.
... Signal...
SKWEE
SQUEAK
DAA
SQUEAK
...
AH! I CAN'T LET MY FOCUS SLIP EVEN FOR A SECOND AGAINST FUKATSU'S DEFENSE!
HE'S PRESSURING ME LIKE IT'S THE LAST MINUTE OF THE GAME!

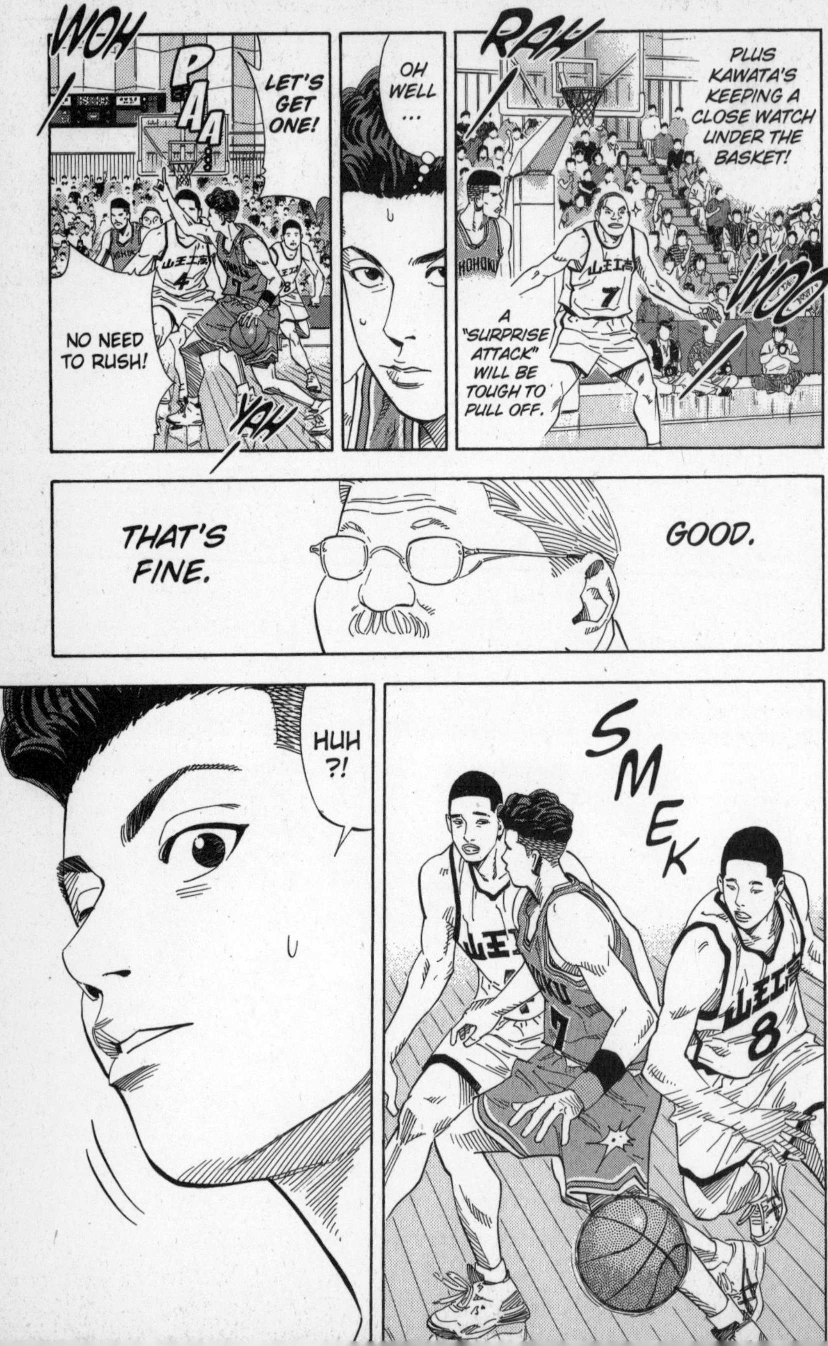
RAH
PLUS KAWATA'S KEEPING A CLOSE WATCH UNDER THE BASKET!
A "SURPRISE ATTACK" WILL BE TOUGH TO PULL OFF.
WOO
OH WELL ...
WOH
PAA
LET'S GET ONE!
NO NEED TO RUSH!
YAH
GOOD.
THAT'S FINE.
SMEK
HUH ?!

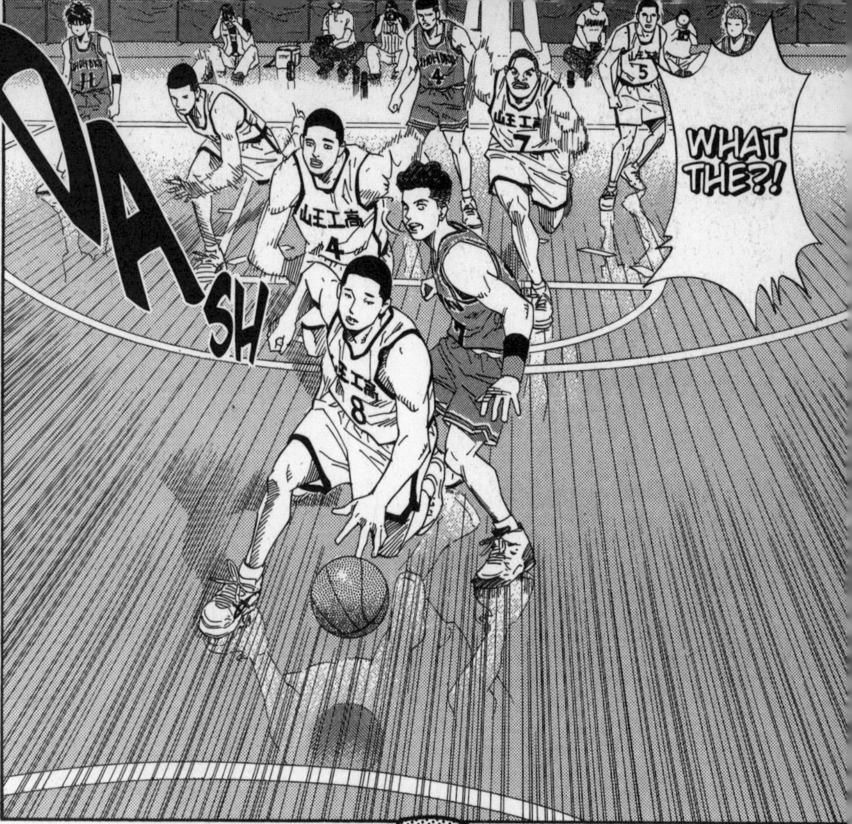
WHAT THE?!
DASH

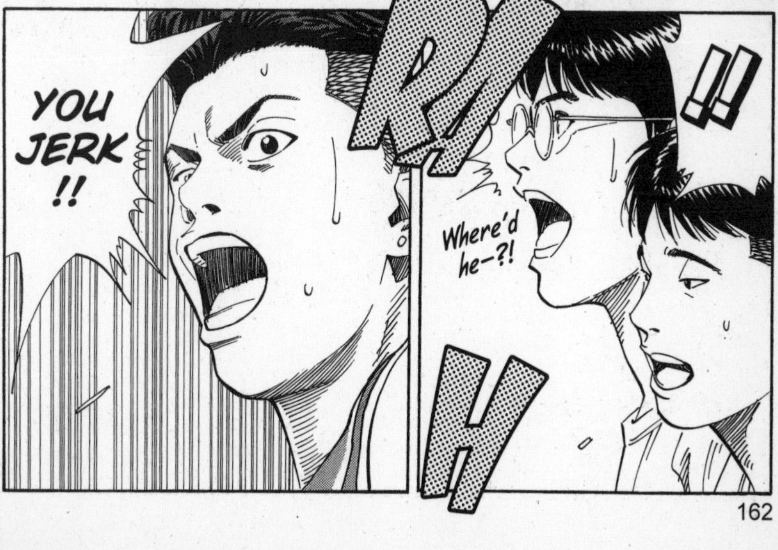
!!
Where'd he-?!
RAH
YOU JERK !!

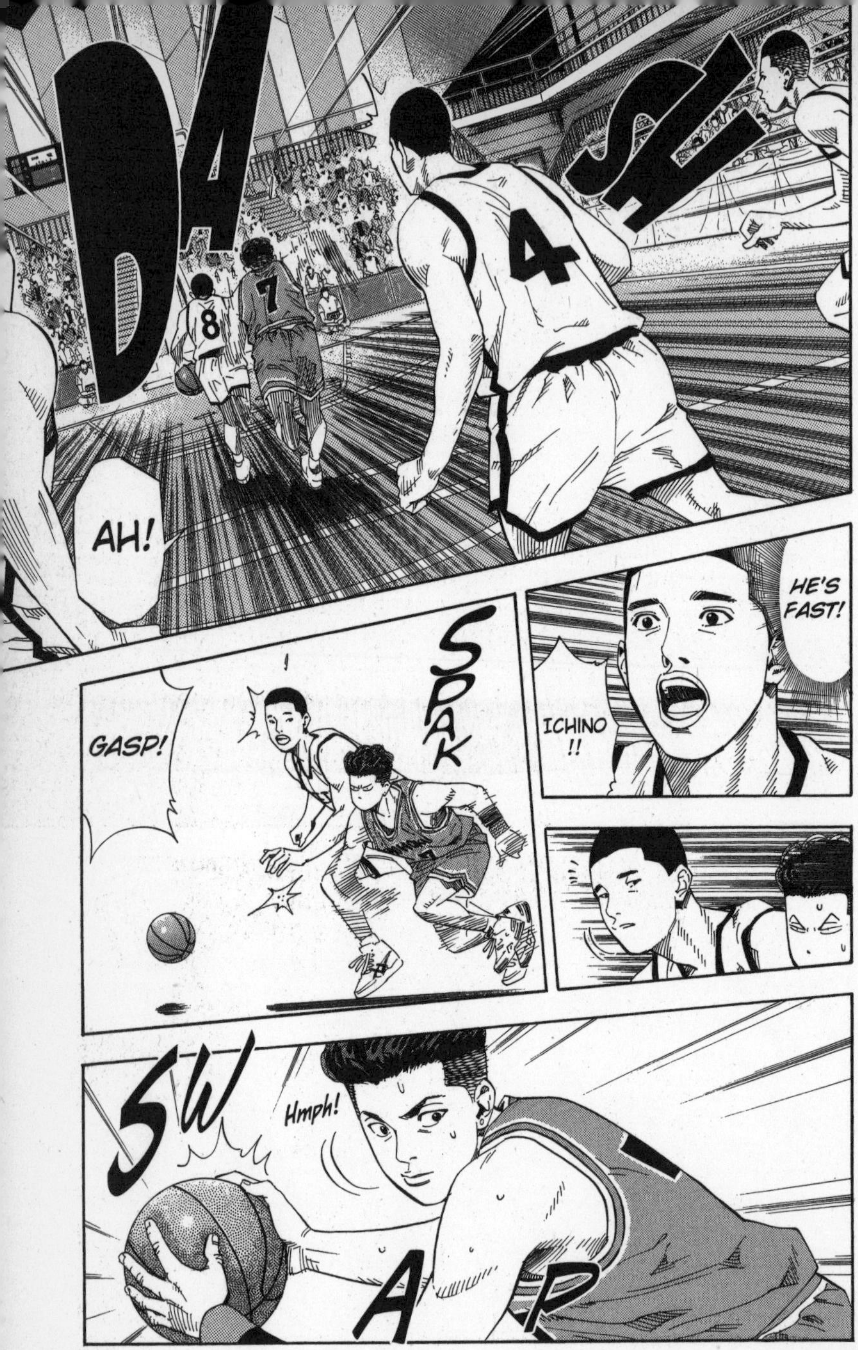
DASH
AH!
HE'S FAST!
ICHINO !!
SPAK
!
GASP!
SWAP
Hmph!

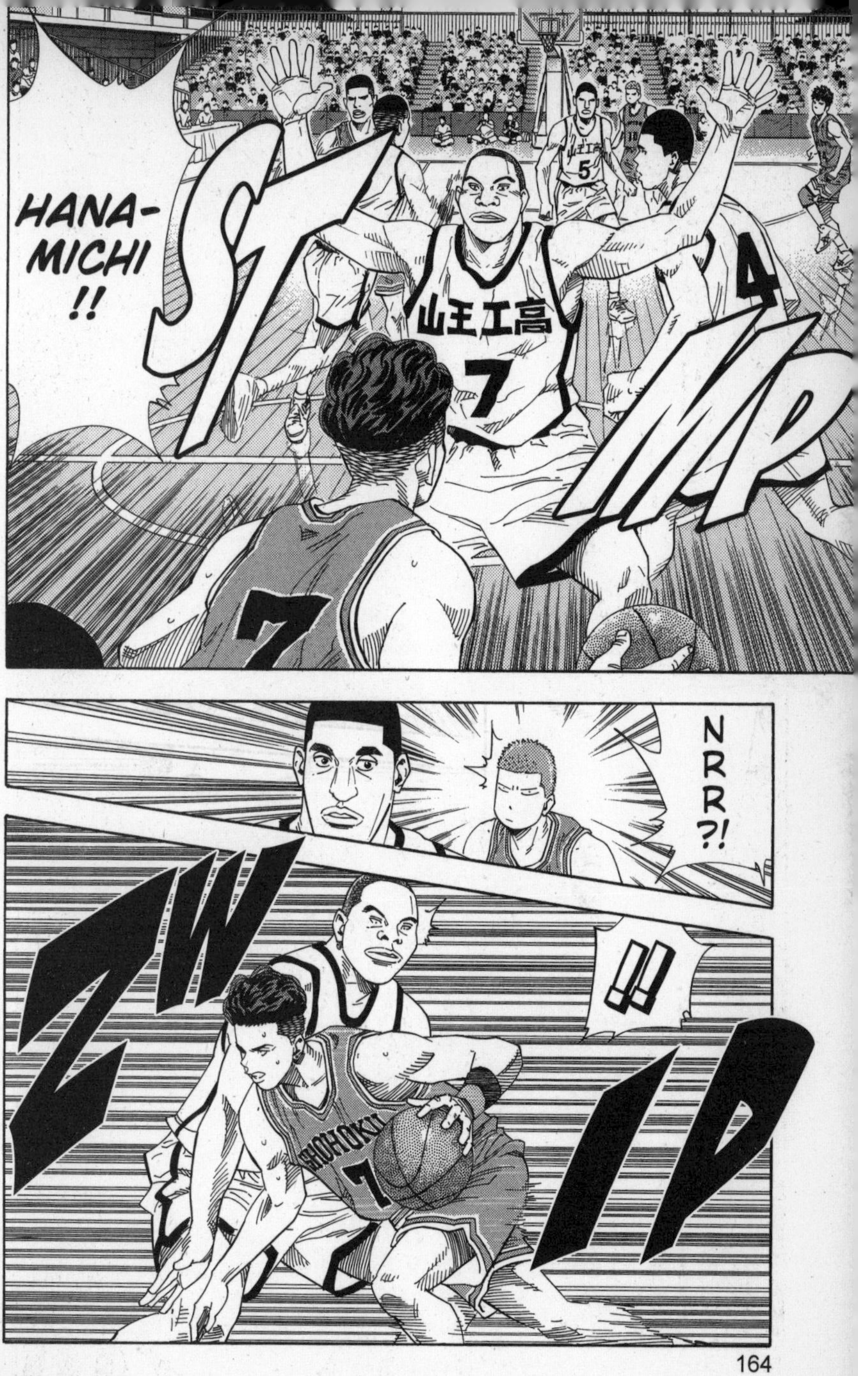
STMP
HANA-MICHI!!
山王工高
NRR?!
!!
ZWIP
SHOHOKU

READ THIS WAY

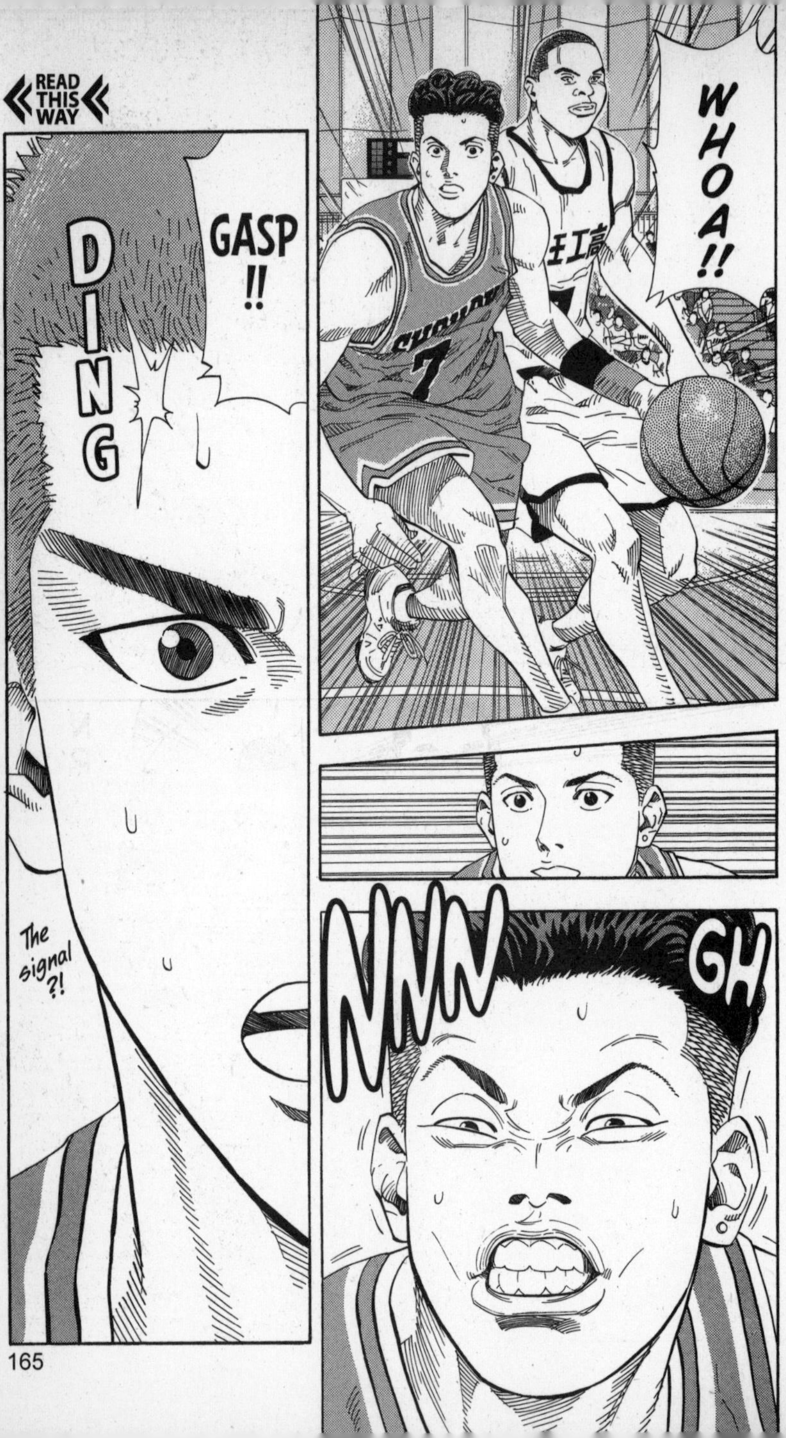
WHOA!!
NNNGH
GASP!!
DING
The signal?!

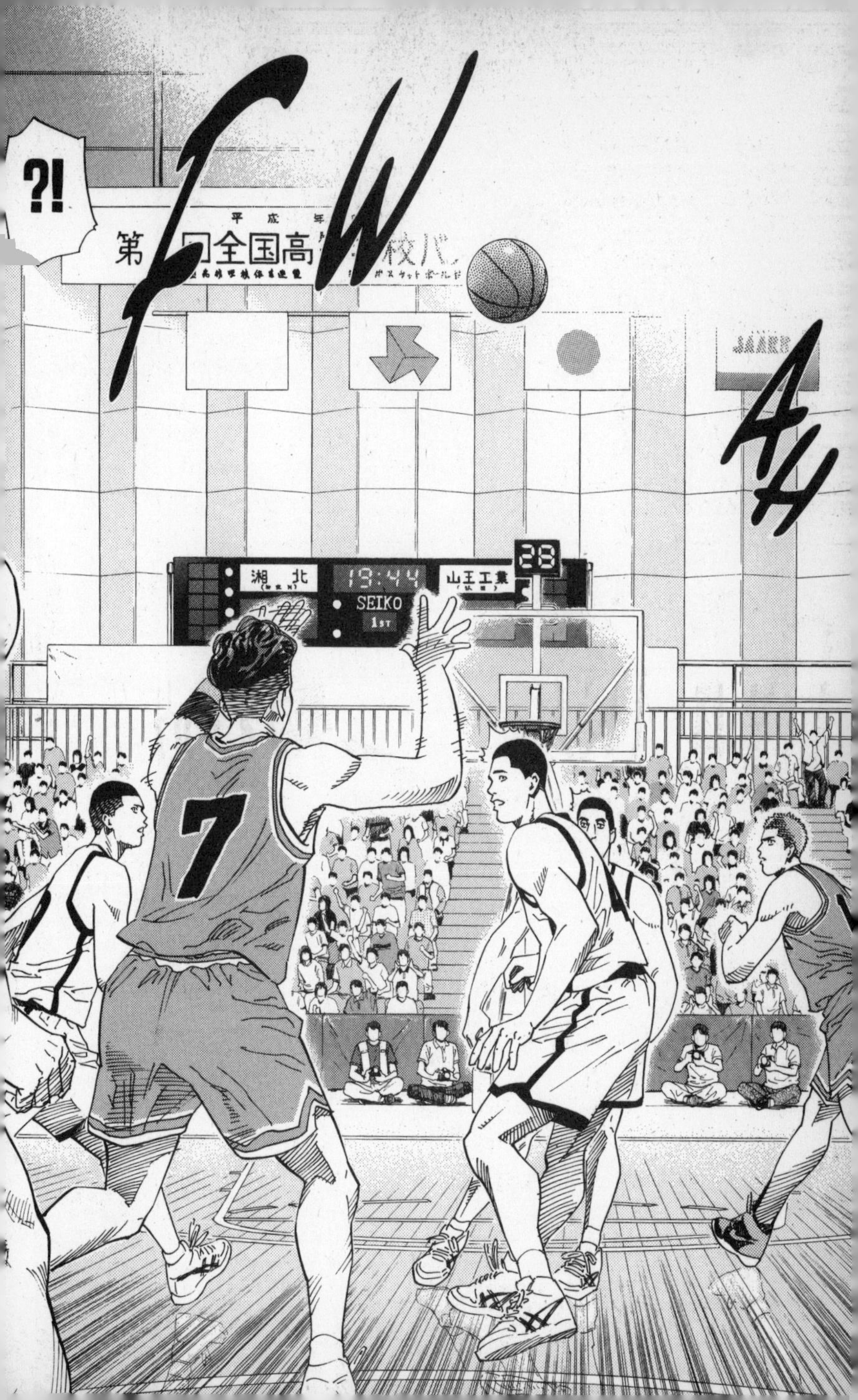

?!
FW
AH
湘北
19:44
山王工業
28
SEIKO
1ST

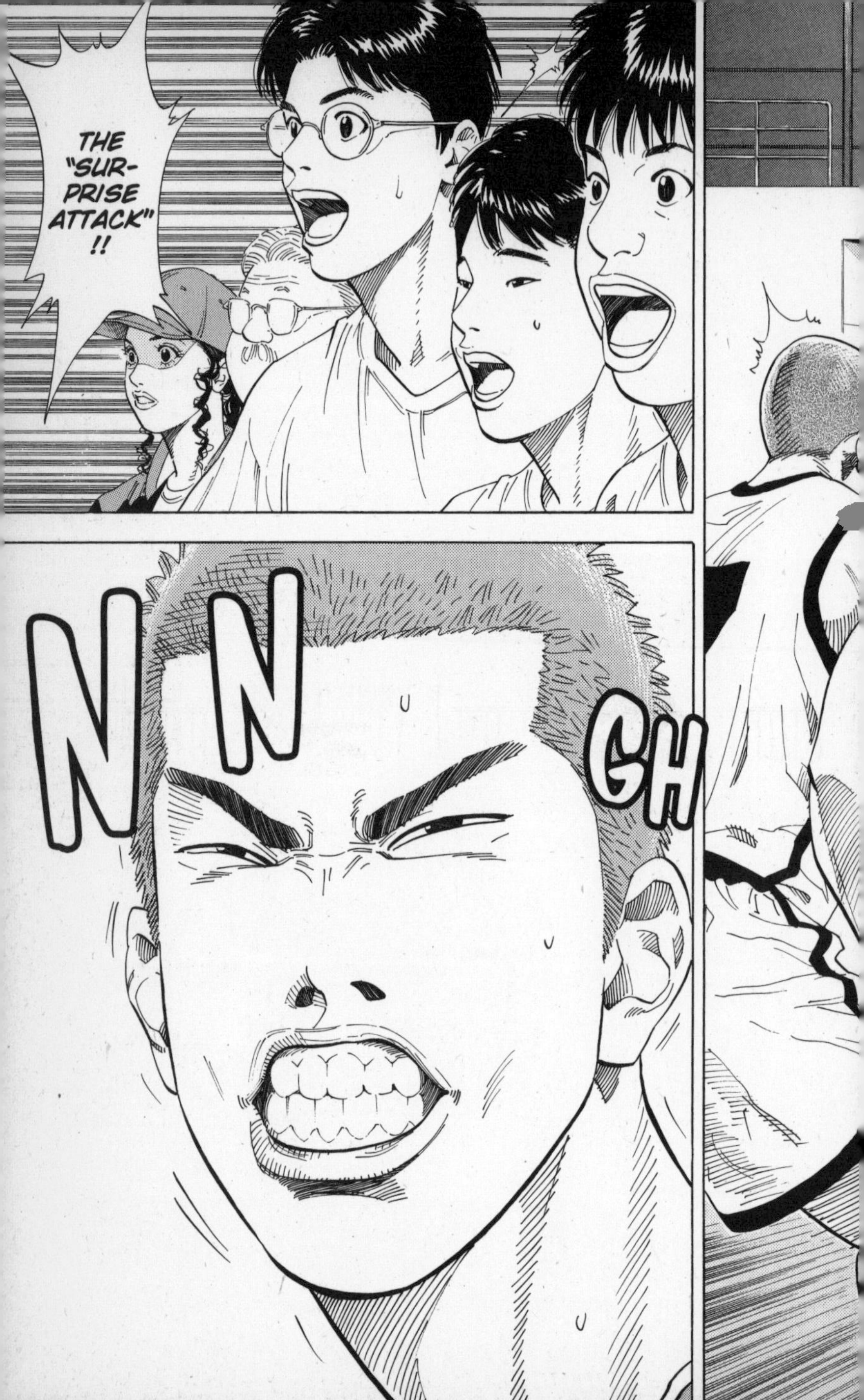
THE "SUR-PRISE ATTACK" !!
NNNGH

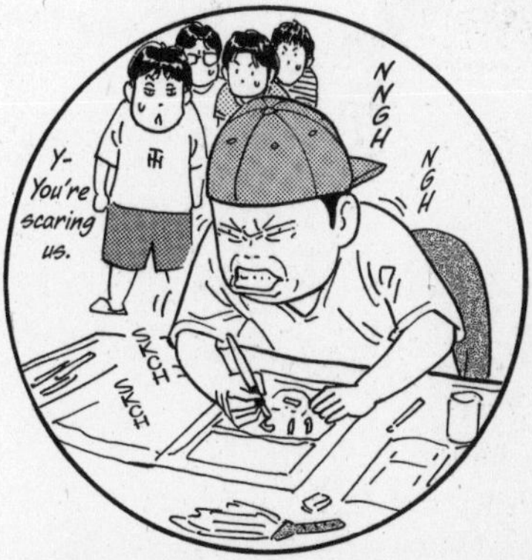
NNGH
NGH
Y- You're scaring us.
SKCH
SKCH

SLAM DUNK

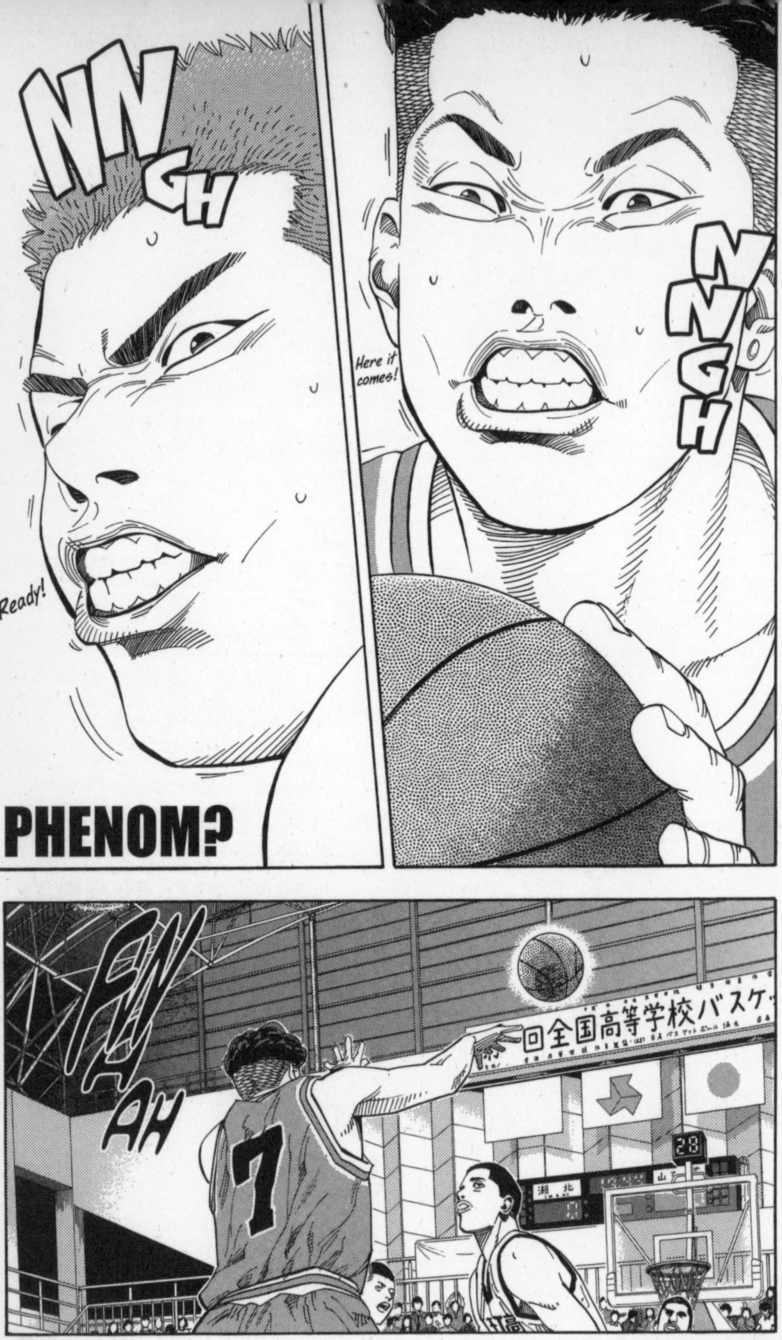
NNNGH
Here it comes!
NNGH
Ready!
PHENOM?
FWAAH
回全国高等学校バスケ
28
湘北

#224 PHENOM?

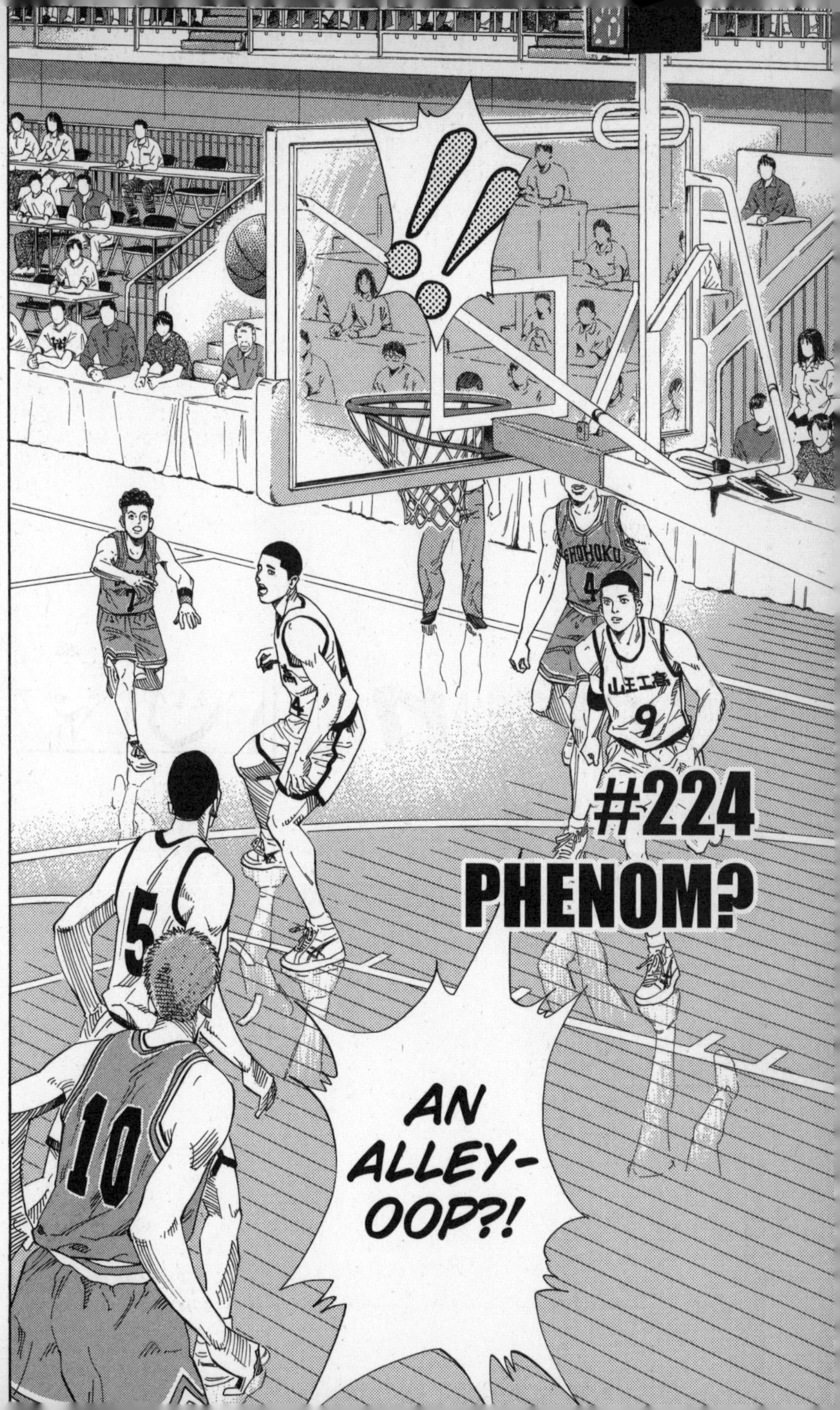
!!
AN ALLEY-OOP?!

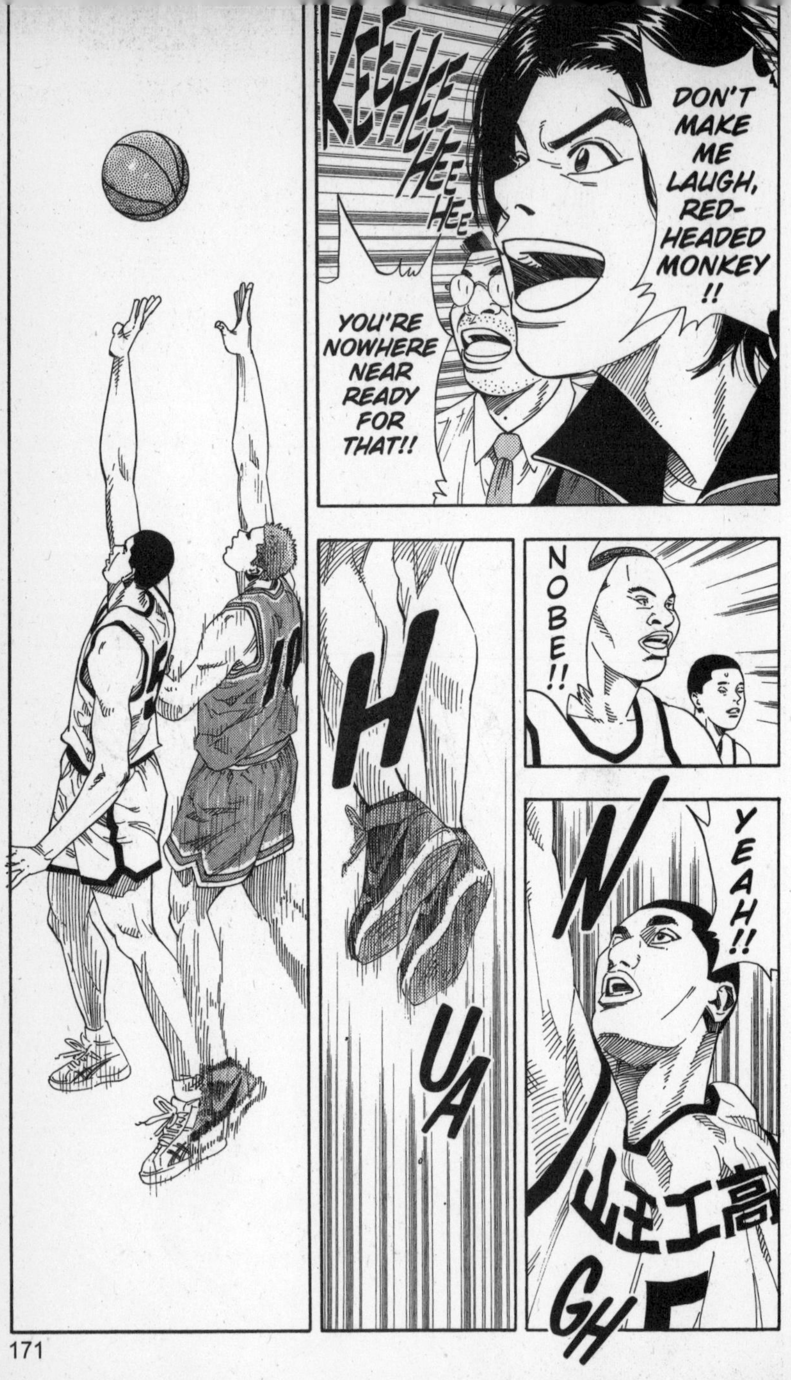
DON'T MAKE ME LAUGH, RED-HEADED MONKEY!!
KEEHEE HEE HEE
YOU'RE NOWHERE NEAR READY FOR THAT!!
NOBE!!
YEAH!!
N
GH
H
UA

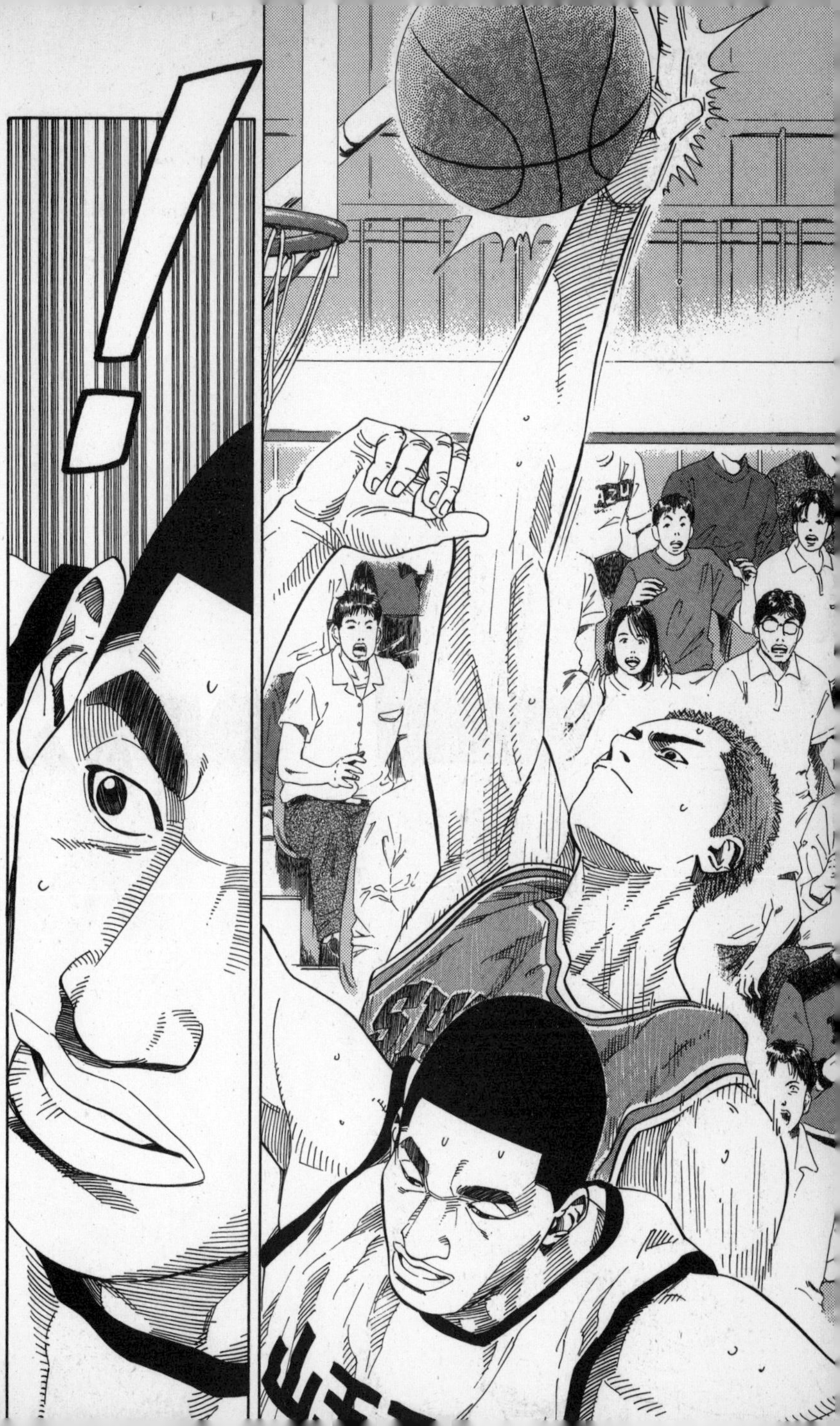
!

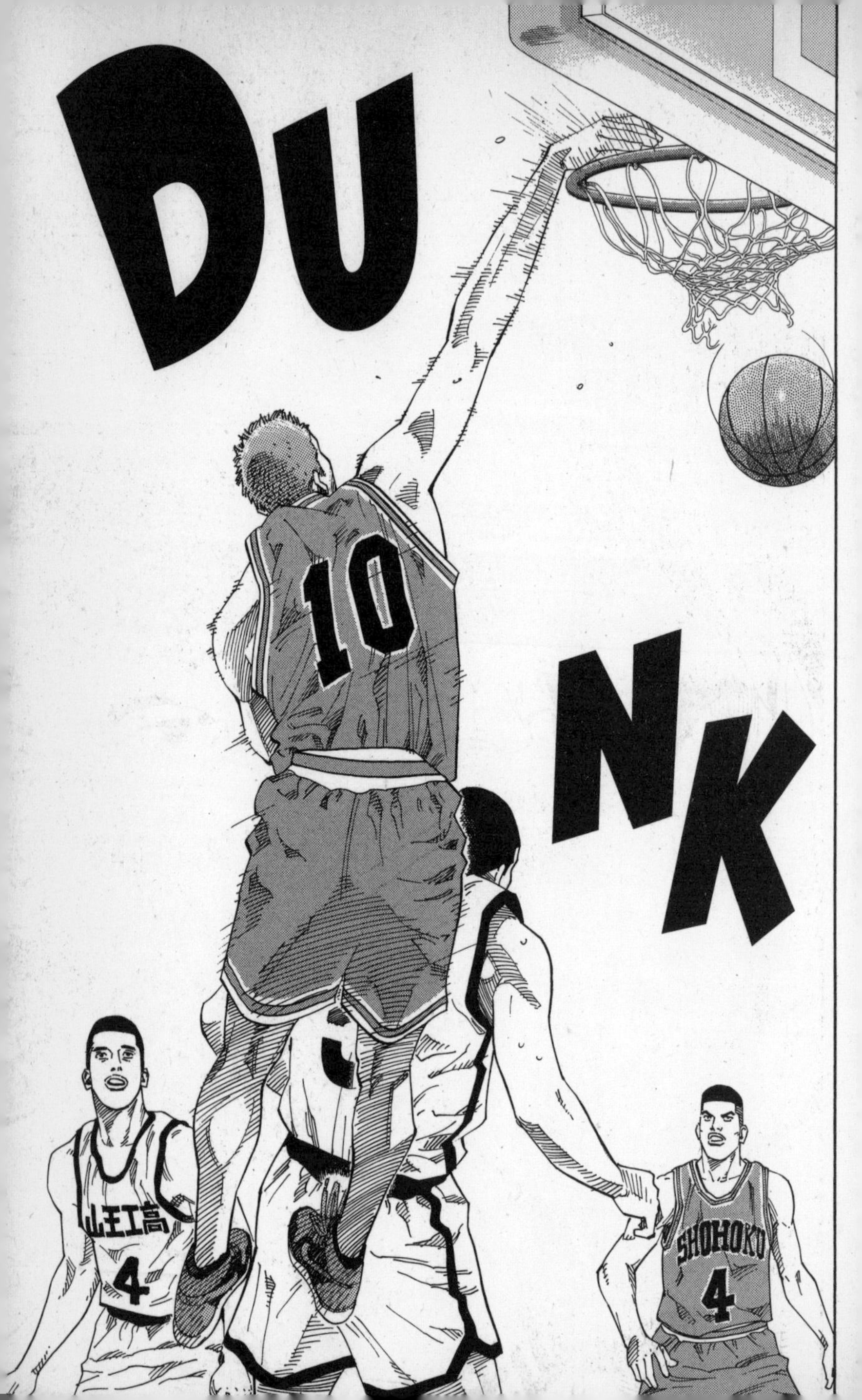
DU
NK
10
SHOHOKU
4
山王工高
4

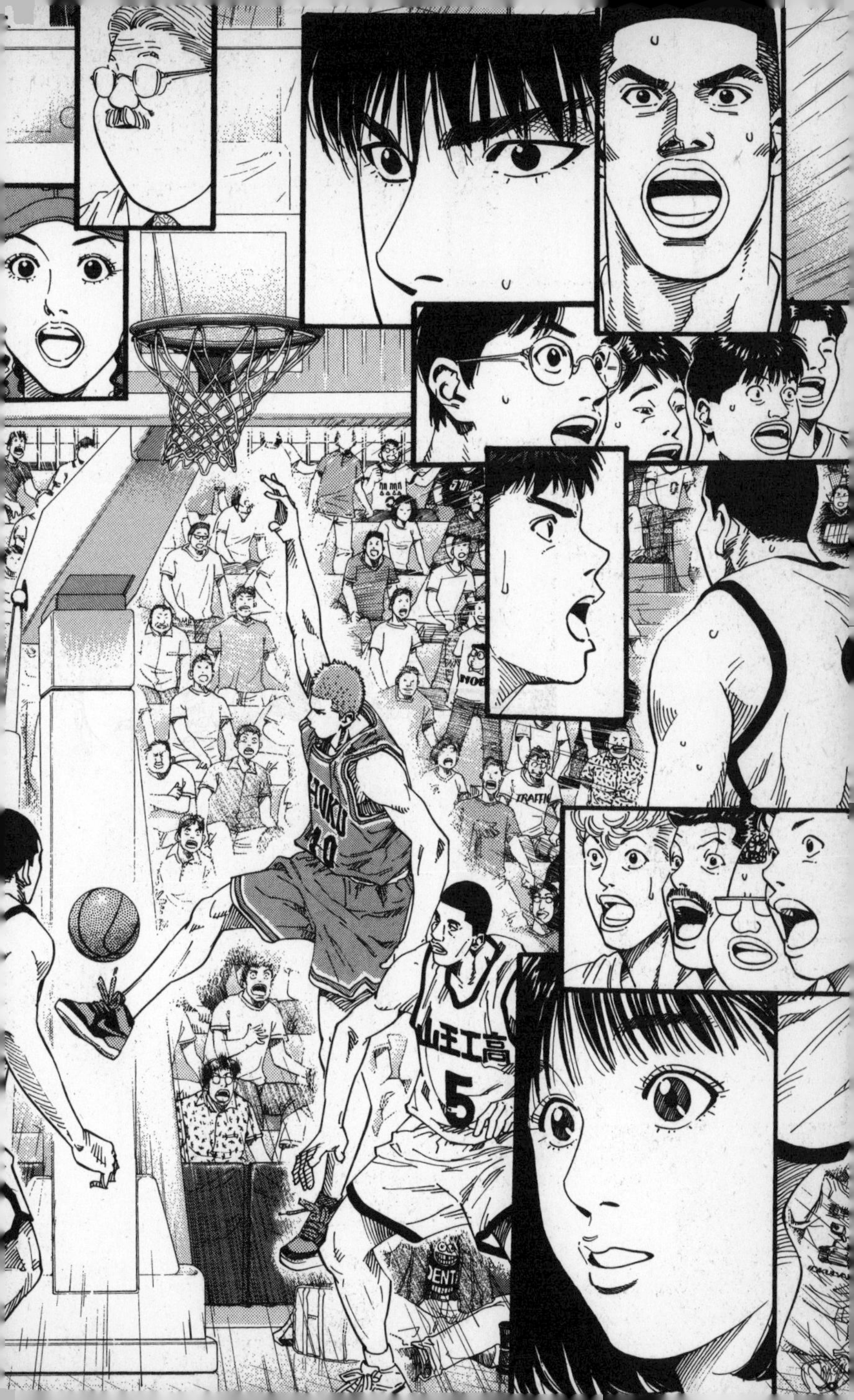
山王工高
5

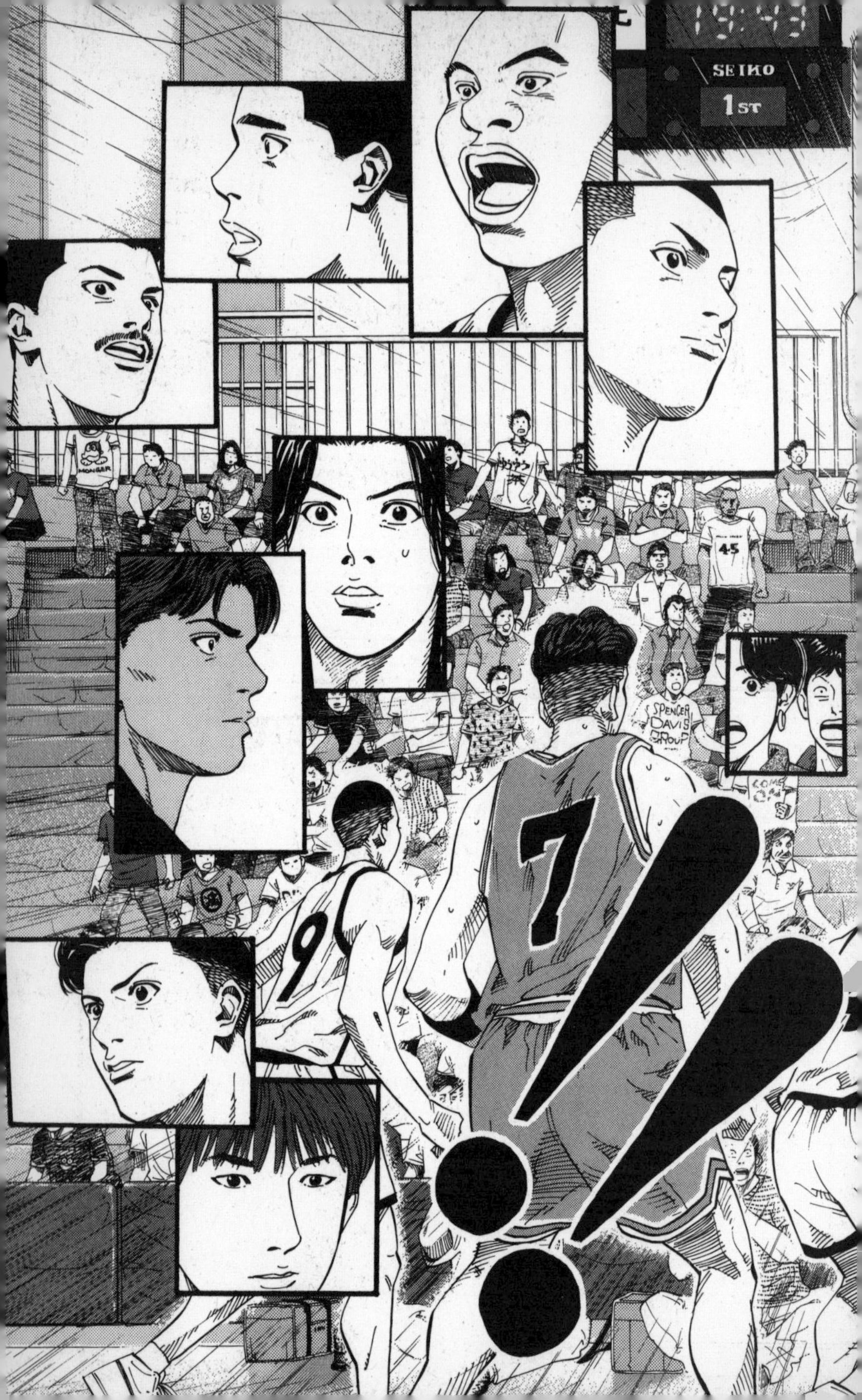
SEIKO
1ST
45
SPENCER DAVIS GROUP

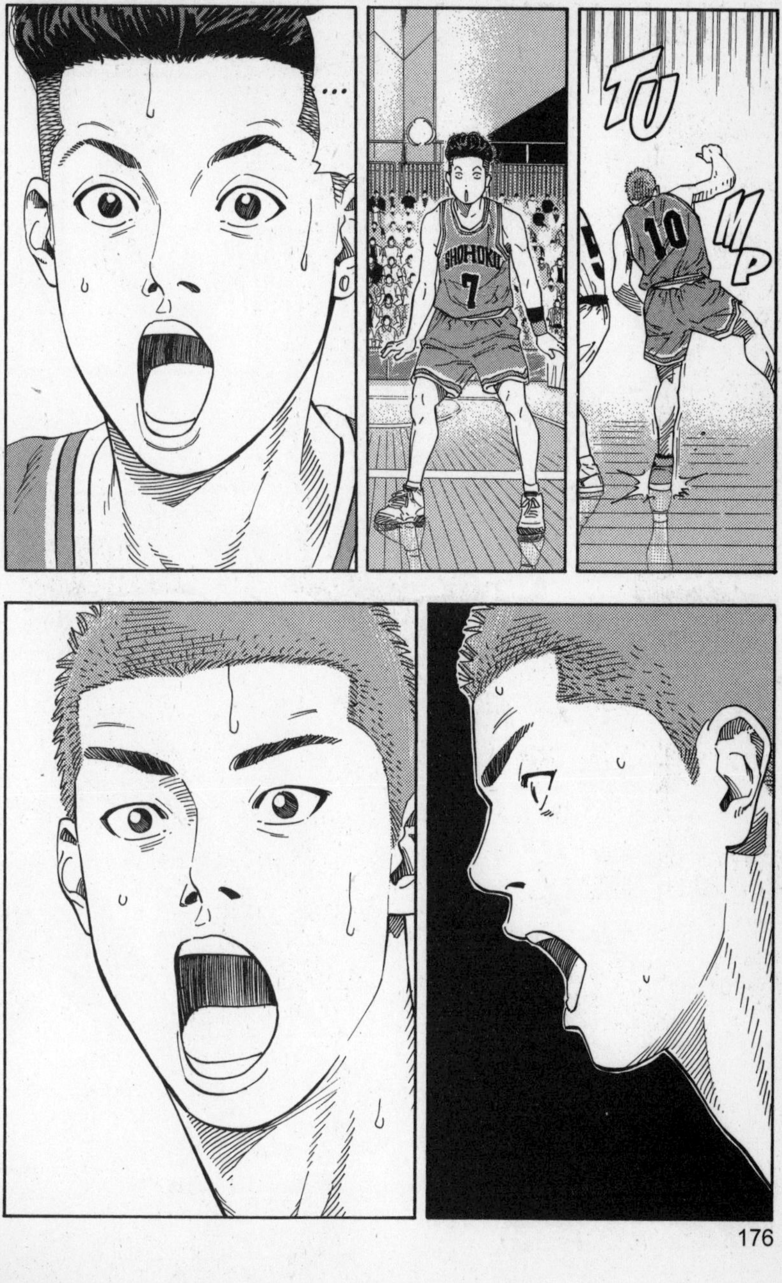
TUMP
...

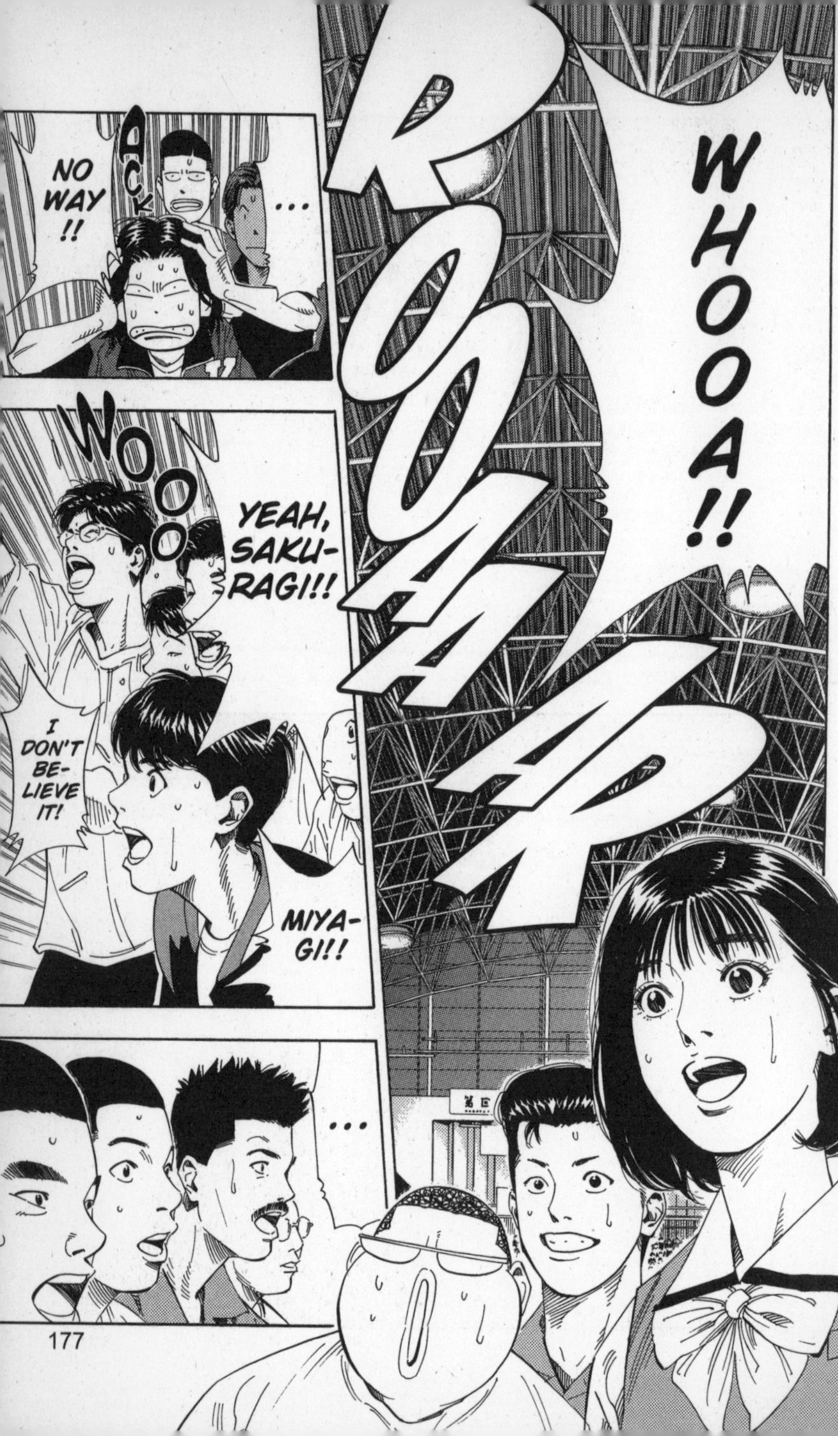
WHOOA!!
ROOAAR
...
ACK
NO WAY!!
YEAH, SAKU-RAGI!!
WOOO
MIYA-GI!!
I DON'T BE-LIEVE IT!
...

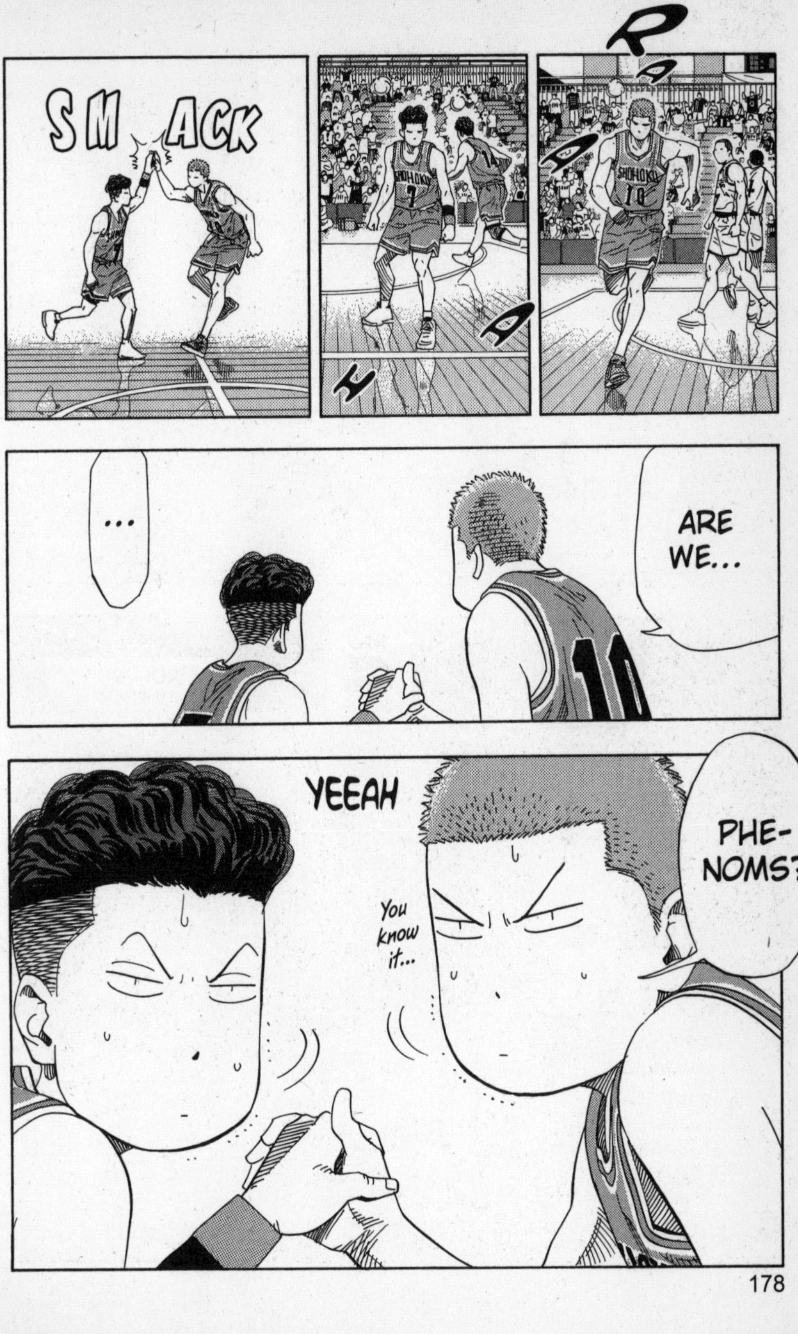
RAAAH
SMACK
ARE WE...
...
PHE-
NOMS?
YEEAH
You know it...

READ THIS WAY

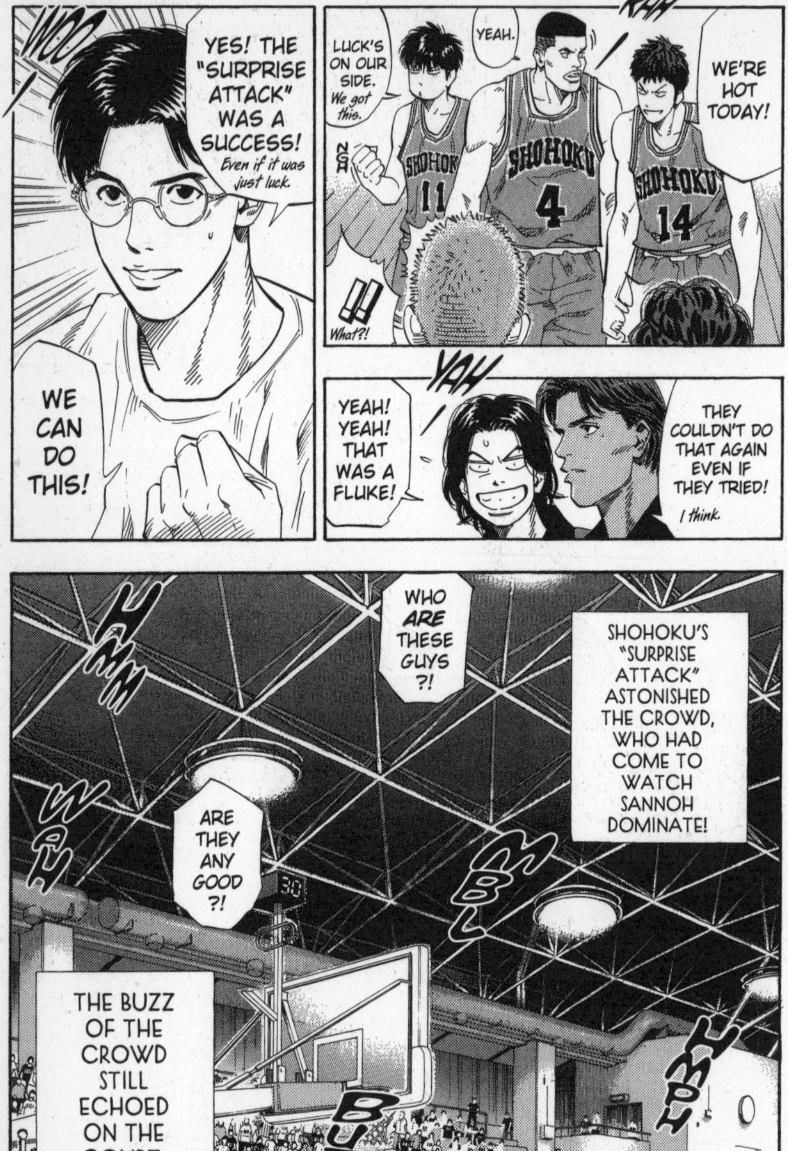
RAH
WE'RE HOT TODAY!
YEAH.
LUCK'S ON OUR SIDE. We got this.
NGH
What?!
THEY COULDN'T DO THAT AGAIN EVEN IF THEY TRIED! I think.
YAH
YEAH! YEAH! THAT WAS A FLUKE!
WOO
YES! THE "SURPRISE ATTACK" WAS A SUCCESS! Even if it was just luck.
WE CAN DO THIS!
SHOHOKU'S "SURPRISE ATTACK" ASTONISHED THE CROWD, WHO HAD COME TO WATCH SANNOH DOMINATE!
WHO ARE THESE GUYS?!
HMM
MMBL
ARE THEY ANY GOOD?!
WAH
HMPH
BUZZ
THE BUZZ OF THE CROWD STILL ECHOED ON THE COURT.

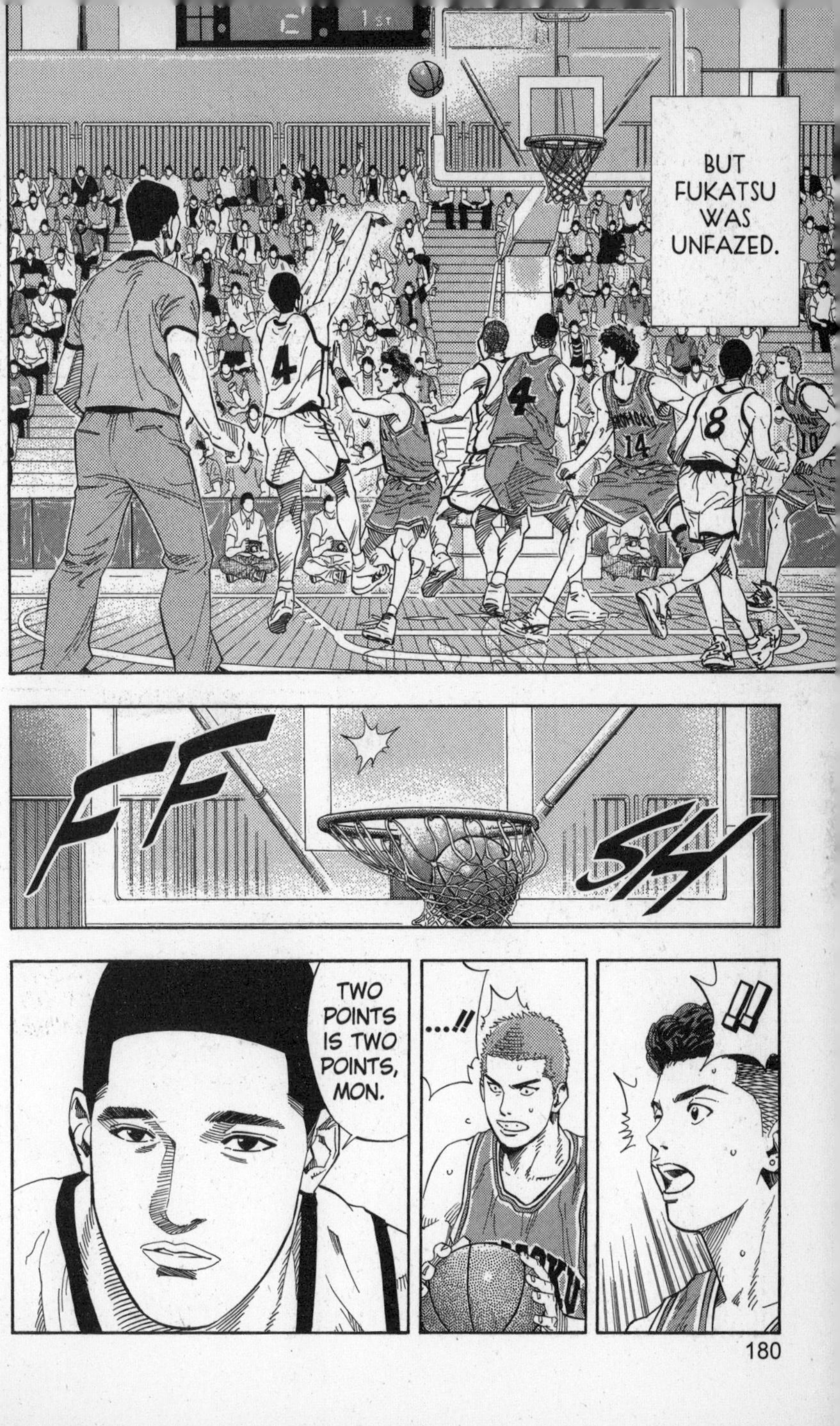
BUT FUKATSU WAS UNFAZED.
FF SH
!!
...!!
TWO POINTS IS TWO POINTS, MON.

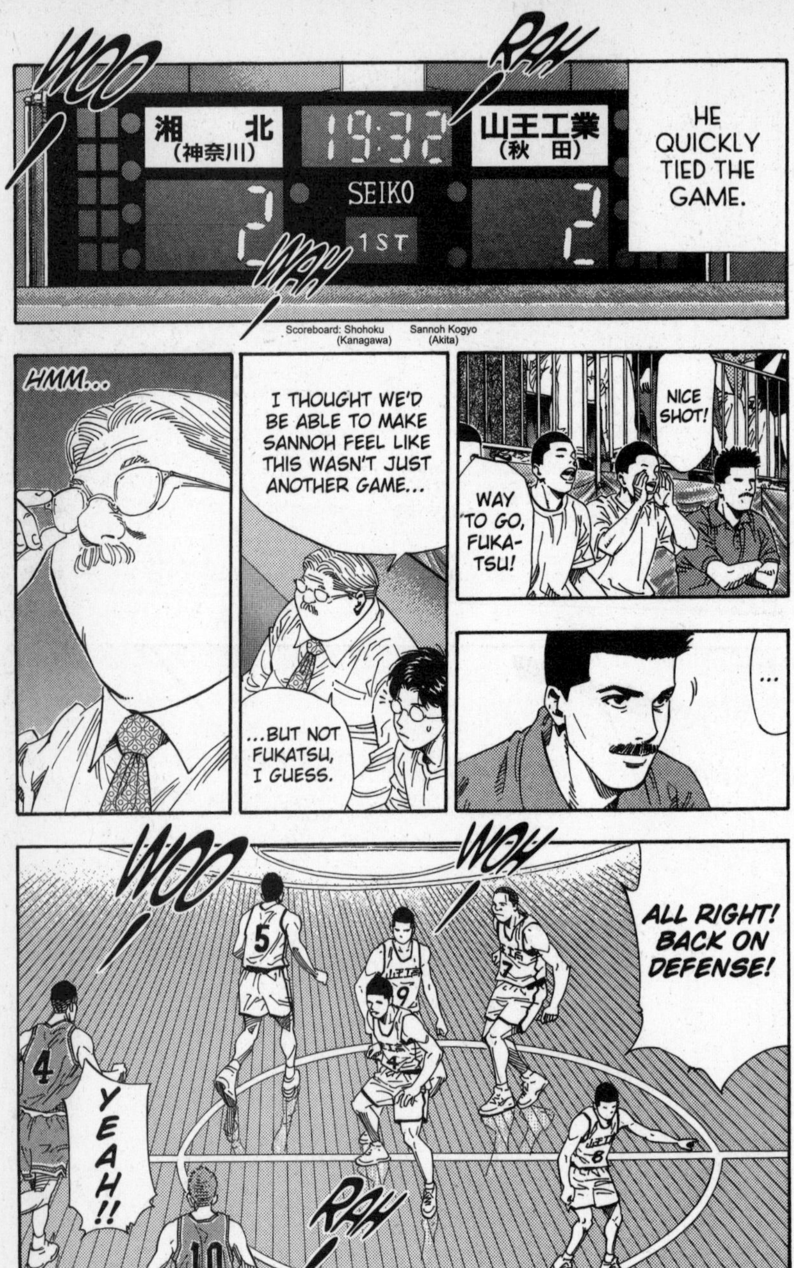
RAH
HE QUICKLY TIED THE GAME.
山王工業
(秋田)
19:32
湘北
(神奈川)
SEIKO
2
1ST
2
WOO
WAH
Scoreboard: Shohoku (Kanagawa) Sannoh Kogyo (Akita)
NICE SHOT!
WAY TO GO, FUKATSU!
...
I THOUGHT WE'D BE ABLE TO MAKE SANNOH FEEL LIKE THIS WASN'T JUST ANOTHER GAME...
...BUT NOT FUKATSU, I GUESS.
HMM...
WOH
ALL RIGHT! BACK ON DEFENSE!
WOO
YEAH!!
RAH

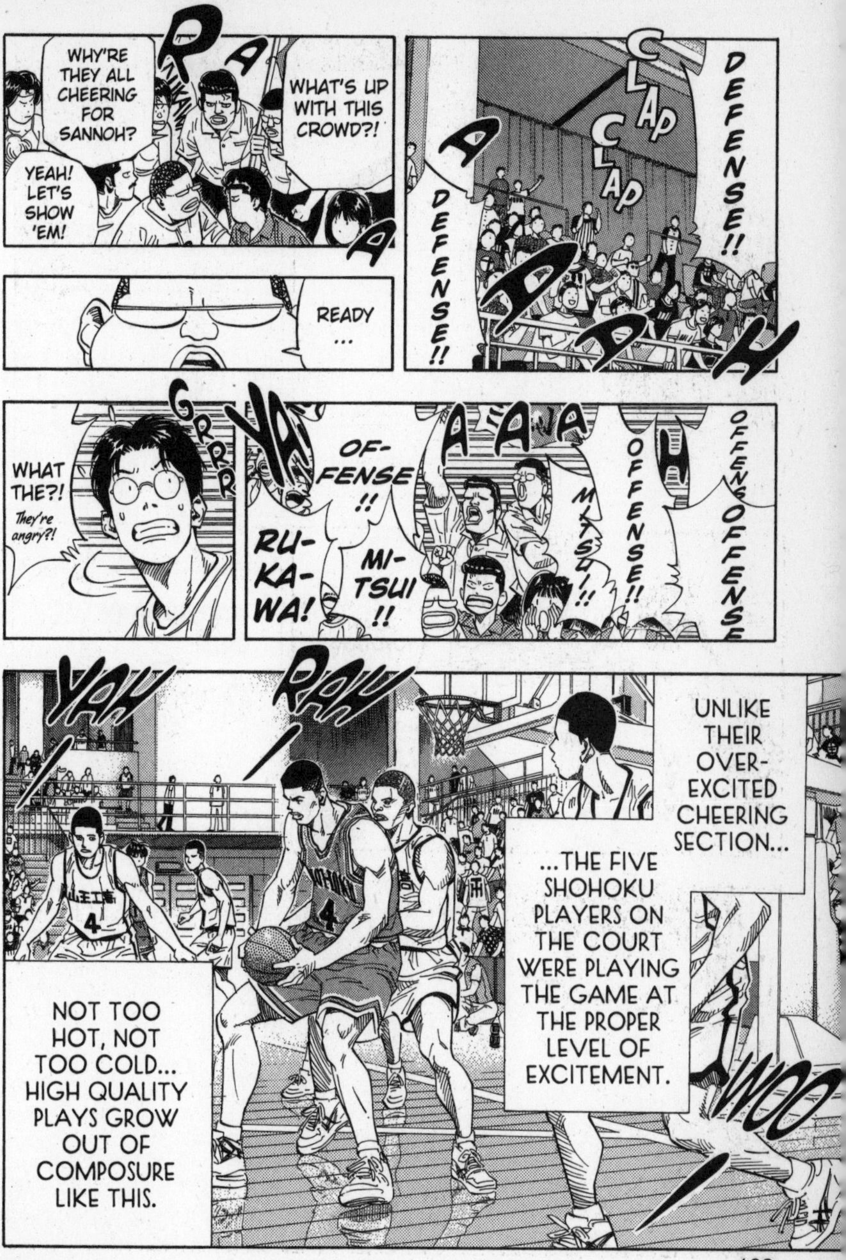
A
CLAP
CLAP
CLAP
DEFENSE!!
DEFENSE!!
AAAH
RA
WHAT'S UP WITH THIS CROWD?!
WHY'RE THEY ALL CHEERING FOR SANNOH?
YEAH! LET'S SHOW 'EM!
A
READY ...
OFFENSE OFFENSE
H
OFFENSE!!
MITSUI!!
AAJA
YA
OF-FENSE!!
MI-TSUI!!
RU-KA-WA!
GRRR
WHAT THE?!
They're angry?!
UNLIKE THEIR OVER-EXCITED CHEERING SECTION...
...THE FIVE SHOHOKU PLAYERS ON THE COURT WERE PLAYING THE GAME AT THE PROPER LEVEL OF EXCITEMENT.
WOO!
RAH!
YAH!
NOT TOO HOT, NOT TOO COLD... HIGH QUALITY PLAYS GROW OUT OF COMPOSURE LIKE THIS.

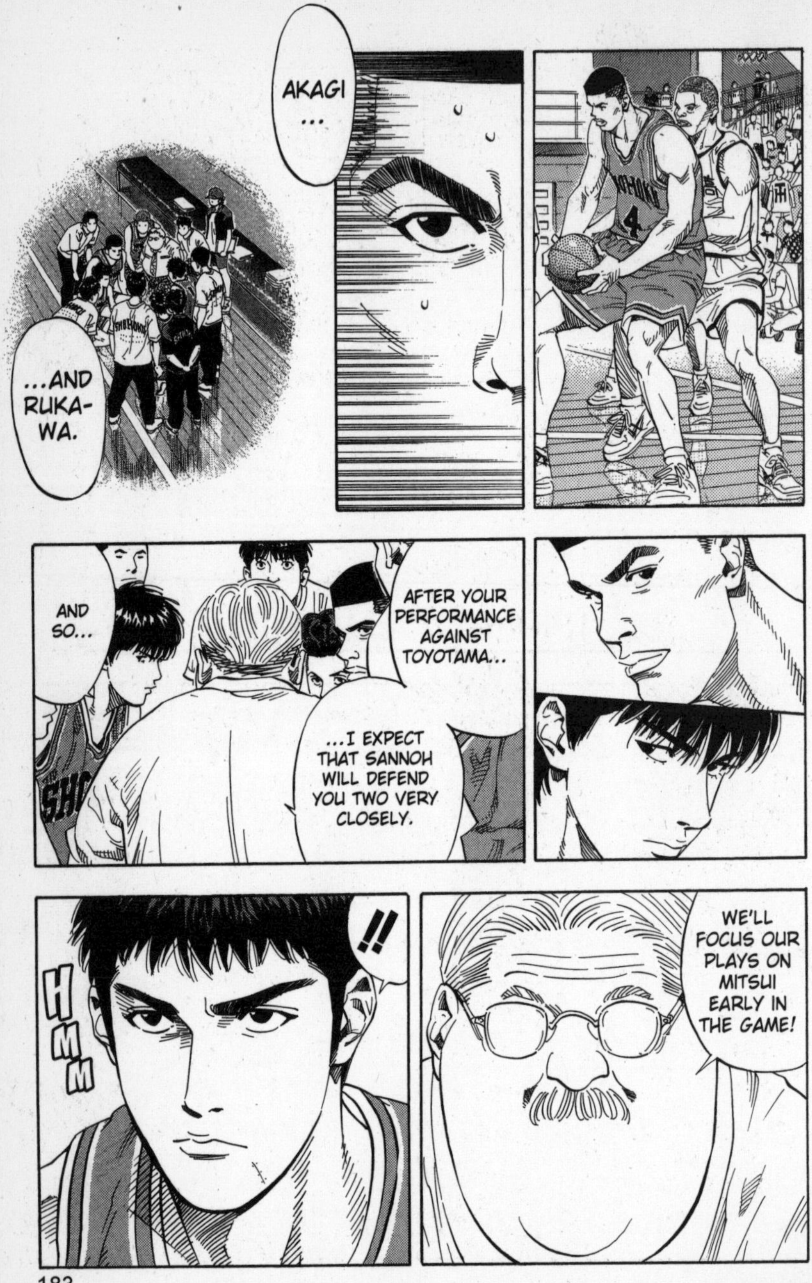
AKAGI...
...AND RUKAWA.
AFTER YOUR PERFORMANCE AGAINST TOYOTAMA...
...I EXPECT THAT SANNOH WILL DEFEND YOU TWO VERY CLOSELY.
AND SO...
WE'LL FOCUS OUR PLAYS ON MITSUI EARLY IN THE GAME!
!!
HMM

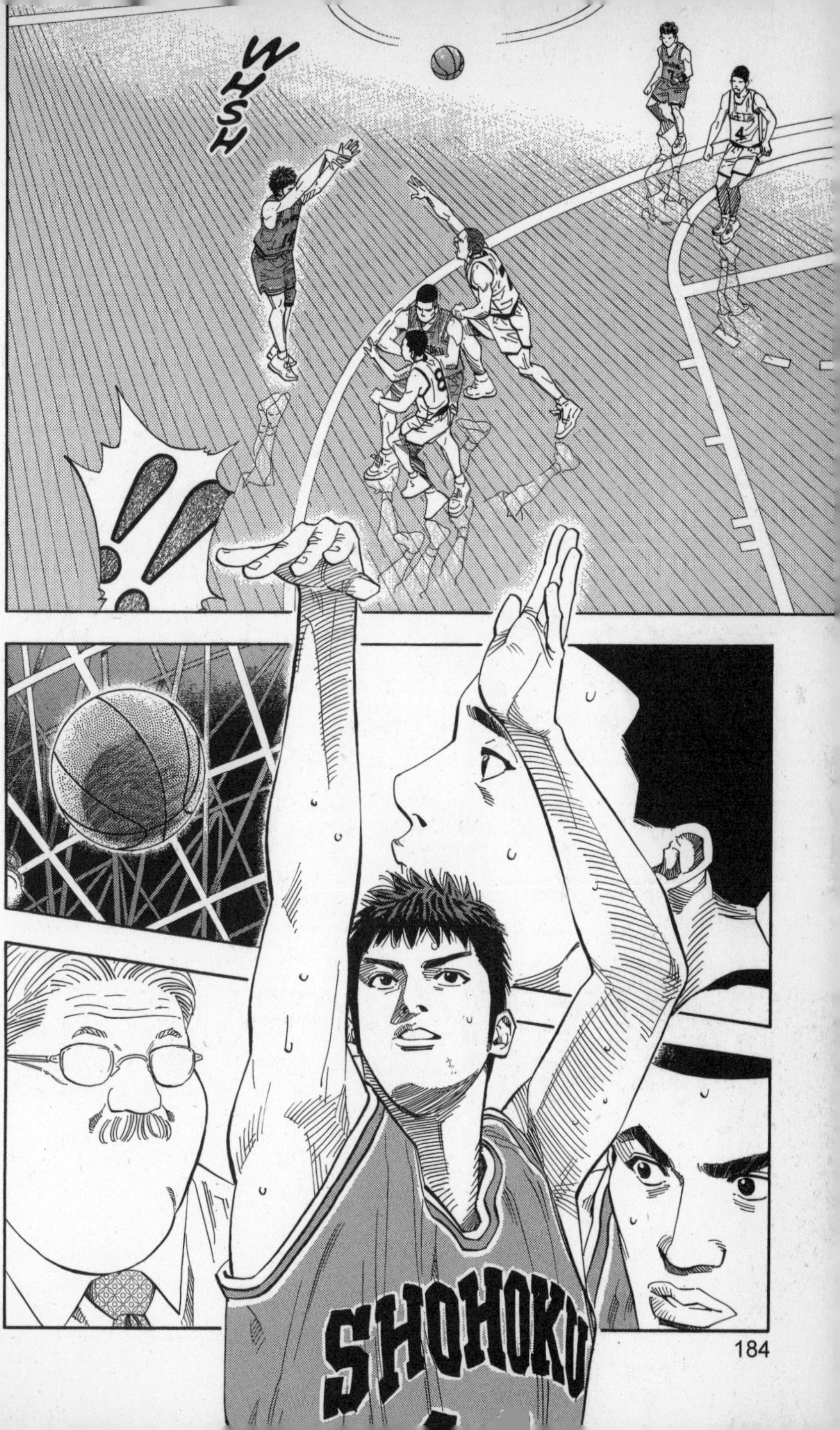
WHSH
!!
SHOHOKU

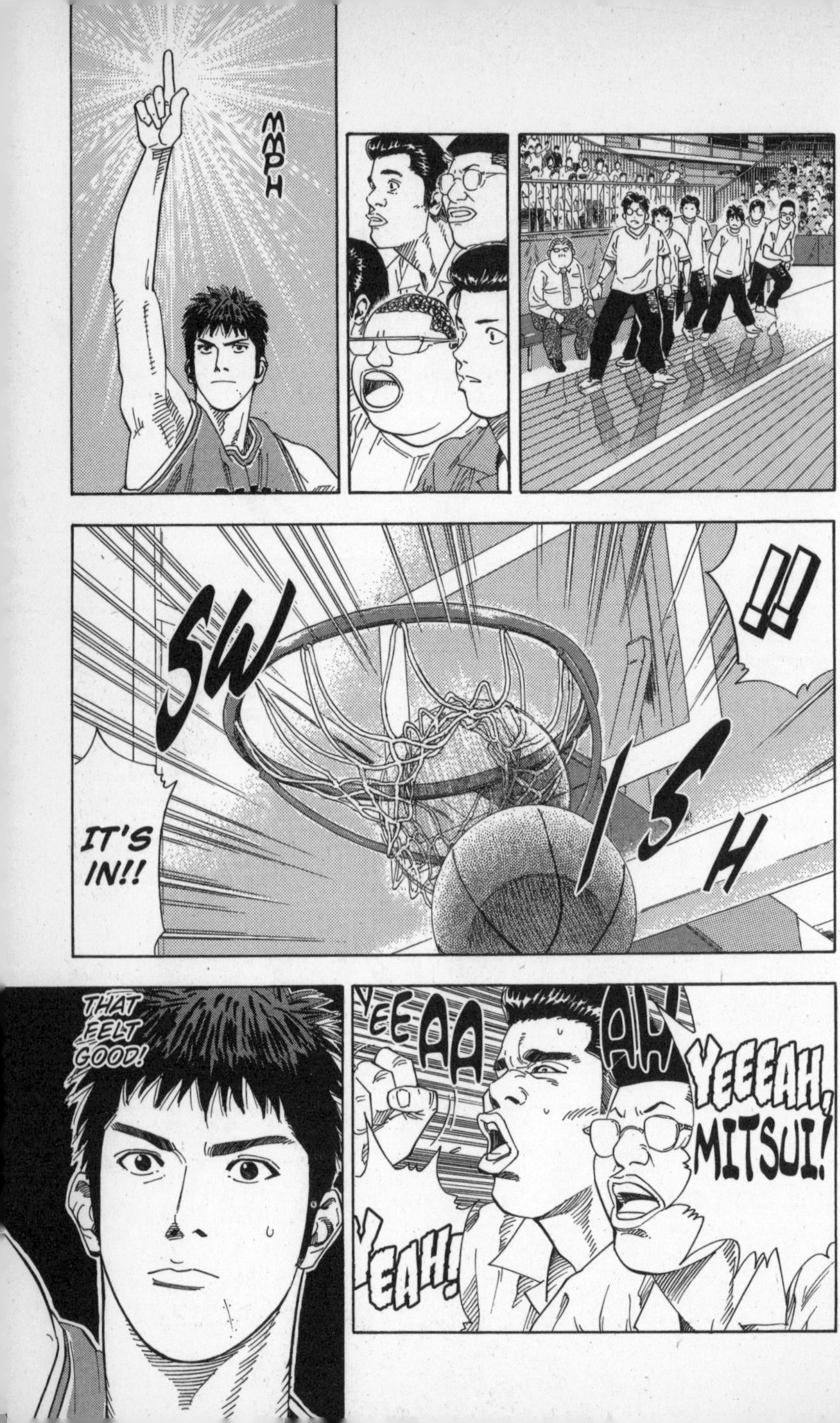
MMPH
!!
SWISH
IT'S IN!!
YEEAAAH
YEEEAH, MITSUI!
YEAH!
THAT FELT GOOD!

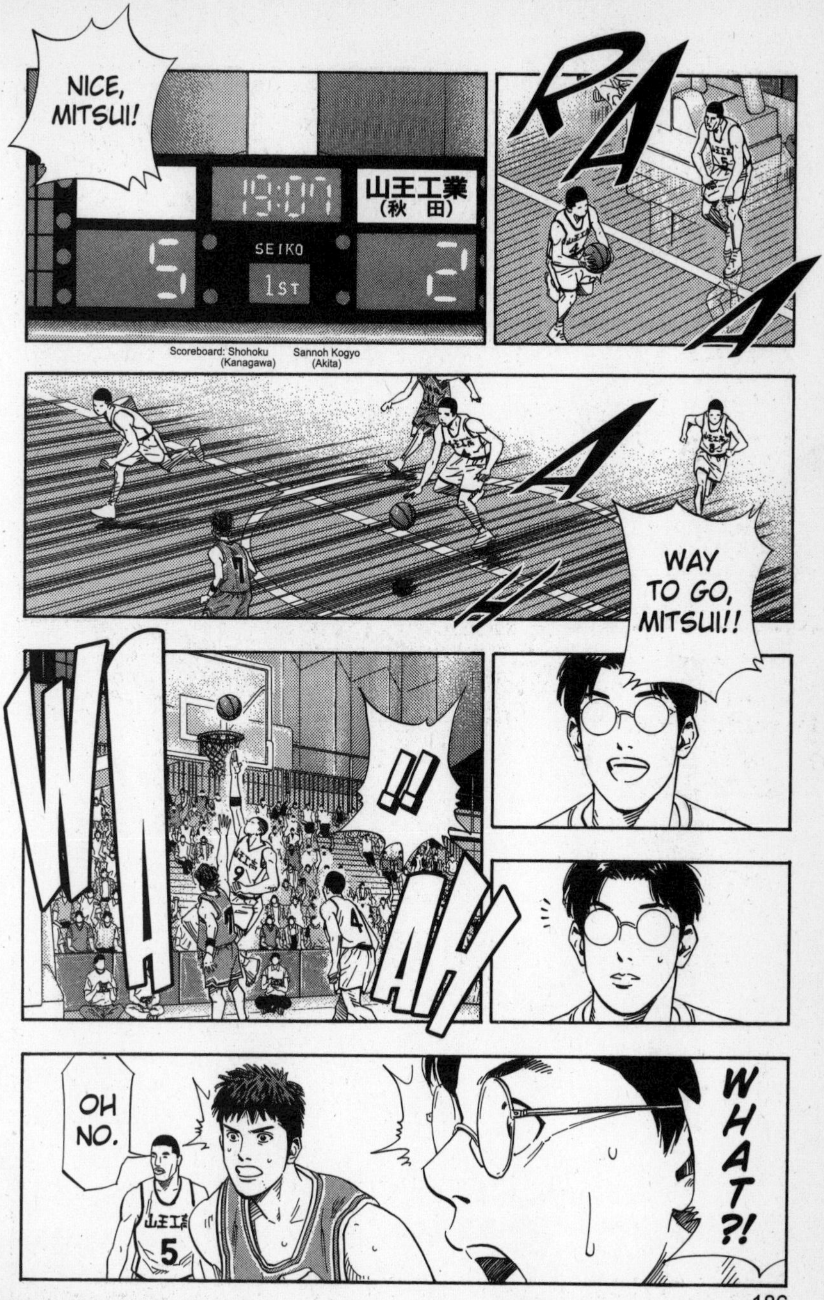
RA
A
NICE, MITSUI!
19:07
山王工業
(秋田)
SEIKO
5
1ST
2
A
H
WAY TO GO, MITSUI!!
!!
WA
AH
WHAT?!
OH NO.
山王工
Scoreboard: Shohoku (Kanagawa) Sannoh Kogyo (Akita)

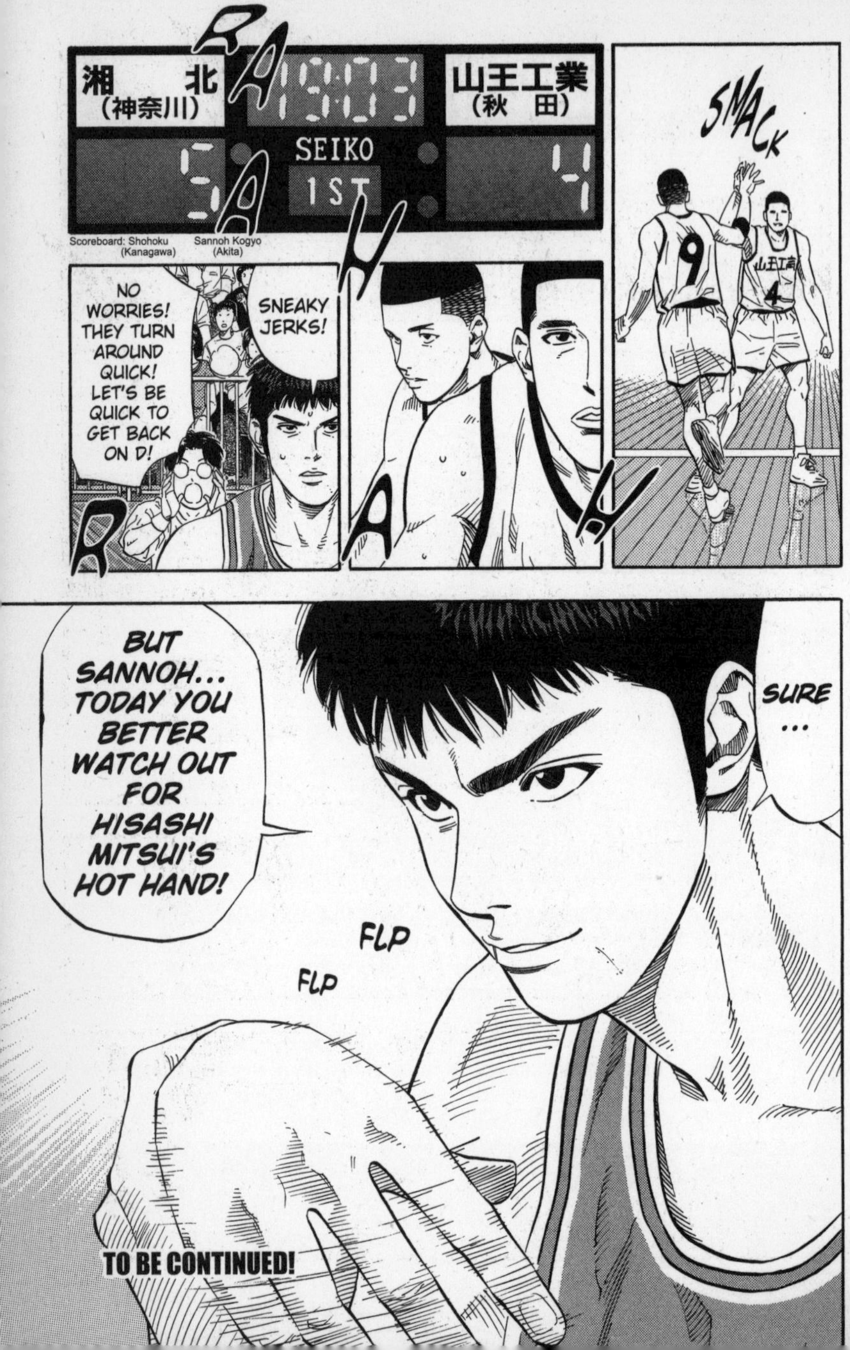
SMACK
湘北
(神奈川)
19:03
山王工業
(秋田)
SEIKO
1ST
5
4
Scoreboard: Shohoku (Kanagawa) Sannoh Kogyo (Akita)
RAAAAHH
SNEAKY JERKS!
NO WORRIES! THEY TURN AROUND QUICK! LET'S BE QUICK TO GET BACK ON D!
SURE...
BUT SANNOH... TODAY YOU BETTER WATCH OUT FOR HISASHI MITSUI'S HOT HAND!
FLP
FLP
TO BE CONTINUED!

Coming Next Volume

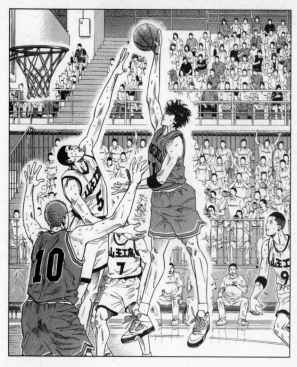

With a slight lead thanks to Mitsui, Shohoku has their hands full as the game against Sannoh heats up. Sannoh's coach Domoto sends in Mikio, a player whose strength and size make up for his lack of experience. Coach Anzai counters by telling Shohoku to run their offense through Sakuragi, and the game becomes a battle between the two inexperienced power players. What Sannoh thought would be an easy win for them is turning out to be a lot more than they bargained for—Shohoku's here and they mean to go all the way to the top!

ON SALE FEBRUARY 2013

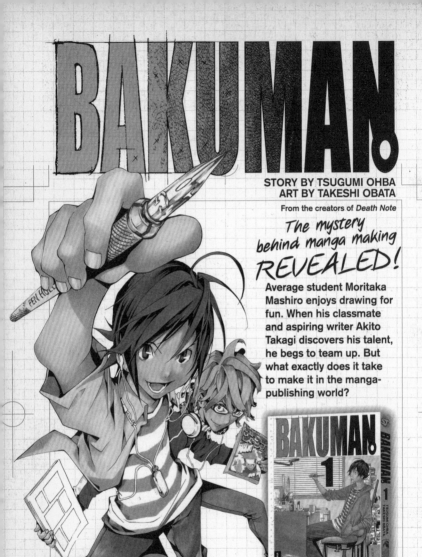

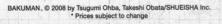

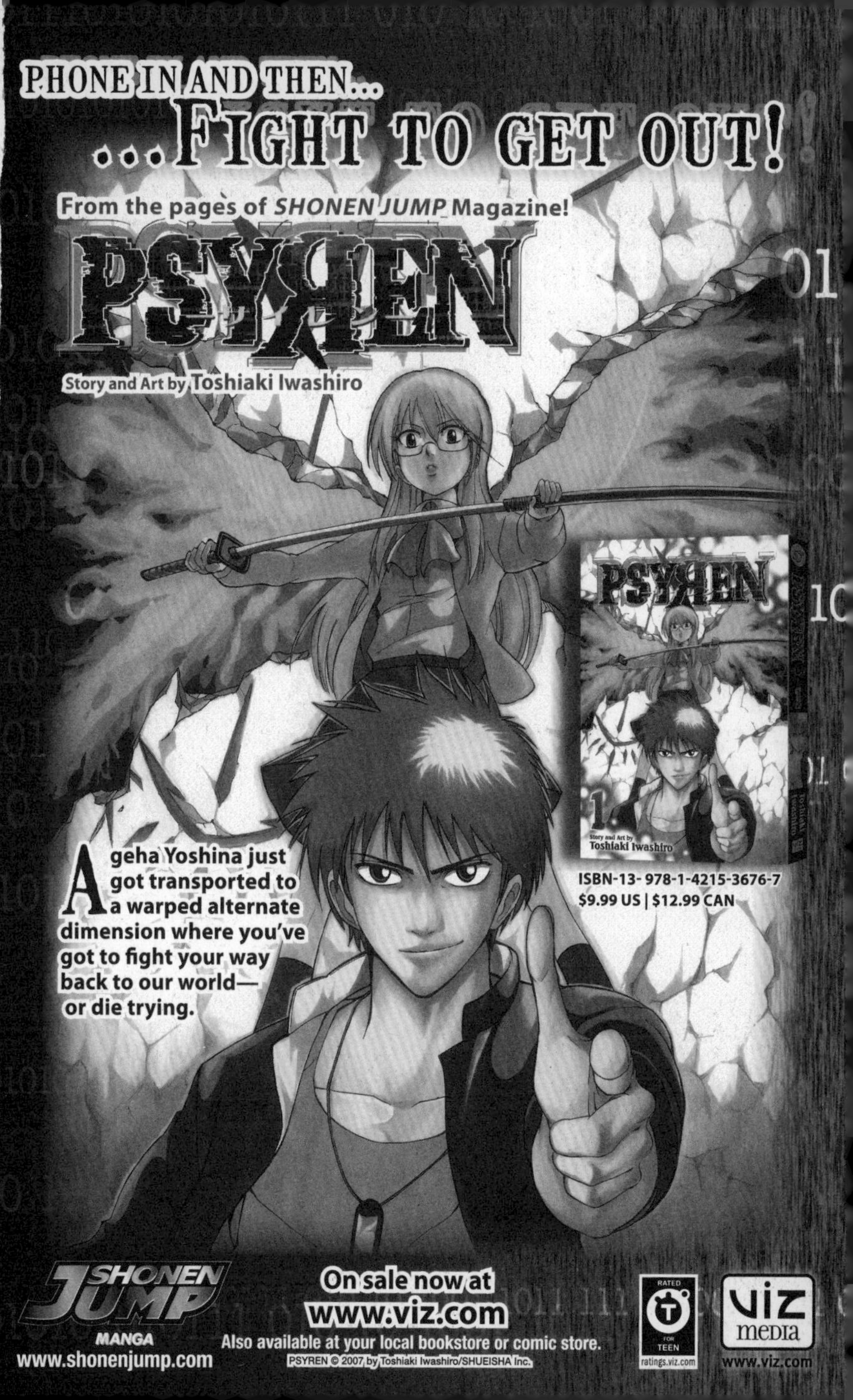
PHONE IN AND THEN...
...FIGHT TO GET OUT!
From the pages of SHONEN JUMP Magazine!
PSYREN
Story and Art by Toshiaki Iwashiro
PSYREN
1
Story and Art by Toshiaki Iwashiro
ISBN-13- 978-1-4215-3676-7
$9.99 US | $12.99 CAN
Ageha Yoshina just got transported to a warped alternate dimension where you've got to fight your way back to our world—or die trying.
SHONEN JUMP
MANGA
www.shonenjump.com
On sale now at
www.viz.com
Also available at your local bookstore or comic store.
PSYREN © 2007 by Toshiaki Iwashiro/SHUEISHA Inc.
RATED
T
FOR
TEEN
ratings.viz.com
viz media
www.viz.com

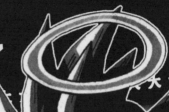
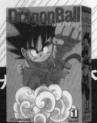

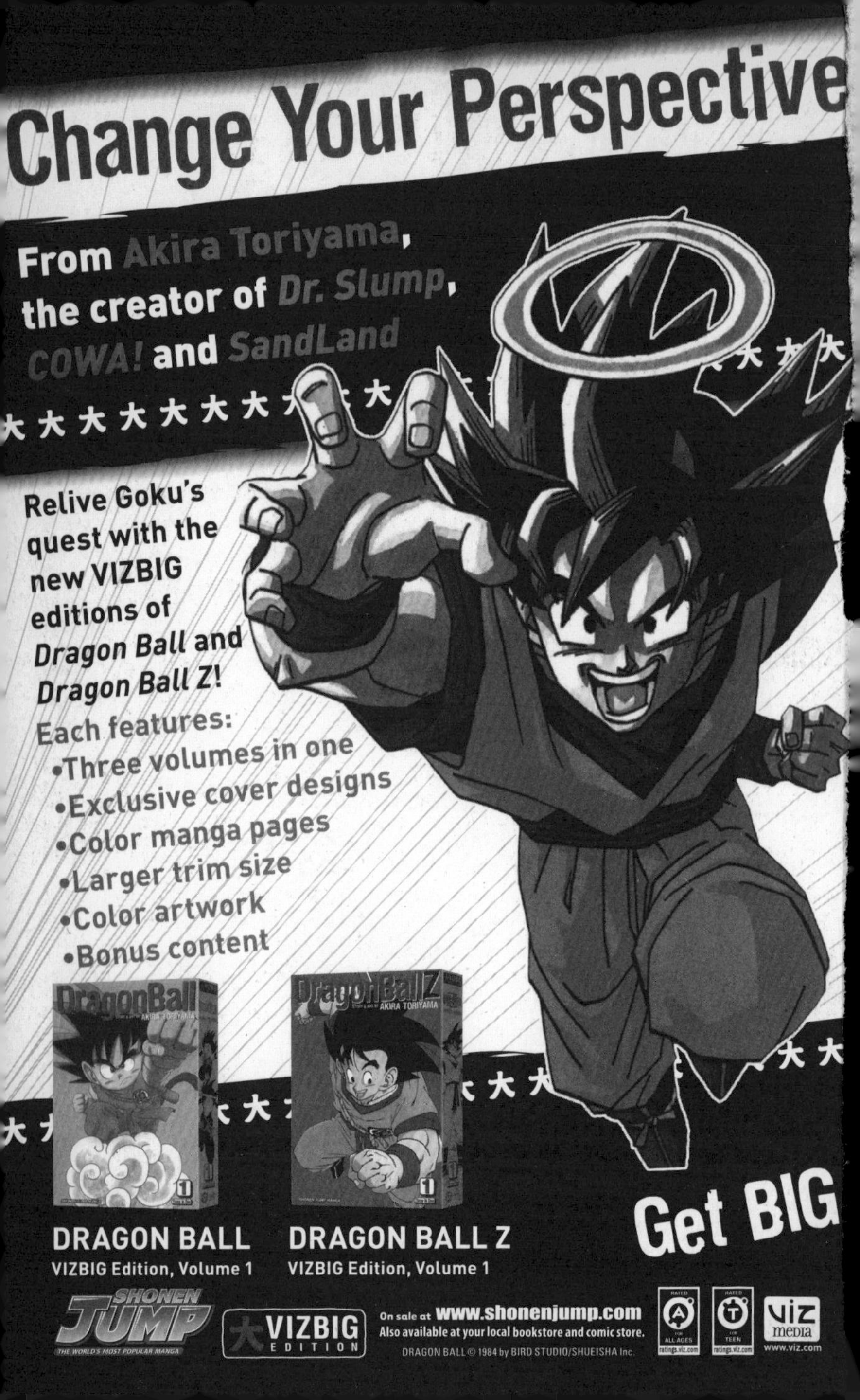

You're Reading in the Wrong Direction!!

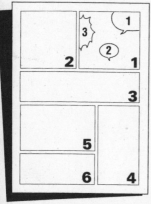

Whoops! Guess what? You're starting at the wrong end of the comic!

…It's true! In keeping with the original Japanese format, **Slam Dunk** is meant to be read from right to left, starting in the upper-right corner.

Unlike English, which is read from left to right, Japanese is read from right to left, meaning that action, sound effects and word-balloon order are completely reversed… something which can make readers unfamiliar with Japanese feel pretty backwards themselves. For this reason, manga or Japanese comics published in the U.S. in English have sometimes been published "flopped"—that is, printed in exact reverse order, as though seen from the other side of a mirror.

By flopping pages, U.S. publishers can avoid confusing readers, but the compromise is not without its downside. For one thing, a character in a flopped manga series who once wore in the original Japanese version a T-shirt emblazoned with "M A Y" (as in "the merry month of") now wears one which reads "Y A M"! Additionally, many manga creators in Japan are themselves unhappy with the process, as some feel the mirror-imaging of their art alters their original intentions.

We are proud to bring you Takehiko Inoue's **Slam Dunk** in the original unflopped format. For now, though, turn to the other side of the book and let the quest begin…!

–Editor

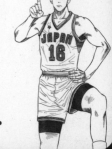

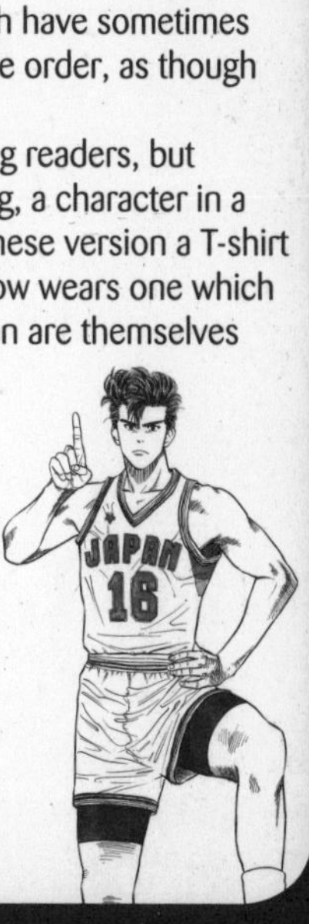